Norfolk Record Society
Volume LXXXVIII for 2024

Socialism in King's Lynn
and
Suffragism in Great Yarmouth

Minutes of the King's Lynn
Socialist and Labour Societies, 1897–1916
and
Minutes of the Executive Committee of the
Great Yarmouth Women's Suffrage Society, 1909–1915

Edited by
Frank Meeres

General Editor
Anthony Howe

Norfolk Record Society
Volume LXXXVIII
2024

First published in 2024
by the Norfolk Record Society

ISBN 978-0-9957736-7-7

Typeset by Carnegie Book Production, Lancaster
Printed and bound by Short Run Press, Exeter

Contents

Illustrations

Acknowledgements

I am grateful to the Norfolk Record Office, county archivist Gary Tuson, for giving permission to transcribe the documents and four images in this volume. The two Yarmouth suffragist images are from Picture Norfolk, and I am grateful to the County Council for permission to publish these. Every reasonable effort has been made to trace owners of copyright material reproduced in this book, but if any have been inadvertently overlooked the publishers would be glad to hear from them.

The idea for publishing the King's Lynn Socialist volumes was originally put forward by the late Alun Howkins: it has been a privilege to bring his original concept to fruition.

I am most grateful to my editor, Professor Anthony Howe, for his many helpful suggestions and comments.

FM, February 2024

Abbreviations

ASE: Amalgamated Society of Engineers
ASRS: Amalgamated Society of Railway Servants
BSP: British Socialist Party
EAF: East Anglian Federation (of Independent Labour Party)
EDC: Eastern Divisional Council (of Independent Labour Party)
EDP: *Eastern Daily Press*
ILP: Independent Labour Party
LA: *Lynn Advertiser*
LN: *Lynn News*
LNL: Land Nationalisation League
M&GN: Midland and Great Northern (Railway)
NAC: National Administrative Council (of Independent Labour Party)
NRO: Norfolk Record Office
NUBSO: National Union of Boot and Shoe Operatives
NUR: National Union of Railwaymen
NUT: National Union of Teachers
NUWSS: National Union of Women's Suffrage Societies
ODNB: *Oxford Dictionary of National Biography*
PO: Post Office
PSA: Pleasant Sunday Afternoon
RCA: Railway Clerk's Association
SDF: Social Democratic Federation
WFL: Women's Freedom League
WSPU: Women's Social and Political Union

Editorial Conventions

\word/	words which have been inserted
~~word~~	words which have been deleted
~~word~~	words deleted within a deletion
underline	underlined text
<margin>	marginal entry or annotation
italics	editorial comment or elucidation in the margins. e.g. *undated*, *signed*, *endorsed*
[*italics*]	editorial remarks within the text
[*word illegible*], [*word inserted*], [*word deleted*]	words which cannot be read
[?]widow	doubt about the transcription of a word
[the other]	words missing through damage to the manuscript which have been supplied
[?the other]	as above, but there is doubt about the first word
[? the other]	as above, but there is doubt about both words
[*? two words*]	missing words which cannot be supplied
[*and*] a larg[e]	words or letters omitted in the manuscript which have been supplied

General Introduction

Edwardian Norfolk is more often associated with the 'Indian Summer' of the aristocracy than with the 'crisis of Liberal England'. But this year's composite volume might well be titled 'The Struggle for Democracy in Edwardian Norfolk'. It illustrates in fascinating detail the battle for social, political, and gender equality from two very contrasting groups, the working people (with middle-class sympathizers) of King's Lynn, forming a succession of socialist organizations, and the well-heeled, middle-class women (with male sympathizers) of Great Yarmouth, campaigning by peaceful means for the vote for women. The editor Frank Meeres brings together two remarkable sets of minutes. The first provides a detailed account of the socialist and labour movement in King's Lynn between 1897 and 1916. The editing of this unique set of documents was begun by the late Alun Howkins (1947–2018), Professor of History at the University of Sussex, Honorary Professor of History at the University of East Anglia, and an acknowledged authority on popular protest and modern English rural society. In April 2014 Professor Howkins gave a conference paper at the University of East Anglia based on the minutes published here, entitled 'Socialism in the Provinces: The King's Lynn Socialist Movement, 1897–1916'. But later, in ill-health, he generously allowed Frank Meeres to take over their editing. Frank's own expertise in the history of the women's suffrage led him directly to the second set of minutes, that of the Executive Committee of the Great Yarmouth Women's Suffrage Society between 1909 and 1915. Together these records provide remarkable insights into grassroots political activism in early twentieth-century Britain.

The Norfolk Record Society is grateful to the Audrey Muriel Stratford Charitable Trust and The Geoffrey Watling Charity for generous grants which have made this publication possible.

Anthony Howe,
General Editor

Minutes of King's Lynn Socialist and Labour Societies 1897–1916

Figure 1. King's Lynn and surrounding villages, 1900.
Source: *Kelly's Trade Directory.*

Introduction

The Minutes of the King's Lynn
Socialist and Labour Societies, 1897–1915

The minutes comprise four volumes in various hands, those of the King's Lynn Socialist Society (1897–98), the Lynn Social Democratic Party (1898–1906), and the King's Lynn Independent Labour Party (1906–1916).[1] When they were still in private hands, they came to the attention of Alun Howkins (1947–2018), social historian, and he recognised their great importance as a record of the early history of Socialist groups and their role in the eventual formation of the Labour Party. The minute books are now in the Norfolk Record Office, together with supporting material including membership records from 1906 and some correspondence (all at NRO, SO 297).

Late Victorian and Edwardian King's Lynn

In 1891, King's Lynn was the third largest town in Norfolk after Norwich and Great Yarmouth. Its population in was 18,360, 12,713 in the parish of St Margaret and 5,647 in the parish of All Saints or South Lynn (both terms are used in the minutes). Lynn's importance was based on trade, its position at the mouth of the river Ouse giving access to the whole of the East Midlands. Facilities were greatly expanded in the later nineteenth century, the Alexandra Dock opening in 1869 and the Bentinck Dock in 1883. It had also become an important railway town: the railway station was rebuilt in 1871 and Lynn was the control centre of the Midland and Great Northern Railway between 1895 and 1936. Traditional industries like brewing, malting and milling were supplemented by two large engineering firms in the mid-nineteenth century (one being Savages, noted for fairground

---

1   NRO, SO 297/1, SO 297/3, SO 297/4, and SO 297/5.

rides and traction engines), a chemical fertiliser factory in 1872 and a large roller-bearings firm in 1893.

In 1896 it was, according to *Kelly's Directory*, 'the great seaport of all the eastern lowlands'. In 1901 out of an employed male population of 6,398 the largest group 1,718 were in transport and related trades including 572 railwaymen and 417 dock workers. Next largest were those employed in the building trades and engineering trades. There were also 230 fishermen. Women's employment was dominated by indoor domestic service followed by dressmaking, millinery and shirt making.[2] In this mixture of traditional and modern working-class groups the railwaymen (here as elsewhere in rural districts and the smaller towns) were to be vital to Lynn socialism. It was also a market town serving an important and prosperous rural hinterland with, again according to Kelly's, 'many excellent shops and good hotels'. It supported a Corn Exchange and markets on Tuesdays and Saturdays.

The King's Lynn Socialist Movement in National Context

Before 1918, it was not possible for an individual to become a member of the Labour Party: this could only be done through one of the groups that made up the party:

The Trade Unions: 'the main force behind the establishment of a party to represent the British workers was the British trade union movement'.[3] Throughout the nineteenth century, craft unions amalgamated to form large national unions, such as the Amalgamated Society of Engineers. The Trade Unions Congress (TUC) was established in 1868, and by 1874 just under a million people were affiliated to it by their trade union membership.

The Fabian Society: a predominantly middle-class debating society founded in 1884 – prominent early members included Sidney and Beatrice Webb, H.G. Wells and George Bernard Shaw. By 1906, it had published more than a hundred tracts and essays. 'It gave British socialism a coherent and practical approach to politics which was neither Marxist nor Liberal and which provided a practical method of advance towards democratic socialism'.[4]

---

2 *British Parliamentary Papers* 1902 (Cd 1305), Census of England and Wales, 1901, County of Norfolk.

3 Rhiannon Vickers, *The Labour Party and the World. Volume 1 – the evolution of Labour's foreign policy 1900–51* (Manchester, 2003), 20. Chapter 2 of this book provides an excellent short introduction to the emergence of the early Labour party.

4 Francis Williams, *Fifty Years March, the rise of the Labour Party* (London, ?1949), 74.

The Independent Labour Party: founded by a conference in Bradford in January 1893. James Keir Hardie was elected Chairman. 'The ILP put together a programme comprising a vague commitment to nationalisation, interventionist social reforms such as pensions, free education, land reform and the eight-hour day, plus the standard radical political causes. This was calculated to be sufficiently socialist to appeal to the activists but not too extreme to offend the unions'.[5]

The Social Democratic Federation: a Marxist grouping founded in 1881 by Henry Hyndman: early members included John Burns and William Morris (who, however, soon broke away from the group). 'The SDF retained, formally at least, the politics of class struggle and a scepticism of the capitalist State, both of which were lacking in the socialism of the ILP.'[6]

When William Morris broke away from the SDF it was to form the **Socialist League** in 1886. This was a small group in terms of numbers but it had a big influence in the development of Socialism, especially in Norwich – in 1887, the Norwich branch had over 150 members – more than 20% of the total national membership. William Morris visited the branch on several occasions, and the anarchist Prince Kropotkin spoke to them in May 1887. Many members of the Socialist League later became significant in the ILP: members of the Norwich branch include several names that occur in this book, including Alf Sutton, Fred Henderson and Herbert Witard.[7]

The Labour Representation Committee was formed on 27–28 February 1900 at a Conference in London, by representatives of these four groupings. Each delegate at the Conference represented 2,000 members. The trade unions had 121 delegates representing more than 545,000 members (not all unions chose to participate). The ILP, with 13,000 members, had seven delegates. The SDF claimed (many people thought rather exaggeratedly) 9,000 members and sent four delegates. The Fabian Society with 861 members had one delegate. The SDF pulled out in August 1901.[8] The Lynn Representation Committee worked at a local level, and on several occasions

---

5 Martin Pugh, *Speak for Britain: a new history of the Labour Party* (London, 2011 edition), 38.

6 Steven Cherry, *Doing Different: Politics and the Labour Movement in Norwich 1880–1914* (Norwich, 1989), 119. For the history of the SDF see Walter Kendall, *Revolutionary Movements in Britain 1900–1921* (London, 1969) and Martin Crick, *The History of the Social Democratic Federation* (Keele, 1994).

7 Cherry, *Doing Different, passim*; David Howell, *British Workers and the Independent Labour Party 1888–1906* (Manchester, 1983), 10.

8 See Frank Bealey and Henry Pelling, *Labour and Politics 1900–1906, a history of the Labour Representation Committee* (London, 1958).

after 1906 Lynn ILP submitted the names of their proposed candidate in local elections for approval.

The groups were working in a common cause, but there were tensions between them as shown in the Lynn minutes. Some, but by no means all, of the Lynn group were members of trade unions, and they gave support to various groups of striking workers. They frequently made use of Fabian educational resources. The Lynn group was originally an independent socialist society, formed on 16 July 1897 under the name of King's Lynn Socialist Society. This was unusual – almost all local groups were affiliated to the Fabian Society, the ILP, or the SDF – but not unique: the *Labour Annual* for 1899 lists Lynn as one of just fifteen independent Socialist Societies.

The first, and many subsequent meetings, of the Society were held at the Rechabites Hall in Coronation Square, Kings Lynn (no doubt through the influence of White, see below). Seven people were present at the first meeting, all of them men. They resolved that three of their number, Messrs Dexter, Rowe and White, 'study the basic rules of other Socialist Societies and draw up from them a basis and rules that in their opinion, would be most suitable as lines on which to conduct this society and to submit the same to the next meeting'.

The seven who attended the first meeting were:

Frederick William White, the most important member of the different Socialist societies in Lynn, was born on 24 December 1869, the eldest of seven children. He began work as a bookstall boy at W. H. Smith on King's Lynn station. As a young man, he was employed by G. M. Bridges at his local scenic studios.[9] White commenced business on his own account in 1894, and was in business as a newsagent in Windsor Road and London Road for 37 years. He was a member of the Rechabite Order, a friendly society, founded in 1835 to promote temperance, and is listed as their secretary in 1904 and 1912 trade directories.

White stood unsuccessfully in the South Ward for Lynn Borough Council in 1905, 1908, 1909 and 1911. He was elected in for the same ward in 1924, and re-elected in 1927 (unopposed) and 1930. He served as mayor of the borough for the year 1930–1: one of his actions as mayor was to oversee the purchase by public subscription of a view of Lynn by Walter Dexter, which is now in the Town Hall.

White married Mary Elizabeth Walker in 1896, born in Stanhoe, and the eldest of a family of fourteen. She survived him. At the time of his death in

---

9 The 1883 trade directory describes Bridges as 'artist' at 9 St John's Street.

1931, White had two surviving daughters, one of whom was Annie Amelia, later Mrs Gent of Heacham: born in 1892, she had worked as his assistant in the shop, and was also a member of the Independent Labour Party. His other daughter was Dorothy Edith White, born in 1895. The three Whites (father, wife and daughter) were among the eleven members still in the Lynn ILP when it was dissolved in 1916. White died on 21 December 1931, just days before his 62nd birthday. His funeral was held at the Primitive Methodist church: the wreaths included one from 'The Down and Outs of King's Lynn'.

Walter Dexter (1876–1958), born in Wellingborough, brought up in Lynn, went to Birmingham School of Art 1892, returning by 1897 to become a founding member of the Lynn Socialist Party: the minutes record that he left the town once more in 1899, but returned to the area later. He is last mentioned in the minutes in 1906. Dexter became a well-known local artist: several of his paintings are in the Lynn Museum. He was one of a number of Lynn Socialists who were not from a Nonconformist background but were rationalists: he was a member of the Rationalist Press Association, founded in 1885 to promote pamphlets and books written by free thinkers.[10]

Dexter was a member of Norwich Woodpecker Club, an artistic society, as was Ethel Leach the Yarmouth suffragist, bringing together key members of the two groups analysed in this book. He married Helen May Chadwick in 1911. He died in 1958 after being struck by a motor-cycle in the Saturday Market Place in Lynn.[11]

Henry 'Harry' Bevis Rowe Born 1866, the son of a King's Lynn mariner. Partner in the firm of Watts and Rowe, letterpress printers, Arab Works, High Street. He was a member of the Oddfellows Friendly Society, a Methodist New Connexion preacher and an activist in the Lynn Working Man's Industrial Co-operative Society. Rowe died on 28 March 1900.[12]

John William Mills, born 1874: in 1901, he was a stationary-engine driver, working at a manure works for fourteen years, living at Frederick Place. He then became a bootmaker at several addresses, North Everard Street, Windsor Road (White's former premises): in 1911, he was a 'boot maker repairer retailer' and lived at London Road. Not a founder member of Lynn

---

10 See Bill Cooke, *The blasphemy depot: a hundred years of the Rational Press Association* (London, 2003). Beatrice Green and Arthur Dorer were also Rationalist Society members.

11 His story is told in Charlotte Paton, *A Portrait of Walter Dexter, an enigmatic man* (Guist, 1994).

12 See his obituary in *Lynn News and County Press* (hereafter *LN*), 7 Apr. 1900.

ILP in October 1906, he joined in February 1907. Like White, he remained in the society until it was dissolved in 1916. He was co-opted onto the Council in 1915, the first Socialist to achieve this. Died from tuberculosis, 16 December 1916.[13]

Robert George Stanford, born 1853, a postman. Married Sarah Anne Rayner at St John the Evangelist, Lynn, 1878; died in Lynn 1914. However, by then he had long left the society: he is not mentioned in the minutes after 1897. He is described as 'late' and as 'postman' of Albert Street, Lynn, in the Lynn Roll of Honour when his son William (one of six soldier sons) was killed in action 18 April 1917.

Charles Grey [sometimes Gray] Rix, a steam engineer draughtsman, born Lynn 1848. At the time of the 1901 census he was living at Valinger's Road, Lynn. His son later became a member as well. Rix senior is last mentioned in the minutes in 1901, but continues to appear in Lynn electoral registers until 1910. At time of 1911 census, he was living in Northfleet, Kent.

Richard Fraser, a postman. Born 1878, Benares, India (his father was killed in Afghan wars). Brought up in Lynn by his grandmother: in 1901 living with his uncle and grandmother at South Everard Street, Lynn. When Lynn ILP was founded in October 1906, Fraser did not join immediately, but, like Mills, he did so in February 1907. Left Lynn for Nottinghamshire in 1907–8; served in Royal Engineers 1915–19; in Mansfield 1930, still working with Post Office. Returned to Lynn soon after, committed suicide at his home 4 Beech Road, Lynn 1934.[14]

At its second meeting on 18 August, the rules and objects of the Society were duly presented, accepted and signed by twelve members, again all male. The new members included three railway workers (two clerks – Arthur Dorer and John Charles Triance – and an engine driver, John Thomas Neave), the first of many railwaymen to join the various Socialist societies.

The society had just one object: 'The education of the Community in the Principles of Socialism'. This was to be achieved by a programme of work which had four points. There were to be 'meetings for the discussions of questions connected with Socialism'; 'further investigation of economic problems'; the 'systematic distribution of Socialist literature' and 'the advocacy of a forward policy in all municipal matters affecting the

---

13 See his obituary in *LN*, 23 Dec. 1916.
14 See *LN*, 10 and 17 Aug. 1934.

social advancement of the people.' The members clearly sought to distance themselves from the political mainstream. The Society's first rule was that candidates for membership 'must pledge themselves to sever all official connection with either political party'. They also initiated for themselves and for a wider public a campaign of socialist education. This began (as it did for so many socialists of their era) with a reading and discussion group based around Robert Blatchford's *Merrie England*, with a chapter to be read and discussed at each meeting. They also involved themselves closely in local trade union issues even if they seem to have lacked many union members. Early in their existence they discussed two current major industrial disputes, passing a motion supporting the Penrhyn Quarrymen (1896–7), and they supported the Engineers lockout (1897–98) with a collection at each meeting and arranged Union speakers wherever possible.[15] However, the defeat of the engineers 'proved the hopelessness of strikes as a method for improving industrial conditions' as the group themselves noted.[16] As Alun Howkins commented, this was a view held by many socialists especially those outside the ILP and does mark them as a quite distinctively socialist organisation. They also subscribed to the fund to support Pete Curran's campaign as ILP candidate in Barnsley in 1897.[17]

On 1 September 1898 the Socialist Society merged with the Lynn branch of the SDF to become Lynn Social Democratic Party.[18] In 1904, a new branch of the SDF was established in Lynn, and the Social Democratic Party changed its name back to the Socialist Society. Under the influence of John James Kidd, the group became part of the Lynn branch of the SDF on 25 March 1905. However, many of the members of the old group were not happy to be part of the SDF and left it to re-form the King's Lynn Socialist Society on 14 January 1906. Just nine months later, Frederick White steered this group into the ILP fold: the group became the King's Lynn Independent Labour Party on 16 September 1906 and kept this name until the dissolution of the branch a decade later. The Lynn branch of the SDF continued after 1906, but its minutes do not survive.

---

15 For Penrhyn, see *Minutes*, below, note 11, for the Engineers, notes 18 and 105.

16 Annual report presented at meeting of 12 Jan. 1899: see *Minutes*, below.

17 See *Minutes*, below, note 33.

18 This name appears to be unique to Lynn, although occasional fusions of Socialist groups are known elsewhere: for example, the ILP and SDF branches in Bristol amalgamated in 1896 to form a Socialist Council. See Keith Laybourn, 'The failure of Socialist unity in Britain c. 1893–1914', *Transactions of the Royal Historical Society* 4 (1994), 153–75: Laybourn (175) notes that the ILP and SDF worked especially closely together in Lancashire, with some people being members of both.

Labour Representation in King's Lynn

Naturally, the Socialist groups hoped to obtain positions of power, both at local and national level. There were three avenues for this in Lynn, all of which are much discussed in the minutes. (Many towns the size of Lynn had a fourth avenue between 1870 and 1902, the School Board, but there was never a School Board in Lynn).

The Board of Guardians

The Board raised a rate to care for the poor within the Borough, either in the Workhouse or by giving an allowance to the needy living at home. The Board was elected by the ratepayers, with an election every three years at which all seats were contested. The Socialist group secured its first electoral success in 1901, with J. J. Kidd being elected to Lynn Board of Guardians. Unfortunately, he then became involved in a sex scandal with one of the nurses at the Workhouse, especially embarrassing as Kidd's wife was also on the executive committee of the Socialist party: Kidd served out his term, and then stood again in 1904 but this time without the support of the Socialist group (who in fact put up three rival candidates). Further elections took place in 1904, 1907, 1910 and 1913 and in each case the group discussed whether or not to put up candidates. None of those who stood was successful.

The Borough Council

There was an election for the Borough Council every year in November. Each councillor took office for three years, so that one third of the council was elected each year. The town was divided into three wards – North, Middle and South – and two people were elected each year, each voter having two votes. Voters could vote for a single candidate ('plumping') or vote for any two candidates they chose. In the first years, the Socialist group did not put up candidates for the Borough Council, instead suggesting that Socialists vote for the candidate the executive committee recommended. In 1902, Kidd stood for South Ward and he stood again in 1903 (the scandal not having been made public) while Dexter stood for North Ward. Later, the group considered every year whether or not to put up candidates for the November election, sometimes putting up a candidate in one, two or even all three wards. None was successful.

Parliament

There were four general elections during the period covered by the minutes – 1900, 1906, January 1910 and December 1910. The group did not feel able to put up a Parliamentary candidate, an expensive project, in any of these elections – in 1909, they did give serious consideration to putting up a candidate at the next general election, but it came to nothing. In other elections they discussed whether to give their support to the Conservative or Liberal candidate, often rejecting both candidates as 'capitalistic'.

Although women could not vote or stand for election in Parliamentary elections, women ratepayers could vote and stand for election in elections for Boards of Guardians and, after 1907, borough councils. Several women did stand for the Lynn Guardians and some were elected: however, all the candidates put forward by the Socialist groups were male.

Foreign Affairs in Local Politics

Foreign affairs caused many tensions among radical groups and their attitudes often made them unpopular amongst the general population, especially when stirred up by a 'jingoist' press. At the very beginning of the century, the Boer War was opposed by many radicals as 'Imperialist' and the minutes record how a meeting led by J. J. Kidd was violently broken up by a mob. The jingoist attitude of the Lynn crowd is illustrated by the way in which the town celebrated the relief of Mafeking in May 1900 – when the news was announced by the mayor, the crowd burst into 'Rule Britannia' and the national anthem, there were processions and a great bonfire in the Tuesday Market Place.[19]

The build up to the First World War also led to tensions, the ILP opposing the arms race between Britain and Germany in the years before the war broke out and denouncing the war as capitalistic. The Parliamentary Labour party did not oppose the war (and its leader Ramsay MacDonald, as an opponent of the war, resigned on its outbreak), but ILP groups like that at Lynn opposed the arms build-up, conscription and the war itself: this may have contributed to the many resignations from the party in 1914, eventually leading to its collapse.

Membership of the Independent Labour Party

No subscription books survive before the autumn of 1906. Before that, names of people wanting to join often appear in the minutes. However, this is clearly not complete as many people, including personalities as prominent as the Kidds, appear in the minutes as members, without any record of

---

19 *Lynn Advertiser* (hereafter *LA*), 25 May 1900, *LN*, 26 May 1900. Lynn was very much a Tory town. In Norwich, in contrast, 'there was enough of a Liberal tradition to avoid the worst excesses of jingoism'. (Cherry, *Doing Different*, 48).

having been formally admitted. Also, there is never any note of any person resigning.

A subscription book survives for members of the Lynn ILP, beginning at its foundation in October 1906, (NRO, SO 297/11). Thirty-eight members joined the new party on its formation. Just five of them were women, four being the wives of members. The only 'independent' woman was Miss Ethel Sporne, and she was one of four people who resigned during the first year (the others resigning were J. H. Jarvis, B. E. Parker and G. Castleton).

The treasurer's book for 1908–9 indicates the complexities of counting the number of members at any given time (NRO, SO 297/7). At the start of the year, there were 63 members in the subscription book. However, fourteen of these paid no subscription during the year, reducing the number of paid-up members to 49. The losses were more than compensated for by 25 new members joining, making a total of 74. However, of the new members, five did not in fact pay any subscription money and three more resigned during the year, reducing the number of paid-up members at the end of the year to 66, an overall increase of just three.

The peak year for membership was 1909–10 when 85 members are listed. Just eight were women, five the wives of members, one a sister, one a daughter, and just one 'independent' woman, Miss Britton. Addresses are given for about half the members: five lived in London Road, three in Windsor Road, and one or two in each of South Everard Street, Greyfriars Road, Friars St, Guanock Terrace, Littleport Street, South Street, Norfolk Street, New Conduit Street, Wisbech Road and Hospital Walk. These were in the main terraced houses in South Lynn, to the south of St Margaret's church not far from the railway station where many worked.[20] The poorest part of Lynn, in contrast, was to the north, the North End, especially associated with fishing families.[21]

Sixteen members lived in towns or villages outside Lynn, usually in the Fens. Six were from Wisbech, and one or two from each of the following: Gaywood, Hunstanton, Heacham, Snettisham (Albert Ducker, coachmaker, and his sister Clara Ann Ducker, both of Kingston House, the latter the only female with an 'out of town' address), North Wootton, Terrington St John, Terrington St Clement, Tilney and Sutton Bridge: some of these are a fair distance from Lynn. No attendance registers survive so it is not known

---

20 John Raby, the son of an engine driver and brought up in South Lynn, later reflected 'my parents were of good, sturdy, independent stock'. (J. W. Raby, *The Allotted Span in King's Lynn, 1879–1949*, (King's Lynn, 1950), 9).

21 Life in the North End is vividly evoked in Caroline Davison, *The Captain's Apprentice: Ralph Vaughan Williams and the story of a folk song* (London, 2022), 13–40.

how often they attended meetings, or how they travelled, perhaps in many cases by railway.

Occupations are not given, but by comparing the names with the 1911 census, it is possible to make an analysis of about fifty of the members. The striking feature is the number of railway workers, 21 in all (fifteen drivers, six railway clerks, firemen and others). No doubt, most – perhaps all – these men were trade unionists.[22]

The Amalgamated Society of Railway Servants (ASRS) played a key role in Labour history at several moments. It was the ASRS who put forward the resolution at the 1899 Trade Union Congress to summon a conference of interested parties to make plans for labour representation in Parliament. As Henry Pelling pointed out, they 'stood to gain very much by representation in Parliament, where so much railway legislation was discussed and enacted.'[23] ASRS secretary Richard Bell was one of the first MPs elected through the Labour Representation Committee in 1900 (along with Keir Hardie of the ILP). However, like many trade unionists he was in sympathy with the Liberal Party rather than the Labour Party: in 1904, he was officially regarded as having lapsed from the LRC, and when the Parliamentary Labour Party was formed after the 1906 general election, Bell did not become part of it, remaining with the Liberals. In 1913, the ASRS amalgamated with other railway unions to form the National Union of Railwaymen, one of the most powerful trade unions in the country.

No other group comes anywhere near the railwaymen in terms of numbers, but seven members can be loosely grouped as housebuilders including painters and plasterers.[24] Small businessmen continued to be important – a tobacconist (White), a draper, a printer, a grocer, a coal merchant.

The middle classes are also represented in the number of teachers, most from outside Lynn: Harry Lowerison at Heacham ran his own school, but the others worked for local authorities: Felix Mendelssohn Walker at Wisbech, James Sparkes and William Woods at Terrington St John,

---

22 Railway workers were highly unionised: 'by 1910 over 116,000 people who worked on the railways were members of a union. Two-thirds of these were members of the ASRS', Alan Haworth and Dianne Hayter (eds.) *Men Who Made Labour* (Abingdon, 2006), 100. For the history of the railway trades unions see Philip S. Bagwell, *The Railwaymen: the History of the National Union of Railwaymen* (London, 1963).

23 Henry Pelling, *A short history of the Labour Party* (London 1961), 9. See also Howell, *British Workers*, 69–83, for the role of railwaymen within the ILP.

24 Compare the early Socialist housepainters in the novel by Robert Tressell, *The Ragged-Trousered Philanthropists*, completed by 1910, published in abridged form in 1914, unabridged form 1956, and essential reading for anyone interested in the history of the labour movement.

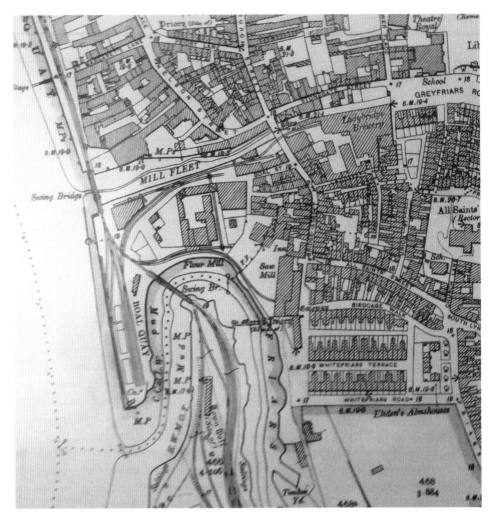

Figure 2. King's Lynn, OS Map six-inch to one mile, 1905. The first meeting
hall was in Coronation Square, the open space below the 'Grey' of Greyfriars
Road, the second in Windsor Road. Many Socialists lived very close, in Windsor
Road, North and South Everard streets and other nearby addresses.
Source: Norfolk Heritage Library.

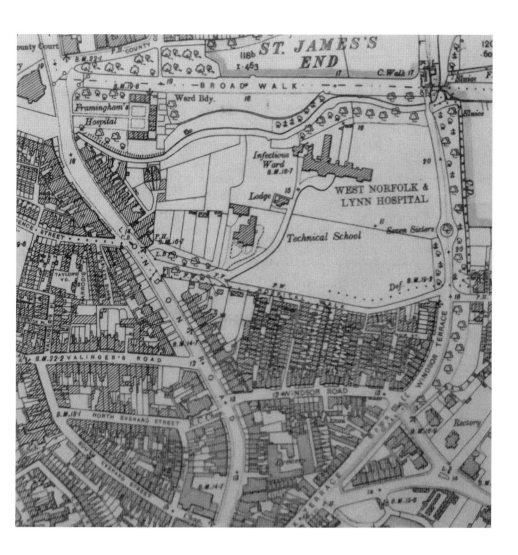

Henry Green at Sutton Bridge and Robert Sporne in Lynn itself: his sisters Susan and Ethel were also Lynn schoolteachers and, at different times, ILP members. Many were no doubt members of the National Union of Teachers, established in 1870.[25] Other middle-class members might include W. Jarvis, an 'architect', and Burns Snodgrass, a 'science student' who lived with his mother, the family being the only one on this list to have a live-in servant at the time of the 1911 census.

The ages of forty-nine members can be deduced from census returns. Twelve were in their mid- or late-twenties, twenty-one in the thirties, eleven in their forties, four in their fifties. The youngest was Snodgrass, twenty-three, while the oldest was Thomas Seapy, seventy-four, a retired stevedore.

Numbers declined after 1908–9: there were forty-two members in 1911–12, thirty-one in 1913–14. By 1915–16, membership had dwindled greatly and the end of the ILP group in Lynn was inevitable. There were just eleven members: Mr, Mrs and Miss White, Mr and Mrs Frost, Mr and Mrs Triance, J.W. Spurling, J. Mills, J. Neave and J. Pooley. Of course, this was primarily due to the special circumstances of the First World War: less than a decade later, Labour formed a government for the first time. The rapid rise of Labour was reflected in Lynn as well. The first-ever Labour Parliamentary candidate was Robert Walker (1878–1969) of the National Union of Agricultural Labourers, who stood in the general election of 1918: in a straight fight with a Unionist candidate, he obtained 9,780 votes, losing by just 366 votes.[26] A quarter of a century later, Lynn had its first Labour Member of Parliament when Frederick Wise (1887–1968) won the seat in the 1945 general election.

At a local level, the first Labour borough councillor was John Mills in the South Ward, co-opted in June 1915 by virtue of a wartime pact between all three parties.[27] On Mills' death in December 1916, another Socialist, John William Raby, was co-opted in his place. When normal elections resumed in 1919, two Labour councillors were elected in the South Ward (Raby and Robert Bunnett) and the number of Labour councillors grew in the 1920s

---

25 See M. A. Lawn 'Organised teachers and the Labour movement, 1900–1930', Open University PhD thesis, 1982: Lawn (13) quotes a contemporary reference to teachers' 'growing interest in socialism'.

26 The constituency had been expanded to include much of the former division of North-West Norfolk, so the votes perhaps included those of radicalised farm workers. See Alun Howkins, *Poor Labouring Men: rural radicalism in Norfolk 1872–1923* (London, 1985).

27 Not everyone was happy with the pact: former mayor Frank Rust Floyd (see below, page 60, note 128) considered standing for the Conservative Party against Mills, but in the end did not submit nomination papers, leaving Mills unopposed. (*LN*, 5 Jun. 1915).

and 1930s: in 1945, Labour secured a majority on the Council for the first time. Four Labour men served as mayors of the borough between 1927 and 1947, three of them twice (Raby, Thomas Asa Frost, Bunnett twice each, White once). All four feature in these minutes, which thus record the march of Socialism in King's Lynn from the humblest beginnings (just seven members in 1897) to positions of power and authority within the borough.

Note on Transcription
The text has been reproduced as exactly as possible, including misspellings in the original; likewise, the original punctuation has been retained.

Layout
Between 16 September 1906 and 19 April 1910 and again between 4 July and 15 September 1910, the minute-taker placed a line space between each paragraph of the minutes. To save space, these have been omitted in the transcription.

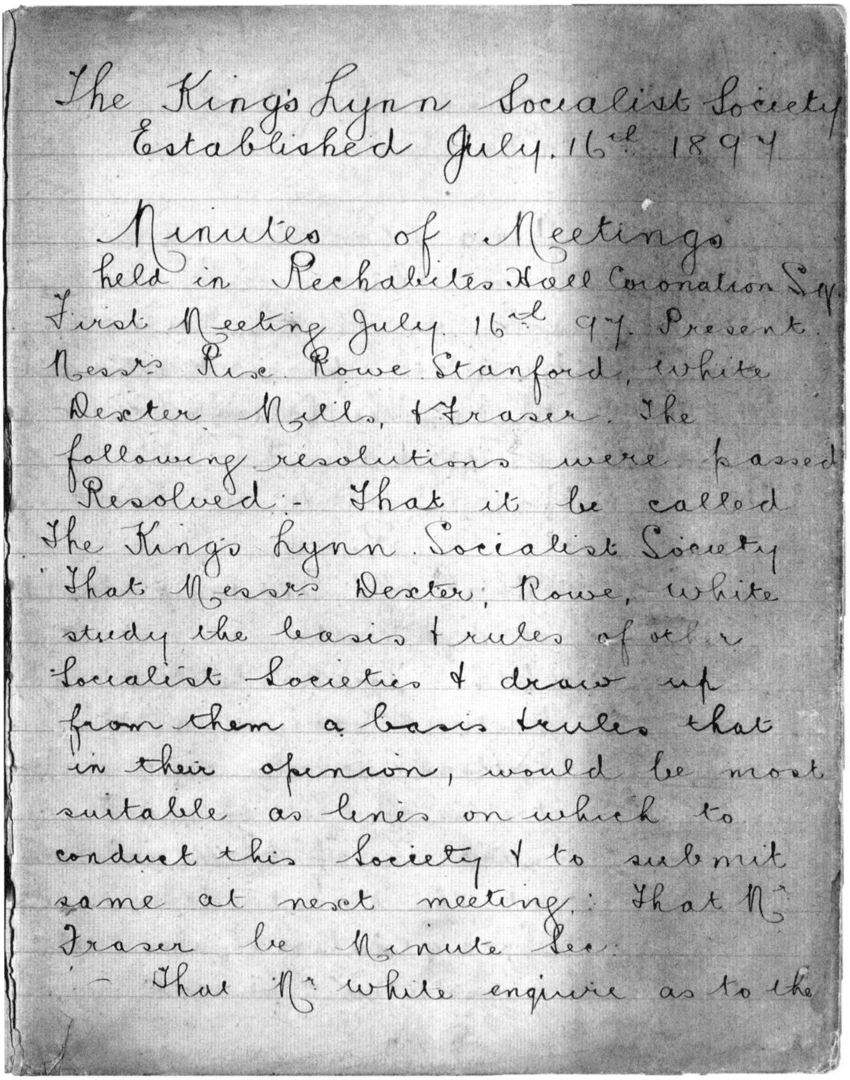

Figure 3. First page of King's Lynn Socialist Society minutes.
Source: Norfolk Record Office, (NRO, SO 297/1).

Minutes of the King's Lynn Socialist Society, July 1897–July 1898[1]

The King's Lynn Socialist Society established July 16th 1897.[2]

Minutes of Meetings held in Rechabites Hall Coronation Square.[3]

First Meeting July 16th '97. Present: Messrs Rix, Rowe, Stanford, White, Dexter, Mills and Fraser.[4] The following Resolutions were passed.

Resolved: That it be called the King's Lynn Socialist Society. That Messrs Dexter, Rowe, White study the basis & rules of other Socialist Societies and draw up from them a basis & rules that in their opinion would be most suitable as lines on which to conduct this society & to submit same at next meeting. That Mr Fraser be Minute Sec.

That Mr White enquire as to the terms upon which we can have the Rechabite Hall for meetings.

---

1 NRO, SO 297/1. On flyleaf, 'R. Fraser 36 South Everard St Lynn'. For Fraser, see Introduction: as secretary, the minute book would be in his care. Also on flyleaf, added in pencil, presumably in August 1914: '1914 Clarion Cycle Club Meet. Mr White went over to Heacham to Ruskin School Lowerisons & broke news war had started'. See below, note 565 for outbreak of the war.

2 The formation of the new society was duly noted in the Socialist press. The *Clarion* at first gave the name of the secretary as Fred Wright, later correcting this to White (*Clarion*, 28 Aug. and 4 Sept. 1897). *Justice* described the formation of an independent party by the local socialists as 'a mistake', opining that such independent groups would soon join the SDF (*Justice*, 7 Aug. 1897).

3 A friendly society, founded in 1835 to promote temperance. Their Hall, according to Hillen, had been built in 1828 as a Roman Catholic chapel by the French refugee P. Louis Dacheux. According to the 1883 trade directory the Roman Catholic school was held there, 'and is now [he is writing in 1907] a socialists' clubroom' (Henry J. Hillen, *History of the Borough of King's Lynn* (Norwich, 1911), vol. 2, 611,644. This part of King's Lynn has been completely replanned: Coronation Square lay roughly where Hillington Square is now.

4 See Introduction for biographies of these seven founding members.

Meeting Aug 18th '97

Mr Rix in chair. 10 Members present.

The Chairman read the Rules of the Society & all present appended their signatures.

The following Resolutions were passed:

Resolved: That Mr White be Secretary

           "   Mr Rowe be Treasurer

That the Secretary should send a letter in the name of the Society to the Head Master & Teachers of the British School congratulating them on the splendid success of their scholars at the recent Scholarship Examination, also that a notice of the resolution be sent for insertion to the Lynn News & Advertiser.[5]

Resolved: that propaganda work be commenced at once by the distribution of Socialistic literature.

The Secretary read a letter he had received from Mr Hunter of Leicester wishing every success & offering assistance as a speaker on Socialism.[6]

Letters for insertion in the Lynn News were read by Messrs White & Rowe.[7]

Walter Dexter Sept 1st 1897

Meeting Sept 1st 1897

Nine Members present. Mr Dexter in chair. Correspondence read by General Secretary. Letters & pamphlets from Land Nationalization League.[8]

---

5 The British School was in Blackfriars Street, built in 1843. The 1900 Trade Directory names Edwin Broome as master, Miss Emma Gowing as mistress. Thirteen of the sixteen successful examinations for scholarships in the town came from this school, and all fourteen candidates from the school taking the Pitman's shorthand exam were successful. See *Lynn News and County Press,* the local Liberal newspaper, published on Saturdays (hereafter *LN* and often referred to simply as *Lynn News*) 21 Aug. 1897. The *Lynn Advertise*r (hereafter *LA*) was the Conservative newspaper, published on Fridays.

6 Hunter not identified, perhaps the A. Hunter of Cedar Road, Leicester who wrote long a letter to his local newspaper, deploring the jingoism of Tory politicians and describing the horrors of war in graphic tones. (*Leicester Mercury,* 17 Nov. 1897). Hunter is not mentioned in B. Lancaster, *Radicalism, Co-operation and Socialism: working-class politics in Leicester 1860–1906* (Leicester, 1987), nor in his thesis under the name William Lancaster, 'Radicalism to Socialism: the Leicester working class 1860–1906' (Warwick University PhD 1982). No Hunter is listed in Nick Newitt's website The Who's Who of Radical Leicester (visited 1 December 2023); www.nednewitt.com.

7 Only White's letter was published, a long letter on the subject of drink: 'To no class of reformers are the evil effects of the drink traffic more apparent than the Socialist'. *(LN,* 21 Aug. 1897).

8 Land nationalisation was official Trades Union Congress policy from 1886, and was supported by both the ILP and the SDF. The Land Nationalisation Society was founded in 1881, Alfred Russell Wallace being its first president.

Letter from Mr Addison of Wisbech wishing success.[9]

The following resolutions were passed:

1 Resolved: That we become members of the L N L the minimum subscription of which is one shilling per annum.

2x That we adopt a forward policy in all matters affecting the social advancement of the people.

3x: That this meeting of Lynn Socialists regrets the fact that the magistrates should have granted a new licence for the sale of intoxicating liquors to the Lynn & County Stores High St being of the opinion that the number of licenced houses is already to [sic] large.[10]

4   The Penrhyn Settlement.[11]

That this meeting of Lynn Socialists congratulates the Bethesda quarrymen upon their vindication of the right of combination, but that we refuse to regard the settlement of the dispute as satisfactory or final inasmuch as there still remains the root cause of the whole trouble viz 'the absolute power of one irresponsible man over the material upon which thousands of workers are dependent & which by every moral right belongs to no <u>individual or class, but to the whole community</u>'.

Letters read for press & one private letter to the Editor asking if he would allow a column to be devoted to Socialism to be contributed by members of this Society.

---

9 Probably William Addison, listed as of Victoria Road, Wisbech, in the 1900 *Labour Annual* 'Directory of Social Reformers': William Addison is certainly the Addison mentioned in SO 297/3. However, there was another 'Socialist' Addison in Wisbech, Charles Henry Addison, recorded as a grain porter in the 1871 census, later superintendent of Wisbech borough cemetery, who chaired a Socialist meeting in Norwich Market Place 26 June 1898 (*Justice*, 16 Jul. 1898). (The latter's son Alfred joined the Northamptonshire Regiment on the outbreak of First World War, dying of wounds 26 Sept. 1914. aged just seventeen.)

10 Early Socialists, many from a Nonconformist background, were acutely aware of how a working man's life could be ruined by drink. Several, including Keir Hardie himself, were lifelong abstainers. For statistics on the number of licensed houses in Lynn, see: https://www.norfolkpubs.co.uk/kingslynn/kingind.htm (visited 16 Dec. 2023).

11 The Bethesda quarries were owned by Lord Penrhyn, who refused to allow the workers to join a union. The long-running dispute led to a strike in 1896 lasting eleven months. There was a further walk-out in 1900, with the quarrymen finally being forced by poverty to return to work in 1903. See Charles Sheridan Jones, *What I saw in Bethesda* (London) 1903: new edition (Llandysul, Wales, 2003) with an introduction by J. Elwyn Hughes explaining the background; see also W Hamish Fraser, *A History of British Trade Unionism, 1700–1998* (London, 1999), 103–4, and for the second strike, Jean Lindsay, *The great strike: a history of the Penrhyn Quarry dispute of 1900–1903* (Newton Abbot, 1987).

Election of Members
William Hancock pro: by Com Mills.[12] \Sec by Com White – elected/. The secretary informed the meeting that Mr J J Kidd was desirous of becoming a member & he therefore pro: him as a member.[13] As no one seconded this a ballot was taken the result being his rejection.

Distribution of Literature
Several hundred leaflets entitled 'What Socialism is and what Socialism is not' were on the table purchased by the Sec for the Society.[14] Each member present took some for distribution.

Meeting Sept 17th 1897
Seven members present. Com Rowe in chair.

New Members
William Hancock elected a member.

Candidates for Membership
William Dennis[15] pro: by Com Rowe, seconded by Com White.   Carried.

Municipal work and programme
Questions for Town Councillors

I Proper Treatment of Labor
1 Will you promote the direct employment of labour by the Council?
2 Where contracting is necessary will you try to put down all sweating, and rigidly enforce the rule of employing only firms which

---

12 William Hancock, probably the man of that name living at Hockham Street, Lynn in 1901, a tar distiller, born 1856. He signed up to the Society's rules on 17 September 1897, the first person after the original twelve signatories to do so.

13 John James Kidd (1866–1920), in 1881 a domestic servant in the house of Charles Plowright, medical practitioner (where he presumably met his future wife, see n. 69); described as florist and seedsman at Windsor Terrace in 1891 census, and as nurseryman at Goodwins Road in 1896 trade directory and 1901 census: he eventually did join and features frequently in the minutes. He may have been rejected initially because his sympathies were with the SDF. *Justice* recorded that a new branch of the SDF was founded at Lynn in the first week of October 1897, with Kidd as its Secretary. It commented that Mr and Mrs Kidd had left the Liberal party to throw in their lot with the SDF: 'both are energetic and enthusiastic workers, and a distinct acquisition to the S.D.F. in East Anglia' (*Justice*, 2 and 9 Oct. 1897: the latter noted that there was already a Socialist Society in Lynn but hoped they would soon become members of the SDF). Kidd was Lynn branch delegate at the SDF annual conference, August 1900.

14 A digest of Robert Blatchford's *Merrie England* (see note 21), printed with this title in several forms after 1895.

15 William Dennis of South Street, Lynn, born 1851, dock labourer. He signed the rules of the Society on 22 September 1897, the fourteenth person to do so (after the original twelve and Hancock).

(a) Pay the Trade Union rate of wages for the particular occupation?
(b) Observe the standard hours of labour, where such standard exists?
(c) Full liberty of combination?

II <u>Artizan Dwellings</u>
(1.) Will you press for ~~the~~ prompt and extensive action by the Council, for the condemnation of unsanitary dwellings under the Artizans Dwelling Acts?[16]
2. Will you support the construction and maintenance <u>by the Council</u> itself of an adequate number of improved dwellings at a fair rental?

III <u>A Democratic Council</u>
1 Will you support a proposal to grant the use of a room in the Municipal Buildings for the meetings of Trade Unions?
2 Will you support any reasonable proposal for evening meetings of the Council & its Committees so that men at work in the day can become effective members?
3 Are you in favour of
   (a) The abolition of aldermen & the formation of the Council exclusively by direct election?
4 Will you press for the effective and regular inspection of every house in the borough so as to secure thorough sanitation?
5 Will you press for the publication of an annual report of the Council's work with a full financial statement of statistics at a cheap rate?
6 Will you vote for the provision of a Free Public Library and reading room for the borough?[17]
7 Will you oppose the sale of the freehold of any land owned by the Corporation?

16 The Artisans' and Labourers' Dwellings Improvement Act of 1875 allowed local councils to buy up slum areas, clear them and rebuild on the site. The Housing of the Working Classes Act of 1890 offered greatly increased loans to councils. See John Burnett, *A Social history of housing, 1815–1985* (London, 1986).

17 The Public Libraries act of 1850 gave large local boroughs the power to establish free public libraries, paid for out of the rates. The power was extended to smaller boroughs such as King's Lynn under an act of 1866. However, King's Lynn did not take up the option. See Thomas Kelly, *History of public libraries in Britain 1845–1965* (London, 1973). Kelly (125 n.) notes that King's Lynn was one of seventeen local authorities that preferred to put money into a subscription library rather than provide a free library. See also below, notes 110, 307.

<u>Engineers Lock-Out.</u>[18]

Pro by Com White on behalf of Com Bloy[19] that the members be invited to make a weekly contribution, to be handed in to the Sec. who would forward same to the Fund organised by the Clarion Newspaper.[20]   Carried Unan.

<u>Literature</u>

Res; That we take the book Merrie England for the study and discussion of its contents.[21] Also that each member should write out a list of Socialistic Literature he possessed & would be willing to lend. In order to form a Circulating Library among the members of the society.

The Sec read the letter by which he informed Mr J J Kidd of the result of his candidature for membership proposed at ~~last~~ the meeting of Sept 1st.

Com Dexter read a letter he had received from Mr Kidd in reference to his rejection as a candidate for membership of the Society. The Sec was instructed to reply to it by letter in the name of the Scty of which the following is a copy:

Mr J J Kidd   Sept 21st

Dear Sir

We are directed to inform you that your letter was read at the last meeting by Com Dexter. We venture to think you are in error in supposing that our Scty did not fully understand your position.

You were pro. by Com White and duly seconded but the proposal was voted

---

18 A lock-out and strike in the British engineering industry took place between June 1897 and January 1898. Henry Pelling calls it 'the first major strike or lock-out in British history'. It began in London after the men demanded a 48 hour week (Henry Pelling, *A History of British Trade Unionism* (London, 1963), 112). See also D. Howell, *British Workers and the Independent Labour Party, 1888–1906*, (Manchester, 1983), 84–94.

19 William Bloy of Wellesley Street Lynn, born 1850, iron turner. One of the twelve original signatories to the rules of the Society, 18 August 1897. He or his son, also William, joined the Lynn ILP in 1910–11.

20 A socialist weekly newspaper founded by Robert Blatchford in 1890 which sold 40,000 copies a week at a penny each.

21 In 1893, the *Clarion* began to serialise Blatchford's *Merrie England*, a key text for many budding socialists. According to Martin Pugh, in the first year alone, the book sold 700,000 copies in its one penny edition and a further 25,000 in a one-shilling version: 'the book stood in a tradition of patriotic literature rooted in the belief that 'at present Britain does not belong to the British; it belongs to a few of the British.' (Martin Pugh, *Speak for Britain* (London, 2011), 28). Echoes of this tradition recurred in the slogan of Labour leader Jeremy Corbyn in the general elections of 2017 and 2019: 'For the Many, not the Few'. Emanuel Shinwell noted that 'It has been rightly said that for every convert to Socialism made by *Das Kapital* there were a hundred made by *Merrie England* in the twenty years that it was essential reading for every thoughtful young man in the working classes'. Shinwell, *The Labour Story* (London, 1963), 43.

upon with the result that the Scty, in their wisdom or otherwise, did not accept you as a member. Com Dexter was willing to pro. you again but having so recently considered & decided upon the ~~subject~~ question we felt it would not be in order to allow the pro. to go before the meeting. We also wish [*sic*] also to say that our Society is not confined to members of one sex. Yours truly

Fred White, Secy
H Rowe (Chairman of Meeting)

The Chairman complimented Com Dexter upon a letter he had written and had had accepted by the 'Reformer.'[22]

Meeting Sept 22nd '97
Cde Dexter in Chair
11 members present. Cde Dennis pro. at last meeting elected a member of the society.
Candidates for Memship – Ernest Cremer[23] proposed by Cde Fraser sec by Cde White.
The following resolutions were passed
That we offer the Rechabites a yearly rental of £10 for the use of their hall.

Letters to Press

The Secy read a letter he proposed sending to the Lynn News in reply to remarks made by the Lynn Advertiser on Trades Federation.[24]

<u>Engineers Lock Out Fund of the Clarion</u>

The Secy received contributions to the above fund amounting to 12/- from members present.
Cde Dennis informed us that Mr Bell of the Amalgamated Union of Labourers was coming to Lynn in order to form a branch of that Society & would be here two months.[25]
Cde Dexter's letter to the Reformer was read by the Minute Secy.

---

22 A London periodical covering social issues. It ran only from March 1897 to December 1904.

23 Charles Ernest Cremer, born 1879, in 1901 an assistant in a draper's shop, boarding in St James Street, Lynn. One of the earliest members, signing up to the rules of the Society 30 December 1897. Married Edith Mary Clift in Lynn, 1902. Last mentioned in the minutes in 1904, when he joined the Social Democratic Party, and later left Lynn: by 1911 the family were living in Walton-on-Thames, Surrey.

24 The article, published in *LA*, 17 Sept. 1897, concerned resolutions discussed at the Trade Union Congress in Birmingham. Replies by Fred White and Walter Dexter appeared in *LN*, 25 Sept. 1897.

25 The Amalgamated Union of Labourers was by 1897 the largest trade union in the United Kingdom with over 20,000 members. Joseph Bell was union corresponding secretary between 1888 and 1898 and union secretary from 1898 to 1923.

Meeting Oct 5th '97

Cde Rowe in Chair. 10 Members present.

Owing to the unavoidable absence of the Minute Secy the minutes were read by Cde White. On the motion of Cde Bloy sec by Cde Dexter the minutes were adopted.

The Secy reported that he attended meeting of the Rechabites & that after some discussion they accepted our offer of £10 for the use of the hall for the coming year.

Cde Mills moved that the Genl Secy be instructed to send the address of the Society to the Editor of the 'Labour Annual' & to order six copies of the aforesaid work.[26] Cde Triance seconded & the motion was carried.[27]

The formation of a "Merrie England Class" was discussed & it was decided that a chapter be read at the following meeting. The Secy said that much of the business might now be left to the Executive so that more time could be given to "Questions connected with Socialism" by members attending the general meetings. Although no resolution was put this was endorsed by the members present.

The Chairman was asked for names of those who would be willing to study "Economics" during the winter months. Cde Dexter moved & Cde sec that the Chairman write to "Fabian Society" for particulars of the correspondence class in Economics &c.[28] This was carried.

The sec having collected contributions towards Engineers Lock Out Fund the meeting closed.

Meeting Wed Oct 13th 97.

~~There was a large gathering of members and friends~~

Com Rowe in Chair. 12 members present many of whom had brought friends to hear Mr S W Belderson of St Martins le Grand Assistant Secy of the Postal Telegraph Clerks Assoc[n] give an address on State Employment &

---

26 *Labour Annual, a yearbook of social, economic and political reformers*, issued under the auspices of the *Clarion* from 1895 onwards. The editor was Joseph Edwards.

27 John Charles Triance, born in Lynn 1873, a railway clerk. At the time of the 1901 census, he is described as a railway collector and canvasser, boarding in Great Yarmouth. His address in 1911 was 50, South Everard St, Lynn. One of the original twelve signatories to the rules of the Society 18 August 1897, he put in many years of loyal service; like White and Mills he was still a member in 1915–16.

28 Fabian Society, political group founded in London in 1884 and one of the groups participating in the formation of the Labour Representation Committee in 1900. Early members included George Bernard Shaw, H. G. Wells, Sidney and Beatrice Webb. Played an important educational role, organising classes and issuing large numbers of 'Fabian tracts', pamphlets on themes of social justice, but remained primarily a London intellectual society.

Socialism.[29] Several P O employees were present. The Chairman introduced Mr Belderson to those present & after a few appropriate remarks called upon him to address the meeting. In the course of his remarks the speaker touched upon the following subjects.

"The State as a model employer. Advantages of Government employment in the PO. The Pension Scheme. The permanent employment. Its disadvantages. No ~~liberty~~ combination recognised, no career remote chance of superannuation owing to the fact of the unhealthy conditions & severe mental strain under which they work. \He also spoke on/ The recent trouble. The many grievances & the Parliamentary Enquiry into same. The Report of the Tweedmouth Committee & the great discontent that prevailed at the findings of the above committee throughout the whole PO service.[30]

In conclusion the speaker advocated the federation of the various associations into one body having for its object the betterment of conditions of labour of the whole Postal & Telegraph Service.

Com Stanford proposed a vote of thanks to Mr Belderson for the excellent address. Cde White seconded. Carried. Mr Belderson thanked those present for their kind attention & said that it had been a great pleasure to him to give an address & would be pleased to do so on another occasion if he were in Lynn. After a few remarks by the Chairman expressing on behalf of the members of their Society his sympathy with the grievances of the P O employees & wishing them success in their agitation, the meeting ended.

The Secretary received contributions to The Engineers Lock Out Fund.

Meeting 20 Oct 97
Present Comrades Rowe (Chairman), Triance, Mills, White, Dexter, Jarvis,[31] Dorer,[32] Bloy.

---

29 Samuel Walter Belderson (1869–1946), parliamentary secretary of the Postal Telegraph Clerks' Association, and active campaigner for its official recognition; considered a 'gentlemanly lobbyist'; gave evidence to the 1904 Bradford committee on Post Office Wages (Cd 2171); an address book in the archive gives his abode in 1898 as 82, Stockwell Road, London SW (NRO 297/9); in 1911, subpostmaster at New Hunstanton; elder brother of William John Belderson, see note 73.

30 Inter-departmental committee on post office establishments, headed by Lord Tweedmouth. The report, published in 1896, ran to over 700 pages.

31 William Jarvis junior was one of the twelve original signatories to the rules of the Society 18 August 1897. An architect, born 1875, of Valinger's Road, Lynn in 1901, later (by 1910) of Myrtledene, North Wootton. At first simply called Comrade Jarvis in the minutes, he is identified with his initial after another Jarvis, J. H. Jarvis, joined the party in 1902. William Jarvis was a founder member of Lynn ILP in October 1906.

32 Arthur Lawrence Dorer (1873–1958), one of eight children of Francis Dorer, a watch

Minutes read by Com White & adopted. On motion of Com White it was agreed that the class in economics & book box should stand over. Comrade Triance proposed that we open a fund for Pete Curran & send encouragement.[33] Seconded by Com Dexter. Carried. Coms White and Triance to write to Pete Curran.

Meeting Nov 5th 1897
Present Comrades Rowe (Chairman), Dennis, Dorer, White, Mills, Triance, Rix & Dexter.
1. The Secretary reported that during the fortnight he had collected £1.1. for the Engineers Lock Out Fund & had forwarded the same to the 'Clarion'.
2. The Chairman read extracts from the 'Clarion' and 'Labor Leader' on the recent municipal elections.[34] He said that Socialists had every reason to congratulate themselves on the results throughout the country. Among the most notable of the Socialists gains were West Ham (where they had won 3 seats), Hull (3), Bristol (2), Southend (2), Cardiff (1), but the most remarkable victory was the splendid success of Fred. Brocklehurst in the Harpuhey Ward, Manchester, who ousted the chairman of the Parks

---

and clockmaker who died in 1874: his widow Maria worked as a laundress while bringing up the children. Dorer became a railway clerk, later becoming Chief Clerk in Lynn of the Midland and Great Northern Railway. He worked on the railways for 45 years and took a leading part in the formation of the Railway Clerks' Association. In 1901 he was living at Paxton Terrace, Lynn. According to his friend John Raby, he was a member of the Fabian Society for many years. He married Beatrice Green (see below, note 213) in 1905: the ceremony was intentionally non-religious. The family were close friends of the Dexters: Dorer and Walter Dexter enjoyed visiting historic churches together while on tours propagating Socialism. In later life, he was involved with the Greenland Fishery Museum in Lynn. See obituary in *LA*, 7 and 14 Jan. 1958; J.W. Raby, *The Allotted Span in King's Lynn, 1879–1949* (King's Lynn, 1950), 80–2; Charlotte Paton, *A Portrait of Walter Dexter, an enigmatic man* (Guist, 2014), *passim.*

33 Peter 'Pete' Curran (1860–1910), trade unionist and politician, a national organiser of the gas-workers' union, a founder member of the ILP and on its National Administrative Council from 1893 to 1898. Also prominent in foundation of Labour Representation Committee. He stood for the ILP in Barrow in 1895 and in Barnsley in 1897: he was unsuccessful on each occasion. A contribution of five shillings from King's Lynn Socialist Society to the Barnsley election fund was noted in the *Labour Leader*, 6 Nov. 1897. See also D. Howell, *British Workers*, 19–20.

34 For the *Clarion*, see above, note 20; *Labour Leader*, Keir Hardie's newspaper founded (under that name) 1888 and edited by him. In 1905, he sold the newspaper to the ILP and John Bruce Glasier took over as editor. For contrasting attitudes reflected in the two newspapers see A. E. P. Duffy, 'Differing policies and personal rivalries in the origins of the Independent Labour Party', *Victorian Studies*, vol. 6 no. 1 (Sept. 1962), 43–65.

Committee by 259 votes.[35] The Secretary also read several extracts relating to the same subject.

3. The secretary read correspondence received from the I.L.P. in which it was strongly urged that the Society should affiliate with the National Party.

4. On the motion of Comrade White, seconded by Comrade Dennis, Comrade Dexter was appointed Municipal Secretary. Comrade Dennis moved & Comrade Triance seconded that Comrade Rowe be appointed Secretary for matters relating to the Board of Guardians.   This was carried.

5. The chairman read a letter by 'Clarion' appearing in the 'Lynn Gazette'[36] of the 5th inst advising the formation of an independent progressive party.

6. The following resolution was passed 'That this meeting congratulates Mr Dexter[37] on his election as Councillor for the Middle Ward, and regrets the fact that owing to the opposition of certain 'leading Liberals' Mr Springall was not also elected'.[38] The Secretary was instructed to forward copies to Messrs Dexter & Springall & to the local press.

7. The formation of a Labor Church was discussed but it was decided to leave the question to be dealt with by a special meeting.[39]

---

35 Fred Brocklehurst (1866–1926), founder member and a leading speaker of the ILP. In 1896, he was imprisoned for giving a political speech in a Manchester park (Boggart Hole Clough) in contravention of a newly-introduced bylaw: hence the sense of triumph in his victory over the chairman of the Parks Committee. He was proposed as secretary to the LRC on its foundation in 1900 but declined as he did not want to move to London. Later moved to the right, standing for the Conservative party in 1910.

36 Local weekly newspaper first brought out in 1883; Rex Stedman, *Vox Populi: the Norfolk press 1760–1900* (Library Association, 1971), 302, states simply that it 'did not survive many issues'. No copies exist in the British Newspaper Library or the Norfolk Library Service.

37 Walter Sothern Dexter (1848–1920), who in 1881 took over the photographic studio in Lynn High St that had been founded by his father in 1853. He was elected to Lynn Borough Council in 1897 as a Liberal, after standing unsuccessfully in 1895. He moved to Felixstowe in about 1907, after selling his High Street property to W H Smith; later moved to Streatham, South London. Member of Lynn Board of Guardians, Stanley Lodge of Oddfellows, sportsman and musician: see obituary *LA*, 18 Jun. 1920. He was the father of the Walter Dexter frequently mentioned in these minutes.

38 Robert French Springall, the second Liberal candidate for Middle Ward: the two men ran in tandem, issuing a joint manifesto. On this occasion he lost by just two votes: he served briefly on the Borough Council in the last years of the 1890s, losing once more in November 1900. Springall, a timber merchant, ran a steam sawmill in Lynn, beside the river Nar.

39 The Labour (also spelled Labor, as always in these minutes) Church was originally founded in Manchester in 1891 by John Trevor, a Unitarian minister. In 1894, the Council of the ILP recommended all its branches to form Labour Churches. (Mark Bevir, 'The Labour Church Movement 1891–1902', *Journal of British Studies* 38 (1999); Jacqueline Turner, 'The Soul of the Labour Movement – rediscovering the Labour Church 1891–1914', University of Reading thesis 2010). The Lynn church probably did not get beyond the discussion stage – it is not among the 79 established churches listed in Turner (pp. 193–4).

Minutes of Meeting Nov 12th 1897

10 Members present. Comrade Rowe in the chair.

1. The minutes of the last meeting were adopted on the motion of Comrade Triance.

2. The sec. read letters received from Messrs Dexter \& Springall/ thanking the members for their resolution etc. Resolved that the same be sent to the local press.

3. The sec read correspondence received from the I.L.P. relating to the question of affiliation.

4. Resolved that we consider the question of affiliation with the I.L.P. at the special meeting which is to be held to consider the formation of a Labor Church.

5. Resolved that the secretaries recently appointed \to/ watch the Town Council & the Board of Guardians on behalf of the Society, be requested to report monthly thereon.

6. The sec. reported that he had forwarded the 4th donation amounting to £1. 1 to the Lock-out Fund for the Engineers, & referred to the death of [*blank*] Fiddy of Lynn, a member of the Leicester branch of the A.S.E.[40]

7. \Comrade/ Dorer moved & Comrade White seconded that a committee (to consist of Comrades Rowe, White, Dorer & Dexter) be appointed to fix a date for the special meeting to be held to consider the question of a Labor Church.   This was carried.

8. Resolved that the secretary be instructed to write to the sec. of the P.S.A.[41] & offer to assist in collecting facts relating to insanitary dwellings.

Minutes of Meeting Nov 27th 1897

9 Members present – Comrade Rowe in the chair

1. The minutes of the last meeting were adopted on the motion of Comrade Rix.

2. The secretary read correspondence received from the I.L.P. relating to affiliation with that body, & much discussion ensued.

---

40 Amalgamated Society of Engineers. Herbert William Fiddy (1871–1897), baptised All Saints church 28 July 1872; living in Lynn in 1881 and 1891 census, where described as 'steam engineer apprentice' (hence the ASE connection); died in Lynn aged 25.

41 Pleasant Sunday Afternoon: the movement was started in about 1875 to provide social opportunities as an alternative to Sunday afternoon drinking and was especially popular with Nonconformist churches: in 1905, it was estimated that there were almost 2,000 such groups with about 250,000 members (*Aberdeen Journal*, 30 Sept. 1905). Documents at the Norfolk Record Office mention a programme of classes, 1892 and an outing to the coast, 1907, by Norwich groups (NRO, FC 13/73 and 90/62): the present minutes indicate that social issues were discussed by the Lynn group.

3. The sec. read correspondence received from the I.L.P. relating to lectures.
4. The sec. read a letter from Harry Snell of the Fabian Society offering to deliver a series of lectures in Lynn if the Lynn Socialists Society will provide a hall, & it was resolved that the sec. be instructed to write to Harry Snell and enquire the latest date on which he will require a definite answer, and in the meantime to make enquiries of the officials of local societies as to the support which they would be willing to give.[42]
5. The Chairman gave an account of the social given by the Lynn Branch of the S.D.F. in the St James Rooms on Nov 24th at which several members of the Lynn Socialists' society were present.
6. The secretary reported that since the last meeting he had forwarded the sum of £1.5 to the 'Clarion' Lock-out Fund for the Engineers.

Minutes of Special Meeting of Members \Dec/ convened to consider the Report of the Labor Church Committee.
Present – Comrades Triance (in the chair), Bush, Dennis, Dexter, Dorer, Fraser, Jarvis, Mills, Rowe, Piper and White (Sec).[43]
1. The minutes of the last meeting were read & adopted on the motion of Comrade Rowe seconded by Comrade Mills.
2. The secretary read correspondence from Comrade Harry Snell relating to Lectures & suggested that the matter should stand over for the present.
3. Comrade Rowe reported that the Committee appointed to consider the Labor Church question had met & that they recommend the Society to

---

42 Henry, later Baron Snell (1865–1944), self-educated secularist and socialist; moved from SDF to Fabians and ILP in 1894; author of various tracts; Labour candidate for Huddersfield; in 1910 London member (Division 6) of NAC; later MP Woolwich (1922–1931); peerage in 1931; Labour leader in House of Lords (1935–1940). See *ODNB*. Although the minutes do not make it clear, he came to Lynn on 7, 14, 21 and 28 March to deliver the four lectures. They were four out of a series of eight that he offered. Titles rejected by the Lynn Socialists were: The Industrial Outlook; Is Over-Population a Cause of Poverty?; The Regulation of the Drink Traffic; Can Government fix a living wage?

43 Bush and Piper are mentioned here for the first time: there has been no record of their admission to the Society. Frederick C. Piper of Saddlebow was one of the twelve original signatories to the rules of the Society 18 August 1897. Not mentioned after 1898, he is probably the F. Piper who joined the SDF in January 1906, and became a founder member of the Lynn ILP at the end of the year. Francis A. Bush, born 1875, was a solicitor's clerk: he lived with his widowed mother in Coronation Square, very close to Rechabites Hall. He was the fifteenth signatory to the Society's rules, signing on 5 October 1897. Later joined the SDF, writing to Mills on 27 January 1906 complaining that his name had appeared as a member of the Socialist Society: 'I am a member of the SDF … [I] am firmly convinced that we can do more good being part of one of the national parties whether ILP or SDF than in standing apart in 'splendid isolation''. Bush is listed as secretary of King's Lynn Horticultural Society in 1904 and 1912 trade directories.

form a Labor Church. On the motion of Comrade Jarvis seconded by Cde Dexter the report was adopted.

4. Cde Rowe proposed & Comrade Dennis seconded that we form a Labor Church, the management of which shall be left to the Executive Committee and which for the present shall be open only to members & their friends.

5. Resolved that for the future the general business of the Society be left to the Executive Committee.

6. Comrade Bush moved that the question of affiliation with the I.L.P. stand over until the result of the ballot now being taken over the question of fusion of the S.D.F. and I.L.P. is published. Seconded by Cde Rowe, this was carried unanimously.

7. Comrade White moved & Cde Rowe seconded that the minimum subscription be reduced to 1d per week. This was carried.

8. Resolved on the motion of Comrade Rowe, seconded by Comrade Piper, that a letter be sent to Comrade Barnes secretary of the A.S.E. congratulating him on the way he has conducted his case for the engineers; the sec. was instructed to forward copies to the local press.[44]

9. Alf. Setchel was proposed by Cde Dennis & seconded by Cde Bush as a candidate for membership of this Society.[45]

Minutes of Committee Meeting Jan 3rd 98
Present – Comrades Bloy, Dexter & White (Sec)
1. The secretary read a postcard received from Cde Russell Smart offering to lecture in Lynn for the Lynn Socialists' Society.[46]

---

44 George Nicoll Barnes (1859–1940), one of the founders of the ILP in 1893. ILP candidate at Rochdale 1895, general secretary of the ASE from 1896. Elected MP for Glasgow Blackfriars and Hutchesontown in 1906; leader of the Labour party, 1910–11; controversial role in wartime Lloyd George coalition government led to break with Labour; see *ODNB*. Barnes was at King's Lynn at a key moment; '[The ASE] held a national strike in 1897 in an attempt to win an eight-hour day but the strike ended in January 1898 without this having been achieved. Nevertheless the strike was successful in establishing the principle of collective bargaining over conditions of employment. This changed the face of British industry, with much world industry being quick to follow. It is this that ensures his place in the history of the working classes.' (Alan Haworth and Dianne Hayter (eds) *Men who made Labour* (Abingdon, 2006) p. 24). See also below, n. 105.

45 Alfred Albert Setchell (1873–1954), in 1891 a general labourer living with his mother at Allen's Yard, Norfolk Street Lynn. By 1901 a docker, and same in 1911.

46 Hyman Russell Smart (1858–1923), educated Dulwich College, an actor before becoming a salesman for a sanitation engineering company; joined SDF and Fabian Society; stood as ILP candidate at Huddersfield in 1895 General Election, and served on NAC; left ILP to join British Socialist Party in 1911 but left in 1912; author, *Trade Unionism and Politics* (Manchester, British Labour Press, 1893); Howell, *British Workers, passim*.

2. The secretary was instructed to write to Russell Smart accepting his offer for Wed January 19th.

3. Resolved that a collection be taken to meet expenses.

4. Comrade Wilson offered to give an address on 'Christ & the Labor Movement' on the following Sunday and it was resolved that his offer be accepted.[47]

5. Comrades Piper & Mills were appointed stewards for the ensuing week.

6. On the proposition of Comrade White, seconded by Comrade Rowe, Comrade W A Wilson was elected a member of this Society.

Meetings of Committee Meeting Jan 17th 98

Present – Comrades Rowe (Chairman), Dexter & White (Hon Sec)

1. The secretary said he would be pleased to entertain Comrade Russell Smart during his stay in Lynn.

2. Comrade Wilson consented to act as chairman ~~on~~ at the public meeting to be addressed by Comrade Russell Smart on the 19th inst.

3. The aftermentioned comrades were appointed Lecturers & Chairmen for the three following Sundays

	LECTURER	CHAIRMAN
Jan	J J Kidd.[48]	Rowe.
Feb 6th	W A Wilson.	F White.
Feb 13th	Triance.	

Minutes of Committee Meeting Feb 27th 98

Present – Comrades Rowe (Chairman), Dorer Dexter & White (Gen Sec)

1.The minutes of the preceding meeting were adopted.

2.The secretary read a letter from the sec. of the Fabian Society relating to the Fabian educational lectures for 1898. The following lectures were chosen:

Monday March 7th   "What a Town Council is & what it can do"

     "   "   14th   "What the Cooperative Movement can do"[49]

---

47 William A. Wilson, signed up to the rules of the Society 3 January 1898. Wilson appears four times on this page, but not subsequently: he is the only one of the eighteen people signing the original List of Rules whose name and signature is crossed through, so probably resigned after a very short time, reasons not given. (NRO, SO 297/2). Not certainly identified, perhaps William A. Wilson of Tilney All Saints, born 1857, mechanical engineer.

48 Although there is no formal note of his admission, the difficulties mentioned earlier have obviously been overcome and Kidd admitted to membership.

49 The Co-operative Movement, which originated in Rochdale in 1844, had developed into the Co-operative Wholesale Society, founded in Manchester in 1863: the Women's

    ”   ”   21ˢᵗ   "Labour in the Longest Reign"[50]
    ”   ”   28ᵗʰ   "The Industrial Outlook"

3. It was resolved that the following gentlemen be asked to act as chairmen:
March 7ᵗʰ Alderman R Green[51]
March 14ᵗʰ Mr Jas. Brown[52]
March 21ˢᵗ Councillor W S Dexter
March 28ᵗʰ Rev G Lansdowne.[53]

Minutes of Quarterly Meeting April 4ᵗʰ
9 Members – Comrade Dorer in the Chair
Resolved that the Annual Report & Balance Sheet made up to the end of
the year be presented in January.
The Treasurer (Cde Rowe) read the ~~following~~ financial statement for the
Quarter.
The Report was adopted on the motion of Comrade Dennis seconded by
Comrade Bloy.
The secretary reported that he had written to the secretary of the Bricklayers'
Union offering in the name of the Society the use of our Hall during the
strike.[54]

Co-operative League was founded 1883, with 32,000 members by 1910: see Percy Redfern,
The Story of the C.W.S. 1863–1913 (Manchester, 1913). The Lynn Society was founded
5 Sept. 1888: Arthur Furbank was a founder member, and its President from January 1910
(*LA*, 13 Jan. 1922).

50 The title of a Fabian Society tract by Sidney Webb, published in 1897. According to
the 1898 *Labour Annual*, it consists of 'a review of the changes in the wages and conditions
of the workers during the sixty years of the Queen's reign'.

51 Richard Green, a builder, Liberal councillor on Lynn Borough Council; later alderman
and twice mayor (1908 and 1922). Lived at Tower Place, later in Tennyson Avenue: an
enthusiastic supporter of William Morris, he named the latter house 'Kelmscott' in his
honour (Paton, *Dexter*, 64). For his daughter Beatrice, see below, note 213.

52 James Brown, born 1848, accountant for West Norfolk Farmers Manure Company;
Lynn borough councillor (Liberal); member of Lynn Board of Guardians; lived at Chase
House, Lynn. He was President of Lynn Co-operative Society in 1895: see *LN*, 7 Feb. 1920.

53 Revd George Lansdown(e), listed by Hillen (as George Lansdown) as Unitarian
minister at the Free Church (Unitarian) Broad Street. Hillen records he was minister there
1897–1900 (Hillen, *Kings Lynn*, 654). The 1900 Trade Directory gives his address as Lake
Rd, Lynn. He does not appear in the 1904 Trade Directory. George Lansdown appears in
1901 and 1911 census as Unitarian minister at Horsham, Sussex. He may have come to
Lynn from Ireland as the census records a daughter born there in 1897.

54 The secretary of the Lynn branch of the Operative Bricklayers' Society (OBS) was
W. Allen. The bricklayers went on strike on 1 April, demanding seven pence an hour
(the employers offered 6½ pence): between 60 and 70 men were involved (*LN*, 2 and
9 Apr. 1898).

Comrade Neave said he had been requested by the Lynn Branch of the A.S.R.S. to enquire as to the terms on which we would be willing to sub let our Hall.[55]

Comrade Rowe moved That we lend the Hall to the A.S.R.S. for their meetings, but as we have no power to sublet they pay us a nominal charge of 1/- for each meeting ~~per wk~~ to cover the expenses of gas & cleaning. This was seconded by Comrade White and unanimously carried.

Minutes of General Meeting April 20th 98

7 members present. Comrade White in the chair.

Comrade Dorer read the report of the N.A.C. to the B'ham Conference and suggested that it be discussed. The Chairman then declared the Meeting open for discussion & after a lively debate Comrade Rowe moved & Comrade Dorer seconded 'that the question of the affiliation of this Society with the I.L.P. stand over'.[56]   This was carried.

Comrade Rowe moved that the secretary be instructed to write to the president of the King's Lynn Y.M.C.A. offering to place the "Clarion" upon the table of the Y.M.C.A. Reading Room. This was seconded by Comrade Dexter & carried.

Minutes of General Meeting May 12th 98

10 members present, comrade Rix in the chair.

On the motion of comrade Rowe seconded by comrade Dorer the minutes of the last meeting were adopted.

The secretary read correspondence received from the secretary of the I.L.P. at Norwich relating to the forthcoming visit of lecturers which it is proposed to arrange to the Towns in Norfolk, and it was Resolved that comrade

---

55 Amalgamated Society of Railway Servants. John Thomas Neave, born 1871, was a railway engine driver, member of ASRS from 1889: another long-serving Socialist supporter, he was one of the original twelve signatories to the Society's rules 18 August 1897, a founder member of the Lynn ILP in October 1906 and remained a member of the latter until it was dissolved in 1915–16.

56 National Administrative Council of the ILP, reporting to the ILP Conference at Birmingham in 1898. This was not a good time for the ILP, William Stewart commenting: 'the I.L.P. was at this time passing through the most depressing period of its history. It had existed for five years. It had fought numerous bye-elections, but had not yet a single representative in Parliament. It had ceased to grow. The number of branches reported year by year remained practically stationary, and many of the branches were purely nominal and consisted in some place of small groups of die-hards who had not room in their vocabulary for the word defeat' (William Stewart, *J. Keir Hardie* (London, 1921), 134). This is the background behind the reluctance of the Lynn group to join. See also Howell, *British Workers*, 315–16.

Dorer be asked to interview the secretary of the I.L.P. at Norwich on behalf of this Society and make arrangements for lectures in LYNN.

It was Resolved that a meeting of members be held on the following Sunday to discuss the cause of the recent rise in the price of bread.

Minutes of Meeting of Members May 19th
9 members present Cde Triance in the chair
On the motion of Cde Rowe seconded by Cde Mills the minutes of the last meeting were adopted.

Cde Dorer reported that he had interviewed the secretary of the Norwich branch of the I.L.P. and moved that we fall in with the suggestion of the I.L.P. as to the forthcoming visit of Comrades Bell & Dobson to lecture in Lynn.[57] This was seconded by Cde Rowe & carried. The secretary was instructed to arrange for two suitable dates on which to hold the lectures.

Cde White moved & Cde Dennis seconded that Cde Dorer be appointed Literary Secretary, & to take charge of the Fabian Book-box. This was carried.

The Literary Secretary was instructed to write to the Fabian Society for a Book-box.

Cde Dorer suggested that the members of this society should get in touch with the local trade unionists & further advocated the formation of a Trades Council for Lynn.

The Secretary reported that he had not yet written to Mr Perry offering to place the "Clarion" on the Table of the Y.M.C.A. Reading Room for special reasons.[58]

---

57 John H. Dobson, organising secretary for ASRS (he had been in Lynn eight months earlier attending the inquest of Walter Frost, a railwayman killed at South Lynn station on 24 Aug. 1897, see *LN*, 28 Aug. 1897); Richard Bell, trade unionist, general secretary of ASRS, 1898–1909, elected M.P. for Derby 1890. By 1904, he had lapsed from support for Labour – this was shown in the 1904 Norwich by-election where he gave his support to the Liberal candidate (Louis Tillett), not the ILP candidate (George Roberts). After the election, he sent a telegram to the Liberal victor: 'Great triumph for progress. Heartiest congratulations.' Bell was re-elected to parliament in 1906 but as a Liberal, so is not one of the 29 MPs who formed the first Parliamentary Labour Party in that year. For Bell, see Philip S. Bagwell, *The Railwaymen: the History of the National Union of Railwaymen* (London, 1963), *passim*.

58 Charles William Perry, born 1857, draper (partner of Alfred Jermyn), a leading figure in the YMCA and PSA in Lynn (see, for example, *LN*, 3 Nov. 1900; also 1896 trade directory which lists Perry as its President). He was also involved in the Forward Association (see n. 263) and according to Raby, its founder (Raby, *Allotted Span*, 108–9); Mayor in 1910. See obituary, *LN*, 9 Jan. 1934.

Cde Dennis proposed & Cde White seconded Edward Osler as a member of this society & it was resolved that he be invited to the following meeting.[59]

Minutes of General Meeting. June 2nd/98
7 Members present – Cde. Rowe in the chair.
1. On the motion of Cde Dennis seconded by Cde Dorer the minutes of the last meeting were adopted.
2. In answer to Cde Dorer the Secretary said that he had received a post card from the Secretary of the I.L.P. at Norwich, saying that Cdes Bell & Dobson cannot at present fix the dates for their forthcoming visits.
43. The Secretary reported that he had written to Mr Perry, on May 24th, offering (on behalf of this Society) to place the Clarion upon the Reading Room Table at the Y.M.C.A. but had not received a reply.
34. The literary sec reported that he had received from the Fabian Society a box of books, a list of which will be supplied to each member, with a note asking members to circulate the information as to loan of the books amongst their friends, with a view to induce them to become members of this Society.
5. Comrade Dennis gave an account of the proceedings which took place at a meeting of the canvassers for a Free Library, held at the Technical School on Saturday May 28th.[60]

Minutes of Meeting – June 9th /98
Present – Comrades Rowe (Chairman), Dennis, Dorer, Mills, Triance, White & Dexter
The minutes of the last meeting were read & adopted.

Minutes of General Meeting July
Present – Comrades Dorer (Chairman), Cremer, Triance, Rowe, Mills, Piper, White & Dexter.
1. The minute of the last meeting was read & adopted.
2. The secretary read correspondence from Comrade Dobson relating to his forthcoming visit, & suggesting that the subject for his lectures for July 27th 28th & 29th should be respectively "Our Food Supply", "The Need for

---

59 Edward Osler; as the name is not common, he is probably the Edward Osler born in Lynn 1864 and baptised at St John's, South Lynn 10 February: his father was a tailor. Nobody of the name (or obvious variants like Ostler) occurs in Lynn census for 1891/1901/1911: there are several Oslers in Southery, 17 miles south of Lynn, including landlords of the *Blacksmiths Arms* there and two on the village war memorial, but no Edward occurs.

60 The Municipal Technical Institute in London Road had been opened in 1894 to provide day and evening classes in science, art and technology.

a Socialist Society" & "Cant, Culture & Capitalism" & it was resolved that his suggestion be agreed to.[61]

3. Resolved on the motion of Cde Dennis, seconded by Cde Triance that the meetings be held at the Walks Gates at 8 p.m.[62]

4. It was decided to ask the following gentlemen to act as chairmen for Cde Dobson – Messrs R. Green, Fisher[63] & Dines[64] & the Revs Lansdowne & Houghton[65] on Saturday May 28th. Cdes Rowe & Dennis offered to act as chairmen in the event of the gentlemen named above not turning up.

5. Resolved that Comrades Dorer, Rowe & White form a sub committee to arrange for the entertainment of Cde. Dobson.

6. Resolved that Cde. White arrange for the distribution of literature at the meetings.

7. The secretary read a letter from the sec. of the Lynn Y.M.C.A. relating to the "Clarion" & it was resolved that the question stand over.

8. The secretary read correspondence from secretary of Lynn Branch of S.D.F. & it was resolved that we meet the members of the S.D.F. at a meeting to be convened by the secretaries, for the discussion of the question of fusion of the local socialist organizations.

[END OF SO 297/1]

---

61 James E. Dobson (b. 1860), an active member of the SDF in Camberwell, London, secretary of its Unemployed Committee before moving to the ILP; elected to the Camberwell Vestry in 1896 and borough councillor when the Vestry was replaced by Camberwell Metropolitan Borough Council in 1900; active in the Honor Hill Protest Committee, 1896–1905, preserving this open space from enclosure. See J. Nisbet, *The story of the "One Tree Hill" agitation, with a short sketch of the history of Honor Oak Hill* (Nunhead, 1905). The Lynn Society's address book describes him as 'Secretary, London ILP Federation' (NRO, SO 297/9).

62 The Walks were (and still are) a historic public recreation area in South Lynn, close to the railway station: public meetings were often held at The Walks gates.

63 Francis (Frank) Archibald Fisher (1870–1921), clothier with shop in Lynn High Street. Home residence 16 Rosebery Avenue, Gaywood in 1901, 8 Whitefriars Rd in 1911. Moved to Norwich (where he had been born) in 1916.

64 Claydon Dines (1854–1925), coal merchant. Primitive Methodist, trustee of Earl of Leicester Oddfellows, on Board of Guardians from 1895: his obituary calls him 'in politics an advanced radical' and a friend of Joseph Arch, the agricultural union leader (see Alun Howkins, 'Joseph Arch', *ODNB*). Like Arch, his radical views were expressed in the Liberal party rather than as a Socialist (*LA*, 3 Apr. 1925).

65 Charles Houghton, born 1859, a Baptist Minister at the Market Street chapel in Lynn, lived at 3 Whitefriars Road (1904 trade directory). At a speech at Lynn Liberal club in 1904, he urged the various radical groups (including the Liberal party) to unite and put forward candidates under a 'progressive' banner. He noted that 'there was a splendid body of men in the railway men who were Radicals to the core – and he thought they only wanted properly handling and they would come into line with the Liberal party.' (*LN*, 26 Nov. 1904).

Minutes of King's Lynn
Social Democratic Party, 1898–1906[66]

Lynn Social Democratic Party Minutes of Meetings Sept 1st 1898.

Introductory note on the formation of the Lynn Social Democratic Party.[67]
A feeling having become manifest with some Members of the Lynn Branch of the S.D.F. and the Socialist Society "that it would strengthen the Socialist movement in the town could an arrangement be come to for fusion between these two existing bodies, a joint meeting was held in the Rechabite Hall Coronation Square on Thursday July 21st to consider the matter. This meeting was adjourned until Sunday July 24th, when it was decided after a lengthy discussion to amalgamate under the name of the Social Democratic Party, and a sub committee – Comrades Dexter, Bush, Kidd, Denny, Cummings & White was appointed to draft rules etc.[68]
This Committee met on Aug 23rd & 24th with the result that a rough draft of object, programme & rules was presented at a General Meeting of Members held in the Rechabite Hall on Sunday Aug 28th and after some additions & corrections had been made were agreed to by those present.

General Meeting Sept 1st
Ten Members present. Comrade J. J. Kidd in chair. Comrade White elected unopposed as General Sec and Comrade H Rowe as Financial Secretary for the year.

---

66 NRO, SO 297/3,4

67 The new party was welcomed by *Justice*, which noted that there were three branches of the SDF in East Anglia (Norwich, Cambridge and Wisbech) and described the new Lynn group as 'an amalgamation of the Lynn S.D.F. and Lynn Socialist Society which I think will work very harmoniously with the S.D.F.' (*Justice*, 21 Jan. 1899).

68 Dexter, Bush, Kidd and White were members of the Socialist Party, and have been mentioned previously. Denny and Cummings presumably spoke for the SDF: Robert Denny born 1872, railway engineer driver, Atbara Terrace Lynn; died in Lynn 19 Dec. 1925 (death notice in *LA*, 25 Dec. 1925); William J. W. Cummings, born 1855, dock labourer, living at Nelson Street in 1901.

The election of Executive Committee was proceeded with Comrades Mr &
Mrs Kidd,[69] Dexter, Triance, Dennis, Denny & Dorer being elected on a
ballot being taken.

Comrades Bush & Rix were elected as auditors & Comrade Piper as
Librarian.

Moved Comrade White Seconded by A. Dorer "that the Executive drafts
a Municipal Programme and submits the same to a General Meeting.
<u>Carried</u>

Moved by Com Denny Seconded Com Piper & Carried "That Members pay
1d a month to an Election Fund.

It was decided "that the various items in our programme be fully discussed
and that Thursday night in each week be recognised as open for debates etc.

Executive Committee Meeting Sept 5th
Com Kidd in the Chair, present Comrades Kidd, & Comrades Denny,
Rowe, Triance & White.

Letter received from J.E Dobson of London relating to his visit. Proposed
by Com Rowe seconded by Mrs Kidd "that a collection be taken at each
of J E Dobson's meetings, meetings to be held at the Walks Gates London
Road. Agreed that a report of meetings be sent accompanied by a note on
the fusion of the two Socialist bodies to the press.[70]

Letter read from the Secretary of the Amalgamated Soc Railway Servants
asking for the use of the hall for their meetings. Agreed that the matter
stand over until an understanding be come too [sic] with the Trustees of
the Hall.

Agreement from the Trustees of the Rechabite Tent was read, and it was
agreed that on the words <u>or lend</u> being deleted the agreement be accepted
Comrades Rowe and White being appointed to see the Trustees.

Proposed by Com' Mrs Kidd "that the Autumn programme be opened with
a Social Evening" seconded by Com' Triance – carried.

Moved by Com' Denny, seconded by Com' Rowe "that a Sub-Committee –
Comrades Mr & Mrs Kidd, Bush & White carry out the arrangements for
the same. The programme for September was arranged.

---

69 Mrs Kidd is the first known female member of the Society, and definitely the first
woman on the Executive committee. Her name was Christiana, born Christiana Plowright
in 1864: her father was a builder's merchant. The Kidds married in 1889. The marriage
survived the difficulties described later, both moving to Letchworth.

70 The local press carried a brief report of the Dobson meetings, adding 'in order
to strengthen the socialist movement in the town the two bodies [unnamed] have now
amalgamated' (LN, 17 Sept. 1898).

Sept 7th 8th 9th J E Dobson Member of Camberwell Vestry London gave three open air lectures at the Walks Gates.[71]

The Meetings were successful and attracted large audiences the subjects were as follows:- "Party Shibboleths", "Socialism and Character", The Czar's Message or Socialism and Peace". At the last lecture, some opposition was organised but the presence of the police – who's protection had been asked for – prevented any serious trouble arising. One or two were\was/ warned by the Inspector of the consequences if they did not desist from using such bad language as was being so freely indulged in, after which the meeting was continued in fairly good order. Questions were asked for at the close of each meeting, several persons took advantage of this and expressed themselves as well satisfied with the replys [sic] given. The Lecturer – Comrade Dobson was very pleased with the success attending his visit.

Sep 15th Comrade Rowe opened a discussion on: "The Payment of Members & Election Expenses out of the Public Funds". Comrade Belderson took the Chair, eighteen present.[72] Comrades Triance, Kidd, Dennis & G W Belderson took part in an interesting discussion.[73]

Sep 18th Sunday Evening. Comrade Rowe read an article from the Social Democrat[74] entitled "Why is Socialism at a discount in England". Comrade Bloy in the Chair. Comrades Kidd, Belderson, Mills, Bloy & White took part in the discussion that followed.

Sep 22nd Thursday evening. A Social Evening at which a Musical Programme & Refreshments was provided was a great success.[75] The hall was decorated with plants kindly lent by Comrades Kid[d]. There was between sixty & seventy friends present. Comrade Bush with several friends gave selections of music & Comrade Fraser & Rowe contributed songs, Miss A & S Sporne also sang,[76] Comrade Belderson recited & Comrade Cumming gave an amusing reading.

---

71 Press cutting attached.

72 William John Belderson (1868–1951), wholesale flower grower and bee-keeper. Address in 1901: The Apiary, Terrington St Clement. William's wife Rose joined the Lynn ILP in 1907.

73 For S.W. Belderson, see above note 29. Among other matters, he spoke of his experiences of deputations to the House of Commons (*LN*, 24 Sept. 1898).

74 Monthly publication by the SDF, started in 1897.

75 Press cutting attached, from *LN*, 1 Oct. 1898.

76 The title Miss rather than Com[rades] probably indicates that the Spornes are supporters but not yet members, (but this may be inconsistency on the part of the secretary). Full names Agnes Mary Sporne (born 1876) and Susan Emmeline Sporne (born 1880), they were the daughters of William Sporne, shopkeeper, and his wife Hannah, of South

Comrade Rowe gave a short address on the object of the party and a short sketch of the history of the two organisations up to the time of fusion into one body.

Comrade Kidd also spoke inviting any friends in sympathy to become members or associates.

After an interesting evening, everyone seeming to have thoroughly enjoyed themselves the friends dispersed after the singing of the Marseillaise.[77]

Sunday Sept 25th Reading from Bellamy's Equality by H Rowe followed by discussion.[78]

Quarterly General Meeting Thursday Sept 29
Comrade Dexter in the chair.
The minutes of the last General Meeting were read and adopted.
The Financial Secretary H B Rowe read his report which was adopted on the proposition of Comrade Dorer seconded by Comrade Bloy.
The General Secretary read a report on the work of the party which was adopted on the proposition of Comrade Rowe seconded by Com Dennis. A Discussion then took place on the question of drawing up a Municipal Programme, it was urged as of the first importance that candidates at the forthcoming November elections be asked to carry out the adoption and opening of the Public Library.
It was suggested also that the principal [sic] of Municipal Ownership; the putting into operation of the Artisan Dwelling Act, a Fair Wage Clause in all contracts, the Fixing of a minimum wage of not less than 20/- a week for Corporation Employees &c &c form part of the proposed Municipal Programme.
It was suggested by Comrade Dorer that a note be inserted in the Clarion inviting comrades who may be contesting for seats on Municipal Bodies to forward copies of Election Addresses.

St, Lynn: Susan was or became a schoolteacher. In 1905, she married J. C. Triance: as Mrs Triance, she is listed as one of the eleven people still members of the Lynn ILP when it was dissolved in 1916. Their brothers Robert and Arthur and younger sister Ethel were also Socialists and are footnoted on their first appearances in the minutes.

77 Written in 1792 and adopted as the national anthem of the French Republic in 1795. Presumably sung in English translation in Lynn. The well-known Labour song 'The Red Flag' had been written in 1899 (appearing in Justice in December of that year), but perhaps had not yet attained its later universality.

78 Best-selling novel by American writer Edward Bellamy (1850–1898), first published in 1897. A utopian work portraying an ideal society in the future year 2000, it was a follow-up to his Looking Backward, 2000–1887 (1888) with the same characters.

Sunday October 2nd F W White in Chair.
Comrade Triance read a most interesting paper on "Militarism". All the members present took part in the discussion that followed.

Monday Oct 3rd. Meeting of the Executive Committee. Comrade Rowe in the Chair. Members present Mr & Mrs Kidd, W Dexter, Denny, Dorer, White.
Comrades Rowe & White reported having signed the agreement with the Trustees of the Rechabites relating to the tenancy of the hall.
Letter was read from the Secretary of the A.S.R.S. – Mr Furbank – intimating that the members of the A.S.R.S. would hold their meetings in the hall commencing January next and agreeing to pay the sum of 2/- for each meeting toward the cost of gas, cleaning & firing, the Secretary expressed the hope that the A.S.R.S which were now holding their meetings at the "Royal Standard public house would benefit by the change made.[79]
The programme for October was arranged copies and of which have since been circulated amongst the members.
Comrade Dexter promised to give a paper in November on Tolstoy's "What is Art".[80]
It was decided that the hall should be opened as a reading room during the autumn & winter each night with the exception of those nights reserved for discussions & the Rechabite Club meetings.

Thursday Oct 6th Comrade Rowe in the Chair. Discussion on the "Clarion Referendum" members present supporting the following questions contained therein:[81]

---

79 Arthur Furbank (1846–1922), Blackfriars Road, Lynn, railway yard foreman, local secretary of the ASRS and one of the founder members of the Lynn Representation Committee in 1903 (see below, note 278). He moved to Lynn in 1871, joining ASRS the following year. In 1913 he stood unsuccessfully for the Borough Council as Co-operative candidate: for his role in Lynn Co-operative Society see above, note 49. See his obituary in *LA*, 13 Jan. 1922. See above (meeting of 4 April 1898) for the earlier agreement with ASRS as to the use of the Hall.

80 Leo Tolstoy (1828–1910), Russian novelist and social thinker. His *What is Art?* was completed in Russian in 1897 and first published in English because of problems with censorship: a translation by Aylmer Maude came out in 1899. Maude (1858–1938) was a personal friend of Tolstoy, and a member of the Fabian Society, serving on its executive between 1907 and 1912.

81 The *Clarion* offered a referendum to members of all socialist-minded groups as to whether the future lay in 'fusion' – a single party made up of a merger of the different groups – or 'federation' – the different groups maintaining their identity but working together. The majority of those replying voted for fusion, but the ILP Conference rejected this, voting for federation.

CLARION REFERENDUM COUPON

DO YOU VOTE FOR:	YES[82]	NO
1. The Establishment of One Socialist Party?	X	
2. The Fusion of Existing Bodies?	X	
3. Federation of Existing Bodies?		
4. The Policy of Running Socialist Candidates at the General Election?	(X)	
5. The Policy of Running Socialists at By-elections?	(X)	
6. The "Strategic" support of Liberals where Socialists cannot be run?	(X)	
7. The "Strategic" support of Tories where Socialists cannot be run?	(X)	
8. The policy of Abstention where Socialists cannot be run?	(X)	
9. Concentration on Specific Palliatives?		

10. If so, mark your approval of the four proposals you deem the most possible and urgent of the following:-

I Referendum and Initiative		
II Taxation of Ground Values	X	
III Increased Succession Duties	X	
IV Eight-hour Day	X	
V Old Age Pensions		
VI Nationalisation of Railways	X	
VII Nationalisation of Land	X	
VIII Nationalisation of the Drink Traffic	X	
IX Payment of Members and Ballot Fees		
X Provision of Work for Unemployed		

Sunday Oct 9th Comrade Dorer in the Chair (11 present).
Comrade Kidd read Peter Krapotkin's "Appeal to the Young".[83] Discussion followed.

---

82 Those marked X have the X in ink; those marked (X) have the X in pencil, perhaps added later.

83 Pyotr (Peter) Kropotkin (1842–1921), Russian activist and revolutionary, spent many years in exile in western Europe after escaping from a Russian prison in 1876. His pamphlet *An Appeal to the Young* was published in 1880, translated into English by H.M. Hyndman. He was in London in 1881, and again from 1886: in May 1887, he spoke in Norwich to the Norwich branch of the Socialist League. He noted how socialism had developed in England in the five years between his visits: 'the year that I then passed in London [1881] was a year of real exile. For one who held advanced socialist opinions, there was no atmosphere to breathe in. there was no sign of that animated socialist movement which I found so largely developed on my return in 1886' (Kropotkin, *Memoirs of a Revolutionary* (1899), vol. 2, 251).

Thursday Oct 13 Chairman Comrade Bush (12 present). Comrade Mrs Kidd read a paper subject "Equal Adult Suffrage". Comrades Rowe, Belderson, Dorer, White, Kidd took part in the discussion that followed, Mrs Kidd replying at some length to the various questions raised in the course of the debate.

Friday Oct 14 Chairman Comrade Kidd.
Special meeting to consider what questions should be put to the various Candidates for the Town Council, the following questions were decided upon as being of pressing importance. 1st to give immediate support Public Library movement
2nd Evening Meetings of the Council
3rd The payment of a minimum wage of 1£ per week to all Corporation Workmen
4th The construction by the Town Council of Workmens Dwellings on land already owned by the Corporation, the same to be let at a fair rental?
Comrade Rowe agreed to see to the printing of the above questions \a copy of/ the same to be sent to each of the Candidates.

Sunday Oct 16 Chairman Comrade Kidd. Comrade Fraser read a pamphlet entitled "A Socialist's View of the Reformation".[84] Comrades Rowe, Dexter, Bush & Mrs Kidd took part in the discussion following.

Thursday Oct 20 Discussion "Compulsory Education" postponed in order to allow members to attend Lecture on Milton by Judge Willis Q.C.[85]

Sunday Oct 23 Chairman Comrade Belderson. Comrade Dorer read a pamphlet subject:- "The Moral Aspect of Socialism".[86] Owing to the length of the reading only a short discussion followed.

Monday Oct 24 Meeting of the Executive Committee. Comrade Dexter chairman.
Minutes of last meeting were read & adopted.
The Secretary then read the replies from Candidates to the list of questions submitted to them by the Party. The replies received were from Messrs Brown, Bettinson & Everitt, in the South Ward, and from Mr Affleck, in the North Ward.[87]

---

84 T. D. Benson, *A Socialist's View of the Reformation* (Manchester, ILP *c.* 1898).

85 William Willis (1835–1911), barrister and judge, said to favour the employee against the employer; Liberal MP Colchester, 1880–85; leading Baptist layman; frequent and eloquent lecturer on Bunyan and Milton. See *ODNB*.

86 *The Moral Aspects of Socialism*, by Sidney Ball, Fabian Tract no. 72 (1896).

87 William Henry Lavender Brown, a builder, elected for the South Ward in 1897; George Young Bettinson, wool merchant; William Everett (the correct spelling), born

It was moved by H Rowe seconded J J Kidd that a general meeting be summoned for Wednesday Oct 26 to decide how the Party should vote.

The programme for November and to Dec 15th was then arranged.

The names of W J Belderson, J German, Ernest E Moy & James Jude were submitted as candidates for membership, and passed unanimously.[88]

Secretary reported the receipt of the latest Fabian Tract on the Liquor Traffic,[89] also I L P News October.

Application was received from Mr Everett's Committee for use of the Hall on Nov 1st. Comrade Triance proposed Comrade Dorer seconded that subject to the consent of the Trustees the hall be let on that day for the sum of 10/-.

General Meeting Wednesday Oct 26. Chairman J J Kidd.

Minutes of last meeting read & adopted.

The revised "Clarion Referendum Vote" was discussed, members deciding to vote in favour of the Socialist Party, by federation of existing bodies for purposes common to all, under a Socialist Joint Committee.

~~Letters~~ Replies from Messrs Everett, Bettinson & Brown in the South Ward was then read & from Mr Affleck in the North Ward, the Secretary reporting the fact that no acknowledgement had been received from Messrs Carpenter, Miles, Thew, Sadler, Savage.[90]

It was moved by Comrade Piper seconded Com Ramm "that we recommend the Members of the Party to support Mr Brown & Everett in the South Ward their replies being most favourable.[91] Moved as an amendment by

1867, corn and cake merchant, of Goodwin's Place, Lynn; William J. Affleck, born 1855, mechanical engineer, of King St, Lynn.

88 J. German was perhaps James German, born 1870, a farm labourer at Benwick, in the Fens: his brother David was living in Victoria Street, Lynn in 1901. Ernest E Moy not certainly identified: the only man of this name in the 1901 census is an engine fitter, born 1877, living in Eton, Berkshire (however, he had been born in Norfolk so had perhaps moved there from Lynn). James Jude, born 1851, a waterman, living in 1901 in Windsor Road, Lynn.

89 Two successive Fabian Tracts on the subject were issued in 1897, both by Edward Pease: tract 85 *Liquor Licensing at Home and Abroad* and tract 86 *Municipal Drink Traffic*.

90 Frederick John Carpenter, a brewer, elected for the South Ward in 1898, mayor 1902–03; William Samuel Valentine Miles, mayor 1893–94 and 1894–95; Frank Sherwood Thew, printer and stationer, Lynn High Street; William Russell Sadler, solicitor, New Conduit Street, Lynn; Frederick William Savage, engineer – the Savage firm is best known for the manufacture of traction engines and fairground rides. The councillors' replies are inserted in the minutes.

91 There is no record of Ramm being formally admitted to the Society and his identity is uncertain: either Frederick Ramm of Lynn Road, Gaywood, painter, born 1860, or Henry Ramm of Guanock Terrace, draper's assistant, born 1863.

Comrade Rowe seconded Comrade Mills "that Members abstain from voting". Eventually after a lengthy discussion it was decided to support Messrs Brown & Everett. Moved by Comrade Piper seconded by Comrade Francis "that the replies of Candidates be sent to the press".[92] Carried. Comrade Mrs Kidd suggested the advisability of purchasing a piano which would add to the attractiveness of our room and would also save the expense of hiring for Socials etc. Mrs Kidd undertook to make enquiries as to price etc. Secretary read a letter from the Secretary South Lynn Club offering the 24 Chairs which have been in use by the party for sometime for 1/6 each.[93] The matter was left over.

Sunday Oct 30 Chairman Comrade Triance. Comrade Dexter read selections from a book entitled "The Coming of the Friars".[94] Discussion followed.

Thursday Nov 3 Comrade Dorer in the Chair. Comrade Rowe read a paper subject "Old Age Pensions".[95] 14 Members present.

Sunday Nov 6 Comrade Triance read a paper on "Disestablishment and Disendowment of the Church". Chairman Comrade Kidd 15 present good discussion followed.

Sunday Nov 13 Comrade Kidd gave an address on "Democracy". Comrades Dorer, Neave, Mrs Kidd, Bush & White took part in the discussion that followed. Comrade Jarvis presided.

---

92 John Edward Francis, born 1869, clothier's assistant, living in Littleport Terrace in 1901. He was clearly an important figure in the party, being mentioned many times in the minutes. However, he is never mentioned after the ILP was formed in October 1906, presumably remaining in the SDF (he is described as 'secretary of the Lynn branch of the SDF' in *LN*, 28 Jan. 1905).

93 The South Lynn Liberal Club, later taken over by the ILP: see note 349.

94 By Norfolk antiquarian Augustus Jessopp, first published in 1885. A friar took an oath of absolute poverty; as Jessopp wrote, 'his life work was not to save his own soul but first and foremost to save the bodies and souls of others'. They could be seen as predecessors of Christian socialism, and this might have special resonance in Lynn where memory of them was preserved in fragments of building, and in place names such as the Friars' Field mentioned below.

95 A much-discussed topic for many years, two leading supporters being Charles Booth, who favoured a scheme paid for out of taxation and Joseph Chamberlain, who favoured a contributory arrangement. There were several reports on the issue in the 1890s: 'at this point, Booth mounted a national campaign for pensions that was supported by the Fabians the Labour Representation Committee, the TUC and the co-operative movement.' (Keith Laybourn, *The Evolution of British Social Policy and the Welfare State* (Keele, 1995), 167). Pensions were finally granted, to those over seventy years old and under certain conditions, under the Old Age Pensions Act (1908).

Secretary read a letter from H W Lee Sec S.D.F,[96] stating that Mrs Rose Jarvis would be at Lincoln on Sunday Nov 27 and offering her services for a lecture on Tuesday Nov 29th.[97] Sec instructed to write for further particulars as to subjects & expense of same.

Piano. Comrade Mrs Kidd urged the desirability of purchasing a piano as soon as possible and mentioned the fact that there was to be a sale the following weekend and that someone should attend with a view to purchasing.

As to means for purchasing it was suggested that members who wished could take shares, the following names were taken of those offering to do so. Comrades Dorer, Rowe, White, Neave, Fraser, Bush, Kidd, Jarvis, Rix. Comrades Kidd & Bush were instructed to attend sale and to bid up to 10£. Arrangements were then made for the opening of the Hall during the week as follows:-

Monday Comrade Rowe   Thursday Mills
Tuesday Mills   Friday Denny
Wednesday Kidd & Triance   Saturday [*blank*]

Thursday Nov 17 Social Evening. This was the second of the season, about 45 friends & Members were present. Comrade Addison of Wisbech presided and in a short speech related some of his experiences during his candidature for the Wisbech Town Council on Nov 1st.[98]

A good programme was gone through the following contributing Comrade Fraser songs, Comrade Rowe & Kidd readings, Comrade Bush conducted the string band which gave selections. Mr Witley "Reading",[99] Miss A Sporne "Song", Mr Frost "Songs". Mr Rix officiated at the piano. The proceeds amounted to [*blank*]

Sunday Nov 20 Comrade Fraser read a paper "In Defence of Capitalism". Comrade Kidd Chairman. Discussion followed. Comrades Belderson, White, Bloy, Mrs Kidd took part.

96 Henry W. Lee (1865–1932) socialist, printer by trade. An early member of the SDF, he became its General Secretary in 1885. In later life, he moved sharply to the right, campaigning against the perceived 'Bolshevik menace' in the years after the First World War.

97 Rose Jarvis (?–1923), politician. She and her husband Tom were leading London members of the SDF. Rose stood for the London School Board in Hackney, 1894. Tom died in 1903. Rose was elected Poor Law Guardian in Croydon in 1904, soon moved to Northampton and was elected to Board of Guardians there in 1906. Later (1920) became first woman member of Northampton Town Council.

98 William Addison had stood as an Independent candidate in North Ward, Wisbech. He finished bottom of the poll with 235 votes, well behind the three successful candidates who each received between 400 and 454 votes. (*LN*, 5 Nov. 1898)

99 John S Witley, born 1859, tailor, of Tennyson Avenue, Lynn.

Wednesday Nov 23. Chairman J Triance. Executive Committee met to hear correspondence re Mrs Jarvis' visit etc. The subject decided upon being "Waste & Want" also agreed that an advertisement be inserted in the Lynn News. Mr & Mrs Kidd agreed to entertain the visitor also \agreed/ that Mrs Kidd should preside at the meeting to be held in the Hall on Tuesday Nov 29th. [*blank*] Francis was adopted as a Member of the Party.[100]

Thursday Nov 24 Comrade Dorer read a paper subject:- "The Artisan Dwelling Act". Chairman F W White.
Discussion followed in which Comrades Triance, Kidd, White took part.
It was proposed that the Mayor & Town Clerk be written urging the importance of at once taking steps to provide houses for the working classes. Comrades Dorer & Triance were appointed to draft a memorial or letter on the subject the same to be presented to a meeting of members.

Sunday Nov 27 Chairman Comrade Mrs Kidd
Comrade Dexter read a paper on Tolstoy's book "What Is Art". The speaker had made most careful extracts and proved himself quite capable of dealing with the subject. A most interesting discussion followed in which Comrades Kidd, Rowe, Belderson and the Chairman took part.

Tuesday Nov 29th
Mrs Jarvis of London gave a Public Lecture in the Hall. Subject: "Waste & Want". Unfortunately owing to many other attractions there was only a small audience present. Comrade Mrs Kidd presided. The Lecturer spoke of the waste of life and energy under a competitive system and showed how by properly organising the means of production for use instead of for profit, existence would not be a constant unceasing drudgery as it is today with many of our people.[101]
Comrades Mr & Mrs Kidd entertained the visitor.

Sunday Dec 4 Chairman Com Neave. Comrade Rowe read part of "Nemo's" reply to "Merrie England".[102] Discussion followed.

Sunday Dec 11 Chairman Com. Triance
Subject "Survival of the Fittest   Speaker Comrade German

Thursday Dec 15
Members attended a debate at the South Lynn Liberal Club, the subject under discussion being:- "Should Party Politics Be Introduced Into

---

100 Advertised in *LN*, 26 Nov. 1898.
101 Press cutting inserted.
102 Nemo (pseud.), *Labour and Luxury. A reply to "Merrie England"* (London, 1895).

Municipal Affairs". Councillor Springall, Mr Gemmell,[103] and several well known Liberals also Comrade Kidd took part in a lively meeting at the end of which on a vote being taken it was decided by a majority of two "that party politics should not be introduced into Municipal Affairs.

Note The Party Held no meetings after this date (15th) owing to the Christmas Holidays and other things being considered against getting the attendance.

Tuesday Jan 3/99 Meeting of the Executive Committee. Comrade Rowe in Chair.
Present Comrades Dorer, Triance, Kidd, Dexter, Denny, White.
Minutes of last meeting read and adopted. The programme for January was arranged. It was also decided to hold a Social Evening at the earliest possible date in the month and to call another meeting of the Committee on Monday Jan 9th to receive reports re Workmans Dwellings from Comrades Dorer & Triance.

FIRST ANNUAL REPORT A YEAR'S WORK FOR SOCIALISM IN LYNN READ AT THE ANNUAL MEETING JAN 12 1899

Comrades In presenting to you a report of the year's work for Socialism in our Town. I think on examining the work done that we – small band as we may be – have no cause for feeling discouraged with what has been accomplished. On the other hand when we take into consideration our isolated position cut off as it were from the outside world – the only information of the progress of the movement being gleaned through the columns of our papers, or the occasional visit from some centre of everyday Socialistic activity of a lecturer – then, I think we have good reason for thinking that after all a good deal has been accomplished, and that our work as a Society has justified its existence. During the year that has past [sic] we have done a good deal to remove any prejudice that may have previously existed against us. The people of Lynn by the opportunity that has been given them of the principles of Socialism expounded by such able workers in the movement as Comrades Russell Smart, Joe Chatterton,[104] Harry Snell, J E Dobson and others – have gained some little knowledge of the existing evils of society and what we Socialists are striving to remedy and remove.
January opened with Engineers still engaged in their struggle against a combination of capitalistic employers for better conditions and shorter

---

103 George Gemmell (1854–1928), draper, Liberal councillor 1901–19 and 1923, alderman 1923–29, chairman of the Liberal Association in 1913. See obituary in *LA*, 14 Sept. 1928.
104 Joseph Chatterton, of the Social Democratic Federation, writer of pamphlet, *The Practicability of Social-Democracy* (London, 1896).

hours. Our members sent several substantial donations to the fund instituted by the "Clarion" for their assistance.

The president of the P.S.A. was also written and asked to devote an afternoon to an address on the Lock Out and to take up a collection to which he consented the result being that two guineas were also forwarded from that Society. The end of this fight proved the hopelessness of strikes as a method for improving industrial conditions.[105]

The chief event of the month was the visit of Russell Smart who gave a lecture in the hall to a full audience the subject being:- "Socialism By Reform Or Revolution". Nine meetings were held during the month besides which members attended and took part in the discussions held at the Cooperative Society's Room.

The month of February brought the welcome news that the Fabian Society London had granted us a course of four lectures with no expense to our society beyond any additional advertising that we might think necessary. It was in the first week of the month that Comrade Chatterton S.D.F gave his lantern lecture in the St James Hall entitled:- "Slaves of Great and Greater Britain" which illustrated the condition of the Cradley Heath Chain Makers etc working under such conditions as would disgrace any form of slave ownership. During the same week Rev R C Fillingham,[106] at a Liberal Meeting, was asked by one of our Comrades to give an expression of opinion on the York Election where Furness the Liberal Candidate adopted was also a member of the Employers Federation fighting the Engineers the

---

105 The lock-out had lasted from July 1897 to January 1898. 'During the six months of the dispute, the trade union movement had rallied around the engineers, providing them with £169,000 in voluntary subscriptions to supplement the £489,000 spent by the ASE on the dispute' … . The consequence of the defeat of one of the most powerful trade unions in the world was evident for all to see; any union could be defeated in the absence of wide trade union support. As a consequence, attempts were made to form federations of trade unions for mutual support.' Keith Laybourn, *A History of British Trade Unionism* (Stroud, 1997), 90.

106 Robert Charles Fillingham, vicar of Hexton near Hitchin from 1891. A controversial figure, he opposed 'Romanism' and ritualism in the Church of England churches, disrupting services including one in St Paul's Cathedral. He also preached in Nonconformist churches, for example, in the Primitive Methodist church at Norwich in April 1904 (*Norfolk News*, 23 Apr. 1904). A radical in politics he declared himself on the side of the Boers in the Boer War and to be a passive resister against the 1902 Education Act. In a public letter in 1906, he wrote 'I am working again in Norfolk constituencies for the Liberal cause, the cause of justice, the cause of Protestantism, the cause of the poor. Every vote given to a Unionist candidate is a vote given for undoing the work of the Reformation and bringing back the curse of Priestcraft in our land.' (*Eastern Daily Press,* hereafter *EDP,* 20 Jan. 1906). When Fillingham was still an undergraduate at Merton College, Oxford, he and a much older man, a clergyman, were accused in the Central Criminal Court of assault and indecent conduct with boys. The clergyman was sentenced to 15 months in prison; Fillingham was acquitted.

question elicited the reply that "if the Liberal Party ignored the claims of Labor, good bye to Liberalism![107]

We were visited during the month by two comrades who happened to be in the Town Comrade Stanton of Manchester[108] who gave a short address on "Our Movement" and Comrade Wilson of Sheffield – an Engineer – who opened a discussion on "The Cooperative Movement". Six meetings were held in the hall during the month.

March was a busy month with us. Besides the ordinary meetings we had the work of organising the successful course of Lectures granted us by the Fabian Society. In this work of advertising a good deal of useful propaganda was done.

About 150 of the most prominent people in the Town had a copy of the syllabus of the lectures and also tracts on a variety of subjects. The subjects of the Lectures were:- "What a Town Council is and what it can do", "The Cooperative Movement", "Labor in the Longest Reign", and "The Industrial Outlook". Of the lecturer Harry Snell we hold very pleasant recollections as to his great talent and ability.

Nine meetings were held during the month.

April 1st witnessed a strike of bricklayers in Lynn, the men who had given a three months notice for an advance from 6d to 7d an hour were offered 1/2d which was refused the result being the strike.

Our Society offered the use of the hall to the men during the dispute and assistance was given them by assisting them in the press etc, the dispute lasted a month ending in a victory for the men.

The dispute pointed to the necessity of a Trades Council being formed in the town. Comrade Rowe read a paper to a meeting of members of the Cooperative Society held in the St James Hall subject "Poverty a cause and its cure".

May. After some correspondence with Comrade Sutton of Norwich and Headley of Yarmouth an arrangement was come to for conducting some joint meetings.[109]

---

107 The York by-election of 1898 marked the growing estrangement between the ILP and the Liberal Party, with the former supporting the Tory Sir Charles Beresford against the Liberal Sir Christopher Furness; Beresford won by 11 votes. Sir Christopher Furness, Baron Furness (1852–1912), a prominent shipowner at Hartlepool, where Liberal MP 1892–95 and 1900–10; see *ODNB*.

108 An address book lists Stanton as S. H. Stanton of Broom Lane, Levenshulme, Manchester (NRO, SO 297/9): according to 1901 census, Sydney H. Stanton, born 1867, traveller in stationery. The Address book calls him 'the Strolling Clarionette', Clarionette being a term for supporters of the *Clarion* movement; Wilson not further identified.

109 Alfred 'Alf' Sutton, member of Socialist League, founder member of Norwich ILP

The Public Library question having reached an acute stage the Town Council were pressed to adopt the Act but there did not seem to be a very great anxiety on their part to do this. The Town Clerk having ruled that they the Council had no power to take poll of the ratepayers, it was decided by the friends of the adoption of the Act to take a voluntary canvas of the Town. On the 23rd of this month it was decided at a meeting of our members it was decided to render every possible assistance and a letter was sent to the Secretary of the Stanley Library Committee offering to help.[110] An offer gladly accepted. Several of our Members attended a meeting held at the Technical School and the Town was mapped out into districts which was allotted out to the canvassers.

During June few meetings were held members being actively engaged in support of the Adoption of the Public Libraries Act. At the Quarterly Meeting of the Amalgamated Society Railway Servants held in our hall Comrade Neave read a paper on "Our Social System", there was a record attendance and a note of the Meeting appeared in the Railway Review.[111]

Comrade Dorer received a box of books from the Fabian Society London which were put in circulation amongst our members Com Dorer acting as Librarian.

July found us still engaged in canvassing the end proved our labour had not been in vain the result being as follows:-

For adopting the Act 1310

Against   678

Neutral   456

On Sunday July 3 L E Quelch S.D F addressed two meetings at the Walks entrance – and again on Monday.[112]

On Wednesday in company with some of the members of the local branch the speakers visited Wisbech and held the first Socialist Meeting there.

1894, secretary to Norwich Trades Council 1897–98, stood for Norwich School Board 1896: unsuccessful but paved way for George Roberts' election to the School Board in 1899. Sutton moved to Bradford and was active in the ILP there. John Milner Headley, born 1869, newsagent and stationer, living at 18, Howard Street North, Yarmouth at time of 1911 census. He is first mentioned in the *Labour Leader* in 1897 and stood (as Jack Headley) for Yarmouth Board of Guardians in 1898 but was unsuccessful (*Labour Leader*, 27 Nov. 1897, 16 Apr. 1898).

110 The Stanley Library, founded by Lord Stanley in 1854; moved to enlarged premises in 1884, at which date it boasted 16,000 books. It was a subscription library, not a free library.

111 The official organ of the ASRS, first published in 1880.

112 Lorenzo [Len] Edward Quelch (1862–1937), younger brother of Harry (see note 122), then a co-opted member of SDF executive, acting as national propagandist.

Sunday 24ᵗʰ – having received a communication from Comrade Kidd suggesting a union of the two local socialist bodies – a joint meeting was held when it was decided in the interests of the movement in the Town it would be better to form one Party and a sub committee was appointed to draw up rules etc.

In the same week following this meeting a series of three meetings was given by Comrade J E Dobson a Member of the Camberwell Vestry London.

The first was held at the Walks entrance the subject being "Our National Food Supply". On the night following the subject was "The Need For a Socialist Party".

On Friday owing to the inclemency of the weather the lecture was given in the hall the subject on this occasion being "Is Socialism Inevitable". The meetings were in every way a success.

In the early part of August we held two meetings at the Walks entrance – which were addressed by Comrade George Belt member of Hull Town Council & Chairman of Hull School Management Committee.[113] Two Committee Meetings were held during the month to draft rules &c, these were presented and adopted at a joint meeting held Aug 28. Sept 1ˢᵗ will be remembered as marking a new era in the history of the movement in Lynn from the fact that it was on this day that the first meeting of the newly formed Social Democratic Party was held a step that neither the members of the old Branch of the S.D.F. nor of the Socialist Society have had any cause for regret in taking. The following week we received another visit from Comrade Dobson of London who addressed three meetings at the Walks entrance. The first night the subject was "Party Shibboleths", on the second "Socialism and Character" and the last "The Czars Message or Socialism and Peace". At this meeting there was an organised opposition and but for the presence of the police who warned one or two of the ringleaders there would have been trouble. As it was the meeting was gone through to the end.

The action of those who had come to create a disturbance only tended to make friends for us. After each meeting an adjournment was made to the hall and a pleasant time was spent on discussing questions affecting the cause.

Wednesday 14ᵗʰ was a notable day for the Town Council received a deputation from the Public Library Canvassing Committee and agreed by a

---

113 George Belt (1865–1930), born Hull, bricklayer by trade, then full-time organiser for ILP. Later in 1899 it became known that, although a married man, he was having an affair with suffragist and socialist Dora Montefiore (1851–1933). See C. Colette, 'Sex and Scandal: the sexual politics of the early labour movement', *History Workshop Journal* 23/1 (1987). He was sacked by ILP, but employed by SDF as Scottish organiser; later moved to London and by 1906 on the ILP list of speakers, living at 33 Mall Rd, Hammersmith.

majority of 11 to 8 to adopt the Act, a result which caused great satisfaction to us who had put in so much time to obtain this desirable result, but as events have turned out our joy was short lived owing to the fact that both the Council and there [*sic*] clerk bungled over the mode of procedure.

On Thursday 22ⁿᵈ a Social Evening was held in the hall between 69 & 70 members & friends being present. A good programme was gone through arranged by Comrades Bush, Fraser, Kidd.

Refreshments were provided at the interval. Altogether ten meetings were held during the month.

October. At our first business meeting a letter was read from the Amalgamated Society Railway Servants intimating they had decided to hold their meetings in our hall on and after January and he also expressed the wish that the Society would benefit by the change, they having previously held their meetings in the "Royal Standard" room.

During the month members voted on the "Clarion Referendum". The most important feature of the result of this was the unanimous feeling in favour of one Socialist Party.

An important meeting was held on Friday Oct 14 when it was decided to put the following questions to the candidates for the Town Council at the Nov elections

To give immediate attention & support to the movement for adopting the Public Libr'y Act.

Evening Meetings of the Council

Payment of a Minimum Wage of 1£ per week to Corporation workmen.

The construction by the Council of Workmens Dwellings on land already owned by the Corporation, the same to be let at a fair rental.

Recent events point to the fact that this our first real action at an Election resulted in the question of Artisan Dwellings being pressed to the front.

Twelve meetings were held during the month.

November Several members attended a meeting of the Town Council at which the Public Libr'y Question was again brought forward in the end the Act was again adopted by the casting vote of the Mayor – Mr Bunkall – a result which has however since again been set on one side.[114]

On the 29ᵗʰ we had a visit from Mrs Rose Jarvis of London S.D.F. who lectured in the hall her subject being "Waste and Want".

---

114 John Thomas Bunkall (1849–1910), born Northwold, proprietor of a leading grocer's shop in Lynn, Liberal town councillor, mayor 1898–99, alderman from 1906. His eldest son, also John, born 1877, took over the business after his father's death. Another son, Frank, was later a member of Lynn ILP.

Another Social Evening was held during the month Comrade Addison of Wisbech presiding who in a short speech related some of his experiences during his candidature for the Wisbech Town Council.

During December nothing of much importance was done by the party one or two meetings were held, and several members attended and took part in a discussion at the South Lynn Liberal Club the subject being "That Party Politics as now introduced into Local & Municipal affairs are prejudicial to the well being of the community". By a small majority it was decided that Party Politics should not be introduced into municipal affairs. The question of Workmens Dwellings was much discussed during the month members taking advantage of every opportunity – letters to the press etc of pressing the matter before the public. Taking a glance back over the work of the year we have every reason for feeling that much has been done for the cause of a lasting character.

F.W. White Secretary

Minutes, Annual Meeting Thursday Jan 12 1899
Secretary's report read and adopted which on the motion of Com Rowe Seconded Com Triance was decided should be entered into the minute book as a record of the year's work. <u>Carried</u>.

Treasurer's report was read an[d] adopted subject to the amount of 4/- part of cost of Fabian Book Box being transferred to the account of the Party.

Comrades Rowe & White were unanimously reelected as General & Financial Secretaries for the ensuing year.

<u>Alteration of rule</u> Comrade Rowe moved that the words "<u>and assistant secretary</u>" be added to <u>Rule 4</u>. Seconded by Com Mills. <u>Carried</u>

Comrade Dorer elected as Librarian.

Comrade Bloy Junr was elected assistant secretary on the proposition of Com Rowe seconded Com Mills.[115]

Comrades Rix & Bush reelected auditors.

The Executive Committee was then elected as follows Comrades Mrs & Mr Kidd, Dexter, Triance, Denny, Dennis, Francis and the two secretaries.

The offer of the South Lynn Liberal Club to sell them 24 chairs (which had been sent by them and had been in use for some time) for 1/6 each was then discussed and it was moved by Com White seconded Com Mills -:- "that members individually purchase the chairs at the price named and bought in as the funds of the Party allowed". Carried

---

115 William Bloy, son of the William E. Bloy who signed up to the Rules of the Society 3 January 1898. This is the only reference in the minutes to a 'Bloy junior' and it is not always clear to which of the Bloys subsequent entries refer.

Housing Question.

Comrade Dorer moved Com Triance seconded that the executive draw up a letter urging the importance of putting the Housing of the Working Classes Act into operation and that copies of the letter and the Fabian Tract bearing on the subject be sent to each member of the Town Council.[116] Carried.

Copy of letter sent Jan 8 to each Councillor:

LYNN SOCIAL DEMOCRATIC PARTY

Dear Sir

We beg your acceptance of the enclosed Fabian Tract and venture to express the hope that you will, as a Member of the Corporation, support the proposition for the immediate construction of **Workmens Dwellings** in this town on **Corporation** or other land.

Although private enterprise may be doing something to meet the pressing demand for more & better houses, thus mitigating the evil of **Slum Dwellings**, it cannot possibly meet existing needs. We further believe there is a necessity for a practical affirmation of the principle that municipalities recognise their obligations in this direction; & since the Act provides that none of the cost need fall upon the rates, we feel doubly sure that the movement will receive your hearty support.

Yours truly F W White.

Sunday Jan 8 Comrade Rowe gave an address subject "A Review of the Year". Chairman F W White.

Monday Jan 9 Executive Committee met. Chair: Comrade Kidd.

Minutes read and adopted.

Agreed that an entertainment be held on Jan 23. Comrades Kidd, Bush & Fraser to carry out arrangements.

Walter Frost was adopted as a member.[117]

The Housing question was then discussed, Comrade Kidd announcing the fact that the Mayor Mr Bunkall and Mr Councillor Springall had moved & seconded a resolution at the Council Meeting held on the previous day that the Council put into operation the Housing Act which was adopted by the Council in 1891.[118]

---

116 Fabian Tract 76, *Houses for the People* by Arthur Hickmott published in 1897.

117 Walter Frost, born 1879, a carpenter and joiner. In 1901, he was living with his father at Chapel Street, Lynn.

118 The motion was defeated. See *LA*, 13 Jan. 1899 and *LN*, 14 Jan. 1899 for report and editorials respectively reflecting Conservative and Liberal opinions.

Sunday Jan 15.[119]
Discussion opened by Comrade Denny subject The Abolition of the House
of Lords.

Wednesday Jan 18
Comrade Triance read a paper, subject: "The Cry of the Children".[120]
Comrade German presided.

Sunday Jan 22nd
Chairman Comrade Kidd Comrade Mills read a paper subject of which was
"The Labor Church" good discussion followed.

Monday Jan 23 Social Evening[121]
Selection by the Gramophone
Short addresses by Comrades Kidd & Rowe

Saty Jan 28
Copy of the Fabian Tract on "Houses for the people" with a letter urging on
the importance of the Council putting into operation the Act sent to every
Town Councillor

Sunday Jan 29 Comrade Denny in the Chair. Comrade Kidd read an article
by H Quelch entitled:- "Municipalism and Socialism" a good discussion
followed.[122]

Monday Jan 30 Meeting of the Executive Committee. Minutes read &
adopted. Programme was arranged for February.
Letter read from Mr Pease Sec of Fabian Society informing us that they
could not grant us another course of Lectures at present, but might be able
to arrange a single lecture.[123]

---

119 A later hand has added '1901?' in pencil but this is incorrect: this and following entries
are for 1899.
120 The talk was presumably developed from the poem 'The Cry of the Children' by
Elizabeth Barrett Browning, which was first published in *Blackwood's Magazine* in 1843,
and which drew attention to the abysmal conditions of child labour in Britain.
121 This entry incorrectly inserted after entry for meeting of 9 Jan.
122 Henry 'Harry' Quelch (1858–1913), socialist activist. Leading member of SDF. and
for three years editor of *Justice*. Attended gatherings of the Second International in Paris
and elsewhere in Europe. Francis Williams describes him as 'a dour and bitter working-class
fighter, whose soul had been seared by the poverty in which he had been born' (F. Williams
Fifty Years March (London, *c*. 1949), 51).
123 Edward Pease (1857–1955), writer, founding member of the Fabian Society in 1884,
and author of several Fabian Tracts. He was also a member of the ILP. He was the Fabian
Society's representative at the 1900 meeting that led to the setting up of the Labour
Representation Committee, on the executive of which he served for fourteen years.

Thursday Feby 2nd Impromptu Speeches by Members. Chairman A L Dorer.

Sunday Feby 5 Discussion, subject "Useful Work, Useless Toil" opened by H.B. Rowe.[124] Chairman F W White

Wednesday Feby 8
Mr Ward Secretary A.S.E. gave a lantern exhibition including a number of views taken by Comrades Triance & Jarvis at Brussels, Antwerp, Rotterdam, Jersey Islands etc.

Sunday Feby 12
Comrade Dorer gave extract from Ald Thompson's (Richmond) report on the Housing Question.[125] Discussion followed.

Sunday Feby 19 Address by J J Kidd "Thou Shalt Not". Chairman A. L. Dorer

Sunday Feby 26 Discussion Subject:- "The Pleasures of Life" opened by R. Fraser F W White in Chair

Monday Feby [27] Comrade Rowe in Chair. Meeting of the Executive Committee.
Programme arranged for March. This was the only business done. Signed Harry B. Rowe Chairman.[126]

Sunday March 5th Discussion subject "Everyday Questions For Socialists" opened by F W White Chairman W Dexter

Thursday March 9th Special General Meeting Chairman Comrade Rowe.
Secretary reported having attended a meeting of the Town Council held on the previous day after giving some account of the proceedings relating to the vacancy for the Town Clerkship &c he reported that a resolution by Mr Brown

---

124 'Useful Work versus Useful Toil' was an address first given by William Morris in 1883, and often repeated by him. It was first published as a pamphlet in 1885, and republished in various editions such as that by the Hammersmith Socialist Society in 1893, selling for one penny.
125 *The housing of the working classes* (Richmond, 1899); William Thompson (1863–1914), born in Southwold; became a schoolteacher in London, and served on the executive of the NUT, 1898–1900; active in local politics in Richmond from 1890 (Mayor in 1908–09), and a pioneer of working-class housing, responsible for first council houses in Richmond; chairman of the National Housing Reform Council on its formation in 1900, and author of several influential works; his funeral was attended by Lloyd George, John Burns and Keir Hardie.
126 On the same day that this meeting was held, the meeting was being held in London that led to the formation of the Labour Representation Committee (see Introduction): there were just nine spectators present in the public gallery! (John Shepherd and Keith Layborn, *Britain's First Labour Government* (London, 2013), 7–8).

that:- "The Friars Field be laid out and sold in building plots",[127] was carried by 9 to 6 those in favour being A. Jermyn who seconded the resolution, Rose, Bettinson, Thew, Bristowe, Floyd, Smith, Brown, Carpenter.[128]
Against The Mayor (Mr Bunkall), Pridgeon, Ream, Bardell, Springall, Sadler.[129]
Dunn & W Miles were present but did not vote.[130]
After expressing the opinion that everything possible should have been done in an attempt to upset this decision the secretary asked those present to give their views and offer suggestions as to what should be done, and read a letter he had sent to A Jermyn. After some discussion it was suggested that a petition should be signed, that a requisition be sent to the Mayor to call a Town Meeting and Comrade Dorer was also asked to write to the Fabian Society London for any advice that they could give us as to our Course of Action in the matter.

Sunday March 12 General Discussion

Thursday March 16 Special Meeting Comrade Rowe in Chair. Petition drawn up against the sale of Friars Field.
Correspondence read from Secretary Lee of the S.D.F London re proposed visit of J Chatterton.

Sunday March 19 Discussion subject:- "All Men Are Liars" Mrs J J Kidd.[131]
Chairman A L Dorer

Monday March 20 Social Evening. A good programme in which Comrades Fraser Rowe and friends took part. Refreshments provided at the interval.

---

127 A field abutting the river Nar: in the floods of November 1897. it was described as 'having the appearance of a lake' (*EDP*, 30 Nov. 1897).
128 See above for Brown, Bettinson, Thew, Carpenter. The other five are Alfred S. Jermyn, draper, mayor in 1897–98 – his shop in Lynn High Street was badly damaged by fire in 1894 and 1897; George Edward Rose, saddler and harness maker, High Street, Lynn, mayor 1906–07; George Bristow, timber merchant, mayor 1899–1900; Frank Rust Floyd, a corn merchant, elected for the Middle Ward 1898, mayor 1911–12; William Robert Smith ship broker.
129 See above for Bunkall, Sadler. William Read Pridgeon, clock and watch maker, mayor 1890–91 and 1891–92; Alfred A. Ream, wine merchant, mayor 1892–93; John Bardell, building contractor, South Ward, also county councillor for the South Ward (1912 trade directory, which gives his address as Melrose House, Goodwin's Road); Robert French Springall, timber merchant.
130 See above for Miles. Edwin A Dunn was a baker, mayor in 1895–96.
131 A striking title for a talk by the only woman on the Executive. It may well be drawn from the Bible; 'I said in my haste, all men are liars' (Psalm 116.11, King James translation).

Sunday March 26 Discussion subject: "Socialism and the teachings of Christ" by Comrade Denny Chairman Comrade Kidd

Tuesday March 28 J Chatterton of the S.D.F London gave a lantern lecture entitled: "Social Democracy On The Screen" unfortunately owing to several other meetings & lectures being held in the Town there was only a small attendance.[132]

On Wednesday 29 Owing to the fact that only a few people turned up at the hall we adjourned to the Walks entrance were [*sic*] a fairly good meeting was held in the open air. Comrade Kidd introduced the speaker J Chatterton who gave a good address. There were a few interruptions but no questions were asked. Comrade Kidd entertained the lecturer during his two days in Lynn.

April 6th Quarterly General Meeting. Comrade Kidd in the Chair. The minutes were read and adopted. Comrade Rowe read Financial Statement which showed that a number of members were in arrears and it was decided that these should be written too [*sic*]. A Resolution was carried "that the question of finance be dealt with by the Executive and a report presented to a general meeting of members".
The question as to when the petition re Friars Field should be presented was discussed and Comrade Kidd was asked to see Mr Councillor Springall and get his advice as to what course would be best to take.[133]
The Secretary reported that the Nar Bank (west side) had been closed to the public although the footpath had been used as long as could be remembered. Mr Bywater had promised to raise the question at the South Lynn Vestry Meeting on the following evening.[134]
William Drayton 9 Bentinck St was proposed as a member and adopted.[135]

---

132 The flyer for the event is pasted into the minute book: it was to be held in Blackfriars' Hall and "Illustrated by Oxy-Hydrogen Lantern".
133 The petition opposed the sale on the grounds that:
    1. It is a reactionary proposal to sell Corporation Land.
    2. It was found when part of the same field was sold a short time since, that the sum realised by the sale was barely sufficient to cover the cost the Town had to pay for Road and Sewer making.
    3. Open air spaces in Towns are regarded as absolute necessities for the maintenance of the health of the inhabitants, especially that of the children.
134 William Bywater, Ingram Cottage, Exton's Road, Lynn.
135 William Drayton, born 1867, occupation in 1901 census given as 'assistant meter' married with three young children.

Sunday April 9
Review of the book "In His Steps" by H.B. Rowe.[136]

Sunday April 16
"Socialism & Liberalism" address by J J Kidd Chairman H.B. Rowe

Sunday May 7
"The Moral need for a Socialist Propaganda" Address by H.B. Rowe
Chairman J. Neave.

Thursday May 11
"Old Age Pensions" by A L Dorer who gave a extracts from Booth's
book on the subject.[137] Chairman J Mills. Discussion followed in which
Comrades Rowe, Bush, Kidd, Mills took part. John Pooley adopted as a
member.[138]

Sunday May 14
Address by J J Kidd Subject:- "The Liberal Candidate for Lynn"

Monday May 15 Social Evening.
This was the last "social" of the season there was a good attendance and
the programme was one of the best. Comrades Bush, Fraser and Mrs Kidd
was responsible for the arrangements which were carried out in a most
satisfactory manner.

Thursday May 18
An Evening With The Poets Comrade Triance

Sunday May 21 Comrade Bush read a most interesting paper entitled:- The
History of Music. The speaker showed a thorough knowledge of the subject
those present expressing the opinion that it was one of the best papers that
had been given. F W White in the Chair.

---

136 An American religious novel, written by Charles Monroe Sheldon, published in 1896
and one of the world's best-selling books. Its full title is *In His Steps: What Would Jesus Do.*
Its themes tie in with the ideas of the Labour Church.
137 See above, note 95. Charles Booth's book was *Old Age Pensions and the Aged Poor: A
Proposal* (London, 1899).
138 John Pooley, born 1864, railway engine driver, member of ASRS from 1888. In 1901,
he was living at Saddlebow Road, South Lynn. A long-term activist, he was one of the eleven
members of Lynn ILP when it was dissolved in 1916 (at which time his address was Queen's
Avenue, Lynn).

Thursday May 25
Comrade Cremer read the pamphlet by Ruskin,[139] entitled:- "The Rights of Labour"[140] J J Kidd in the Chair

Sunday May 28
Paper by H B Rowe subject "The Fallacy Of Saving". Comrade Denny presided.

June 22 Meeting of the Executive Committee.
Comrade Rowe gave a rough statement as to the financial position of the party and it was arranged that the quarterly general meeting should be held on Thursday June 29th. Comrades Francis & Denny moved & seconded that the Committee recommend the appointment of a Collector.   Carried
~~W~~ S Catty was adopted as a Member.[141]

Thursday June 29 General Meeting.
Chairman Comrade Kidd.
Minutes read and adopted.
The Financial Secretary gave a report as to our position. Some discussion followed the general tone of which was one of satisfaction with the statement read but that efforts should be made to increase our membership.
The General Secretary's Report showed that two or three important matters would stand as record of the work done in the past quarter: namely the fact that through Comrade Kidd's efforts the Clarion Labour Leader and Justice had been accepted and were now laid on the table of the Public Library:[142] That the decision of the Town Council to sell Friars Field in building plots had been rescinded through the efforts of the society who memorialised the Council the said memorial undoubtedly influencing the Corporation to reconsider their decision.[143] Comrade Denny proposed and H B Rowe seconded that Mrs Kidd be appointed collector.

---

139 John Ruskin (1819–1900), art critic and social thinker. His works had an enormous influence on socialist thinking; Tolstoy called him 'one of the most remarkable men not only of England and of our generation, but of all countries and times'. His long-term influence is shown in the references to Ruskin College and the Ruskin School in these minutes.
140 Full title, *The Rights of Labour according to John Ruskin arranged by Thomas Barclay*. This undated pamphlet consists of extracts from Ruskin's work on economics, *Unto this Last*, published in book form in 1862, previously as a series of articles.
141 Not identified: no one of this name in 1901 or 1911 census. Perhaps an error for William Catton, born 1855, in 1911 census an engine driver living at Exton's Place, Lynn.
142 For *Clarion* and *Labour Leader*, see above, notes 20 and 34. *Justice* was the newspaper of the SDF, founded in 1884.
143 The petition was signed by between 500 and 600 ratepayers: as a result, the Borough Council rescinded its decision to sell the land for housing. The original debate on the matter

Alteration of Rules. Comrade Rowe proposed Comrade Denny seconded "that rule 4 be altered to read: Treasurer, Secretary, Collector, two auditors & Librarian". Rule 5 to read "There shall be an Executive consisting of the General Secretary, Treasurer, Collector & six members etc".
Comrades Rowe & Kidd moved & seconded that "the Executive meet and draw up a programme for July.

Sep 14 General Meeting Com Dorer in the chair.
Minutes of last meeting read & adopted.
The programme for the two remaining Thursdays in the month and for Oct was then arranged.
Two vacancies on the Executive Committee by having occurred by Coms Dexter & Triance leaving the Town,[144] the names of Comrades Bush & Mills were proposed to fill their places on the proposition of Com Rowe seconded by Com Dorer.   Agreed
Moved by Com Bush seconded by Dorer:- That a Correspondence Class be formed in connection with either Ruskin Hall,[145] or the Fabian Society and that Comrade Rowe take charge of the class".   Carried
The Secretary reported having written the landlords calling attention to the condition of the hall.

Thurs Sept [21] Discussion
Subject "The Transvaal" opened by Mrs Kidd.[146]

Thursday Sept 28 Quarterly General Meeting.
Comrade Mills in the Chair. Minutes read and adopted.
Comrade Rowe read particulars of the Ruskin Hall Correspondence Classes.

---

is fully reported in the local press; the most vociferous opponent was Springall, who pointed out the need for a public space in a part of Lynn where many houses did not even have a back yard let alone a back garden (*LN*, 17 Jun. 1899).

144 Neither stayed away long. Triance reappears in the minutes from February 1903. He may have spent some or all of the interim in Great Yarmouth: the 1901 census records him as a boarder in Shuckford's Buildings in that town, and his occupation as 'Railway Collector and Canvasser'. Dexter reappears in the minutes from October 1903, but may not have been away from Lynn all that time. In the 1901 census he is recorded as being at 23 High Street Lynn, in his father's house, and he is described as 'W. Dexter junior, Studio, KL', in an art exhibition of June 1901. Sources mention an undated stay in Belgium and Holland by Dexter after he had finished his time at Birmingham: this could fill the gap between 1899 and 1901.

145 Ruskin Hall, Oxford, now Ruskin College. Set up in 1899 as a workers' college.

146 Territory in southern Africa disputed between the British and the Boers, one cause of the outbreak of the (Second) Boer War in October 1899. See Thomas Pakenham, *The Boer War* (London, 1979), and for the Labour viewpoint Rhiannon Vickers, *The Labour Party and the World: the evolution of Labour's foreign policy 1900–51* (Manchester, 2003), 43–6.

The Treasurer – Com Rowe – gave a statement as to the financial position of the society which was considered fairly satisfactory, and the report adopted.

Comrade Kidd moved, Comrade Mills seconded: That a public meeting be held on the Market Place on Friday Oct 6th on the Housing Question". Carried. Comrade Kidd to arrange for same.

Thursday Oct 5th. Social Evening. Comrades Bush & Fraser undertook arrangement of programme and Mrs Mrs [sic] Kidd the providing of refreshments.[147]

The Housing Agitation. Comrade Kidd was responsible for the successful organising of a public meeting held on the Saturday Market on Friday Oct 6th.[148]

Sunday Oct 15 Discussion "The Commercial Conscience" opened by F White. Chairman Com Denny

Monday Oct 16 Housing Question
Another successful meeting was held on the Saturday Market Place. Mr C Dines presided. The speakers were Comrade Kidd, Rev Lansdowne, Mr W Kidd[149]
Councillor Floyd made some rambling remarks in opposition which Councillor Springall very easily disposed of, the crowd hugely enjoying the way he dealt with the subject. During the meeting Councillor Carpenter who had undoubtedly taken an overdose of stimulants to give the necessary courage – made a mixed medley of statements relating to his attendance of Council meetings and attention to the business of the Town quite outside the subject before the meeting and after being called to order by the chairman gave up any further attempt to speak.[150]
It was decided to hold another meeting the following week.

---

147 Press cutting inserted. The local press noted that at the meeting it was announced that a correspondence class would be started in connection with the Fabian Society and open to non-members, the subject either 'Economics' or 'Local Government' (*LN*, 14 Oct. 1899).

148 Press cutting and handbill inserted. Also reported in *Labour Leader*, *Clarion* and *Justice*.

149 William Kidd born at Wiggenhall St Peter, 1859, in 1896 trade directory and 1901 census a greengrocer living at Windsor Road, in 1911 fruiterer and florist, same address.

150 As a brewer, Carpenter was especially vulnerable to claims of alcoholic indulgence. This was not confined to his Socialist opponents: when Carpenter was proposed for mayor in 1902, Liberal councillor and temperance campaigner Alfred Jermyn opposed his election because of his profession.

Sunday Oct 22nd. Discussion subject:- "Constructive Socialism" by Com Denny Chairman Comrade Dorer.

Monday 23 Housing Meeting Walks Gates
this was the third held during the month and the interest in no way abated. A good attendance of the public who followed with interest the remarks of the speakers.
Mr Mason[151] presided and the same speakers as at the previous meetings Kidd, Springall, T.F. Cox,[152] Revd Lansdown again pointed out the advantages of Corporation Dwellings.
The meeting passed a resolution to use every effort to return Councillor Springall again to the Municipal Chamber on Nov 1st.
A collection was taken which nearly covered the amount spent in organising the meetings.

Sunday Oct 29.
Arrangements made for opening the Fabian Correspondence Class on the following Thursday. Programme arranged for November.

Thursday Nov 2.
First meeting of Class to study "Local Government" in connection with Fabian Correspondence Classes.

Sunday 5th.
Paper by Comrade Rowe subject "Life In Our Villages". Chairman F.W. White

Thursday 9th.
Local Government Class subject under study "Sanitation etc.

Sunday 12 Comrade Dorer in chair.
Comrade Kidd introduced the subject of "Sanitation, Education and the Poor Law" followed by discussion.

Tuesday Nov 14 Meeting of Executive Committee. Comrade Bush in the chair.
Present Comrades Denny, Kidd, Mrs Kidd, Mills, Francis, White, Rowe.
Minutes read and adopted.
Secretary read a communication from the Secretary newly formed branch of the Railway Clerks Association asking for terms for use of hall for future

---

151 Not identified: no obvious candidate in trade directories or local newspaper reports, nor among the various Masons in census returns.
152 Thomas Fuller Cox, born 1855, engineer store-keeper, living at 4, Exton's Road at time of 1901 census.

meetings.[153] After some discussion Comrade Francis moved Comrade \Mrs Kidd/ seconded that "the hall be lent to the said Association on the same terms as the A.S.R.S. that is 2/- for each meeting. Comrade Denny moved an amendment that the charge be 2/- without gas and firing. The resolution was carried.

Treasurer then read rough statement as to financial position & Comrade Mills moved a resolution that the Treasurer & collector meet and draw up an estimate of the Society's income and expenditure to Dec 30 and report to the next meeting of the executive. Carried.

Meeting was then adjourned to following week.

Thursday Nov 16
"Local Government Class"

Sunday Nov 19
Discussion subject:- Life In Our Villages by Comrade Rowe. Chairman F.W. White

Wednesday Nov 22 Adjourned Meeting of Executive Committee.
Comrade Bush in the Chair.
Minutes read and adopted.
Financial secretary Rowe presented a report showing that the estimated receipts for quarter ending Dec 31 would after paying all liabilities including Election Fund and the bill for Chatterton's Lantern Lecture leave the society with a probable deficiency of 2/10/0.
The meeting then proceeded to arrange program for December and decided that a Social Evening should be held on the 6th and that an effort should be made to make a profit on same towards wiping out the deficiency.

Sunday Nov 26
Discussion "Secondary Education" opened by Comrade Denny. Comrade Rowe Chairman

Wednesday Dec 6
Social Evening. Musical program arranged by Comrades Bush & Fraser. Refreshments supplied at the interval by Comrade Mrs Kidd & Friends.

Dec 10 Discussion opened by Comrade Denny subject:- "How it might be done".

---

153 The Railway Clerks Association was founded in 1897 in response to the apparent unwillingness of Richard Bell of the ASRS to enrol clerks into its ranks: see Bagwell, *Railwaymen*, 238. Dorer was a member of this union.

Jan 10 [*1900*] Executive Committee met.

Program arranged for remainder of Jan and for Feby.

Decided that the Annual Meeting be held Jan 18th and that special urgent notices be sent out urging members to attend.

Jan 25 Annual Meeting. Comrade Dorer in the Chair. Minutes of last Annual Meeting read and adopted. General Secretary then read report of the work of the Party during past year and it was moved and carried that the same report be entered in the minute book. Financial Secretary Com Rowe then presented the financial statement which showed a deficiency of about 15/-. Report adopted on the proposition of Com Mills seconded Com German subject to being audited and presented to a meeting of the executive. The election of officers then proceeded with. On the motion of Com Rowe seconded Com Kidd the General Secretary F W White was reelected for ensuing year. The appointment of Assistant Sec'y left to a future meeting. Com Rowe re-elected <u>Financial Secretary</u> Mrs Kidd to be collector.

<u>Executive Committee</u> JJ Kidd, Denny, Francis, Mills, German, Cremer & the collector & Secretaries.

<u>Librarian</u> Comrade Dorer

Auditors Comrade Bush [*added in pencil*]

Com Kidd moved Com Cremer seconded that:- A memorial be drawn up and signatures obtained requesting ~~that~~ the Public Library Committee rescind their resolution excluding papers presented. <u>Carried</u>.

Petition from London Trades Council read and it was agreed to obtain signatures thereto.

<u>Report read at Annual Meeting Jan 25th 1900</u>

The month of January found the members of the Socialist Party actively engaged in agitating on the housing question.

At a Meeting organised by the Friends Society[154] Comrade Dennis & Kidd carried a resolution which was forwarded to the Town Council and a copy of the Fabian Tract "Houses For The People" was sent to every member of the Corporation.

The Mayor moved & Councillor Springall seconded that the Town Council put into operation the Housing Act which the Council had adopted in 1891. Defeated.

Letters from members appeared in the Press including extracts from Ald' Thompson's (Richmond) sent by Comrade Dorer.

---

154 Society of Friends (Quakers) had a small but active group in Lynn.

During Feby usual meetings were held and a meeting held at South Lynn Club on the Housing Question was attended by our members who took an active part in the discussion.

March The principal work of the month was that of obtaining signatures to a petition to the Town Council to rescind a resolution to sell Friars Field in building plots passed at a meeting held on March 8th.

During the month J Chatterton gave a Lantern Lecture at the Blackfriars Hall entitled "Social Democracy On the Screen".

On the following evening 29th a meeting was held at the Walks Gates addressed by Coms' Chatterton & Kidd.

April The most important item of interest was the acceptance by the Library Committee on the casting vote of the Chairman Councillor Springall of the "Clarion" "Labour Leader" & Justice. These had been offered by members and to Comrade Kidd who was a member of the Committee belongs the credit of the success of this move.

May 1st The Public Library was opened a result of the hard work and agitation of members and other friends who took a voluntary canvas of the Town in the previous year.

May 10th a petition was presented to the Town Council against the sale of Friars Field (Corporation Land) for building plots, a result of this agitation was the rescinding of the resolution to sell the land.

The first week in August we received a visit for Comrade Dobson of London who lectured at the Walks Gates the subjects were "No Room to Live", "Waste", "Socialism & Drink" all three meetings were well attended.

During October a correspondence class was opened in connection with the Fabian Society London the subject of study being "Local Government".

All through the month a very active agitation on the Housing Question was organised Comrade Kidd being largely responsible. Several well attended open air meetings was held on the Saturday Market & Walks Gates addressed by Messrs Dennis, Springall, Kidd and others. Councillor Springall so upset the property owners in the town that on Nov 1st a successful effort was made on their part and he lost his seat on the Council.

During December usual meetings was held. Taking a brief survey of the whole year's work it hardly compares with the previous one but much good was done from an educational point of view justifying our existence as a society.

F.W. White Secretary

March 1 Meeting of Executive Committee.

Minutes read and adopted. Decided to at once prepare petition and to commence obtaining signatures to same re exclusion of presentation papers by Library Committee.

Com' Bloy adopted as Assistant Sec'y. Programme for March was then arranged.

Discussion was raised by Com Kidd as to whether we could not get some alteration of our terms of tenure of hall. Secretary was instructed to write the Rechabites on the subject.

March 8 Discussion Subject "What Socialism Is" Com Kidd

March 11 Sunday
Comrade Rowe read some chapters from Nunquam's book "Dismal England".[155] Comrade Kidd in Chair. This proved to be the last discussion opened by Comrade Rowe.

March 15 Impromptu speeches by Members. Subjects "Antagonism" by Com Kidd "Christianity & the war in South Africa by Com Dorer "The War Fever" Com White etc etc'[156]

Sunday 18 "Self Help" discussion opened by Comrade Mills

Sunday 25 Discussion opened by Com' White. Subject Imperialism, Militarism, Conscription.

Death of Comrade Rowe Financial Sec'y
March 29th Under the most sorrowful circumstances in the history of the Society a special general meeting was held to consider what tribute we

---

155 By Robert Blatchford, published in 1899, following up his *Merrie England*, which originally was also published under the pseudonym Nunquam, (a Latin word meaning 'never').

156 The Boer War split early members of the Labour movement, just as did the First World War fourteen years later. The ILP put forward an anti-war motion to the annual conference of the LRC in February 1901: it was unanimously agreed to. However, the Fabian Society voted against issuing a resolution condemning the war (which brought about the resignation of sixteen of its members including J. Ramsay MacDonald): 'The socialists were divided: the Fabians were inclined to support it, but the ILP and the SDF came out on the side of the 'pro-Boers' and incurred great hostility. MacDonald and Hardie, in deploring the attack of a large nation on a small, were hardly to be distinguished from the Liberal Radicals. With the latter they accepted the Marxist analysis of the SDF – the war had been brought about by the machinations of international armament rings sponsored by international financiers.' (Vickers, *The Labour Party and the World*, 46, citing Frank Bealey, ed., *The Social and Political Thought of the Labour Party* (London, 1970), 11). Their anti-war stance made the Socialists extremely unpopular: 'the country was in a jingoistic fervour which rose to a climax in the South African War; and the Socialists suffered, not only because their primary concern was with domestic politics, but because in most cases they actively opposed the war' (Henry Pelling, *A short history of the Labour Party* (London, 1961), 4–5).

could pay to the memory of our Comrade Rowe who died on the morning of Wednesday March 28th.[157] Comrade Kidd presided. There was a fair attendance. The Chairman explained the object for which the meeting had been called and after testifying to the loss sustained through the death of our Comrade asked for suggestions as to what form our tribute should take.

Comrades Bush & Dorer in a few words spoke of the valuable services our comrade had rendered to the cause and the loss his death had occasioned.

It was decided that a wreath should be sent with a letter of condolence to Mrs Rowe and that an enlarged portrait be obtained to hang in the hall, the cost to be defrayed by subscriptions.

Comrades Kidd, Denny, Francis & White was appointed as a deputation to represent the Society at the funeral. Members to be notified as to time in order that as many as possible should attend.

Resolution to be sent to local paper and a note inserted in the Socialist papers.[158]

Com' Mrs Kidd was appointed Treasurer pro tem.

Sunday April 8 Discussion opened by Com' Denny. Subject:- "The coming force in politics".

April 12 General Meeting Comrade Kidd in Chair.
Minutes read and adopted.

Comrade Kidd reported on the presentation of the Petition to the Library Committee re excluded papers.

Appointment of Treasurer & Trustee deferred. Mrs Kidd gave a statement as to financial position which was considered satisfactory. Proposed, seconded and carried: that we cancel our liabilities to the Election Fund and start it afresh as from Jan 1.

Comrade Mrs Kidd reported that 1/11/- had been collected to Comrade Rowe's memorial Fund after paying 10/6 for wreath left 1/0/6 in hand for purchase of portrait for the wall.

April 19 Discussion opened by Comrade Dorer Subject:- "What the Municipalities have done".

April 22 Discussion subject "The I.L.P. and the War in South Africa" opened by F W White

---

157 See Introduction.
158 Rowe's death was noted in the *Labour Leader*, 7 Apr. 1900, and a notice by F.W. White appeared in the *Clarion* on the same date.

June 15 Meeting of Executive Committee.

Minutes read and adopted.

Moved by J.J Kidd seconded by Com Francis that the "Secretary write the Rechabites for an immediate answer to the request to sub let the hall. Carried.

Comrade Kidd was appointed trustee in place of our late Comrade Rowe, subject to the approval of next General Meeting.

Aug 29

Comrade Kidd addressed a large open air meeting at the Walks Gates dealing with "The Library Scandal" the refusal of Messrs Bunkall & Jermyn's offer of the Union Chapel, and the exclusion of labour papers from the reading room.[159]

Aug 30 General Meeting.

Minutes of previous meeting were read and confirmed. It was reported that the memorial to the Public Library Committee had been successful and that periodicals etc will now be accepted on presentation subject to approval of Committee.

Correspondence was read from several speakers offering to come to Lynn and it was resolved to accept the services of Comrades Anderson of York & Buckeridge of Lincoln.[160]

It was decided to discontinue taking the Fabian book box.

Sept 12 Comrade Kidd addressed a meeting at the Walks gates taking for his subject:- "Corporation Waste, Work & Wages"

Sept 15th. In accordance with arrangements Comrade Buckeridge commenced what was intended as the first of a series of open air lectures in Lynn. The meeting however ended in such disorder amounting to almost a riot through the lax way in which the police acted – that the other meetings had to be abandoned.

[NEWSPAPER ARTICLE INSERTED]
SOCIALIST ORATOR MOBBED AT LYNN.

Mr J.J. Kidd of Lynn, a well-known nurseryman and an active member of the Social Democratic Federation was the central figure of some

---

159 Union Baptist Chapel, built 1859, became redundant after a new chapel was built in Wisbech road in 1901. The building was converted to a museum in 1901: Lynn Museum still occupies it.

160 Anderson, not identified; James Benjamin Buckeridge, born Lambeth 1860, in 1901 living at 14 Spital Street Lincoln. The census described Buckeridge as 'store keeper engineers'.

lively scenes on Saturday night. The local branch of the federation have arranged for a series of open-air lectures, and one of them was fixed for Saturday night, and located on the Saturday Market place. The lecturer was announced on handbills to be Mr J.B. Buckeridge of Lincoln. A crowd of several hundreds who were attracted to hear the discourse allowed the speaker to proceed with little interruption until he made references to the Boer war. Cries of resentment rose from the listeners, and thereupon it is stated, Mr Kidd, mounting upon a stool, proceeded to harangue the crowd in excited tones. With hoots and cries they rushed upon him, and he was swept off his stand and severely hustled. Some onlookers state that he was several times thrown to the ground. The orator from Lincoln appears to have escaped. Inspector Edwards and several other police-officers quickly went to the protection of Mr Kidd, and, forming a cordon round him, escorted him to the Stanley Public Library. Mr Kidd had by this time been joined by his wife, and the crowd who followed attempted no violence, respecting perhaps the presence of the lady, and contented themselves with hooting and yelling. On arrival at the library Mr and Mrs Kidd entered the building, while the police stood on guard at the door to prevent the crowd, who surged around, from gaining admittance. It wanted an hour to the closing of the library, and the crowd settled to wait until as they believed the object of their execrations would have to leave, singing patriotic songs meanwhile. However, their design was defeated, for Chief-Constable Payne, who arrived in a short time, succeeded in getting Mr Kidd away over a wall at the rear, and they took refuge in some almshouses. At the closing of the library the crowd moved round to Mr Kidd's house to await his coming, and a large number of panes of glass were also broken in his greenhouses. Eventually the watchers departed, and the fugitives were enabled to come from their refuge.[161]

[END OF INSERTION]

---

161 Newspaper not identified. Another local newspaper (Conservative-leaning) was dismissive, describing Buckeridge as a 'stump orator' and stating that the crowd 'were by no means overwhelmed with a sense of the blessings which were to rain upon themselves under a socialistic regime' (LA, 21 Sept. 1900). The events in Lynn – smashing of windows and property, with meetings broken up by mobs while the police looked on – were typical of actions by jingoists against 'pro-Boers' as anti-war speakers were known. See Bernard Porter, 'The pro-Boers in Britain' in Peter Warwick, South African War (London, 1980), esp. 239. More than three decades later, J. W. Raby, then mayor, recalled that the breaking of Kidd's windows was one of the things that brought him into the Labour movement (LN, 10 Mar. 1936).

General Election
Sep 20th A meeting of members of Executive decided to issue a recommendation to members to abstain from voting for either Mr Bowles the Tory or Mr Booth the Liberal.[162]

Sepr 30 Sunday Morning
Meeting of executive Committee. Present Comrades Kidd, Francis, Bush, Denny, White.
A long discussion was carried on as to whether the previous recommendation sent out re Election should be withdrawn. It was ultimately decided:- that in view of the official statement by Joseph Chamberlain that every seat won by the Liberals would be regarded as a vote of censure on the Government's South African policy"[163] – to advise our Members to vote for Mr Booth. Secretary announced the receipt of 17/- in contributions for members to the Central Election Funds and it was agreed to send 8/6 each to the I.L.P. and S.D.F.
A Letter was also written to the President of the Lynn Liberal Association announcing the decision of the Executive.

Election result in Lynn
Bowles (Conservative)   1499
Booth (Liberal)   1332
                Majority   167

---

162 Thomas Gibson Bowles (1842–1922), journalist and politician, known as 'Tommy' or 'Tap'. Founder of *Vanity Fair* and *The Lady* magazines. He was elected Conservative MP for Lynn in 1892 and re-elected in 1895 and 1900. He lost the seat in the 1906 general election, standing as an independent (pro-free trade) Conservative. He then moved to the Liberal Party, standing for Central Glasgow in March 1909. He stood as a Liberal in Lynn in January 1910: his candidature led to some disputes within the ILP, described later. He won the seat but lost it again in the December 1910 election. Bowles had another claim to fame: his daughter Sydney was the mother of the Mitford sisters (of whom the best-known were Nancy, Diana, and Unity Mitford). See *ODNB*.
Frederick Handel Booth (1867–1947), part of the Manchester cotton goods manufacturers of Booth and Sons. Like Bowles, he was not a local man – he had addresses in Bakewell, Derbyshire and in London. He became Liberal MP for Pontefract in 1910. He was involved in scandal in 1917 when a German born businessman John (formerly Johann) Gruban accused Booth of defrauding him of his company, and having him interned. Gruban won the case and was awarded £4,750 damages by the court.
163 Joseph Chamberlain (1836–1915) was colonial secretary in Lord Salisbury's Conservative government. He advocated fighting the 1900 general election on a single issue, British military victory in South Africa: because of this, it has become known as the 'Khaki' election.

Oct 17 Comrade Kidd addressed a meeting at the Walks Gates his subject being:- "High Rates & the Remedy".
The audience was fairly orderly to the end but at the close our Comrade was severely hustled, the police allowing the crowd to get the upper hand. Later some hundreds of lads rushed to his house and smashed windows to their hearts content the police carefully keeping back until they had wreaked their vengeance howling the while. Without a doubt this will stand as one of the most disgraceful occurrences of a year of similar outbreaks, the direct result of the jingo war fever.[164]

Oct 25 General Meeting Comrade Denny in Chair.
Minutes read and adopted. A resolution was passed sympathising with Comrades Mr & Mrs Kidd in the treatment received at the hands of the mob on [sic]. It was agreed that the expenses of Comrade Buckeridge Lincoln be paid out of Election fund. Financial Secretary then presented a rough statement of accounts which showed that our income to end of September would cover expenses. Comrade Dorer moved Comrade Francis seconded that in the forthcoming Municipal Elections our members be recommended to plump for Bunkall, Dexter & Everett for the South, Middle, and North Wards.   <u>Carried</u>.

Comrade Dorer in Chair. Minutes of last meeting read and adopted.
Dec 5 Meeting. Programme arranged for December.

Dec 9 Comrade Denny read an article from "The Ethical World"[165]

     " 12 Comrade Francis read a paper entitled "Corruption in American Politics"

     " 16 Comrade White read A. M Thompson's pamphlet – "The Only Way to Democracy"[166]

     " 23 Comrade Mills gave selections from Burns' Poetical Works.[167]

---

164 Press cutting inserted.

165 Ed. Stanton Coit and John A. Hobson (London, 1899).

166 Alexander Mattock Thompson (1861–1948), *The Only Way to Democracy* (London: Clarion Newspaper Co. 1900).

167 Robert Burns (1759–1796) Scottish poet whose radical ideas (support of the French Revolution, approval of Thomas Paine's *Rights of Man*) made him popular among early Socialists. He was a special favourite of fellow-Scot Keir Hardie, who once wrote 'I owe more to Robert Burns than to any man, alive or dead.' The Norfolk Record Office has a copy of Burns' poems that Hardie presented to George Roberts in 1906 (Stewart, *Hardie*, 19; Frank Meeres, *George Roberts MP* (Lowestoft, 2019), 33).

<u>1901</u>

Jan 2 The Party opened the new year with the most successful and enjoyable "Social" yet held. The hall was tastefully decorated by Comrades Kidd who also lent the plants.

The company indulged in all kinds of games interspersed with music and refreshments.

Comrade Walker was present from Wisbech who upon leaving was thanked for attending.[168]

Not the smallest item of interest during the evening was the appearance of No 1 of the "Norfolk Socialist Review",[169] which had been looked forward too with some amount of curiosity as to the form it would take. The successful issue of this publication must have entailed an immense amount of labour on its Editor Marcus M Isserliss.[170]

Jan 9 Comrade Kidd opened the usual discussion. Labour Hymns were sung for the first time and added greatly to the attractiveness of the meeting.

13th Comrade White read an article by Comrade Vanderweld "The Nineteenth Century".[171] Labour Hymns sung.

Jan 17 Com Denny in the Chair. An informal meeting was held when a discussion took place upon the fact having come to our knowledge that the Rechabites had offered to sublet the Hall to the Good Templars on alternate Tuesdays which was considered a breach of our rights as sole tenants. After a lengthy conversation the following resolution was carried:- That a letter be written to the Rechabites informing them that considering we the Socialist Party pay £10 per annum rent the full value of the hall, all sub-letting must be in their hands. If however the Rechabites desire on any Tuesday evening or part of such evening to sub-let the Hall the proceeds from such letting shall be deducted from the rent of £10 per year paid by the Socialist Party.

---

168 Felix Mendelsohn Walker of Strad House, Wisbech, schoolmaster, born 1880, a member of Lynn ILP from October 1906. The name 'Strad House', and the giving of three brothers the names of famous musicians as second names, may be explained by the description in the 1891 census of their father Jeremiah Walker as 'joiner and violinist'.

169 *Norfolk Socialist Review*, a monthly journal issued by the Norwich branch of the SDF. It appears to have been issued for just three months, from January to March 1900, then ceasing publication with a financial loss to its subscribers: see A.G.M. of January 1902 in this volume.

170 Marcus Maurice Isserlis (1872–1952), printer and stationer by occupation and Socialist activist. Born in London of Austrian parents. In 1902, he was sentenced to six months hard labour for obtaining money under false pretences, about that time changing his name to Mark Graham Maurice.

171 Emile Vandervelde (1866–1938), Belgian socialist leader and author, President of the Second International 1900–1918.

The terms of this resolution to come into operation on and after the 29th day of January 1901, and that an agreement be immediately drafted and signed by both parties and thereby avoid misunderstandings in the future.

It was also agreed that thanks be tendered for the donation of 2/6 from the Rechabites towards the cost of cleaning the room.

Jan 20 Comrade Denny in the chair.

Comrade Fraser read a paper entitled "Fallacies of the poverty problem".

At the close of the discussion E. Cawston & W Frost were adopted as members of the Party.[172]

Annual Meeting Jan 30 1901
Comrade Dorer in the chair.
Minutes of last annual meeting read and adopted.
The general Secretary then read the report which on the proposition of Comrade Bush was ordered to be transcribed in the minute book.

Comrade Mrs Kidd the Financial Secretary then presented her report which showed a small balance in hand. The Election Fund also showed a small balance. The report was adopted on the proposition Com' Mills seconded by Com' Denny.

The Chairman then called on the General secretary who on behalf of members of the Party presented to Comrades Mr & Mrs Kidd two volumes: "Economics of Socialism" by Hyndman,[173] and "Annals of Toil" by Morrison Davidson,[174] as a mark of sympathy for the brutal treatment received at the hands of jingo mobs during 1900. The presentation was a complete surprise to our Comrades who both responded remarking that no treatment that they had received would deter them in their work for the cause of Socialism.

The re-election of Officers & Committee was then proceeded with. On the motion of Com' Kidd seconded by Com' Bush, Com' White was re-elected General Secretary. Com' Mrs Kidd was re-elected Financial Secretary. Comrade Dorer was elected to the Committee in place of Com' Cremer the

---

172 Edgar C. Cawston, born 1865, draper, lived in St James Street; for Frost, see above note 117.

173 Henry Mayers Hyndman (1842–1921), politician, orator and founder of the Social Democratic Federation in 1881. His *Economics of Socialism: being a series of seven lectures on political economy* was published in 1896. See Chushichi Tsuzuki, *H. M. Hyndman and British Socialism* (Oxford, 1981).

174 John Morrison Davidson (1843–1916), Scottish-born journalist and radical. His book, *The Annals of Toil; being labour-history outlines, Roman and British* was published in London in 1899.

names thus being Comrades Denny, Francis, Mills, Dorer, J.J. Kidd & the two secretaries.

Comrade Bush was re-elected Auditor & Fraser Assistant Sec'y.

The financial Secretary then read over the membership roll with amount of subscriptions paid by each member and it was decided that two members should be seen as to their intentions.

This concluded the business.

General Secretary's Report

Comrades The year 1900 opened not very happily for Socialists. To their everlasting credit a firm stand had been made against the Capitalist War which was now in full swing in South Africa. In consequence of their attitude they were often marked out for the vengeance of jingo mobs instigated by an unscrupulous press whose proprietors, shareholders and other interested persons stood to gain by forcibly taking away the independence of these two Republics, the Transvaal and Orange Free State. Locally the same spirit was gradually being fanned into a flame until in June it burst out, the occasion of the British troops march into Pretoria being made the excuse for organising the so called patriotic demonstration.[175] Numbers of howling people – many holding prominent positions – parading the town till long after midnight and under cover of the darkness smashing windows and doing other damage Comrades Kidd & White being amongst the sufferers. The Corporation in this instance after the presentation of a memorial agreed by a majority of one to pay all claims.

This proved to be the beginning of a series of similar disgraceful scenes which on October 17 reached its height.

On this occasion Comrade Kidd held a meeting at the Walks Gates taking for his subject:- "High Rents and the Remedy". The meeting was fairly orderly till the close when on leaving our Comrade with his wife was followed by a mob bent on mischief the police seeming quite incapable to check their movements and they were allowed to rush in a body to Com' Kidds house & nurseries and smash windows to their hearts content. At subsequent police court proceedings magistrates gave their blessing to the organisers of this outbreak Councillor W H Brown paying a fine for one of the lads.

Our Comrades are deserving of our gratitude and sympathy in their endeavours to maintain their right of Free Speech.

---

175 The British took Pretoria from the Boers on 5 June 1900. Opposition to the Boer War by the Labour movement and a part of the Liberal Party made both extremely unpopular among the 'jingoist' elements in society, but the shared experience arguably helped the Liberal and Labour groups to work together later (see, for example, Sir Robert Ensor, *England 1870–1914* (1936), 229–30).

In the month of March we sustained a great loss by the death of Comrade H.B. Rowe who was one of the pioneers of the movement in Lynn and acted as Treasurer up till the time of his death. Members attended \the funeral/ and a beautiful wreath placed on his grave.

In spite of the general apathy of the people some good work was accomplished during the year.

During May an attempt was made to organise the labourers of Lynn several meetings were held Comrade Kidd assisting on each occasion but the men appeared to be satisfied with their 4d an hour and little resulted from the effort.

A petition to the Public Library Committee resulted in the rescinding of the resolution refusing to accept presentation papers.

The proposal by <u>interested</u> Councillors to build on Friars field – Corporation land – was again brought up and ended in a Local Govt Enquiry being held in December, as a result it is expected the idea will be squashed and the field kept open as a "lung".

A General Election took place in October our Party taking little interest locally owing to the fact that both Liberal & Tory candidates fought as "Imperialists".

In the country Socialists polled well Keir Hardie being returned for Merthyr Tydvil,[176] Bell (A.S.R.S.) for Derby,[177] & John Burns for Battersea.[178] Our comrades subscribed to the I.L.P and SDF Election funds.

Usual meetings were held during the year and altogether I think we may congratulate ourselves on the fact that whilst all over the country other organisations showed an apathy and indifference to reform work owing to the jingo wave that swept the country – Socialists kept up the work of educating the people and propagating their principles in every way. As Secretary I must say that is with some satisfaction that under the most

---

176 James Keir Hardie (1856–1915), a key figure in the early development of the Labour Party. M.P. for West Ham, elected in 1892 as 'an independent supporter of the Liberal Party' who would put 'the claims of Labour above party'. Lost seat 1895. MP for Merthyr Tydfil from 1898. He wrote articles against the Boer War in his newspaper *The Labour Leader*, and held anti-war meetings, at several of which he was in danger of physical assault; the first leader of the Parliamentary Labour Party after 1906. His friend and biographer William Stewart called him: 'an incorruptible man of the common people, who, in his own person, symbolised the idea of independence, and in his message proclaimed the practicability of Brotherhood.' Stewart, *Hardie*, 374.

177 Richard Bell, see above, note 57.

178 John Burns (1858–1943), trade unionist and politician. Like Bell, he soon found himself in sympathy with the Liberal party, rather than Labour – in 1905, he became a Cabinet Minister as President of the Local Government Board. However, he did uphold the anti-war tradition, opposing the Boer War and, later, Britain's entry into the First World War.

trying circumstances of the past year we find ourselves in the position we occupy today. Hardly a single household but knows of the existence of a Socialist organisation, and although in ignorance of our principles, their [*sic*] are many who sympathize with our efforts to raise the standard of life of the workers and admire those who at the expense of persecution and boycott in business from time to time endeavour to spread the gospel of Socialism. Fred Wm White Secretary

Feby 2 No 2 Norfolk Socialist Review published

Feby 7 "At Home" social evening members and friends spent an enjoyable evening. Songs were rendered by Messrs Fraser & Cawston & Miss A Sporne. Refreshments were supplied and games indulged in, the company breaking up at midnight.[179]

Sunday 10th Comrade White read a paper:- "A Lesson in Economics from Nature". Comrade Fraser in chair. Discussion followed. Secretary Cambridge Labour Church present.

17th Comrade Fraser read part of a criticism of Merrie England by Nemo.

Monday Feby 25 Meeting of Executive Committee. Comrade Francis chairman.
General Sec'y read a communication from the Rechabites re terms of agreement and informing us that JJ Kidd had been accepted as guarantor in place of H B Rowe deceased. It was agreed that the matters relating to agreement stand in abeyance.
At the request of Com' Dorer the Secretary read the rules and objects of the Party and it was decided that members should have a copy of same and sign a declaration accepting same.
Comrade Dorer moved, Comrade Fraser seconded "That we run one or more candidates at the Board of Guardians' election in March, a special meeting being summoned to consider.   Carried.
Comrade White moved, Com' Dorer seconded that Com' Kidd obtain as much information as to probable cost &c &c and submit at the special meeting to be held ~~Thursday~~ \Wednesday/ Feb 27.

Wed'y ~~Mar~~ 25\Feby 27/ Special general Meeting to consider advisability of contesting the Board of Guardians Election.
Comrade Denny in the Chair.

---

179 A slightly different version of this minute appears struck through between the minutes for 17 and 20 January.

Com' Dorer moved Comrade Neave seconded "that Com' Kidd be adopted as candidate for the South ~~Wa~~ Lynn Parish. <u>Carried</u>
Com' White & Mrs Kidd declined to stand
Com' Kidd proposed and Francis seconded that Dorer be a Candidate for St Margarets Parish. Com' Dorer declined on grounds of inability to carry out duties.
Comrades Kidd, Dorer & White were appointed to get all information necessary regarding time of election, draw up address &c

March 3 Comrade Kidd gave readings from Shakespeare.

March 7 Mrs Kidd opened the discussion.

March 10 Com' White read a paper subject:- "Social democrats and the administration of the Poor Law"

March 14 Comrade Kidd's claim for damages against the Corporation arising out of the riots of the previous year was heard in the County Court before Judge Willis. Comrade Kidd conducted his own case. The Judge severely condemned the authorities and said that if Mr Kidd had complied with the Act by sending in detailed claim within the 4 days stated therein he should have awarded him damages and costs against the Corporation not having done so he must dismiss the claim with costs.[180]
<u>A Moral Victory</u>

Mar 17 Comrade Kidd read an article on the Life of William Morris.[181] Com' White in the chair.

Mar 21 Members had a long night directing addresses to the Electors on behalf of Com' Kidd.

Mar 24 Com Mrs Kidd read selections from "Shelley".[182] Comrade Dorer in the Chair. Discussion followed at the close of which arrangements was made for the morrow which was the date fixed for the Board of Guardians Election.

---

180 The figure has been amended: it is not clear what was originally written.
181 William Morris (1834–1896), artist, writer, socialist. Many biographies, but not all give due weight to his political aspect, for which see E.P. Thompson, *William Morris: romantic to revolutionary* (London, 1955, revised edition 1977). The 'Life' referred to is presumably J. W. Mackail, *The Life of William Morris* (2 vols, London, 1899).
182 Percy Bysshe Shelley (1792–1822), romantic poet and radical thinker, believer in non-violent protest, advocate of vegetarianism. For his political views, see *Red Shelley* (London, 1981) by socialist writer and activist Paul Foot.

It was decided to recommend our members in South Lynn to support Messrs Green Springall and Kidd and in St Margarets to support 11 candidates.

[*INSERTED Kidd's election leaflet* see Plate 3]

Board of Guardian Election March 25 1901
First contest in which a Socialist candidate stood for election. <u>South Lynn Parish</u> candidate JJ Kidd polled <u>213</u>. <u>Elected</u>.[183]

Wednesday March 27 Social Evening.[184] This was a pleasant event and was made the occasion for celebrating our splendid victory at the Guardians Election. The hall was filled and the greatest enthusiasm prevailed. Comrades Mrs Kidd, Fraser & Turner gave the well known farce "Box & Cox" in fine style.[185]
At the close short speeches were made by A.L Dorer, J J Kidd, Mrs Kidd and the Secretary FW White and the company sang Edward Carpenter's hymn "England Arise".[186]

April 14 Com' White in Chair.
Com Kidd gave an address subject:- "The aims & claims of Socialism"

April 15 Meeting of Executive at Com Kidds. Com Kidd in chair.
Minutes of previous meeting read and adopted.
Mrs Kidd gave a rough statement as to the financial position which was considered satisfactory. The cost of the candidature of Com Kidd at the Guardians Election amounted in all to 2/4/5. Comrade Dorer moved:- That members be invited to subscribe to the election fund and wipe out liabilities of same. Com Denny seconded. <u>Carried</u>.

---

183 Kidd finished seventh out of seventeen candidates, the top eight being elected to the Board. The result was very close – Kidd was just nine votes ahead of the best unsuccessful candidate. The minutes include press cuttings of the result and a report from the *LN* (30 Mar. 1901) concerning the 'Sweeping Progressive Majority' returned.
184 Press cutting inserted.
185 Farce by John Maddison Morton, first performed in London in 1847, based on an earlier French work. It was extremely popular, gave the title phrase to the English language, and was frequently performed by amateur groups. A comic opera based on it was produced in 1866 with the title 'Cox and Box'. Its political applications were realised by 1870 when comic magazine *Punch* portrayed rival party leaders Disraeli and Gladstone as Box and Cox. Frederick Turner, born 1857, was a postman, living at 25 Regent Street. His son, also Frederick became a member later.
186 Edward Carpenter (1844–1929), socialist – he was a founder member of the ILP – pacifist, vegetarian and early advocate of gay rights. He wrote the anthem 'England Arise' in 1893, and it has been much sung at Socialist gatherings ever since.

Letter read from Anderson of York offering to come to Lynn if date could be arranged

The action of the Town Council in relation to outside public meetings was then discussed at some length and it was decided that a meeting be held in the following week at which a resolution should be submitted condemning their action in attempting to prevent public meetings in open spaces.

It was decided that the first Thursday in each month be set aside for the discussion of general business and any matters of local interest relating to the various public bodies.

Comrade Dorer moved Com White seconded:- That it be ascertained who are the retiring Town Councillors next November Carried

Secretary recorded an application from the Good Templars as to our charge for use of piano for one night. Agreed that the charge be 2/6.

Quarterly General Meeting
April 18th Comrade Neave in the chair.
<u>New members</u> William Drew Guanock Terrace proposed by J Mills seconded by Com Denny.[187]
Samuel Reynolds Horsley Hockham Street proposed by F W White \seconded by Com Dorer/.[188]
Miss Burke proposed by Com Turner seconded by Com Fraser.[189]
G.G Rix Valingers Road proposed by Com Turner seconded by Mills.[190]
<u>All adopted</u>

Com Mrs Kidd then presented the financial report for the quarter which was adopted.

---

187 William Drew, born 1875, a stone mason: in 1901 he was still living at Guanock Terrace, Lynn. For confusion between him and fellow member Robert Drew, see below, note 232.

188 Either Samuel Reynolds Horsley, born 1853, builder, or his son of the same name and address, born 1878, a bricklayer: in 1901, the family was living in Guanock Terrace, Lynn.

189 Frances Ann Burke, born 1880, the daughter of an Islington harness maker. She thus became the second woman member, as far as is recorded, and the first who was not the wife of an Executive member. . She had become a schoolteacher by the time of the 1901 census, in which she is recorded as a visitor at the home of Frederick Turner, postman, of Regent St, Lynn. She must have moved to Lynn as she is mentioned later in the minutes: in December 1903, she married Turner's son Frederick Robert Turner, a Lynn hairdresser. By the time of the 1911 census they were living in Lynn with a small child – and could afford a live-in nursemaid! However, by then they had long left the Society, not appearing in the minutes after 1906.

190 George Graham Rix, born 1882, a baker and the son of Charles Grey Rix, a founder member of the Society.

The cost of our contest at the Election of Guardians amounted to just over two pounds.

Com Dorer moved & Mills seconded "that members be invited to subscribe towards the Election fund. Carried

The Secretary then briefly referred to the action of the Town Council with relation to public meetings held in the open and it was decided after some discussion that a meeting be advertised for Monday April 22nd at the Walks Gates at which a resolution should be presented to the audience condemning the Councils action in attempting to interfere with the right of Free Speech.

It was decided that a Social Evening be held on Wednesday 24th and on the proposition of Com Mills the following names were appointed as a Standing Committee to arrange Socials & if possible one walk out to some spot in the country once each month during the summer.

Cmrades Denny Fraser Turner Rix Mills Mrs Kidd.

It was suggested that the committee correspond with Lowerison of the Ruskin School Hunstanton with a view of arranging a meeting at Rising Castle where he might give the members a historical address.[191]

Alteration of rule Com Mrs Kidd proposed & Com Mills seconded that the rule which states:- "that an audited account be presented each quarter be altered to read annually.   Carried

It was decided that the first Thursday in each month be set on one side for general business and any matters of local interest.

April 24 Social Evening

April 22 A Meeting was held at the Walks Entrance to protest against the action of the Watch Committee in their attempt to interfere with the right of public meetings in public places.[192]

---

191 Bellerby Harry Lowerison (1863–1935), son of Durham coalminer, teacher and leading member of the Fabian Society. In 1899, he was sacked by Hackney School Board for his political activities, then setting up the Ruskin School first in Hunstanton but moving to Heacham in 1902. This, an experimental and communal school for boys and girls, was helped by money from readers of the *Clarion*, for which he wrote many articles. The School Magazine for 1902–03 states that there were 28 boys and 10 girls [at its peak, in 1909–10 the figure was about 50] on the roll, and six teachers including Lowerison himself, who is referred to as 'Pater'. There is a great stress on outdoor and practical activities such as nature study, gardening, pottery. The motto of the school is given as 'Justice and Gentleness' (NRO, SO 297/16). The school closed in 1926: there is a painting it, by Edward Gosling, in King's Lynn Museum.

192 The Watch Committee attempted to limit public meetings in the town (*LA*, 26 Apr. 1901).

Comrade Smith Secretary Norwich Branch S.D.F addressed the large crowd which gathered round listening very attentively to the end. A resolution was proposed by Com Kidd seconded by Com' Denny condemning the action of the Council and <u>carried</u>.[193]

Comrades afterwards retired to the hall and indulged in a general conversation.

April 25 Com Mills in the chair.
Com' Dorer opened the discussion subject "Education"[194]

Thursday May 2 Monthly Meeting.
Minutes of last meeting read, adopted
New Members Com Turner proposed Com Mrs Kidd seconded <u>Mr F Turner 25 Regent Street</u>.[195]
Mrs Kidd proposed Com Turner ~~proposed~~ seconded <u>Harry Crow Bridge Street</u>.[196]
<u>Adopted</u>
Treasurer reported that the Guardian election fund amounted to 1/8/0 to date. Program for May was arranged. Meetings to be held at Com' Kidds nursery weather permitting. Comrade Turner was appointed Literary Secretary.

Sunday May 26 Meeting at Com Kidds'.
Comrade Mills read:- Should women have the vote" discussion followed.

---

193 Walter Robert Smith (1872–1942), founder member of the Norwich branch of the SDF 1894 (the same year as the Norwich branch of the ILP was founded). Smith, one-time President of Norwich branch of National Union of Boot and Shoe Operatives, was elected to Norwich Board of Guardians for the SDF in 1904. Elected to Norwich City Council as 'Socialist and Trade Union' candidate in 1904, then joined ILP becoming its third member on the Council (after Witard and Holmes, see notes below for both). In later life a Labour M.P., government minister, and, in 1934, Chairman of the Labour Party. His ability to bend with the current trends within Labour led to his enemies calling him 'Wily Walter'.

194 The whole topic of education was being hotly debated at this time. The result was the Education Act of 1902, which abolished the School Boards and made local authorities responsible for providing schools: the Act was opposed by many Socialists. See Brian Simon, *Education and the Labour Movement, 1870–1920* (London, 1965), 165–295.

195 Frederick Turner junior, born 1879, a hairdresser, and son of Frederick Turner who here supports his membership.

196 Either Henry 'Harry' Crowe, born 1852, boiler maker, or his son of the same name, born 1877, recorded as a sewing machine agent in 1901, and as a post office clerk in 1911: the family was living in Bridge Street at both dates. A Henry Crowe was admitted to the ILP in 1908, address given as Bridge Street in subscription book: he could also be either the father or the son.

May 26 Sunday The first meeting of the summer season was held at Com'
Kidds garden. Comrade Mills opened the discussion, subject:- Should
women have the vote".

<u>Whit Monday</u>
Several Comrades visited the <u>Ruskin School home, Hunstanton</u>. In the
afternoon Comrade Hy Lowerison gave us a lecture on the geological
formation of the cliffs. Grand weather prevailed and \an/ enjoyable time
was spent.

June 2nd Discussion opened by Mrs Kidd Subject "Competition"

June 16 Discussion, Subject: Socialism & Christianity" opened by R Fraser.
Comrade Neave in Chair

June 23 Sunday. About 20 Members & friends visited <u>Rising Castle</u> to meet
Harry Lowerison who had promised a lecture. Owing to the strong wind he
was unable to "bike". However those that were present enjoyed the outing
some partaking of tea inside the Castle and some 'neath the shade of its
walls.

June 30 Discussion "Was Jesus A Socialist" opened by Mrs Kidd

July 7 Discussion subject "Ingersoll & Religion"[197] J.J. Kidd

July 14 Comrade Mills read Dennis Hird's pamphlet "Was Jesus a
Socialist".[198] Comrade Dorer in the chair.

July 18 Quarterly General Meeting held at Com' Kidds Garden. Comrade
Fraser in the chair.
Minutes of last meeting read and adopted.
<u>New members</u> Comrade Fraser proposed & Mills seconded H.C. Shears
Wellington St as a member of the party.[199] <u>Adopted.</u>
It was agreed that new members be seen by the financial secretary.
A rough statement was read by the financial secretary showing a small deficit.

---

197 Robert G. Ingersoll (1833–1899), American writer known for his agnostic thinking.
198 Dennis Hird (1850–1920), former Anglican minister, a leader of the Christian
Socialist movement and first Principal of Ruskin College, Oxford, from 1899. He delivered
a speech on this theme in 1896, which was printed under the name *Jesus the Socialist* in 1908
and sold over 70,000 copies. This is presumably an earlier version, its title interrogatory
rather than affirmative.
199 Henry Charles Shears, born 1883, a telegraph messenger, Wellington Street Lynn
(subscription book and 1901 census). Shears was a founder member of the Lynn ILP in
October 1906, but left Lynn after a couple of years: he last paid his subscription in January
1908. In 1911, he was living in Sheffield, occupation postal clerk, still there in 1921.

Correspondence was read from the Secretary I.L.P. Norwich inviting our cooperation in arranging a visit from J E Dobson of London and from T Anderson York and it was decided that we could not entertain these offers at present.

It was recommended to the Outings Committee that they arrange a visit to Comrade Belderson's Terrington St Clements for Sunday July 28th weather permitting.

Sunday July 21
The Secretary (Com' White) gave an account of his trip into Holland and up the Rhine to Mainz in company with Comrades Triance & Dorer.

Sunday 28th Several comrades tramped to Terrington St Clements beautiful weather prevailing. Comrade Belderson and his good wife provided a good tea in their garden after which the company having "taken the veil" our Host gave ~~the~~ an interesting description of his various hives and how the bees work. After an enjoyable time Com' Kidd thanked our friend for his kindness and the comrades started off to walk home.

Sepr 5 Meeting Executive Committee. Chairman Com Francis.
Present Mr & Mrs Kidd, Fraser, Denny, Dorer & White.
Minutes of previous meeting read & adopted.
Com Dorer read a letter he had received from S.D. Shallard (Fabian lecturer) asking what chances there were of running a course of lectures at Lynn.[200] After some discussion Com Kidd proposed & Com Mills seconded that we accept the offer. Carried
Com Dorer read the list of lectures and the syllabus of each.
Com Kidd informed meeting that W.R. Smith of Norwich would be in Lynn on Sunday and would be prepared to speak for us, he also stated that he was accompanying Smith on a lecturing trip to Wisbech, Peterboro & Cambridge under the auspices of the S.D.F.[201]

Sept 12 Monthly general meeting.
Comrade Mills in the Chair.
Minutes read. Discussion as to the arrangements for Comrade Smiths meetings to be held on the site of the Millfleet on Sunday at 3 & 8.[202]

---

200 Sidney Dillon Shallard (born 1869) journalist, member of SDF, and Fabian Society, and on the NAC of the ILP. Arrested while campaigning for election to the London School Board in 1891, spent a week in prison, eventually released without trial.
201 Flyer attached in minute book.
202 A former tidal inlet of the river Ouse: in 1896, the Corporation had borrowed £12,846 to fund having part of it filled in. The newly-formed street was just to the north of Coronation Square.

Comrades Denny, Francis, Walker of Wisbech and Cooke of Lincoln promised to distribute literature and take collection.

Mrs Kidd proposed & Com' Dorer seconded that 3/- be spent on leaflets to distribute.

Com Neave proposed Dorer seconded that we again hire a piano for season the terms etc to be left to Mrs Kidd & Bush to arrange with Mr Street who supplied the instrument last season.

Discussion then ensued as to the prospect of meetings, lectures etc for the Autumn & Winter.

The Fabian Lectures are expected in weeks ending Nov 25 Dec 2, 9, 16, it was also agreed that the Secretary write to H Lowerison for a fixture\terms for/ if possible. Several other important items were mentioned as being arranged by other organisations. Programme arranged for remainder of month.

Bethesda Fund Secretary reported the anxiety on the part of some of the members to subscribe to this fund and it was recommended that the Secretary put a footnote to the programme to be issued inviting subscriptions.[203]

Sunday 15 Comrade W R Smith addressed two good meetings on the site of the Millfleet. In the afternoon taking as his subject "The Good Time Coming" in the evening "Socialism the only hope of the workers". Comrade Kidd presided at each gathering which was large and orderly.

On the Monday Comrade Smith commenced a series of meetings in the neighbourhood on mostly "new ground" having the usual experiences at some of the places.

Comrades Kidd & Denny had an exciting time at Wisbech having to seek protection from the police.[204]

Sunday Sepr 22 Discussion in the hall. Mrs Kidd subject "Ruskin on War".

Monday Comrade Kidd addressed a large meeting on the Old Millfleet subject:- "The Survival of the Fittest". After the meeting a section of the crowd made an attempt to create a disturbance but were dispersed by the police.

Thursday Comrade Dorer read a paper from "Fields, Factories & Workshops".[205]

---

203 See above, note 11.

204 The three men (Smith, Kidd and Denny) tried to speak at Market Hill but an antagonistic crowd who dragged them off the box on which they were standing: 'at length, supported by a couple of members of the police force and followed by a large crowd of youths and boys, the speakers were conducted to the Police Station as a matter of protection.' (*LN*, 21 Sept. 1901).

205 Pyotr Kropotkin, *Fields, Factories and Workshops* (London, 1899). For Kropotkin, see above, note 83.

<u>Oct 3</u> Quarterly General Meeting. Chairman Comrade Denny.
Minutes read and adopted.

Communication read by Secretary from Harry Lowerison relating to his proposed visit and giving a list of subjects of Lectures. The meeting decided on the proposition of Com Mills & Bloy that "Ants" would be the subject most likely to attract. Secretary was instructed to write Comrade Lowerison and ascertain probable expense.

Financial Secretary then read a rough statement of accounts which was considered satisfactory.

<u>New Members</u>. W. Finbow was proposed by Comrade Bloy & seconded Mills.[206]

Discussion then ensued re Fabian lectures, Comrade Dorer stating that that Society was in correspondence with the Cooperative Society[207] offering the services of S.D. Shallard. It was ultimately agreed that if the Cooperative Society was willing to run the lectures it would be better as they would be more able to engage a suitable hall. Comrade Dorer was asked to use his influence in that direction.

Comrade Kidd agreed to ask Mr Belderson of Terrington to give us a lecture during Oct

And it was also decided that a Social Evening be held at the latter end of the month.

Oct 10 Comrade White read selections from Nunquams "Tales For Mariners".[208]

Oct 13 Comrade Kidd opened the discussion

Oct 17 Comrade Dorer gave a paper

Oct 20 Comrade Mrs Kidd read selections from Blatchford's "Dismal England"
Oct 24 Comrade Belderson of Terrington gave a lecture on "Bees", owing to the inclement weather there was not a large attendance. Our comrade brought with him a model hive, specimens of comb, wax &c with which to illustrate his lecture and the company who had braved the elements were amply repayed. A long report of the lecture appeared in the Lynn News.[209]

---

206 William Finbow, born 1885, machinist in a wood mill, in 1901 he was living with his parents in Stanley Street, Lynn.

207 Co-operative Society, see n. 49. Many members were Socialists but others supported the Liberal Party, and the Co-operative Union chose not to affiliate to the Labour Party or the LRC: see Haworth and Hayter, *Men who made Labour*, 261–2.

208 Published by the Clarion Newspaper Company in 1901: as above, Nunquam was the pseudonym of Robert Blatchford.

209 Bees were an especially appropriate subject for a Socialist group because of the way in

Oct 31 <u>Social evening</u> this the first social of the season was a success, a good programme of music was gone through by the members and friends, and Com' Kidd gave an exhibition of sleight of hand tricks, thought reading &c. Com' White officiated as chairman.

<u>Nov 7</u> Harry Lowerison of the Hunstanton Ruskin School House kindly came over and gave us a lecture on "Ants". Comrade Kidd presided. A goodly number of members and friends enjoyed the homely way in which our Comrade gave us of his store of knowledge of the wonders of the "Ant Kingdom" and a report appeared in the columns of the "Lynn News".[210]

Nov 10 Comrade Fraser "Poverty & Pride" followed by discussion

Nov 14 Monthly General meeting as there was only a few members present and no matter of importance to discuss. Games were indulged in.

Nov 24 Discussion opened by Com' Turner Subject:- "A Criticism of Ruskin"

Dec 8 Monthly Meeting Mills in chair
Programme arranged for December
Members attention to be called to the Debates at Y.M.C.A.
Recommended that the entertainment committee meet to arrange social or other form of entertainment to open New Year with.
Members attention drawn to the Recommendation book at the Library by Com' Dorer who asked that titles of books should be written down from time to time.

Sunday Dec 15 Comrade Dorer read the Fabian Pamphlet:- "Twentieth Century Politics".[211] Discussion followed.

Sunday 22 Comrade Mills gave an interesting reading on the "Life & Writings of Carlyle.[212]

---

which a hive is organised. In the *Labour Prophet*, July 1893, Eleanor Keeling recommended them as a subject for children's education – 'all the workers share the honey' (Turner, 'Soul of Labour', 143). The Lynn newspaper carried a detailed report, but made no reference to bees as an example to Socialists (*LN*, 2 Nov. 1901).

210 The social life of ants was also recommended as an example to children by Keeling. The account of Lowerison's speech in the press shows that he drew this parallel (*LN*, 16 Nov. 1901: the cutting is pasted into the minute book).

211 Fabian Tract 108, *Twentieth-Century Politics; A Policy of National Efficiency*, written by Sidney Webb (1901).

212 Thomas Carlyle (1796–1881), historian and philosopher. His many books included *The French Revolution: a history* (1837) and *Past and Present* (1843). He is known for his theory of the importance in history of the 'Hero' or 'Great Man': 'the Great Man was always

Annual Meeting Jan 23 [*1902*]

Comrade Dorer in the chair.

Minutes of last annual meeting read & adopted.

The General Secretary then read his report which on the Motion of Comrade Denny was adopted and ordered to be entered in the minute book.

Mrs Kidd Financial Secretary then presented her report which showed a small balance in hand and also a balance in the Election Fund of about a guinea. Adopted on proposition of [Com Mills] Com Miss Burke and the thanks of the Party was tendered to her for her services during the year

Election of officers Com White was unanimously re-elected as General Secretary and Comrade Mrs Kidd as Financial Secretary.

Comrade Fraser having refused assistant secretaryship Comrade Francis was proposed by Mrs Kidd, Com' Neave seconding and elected unanimously.

Comrade Bush was re elected auditor.

A Ballot was then taken for six members to form Executive seven names having been proposed the result was that Comrades Dorer, Denny, Turner, Drew, Mills, Kidd were elected.

Entertainment Committee Fraser, Turner, Mills & Mrs Kidd with power to add.

The Secretary then gave a statement with respect to the Norfolk Socialist review estimating his loss at 3/- or 4 doz copies and that the Party had guaranteed to be responsible for 50 copies of each number. After a few remarks and enquiries Com Kidd moved & Denny seconded that the Secretary be reimbursed to the amount of 3/-. Carried.

A discussion then took place as to the advisability of forming a Choir to take part in our meetings and Com Kidd proposed Com Mills seconded that:- that an instruction be made to the Executive to take steps to form a choir. Carried.

A further recommendation that the Executive draw up a programme of meetings &c covering three months was also carried.

New Member Com White proposed the name of Miss Beatrice Green as a member Com' Neave seconded.[213] Carried.

---

as lightning out of Heaven; the rest of men waited for him like fuel, and then they too would flame'.

213 Beatrice Green, eldest of eight children, attended Lynn High School for Girls, and became one of the first girls from the school to go to university: she studied Classics at Aberystwyth, and subsequently taught at Queen St School in Lynn. In 1901, she was living with her father Richard Green, see above, note 51. The family were Rationalists: in later life, Beatrice recalled sitting on the knee of atheist MP Charles Bradlaugh when he visited her parents! She married Arthur Dorer in 1905. Teacher at Lynn High School 1918–38 and later served for 31 years on the Town Council's Library Committee. See her husband's

Comrade Mills then rose "to call attention to the confusion arising through our name being wrongly reported" he stated that several times our meetings had been reported as under the auspices of the S.D.F.

Comrade Kidd stated that he was annoyed at what had occurred ~~and~~ but it was through the carelessness of the press. After some further remarks he proceeded to outline a plan for members to attach themselves to the S.D.F & I.L.P. which he considered it was the duty of all to do in order to keep in touch with the national organisation.

~~However~~ The Secretary followed remarking that the differences that existed between those bodies had up to the present been kept out of our local movement which had not experienced a jarring note but that if members were to do as suggested we should import those differences into our own ranks. He hoped the time would soon come when this bitterness between the two different sections would cease to exist.

Com' Dorer then spoke stating that he would not join either organisation. The hour was now very late or he would give his opinion of the regrettable state of affairs.

The matter was allowed to drop the time being late eleven o'clock.

Report of Annual

General Secretarys Report read at the Annual meeting held Jan 23rd 1902.

Comrades The past year has been the most successful in every way since our organisation was started and I have none of the lamentable incidents to report arising from the outburst of jingoism which I had last to record.

On the other hand I think there is a growing evidence that the prejudice against us is surely if slowly becoming a thing of the past.

We began the year by introducing music at our gatherings which undoubtedly had the effect of brightening our meetings which were fairly well attended.

In the month of January number one of the "Norfolk Socialist Review" made its appearance an event which had been looked forward too but which after all did not I think fulfil expectations.

During February meetings were all well attended.

On Feb'y 27 an important meeting was held to consider the desirability of running a Candidate or candidates at Election for Board of Guardians in March, after several names had been submitted it was finally decided to run Comrade J.J. Kidd for South Lynn.

On March 6th a party of our members paid a visit to Norwich when a united gathering of members of the S.D.F, I.L.P. and socialists of the district

---

obituary, *LA*, 7 and 14 Jan. 1950 and her own, *LA*, 27 Jan. 1971; see too Paton, *Walter Dexter*, 64.

was held in the <u>I.L.P. Institute Elm Hill Norwich</u>. Speeches were made by Comrades Roberts[214] (in the chair) Member Norwich School Board, Henderson[215] Wroxham School Board, W.R. Smith, Secretary S.D.F., and several other comrades including those from Lynn.

March 14th was a day of interest as this was the date fixed for the hearing of Comrade J.J. Kidd's action against the Corporation – under the Riot Act – for damages received during the jingo outbreak.

Comrade Kidd conducted his own case which was heard by Judge Willis in a crowded court. At the close of the case the Judge strongly condemned the action of the authorities and made a speech on the right of public meeting. The case was proved against the Corporation but the Judge could not award damages owing to the fact that Comrade Kidd had not sent details of his claim at the same time that he notified the authorities that he intended suing. <u>Public interest in this case and the sympathy of many people had much to do with the result of the Guardian Election which saw Comrade Kidd elected with 213 Votes. The way in which this our first fight was worked surprised outsiders.</u>

A well printed address bearing a photo of our Candidate was sent to every elector and willing workers who gave up their time were well repaid when the result was announced [Plate 4].

---

214 George Henry Roberts (1868–1928). A printer by profession, his election to the Norwich School Board in 1899 was the first democratic success for Labour in East Anglia. Joined Norwich branch of ILP in 1896 when he returned to the city after working in London, became President of the branch 1899. A full-time official of the printers' union the Typographical Association from 1904. Elected M.P. for Norwich 1906, served in wartime coalition governments under Asquith and Lloyd George, left Labour Party in 1918, stood for Norwich (successfully) as an Independent in 1922 and (unsuccessfully) as a Conservative in 1923! Known for his oratory, not always appreciated: Norwich newspaper editor Edward Burgess called him 'an ambitious windbag'! (Frank Meeres, *George Roberts MP: a life that 'did different'* (Lowestoft, 2019), *passim*.

215 James Frederick 'Fred' Henderson (1867–1957), Norwich socialist politician and writer, long-term member of Norwich City Council, and later served as Lord Mayor. Best known book was *The Case for Socialism* first published in 1908 and reissued in many editions since. Also highly-rated poet, books including *Love Triumphant* (1888) and *By the Sea and other poems* (1892): correspondence at the Norfolk Record Office suggests he was even considered for the post of Poet Laureate! He was elected to Norwich City Council as a 'Progressive' candidate in 1902 and referred to himself as the first Socialist on the Council (NRO, HEN 43/86). However, at this stage he was a Liberal rather than a member of any Labour grouping: in the 1904 Norwich Parliamentary by-election, he urged voters to support the Liberal candidate rather than Roberts, the ILP man. He joined the ILP in 1906. 'Many ILP members assessed Henderson as a 'Wobbler'. This underestimated his own self-interest while nicely summarising his political situation'. (Steven Cherry, *Doing Different* (Norwich, 1989), 118).

A Social Evening was held at which a large number of friends were present to celebrate our success.

April was a busy month with us meetings being very well attended.

A large meeting held at the Walks Entrance was addressed by Comrade Smith of Norwich and a resolution was passed condemning the action of the Watch Committee in attempting to interfere with the right of outdoor public meetings.

Easter Monday a number of our members paid a visit to Ruskin School Home Hunstanton and in the afternoon Harry Lowerison gave an interesting lecture on "The Geological Formation of the Cliffs".

During the summer months meetings were held at Comrade Kidds Nursery. A picnic was held at Castle Rising where a goodly company had tea in the grounds. Several members accepted an invitation from Comrade Belderson to visit his place at Terrington and tea was provided in his garden after which the company inspected the bee hives Comrade Belderson's description of which proved very interesting.

During September several outdoor meetings were held on the site of the old Mill Fleet which were addressed by Comrades Kidd and W. R Smith of Norwich good crowds gathered on each occasion.

During the autumn by way of a change from the usual subjects we had lectures from Comrade Belderson on "Bees" and Harry Lowerison favoured us with an interesting lecture on "Ants".

Besides the ordinary business of the Party I ought to mention the activity of individual members in various directions. Comrade Kidd has devoted a considerable amount of time to his work as a Guardian.[216] Comrade Dorer in connection with the Cooperative Society and also \his/ letters in the Press

---

216 His work in this field was described in the local newspaper: 'Mr Kidd had during the past year made 79 visits to the workhouse; and although he was frequently thwarted by some of the older members with being new to the Board and therefore ignorant of the workings of the house and the Poor Law, he had found that he had in one year learned more than those of the 'fossil order' who had been there nearly 20 years. There was a tendency to increase the salaries of and enrolments of the head officials, and on the other hand there was a manifest endeavour to keep down the wage of other employees and be stingy with the poor.' (*LN*, 28 Mar. 1902, quoted in NRO, SO 297/28). He caused controversy on several occasions, in 1901 visiting every Sunday with his wife, their visits allegedly stirring up the inmates to write rude words on the walls; in 1902 he accused two nurses of keeping back the brandy allotted to infirmary inmates and drinking it themselves. He also raised several cases illustrating the terrible conditions within the Workhouse: one old man sat by an infirmary bed where a patient was dying: as soon as the patient was dead, the bed was disinfected and the old man put in it (he died a few days later). Men ('tramps') were given a meagre allowance of water, bread and cheese – and then expected to break 7 cwt of stones. However, Kidd's frequent visits to the Workhouse may have not been entirely out of concern

~~from~~ bearing on Municipal questions, other members have also contributed letters to the Press from time to time. The work of the year has been very satisfactory and will not be without its good results in the future.

Minutes of Lynn Social Democratic Party <u>January 1902</u>[217]

Jan 2nd Meeting of Executive Committee
<u>Chairman Comrade Mills</u>
Secretary stated that the meeting was called to consider advisability of holding a first class social supper or fraternal gathering. After some discussion it was decided that: We hold a Supper & Fraternal Gathering on Wednesday Jan 8, that the charge be 1/- each. <u>Agreed</u>.
Meeting then discussed arrangements to be made and decided that the whole catering be left to a committee Mrs Kidd, White & Mills with power to add.[218]
Comrade Kidd & Dorer with the Secretary were appointed to draw up the programme. Comrade White proposed Comrade Belderson as Chairman and Bush as Vice Chairman for that evening. <u>Carried</u>

Sunday Jan 5 Address by Comrade Kidd:- Ethics & Socialism

Jan 8 Wednesday. Supper & Fraternal Gathering
About forty sat down to a well spread table. Com Belderson presided and Comrade Bush occupied the vice-chair.
After the "solids" had been disposed of three toasts were submitted as follows:-
The local organisation by Com Belderson responded to by Com White Secretary
The National Movement by Com' Denny responded too [sic] Com Dorer.
The International Movement submitted by Com Mills responded too [sic] by Com' Kidd.
The toasts disposed of games was indulged in with vocal and instrumental interspersed until 2 a.m. when the company joined hands and sang Auld Lang Syne before breaking up. The most successful gathering of the kind held.

Jan 12 Address by Comrade M Isserlis of Norwich subject:- Scientific Socialism. Discussion followed.

---

for the poor, as later events were to show: see below note 257; NRO, C/GP 13/689; *EDP*, 5 Oct. 1901; 18 Mar. 1901; 20 Sept. 1902; 12 Dec. 1903.
 217 Second volume of minutes begins here (NRO, SO 297/4).
 218 Mary E. White, born 1868, Frederick White's wife; Susannah Mills, born 1874, John Mills' wife.

Jan 16 Meeting of Executive Committee Comrade Denny in the chair. Minutes of last meeting read and adopted.

The Financial Secretary was unable to present a statement of account but reported that there would probably be a small balance in hand and that her accounts would be audited before the Annual Meeting which was fixed for Jan 23.

Secretary read a letter from Rev Spriggs-Smith Terrington offering to lecture on Militarism and it was decided that nothing be arranged at present.[219]

Secretary reported that at a meeting of the Town Council in Committee it had been decided to recommend an increase in the Town Clerk's salary and that Comrade Kidd had sent an advertisement to the Lynn News calling a protest meeting for the following Wedy evening. Agreed that his action be approved.

Com Dorer proposed and Com' Mills Seconded that the Secretary write the Norwich SDF & ILP secretaries with a view to arranging a joint convivial gathering.

Com Mills proposed and Com' Francis seconded that a programme for three months be drawn up and copies sent to any sympathisers. Carried

The agenda for the Annual Meeting was then arranged.

Wedy Jan 22nd. A meeting was called by advert. in the Lynn News to protest against the increase to the Town Clerk's salary". Comrade Dorer occupied the chair and Comrade Kidd placed the facts before the small audience which gathered. A resolution of protest was passed.[220]

Thurs Jan 23
Annual Meeting
Comrade Dorer in the chair
Minutes of last meeting (annual) adopted.

The Secretary then presented his report of the work of the party during the past year which on the motion of Comrades Denny & Turner was ordered to be inscribed in the minute book.

The Financial secretary Mrs Kidd then read her financial statement which showed a small balance in the general fund of 1/0/0½ also a balance in the Election fund of 1/5/2 on the motion of Com Mills seconded by Miss Burke

---

219 Revd William Spriggs-Smith (1847–1914), vicar of Terrington St John in west Norfolk at time of 1896 and 1904 trade directories; author of tracts such as *Peace-Goodwill versus war-illwill: notes of an address delivered at the General Peace Meeting at Holbeach, Nov. 26th 1895* (1895).

220 Just six ratepayers attended, along with a few youths hoping 'for a bit of fun' (*LN*, 25 Jan. 1902).

the report was adopted and the best thanks of the meeting awarded her for her services during the year.

Election of officers. On the motion of Com Kidd seconded by Com Turner Com White was re-elected General Secretary. Comrade Neave proposed and Comrade Dorer seconded that Mrs Kidd be Financial Secretary. Carried.

Assistant Secretary. Comrade Fraser \having/ expressed a wish not to take this position Com Dorer proposed Com Francis Comrade Neave seconded. Carried.

Comrade Bush was unanimously re-elected auditor

Committee After a ballot Comrades Dorer, Denny, Mills, Drew, Kidd, Turner were elected.

Socialist Review. The Secretary reported that there had been a loss of 3/- on the sales of the Norfolk Socialist Review. Some discussion followed in which it was stated that the party had made themselves responsible for fifty copies each month. Com Kidd moved that the Secretary be paid the sum of 3/- loss, seconded Com Denny. Carried

Comrade Mrs Kidd Comrade Mills seconded "That an instruction be made to the Executive to form a choir or musical party. Carried

Comrade Mills proposed Comrade Denny seconded "that the Executive draw up a programme of lectures & covering three months and that copies be sent to sympathisers as well as members. Carried.

New Member On the proposition of Com White Miss B. Green was adopted as a member.

Comrade Mills then drew attention to the confusion that arose through our name being variously reported as S.D.F. etc, a lengthy discussion followed in which nearly all present joined but owing to the late hour the matter dropped.

Sunday Jan 26 Comrade Fraser read Ingersoll's Lecture on Shakespeare.[221]

Wedy Jan 29 Meeting of Executive Committee Comrade Dorer in the chair. Minutes read and adopted.

Secretary called attention to the instruction from the Annual Meeting that a choir or musical party be formed and on the proposition of Com Denny seconded by Com Denny [sic] the Secretary was appointed leader and arrangements left to him.[222]

The programme for three months was drawn up with two or three vacant dates which the Secretary was instructed to fill in as soon as possible.[223]

---

221 Ingersoll, see above n. 197. His *Shakespeare: a lecture* was first published in 1895.

222 One of these names must have been written in error: perhaps one should be Dennis.

223 The completed programme is inserted after the minutes for 10 April 1902.

Letters was then read from H. Lowerison and Mrs Despard (London) offering to lecture for us and their it was agreed that their services be thankfully accepted.[224]

Sunday Feby 2 Comrade White in the chair.
Comrade Kidd gave a lecture entitled "Blessed be ye poor"
(This was one of two lectures as delivered by him at Nottingham Labour Church.)

Thurs Feby 6 Monthly general meeting. \Comrade Neave in chair./
Minutes of last meeting read and adopted.
<u>New Members</u>. Com White proposed Com Mills seconded Miss S Sporne be accepted as a member of the party. C Triance was proposed by Com Dorer and accepted.[225]
Secretary read a letter from H. Lowerison stating that he would be here on Sunday Feby 9th.
Re proposed visit to Norwich Secretary stated the Norwich Trades Council were meeting on the date named and this would prevent many Norwich Comrades from being present. Agreed that the outing be fixed for another date.
It was decided that a Social Evening be arranged for Wedy Feby 26.

Sunday Feby 9th Comrade H Lowerison of the Ruskin School Home Hunstanton gave a lecture entitled "Parasitism". Comrade Dorer occupied the chair.
After the opening hymn the Chairman introduced the lecturer to those present but before calling on him for his lecture Miss Sporne sang "The story of a rose".[226]
Harry Lowerison then gave his lecture which was much enjoyed by the goodly number of friends present.
Miss Green played a pianoforte selection.

---

224 Charlotte Despard (1844–1939), Anglo-Irish suffragette and Sinn Fein activist; at this stage known as a Socialist speaker, and a Socialist Poor Law Guardian for Lambeth from 1895. Her social concerns (and the fact that she came from a wealthy background) were demonstrated when she travelled at her own expense to Canada to investigate the conditions of Lambeth children who had been sent there at the Guardians' expense (see Patricia Hollis, *Ladies Elect, Women in English Local Government 1865–1914* (London, 1987), 257). She later became better known for her work in promoting women's suffrage. See below, page 260, note 3 and page 277, note 17.

225 Susan Emmeline Sporne, see note 76. C. Triance is presumably an error for J. C. Triance, see above, note 27. If he was known by his second name (Charles), the error would be a natural one.

226 American popular song, composed by Andrew Mack in 1899. Full title: 'The story of the rose (heart of my heart I love you)'. Much sung by barber-shop quartets.

Sunday Feby 16 Comrade White in the chair.

Comrade Fraser read a pamphlet by Grant Allen subject:- "Natural Inequality".[227] Discussion followed.

April 10th Meeting Executive Committee Comrade Mills in the Chair.

Minutes read and adopted. Secretary reported that he had received an application from the Fanciers Society for use of the Hall one night each month and asking for terms.[228] Comrade Dorer Comrade Denny seconded "That the use of the hall be granted on condition that no large shows be held for 30/- the year".

Secretary reported that the Penrhyn Quarrymen's Male Choir would give a concert in the Music Hall Lynn on May 28th and it was agreed that we give every all possible assistance.[229]

The items for the agenda Quarterly General Meeting was arranged as follows The Education Bill,[230] Housing Question, Sale of Literature at Meetings, Whit Monday Outing.

Quarterly General Meeting April 10 Comrade Triance in the Chair.

Minutes read and adopted.

The advisability of holding a special meeting to discuss the Government's new Education Bill was considered and it was agreed that the Rev Osborne be invited to address a meeting in the hall on April 17th.[231]

Whit Monday Outing

Com Mills proposed Comrade Kidd seconded that we hold a picnic at Harry Lowerison's School Grounds. Mrs Mills, Miss Spence & Mrs White volunteered to provide for the party.

Housing Question Comrade Dorer brought forward the suggestion that a special Slumming Committee be formed which should during the summer months ascertain all particulars as to ownership, condition of properties

---

227 Charles Grant Allen (1848–1899), extraordinarily prolific Canadian journalist and writer, author of serious scientific and factual subjects as here, but better known for sensational detective and horror stories. Best known today for his novel *The Woman Who Did* (1895). His book *Natural Inequality* was published (Manchester, National Labour Press) in 1897.

228 Not identified. 'Fancier' is most commonly applied to pigeon enthusiasts, but may refer to other species such as the rabbit or (especially in Norfolk) the canary.

229 See above, note 11.

230 See above, note 194.

231 Alfred T. Osborne (born 1840), a Lynn Baptist minister, lived at Exton's Road, South Lynn. A press cutting 'Lynn Socialists and Education', relating to an earlier address by Osborne, 20 Feb. 1902, is inserted in the minutes.

&c and draw up a detailed report thereon. After discussion the following agreed to act R W Drew,[232] Mills, Triance, Dorer, Mrs & Mr Kidd Francis & White.

Note the programme from February to May must be taken as the most successful yet carried through good attendances was the rule at all meetings Owing to the Whitmonday holiday being wet and cold the picnic to the Ruskin School Heacham had to be put off but a tea, social evening & supper was held in the hall which was well carried out by those responsible for the arrangements.

June 8 General Meeting Comrade Kidd in the Chair.
Minutes of last meeting read and adopted.
New Members Mr Barker & Miss Spaxman proposed by FW White seconded J Mills.[233]
E Lyon[234] proposed by Mrs Kidd seconded R Fraser
R Sporne proposed by J Neave seconded J Pooley[235]

Secretary reported that the Norwich Clarion Cycling Club were arranging a run to Lynn on Sunday June 15th and that if Roberts of the Norwich School Board accompanied them they would hold a meeting.[236]

---

232 There were two members named Drew, William Drew (see above, note 187) and Robert J Drew, which caused occasional confusion as in this entry. Where both appear, they are distinguished by their initials: however, William soon drops out of the record and all the many subsequent entries to 'Drew' are to Robert. Robert, born 1872, lived at Guanock Terrace at the time of the 1911 census: his wife, also frequently mentioned, was named Eleanor. Robert was a housepainter.
233 Barker not identified (several possibilities in 1901 census); Ethel Spaxman born 1882, dressmaker, lived with her parents in Wisbech Road: her father was a millwright and stone dresser.
234 Ernest Lyon, born 1879, gardener, lived in Windsor Row. Lyon is spelled this way ten times in the minutes, but spelled Lyons eleven times: on several occasions the context makes clear that all the references are to the same man. At the time of the 1911 census he was working as a gardener in North Creake. According to the Lynn Roll of Honour he worked at West Norfolk Farmers' Chemical Works: he was killed at Suvla, 28 August 1915.
235 John Pooley born 1865, an engine driver, lived at Wisbech Rd, West Lynn: he was to remain in the Society until its dissolution in 1915–16. Robert William Sporne (born 1882), yet another child of William and Hannah Sporne: like his sisters Susan and Ethel he was a school teacher: by 1911, he was teaching at Letchworth and by 1917 he was headmaster at Towcester school.
236 Clarion Cycling Clubs were first formed in 1894 in connection with the newspaper of that name: they promoted comradeship, healthy living and the Socialist cause. Christabel and Sylvia Pankhurst were members, the latter capturing the atmosphere in her memoirs; 'Crowds of young men and women, generally rather ostentatious in their lovemaking, in what was then the Clarion way, came down there, and crowds of 'Cinderella' children were brought in

Arrangements was left over until definitely known as to their coming.

<u>Summer Programme</u>. After a lengthy discussion it was agreed that Meetings be held twice a week (Thursdays & Saturdays) at Com Kidd's nursery and that evenings be devoted to Shakespearian readings & "Britain For The British".[237] Alternately if wet in the hall. It was further proposed that an outing be arranged for Coronation Day June 26th and that the secretary see Mrs Drew with a view to engaging the "Leader" for a trip to the Cockle Sands.[238] Comrade Miss Green announced that the first Shakespearian reading would be "The Merchant of Venice".

July 2nd W. R. Smith of Norwich lectured at the Walks Gates to a good crowd.

July 3rd Quarterly General Meeting held at Comrade Kidd's Nursery.
Comrade Dorer in the Chair.
Minutes of last Quarterly Meeting read & passed on the motion of Comrade Mills.
Arising out of the minutes a lengthy discussion ensued as to the methods to be adopted by the Slumming Committee in the collection of information. Attention was drawn to the useful statistics supplied in the last report issued by the Medical Officer showing the wide difference in the death rate of the crowded areas as compared with the suburban districts. No decision was arrived at as to when the Slumming Committee should commence work but an effort should be made to meet at an early date. Comrade Kidd then called attention to the resolution of the Kelmscott Club London re Socialist Unity,[239] and proposed that a letter be drafted and forward to the sub committee of the Club supporting this action.
Seconded by Com Mills & carried.

relays for a week's holiday. Robert Blatchford spent a few days there with his daughter, keeping exclusively to his chosen circle of friends, as he always did' (Sylvia Pankhurst *The Suffragette Movement* (1977 edition), 140). George Roberts was elected to the Norwich School Board in 1899, in the process becoming the first Socialist elected to any public position in East Anglia.
237 *Britain for the British* by Robert Blatchford, published in 1902. The title is confusing: the book is not concerned with immigration. Blatchford's point was that Britain did not currently belong to **all** British people but just to a wealthy few who employ the rest as servants or as workers: 'it is because Britain does not belong to the British that a few are very rich and the many are very poor … . The remedy for this state of things – the *only* remedy yet suggested – is *Socialism*.'
238 The coronation was in fact postponed from 26 June to 9 August but the nautical outing took place anyway and is described in the Chairman's end-of-year report. Press cutting inserted.
239 The Kelmscott Club was a London organisation which aimed to unite the various Socialist organisations, from the Fabians to the SDF. It was based in Hammersmith and

July 6 Members to the number of about 20 met Harry Lowerison at Rising Castle. After tea the party was conducted over the Castle and to other spots of historic interest in the neighbourhood.[240]

July During the month meetings were held at the Nursery Goodwins Road On the 20th Comrade Roberts and two or three members of the Norwich C.C.C.[241] visited Lynn several members met our comrades at the house of Comrade Kidd in the evening and a pleasant time was spent.

Aug 3 Mr Amstell Secretary of the London Cosmopolitan Club,[242] who was passing through the neighbourhood on a holiday kindly gave an address to members on "The History of the Socialist Movement"

Aug 23 Several members from Lynn met at Norwich to meet Phillip Snowden.[243] A Social Evening was held in the evening at the Labour Institute. Comrade Roberts in the Chair. The toast of the evening was proposed by Roberts "Phillip Snowden & the N.A.C of the I.L.P." and coupled with it "The Lynn Comrades". Snowden responded for the N.A.C & White for Lynn Comrades.

Sunday 24 Phillip Snowden gave two fine lectures to large crowds in the Norwich Market Place. The Lynn contingent were Mr & Mrs Kidd, Dorer, R Sporne, S Sporne, Mills, Turner, White & two friends. In the evening after the lecture an adjournment was made to the Institute w[h]ere a few

---

was founded in memory of William Morris (the name comes from the name of his London house, itself taken from a country house that he formerly inhabited). The secretary in 1902 was E. J. Nevill. The King's Lynn letter, written by White and dated 5 July, is inserted in typescript in the Minutes, with a press cutting from the *Clarion*. It also appeared in *Justice*, and prompted a reply to the Lynn group by Nevill: 'such communications encourage us to pursue our efforts to secure unity of action, and in this effort we shall succeed notwith-standing the action of the few who will quickly go under if the rank & file have a little more courage to express their convictions' (NRO, SO 297/24)

240 Press cutting inserted.

241 Clarion Cycling Club.

242 The Cosmopolitan Club, which ran from 1852 to 1902, was a club that prided itself upon conversation: its members were mainly literary figures, politicians, usually Liberal and including several members of Gladstone's cabinets, and civil servants. S.V. Amstell was a leading member of the SDF, a member of their London Committee, delegate for Enfield branch at SDF 1908 Conference and writer of articles published in *Justice*.

243 Philip Snowden (1864–1937), joined the ILP in 1895, its Chairman 1903–06, stood unsuccessfully for Blackburn in the 1900 election, elected in 1906. Part of the Labour group opposing Britain's entry into the First World War, later Chancellor of the Exchequer in MacDonald's governments. In the early years, probably the most popular speaker within the Party apart from Keir Hardie himself, hence the continued (and unsuccessful) attempts of the Lynn group to book him.

short speeches were made by Norwich & Lynn Comrades who before leaving to catch the train thanked all the friends who had contributed to their comfort. Lynn was reached about 2 a.m.[244]

Aug 31 Monthly Business meeting. Owing to wet weather this meeting was held at Comrade Kidd's house. Comrade Neave in the Chair. After some discussion it was decided to hold the meetings at our hall during September Thursdays at 8 Sundays 7.30 a programme for the month was drawn up.
The condition of the hall cleaning &c was then discussed and it was agreed that Com' Kidd & White see what was required to be done and call the attention of the Rechabites to the same.

Thursday Sep 4 Shakespearian Reading "Twelfth Night" by Members
Sunday Sep 7 First meeting in the hall "Impressions of our Norwich visit". Members
Thursday 11 "Twelfth Night" Shakespearian reading
14 Address "What is Capital" by J J Kidd, J Mills in the chair.
15 Comrade Kidd addressed a large meeting at the Walks Gates on local topics.

Sep 18 Business Meeting. Com Kidd in the chair.
Minutes of last meeting read and adopted.
Secretary reported that he with Com Kidd had looked round the hall and a list of necessary repairs had been drawn up and submitted to the Rechabites who had since intimated that they intended having the hall colored & painted and sundry repairs done at once. It was agreed that our outside sign board be painted. Com Drew undertook to see it done.
Com White proposed Com Turner seconded:- That we hire a piano commencing with the first week of October. Agreed.
It was decided that memorandum forms be printed bearing the name of our party and a brief declaration of principles. Recommended for the consideration of the Executive the advisability of having membership cards with rules printed thereon.
It was decided to issue a programme to December and a number of names were suggested of those who should be invited.[245]
Proposed as a recommendation to the Executive that we offer papers from our members to the various societies in the town such as the Congregational Guild, Friends, Liberal Club &c

---

244 A leaflet relating to the meetings and press cuttings from the *Clarion*, 5 Sept. are inserted.
245 This is inserted in the minute book preceding the minute of 31 December, together with a press cutting of Beatrice Green's lecture on the Education Bill.

Sunday 21 Paper by Mrs Kidd subject "The Socialist Outlook" Com' White in the chair

Thursday 25 Comrade Dorer gave a paper the subject of which was:- The Times attack on Municipal Socialism.[246] Com White in the chair.

Monday 29 Com Kidd addressed a noisy meeting. Com' Roberts of Norwich presided the subject being "The Brandy Question". A crowd afterwards attempted to hustle the speakers but ultimately order was restored, though at one time things looked rather ugly.

Sept 28 Paper:- "Socialist Policy what should it be" by Com White. Miss Burke in the chair.

Oct 2 Meeting of the Executive Committee Com Denny in the Chair.
Secretary read letters from Mrs Despard & Harry Lowerison offering to lecture for us. Agreed that their services be thankfully accepted.
Secretary reported that the Rechabites would commence cleaning the hall at once.
Comrades Dexter & Kidd were appointed to go through our rules with a view to printing more forms & membership cards.

Oct 5 Pamphlet read by Com' Turner subject:- The Christian, Atheist & Socialist.[247] Com' Barker in the Chair.

Oct 9 Quarterly General Meeting Comrade Dorer in the Chair.
Minutes read and adopted.
Arising out of the minutes questions were asked as to what had been done by the Slumming Committee. Secretary reported that nothing had been done but
New members Com W Dexter proposed his brother Owen Dexter as a member of the Party Com' Kidd seconded.[248] Carried

---

246 *The Times* ran a series of articles on the subject between 19 August and 25 September 1902: the articles criticised the way that Socialists – specifically the SDF, ILP and Fabians – on municipal councils were using their powers to control local affairs, such as wage rates and housing and educational matters, and the increase in rates that these involved. The articles were anonymous but were actually written by E. A. Pratt and were published as a book *Trade Unionism and British History* in 1904.
247 *The Christian, the Atheist and the Socialist: where they agree and where they differ* is a tract by Joseph Shufflebotham (London: Twentieth Century Press, 1891).
248 Owen Dexter (1881–1952). Four years younger than Walter, he is described as 'photographer' in the 1901 census, and as 'illustrator of works and painter of pictures' in 1911. In later life he practised his art in London: married Agnes Green (the sister of Beatrice Green, see above, note 213) there in 1927, when both were in their forties.

Com' Mrs Kidd gave a rough statement of accounts which showed a substantial balance which was considered very satisfactory. The Election Fund amounted to £2. 0s. 9d.

Municipal Elections Comrade W Dexter moved that "we contest one of the Wards at the forthcoming November Elections". Comrade Turner seconded. Com' Dexter said that the present time gave us an opportunity that we ought to avail ourselves of. Comrades Neave, Denny, Dorer & White also spoke to the resolution. Com' W Dexter proposed & Com Turner seconded the nomination of Com' Kidd as a candidate.

Comrades Dexter, Dorer & White were also nominated but each declined to stand. Comrade Denny proposed "that we fight the South Ward with Comrade Kidd as candidate. Comrade Lyon seconded <u>carried</u>.

Comrade Kidd the candidate then spoke on the prospects and what would be required of our members in the way of help.

Com' White proposed Comrade Dorer as Election Agent. Com' Dexter seconded. <u>Carried.</u>

Comrades Dorer & Dexter were appointed to meet Comrade Kidd at his residence on the following Saturday evening to draft an address &c which should be presented to the members for their approval at seven on Sunday evening.

Comrade Kidd then brought forward a proposal that we pay Com' Roberts of Norwich his train fare on the occasion of his attendance at the meeting held at the Walks gates on "the Brandy Question" \over/ which he presided. Com Dorer moved & Com Mills seconded "that the treasurer be authorised to pay his fare. <u>Carried</u>.

Sunday Oct 12 Comrade Dorer in the chair. Comrade Kidd (candidate for the South Ward) read a rough draft of his election address and submitted it to the meeting after a slight alteration it was approved.

The Chairman then asked for volunteers for the house to house distribution of addresses to which the following responded:- Miss Spaxman, Miss Burke, Messrs Barker, Drew, Francis, Denny, Lyon, White, Triance, Miss Green. This concluded the business.

Comrade Kidd followed with an address on "Studies from [?]Criminal Life".

Sunday Oct 19 Com' White in the chair. Comrade Triance read a paper entitled "The Economic Lie" from Max Nordau's Work.[249]

---

249 Max Nordau (1849–1923), writer, philosopher, and co-founder of the World Zionist Organisation. *The Economic Lie* comprises chapter five of his great work *The Conventional Lies of our Civilization* (1884): the chapter was published as a separate work in 1904.

Monday Oct 20 Active work in connection with our contest in the South Ward commenced by the distribution of our Candidate's address door to door.[250] In the evening a meeting was held and questions drawn up to submit to the Candidates in the Middle Ward.

Sunday 26 Mrs Kidd read a paper on "The Religious Lie". Comrade Neave in the chair.[251]

Monday 27 Comrade Kidd addressed a meeting of electors in our hall. Comrade Dorer occupied the chair there was a good attendance and great attention was shown in the points touched upon by the candidate. A few questions was put at the end.

Wednesday Oct 29 Saw members busy distributing the leaflet "why you should vote for Kidd" throughout the South Ward.[252]

Thursday 30th Meeting to consider replies received from Middle Ward Candidates. Comrade Dorer in the chair. After reading replies from each Candidate (Messrs Bunkall, Floyd & Parsons) it was decided to reco support Bunkall and leave it to the option of our members if they cared to divide their votes between Bunkall & Parson.
Election Day Mr R Scuter was appointed Personation Agent[253]
Scrutineers at the counting. Comrades Dorer, Dexter, Triance.

Nov 1 Election Day opened fine.
A good deal of interest and much curiosity was expressed as to the amount of support our Candidate would get. No canvas had been taken, and the views of our candidate having been put before the electorate the result was left entirely in their hands.
Towards evening it was seen that the Tories were straining every effort to get up their supporters many of whom showed signs of having drank "not wisely but too well". As the time drew near for the poll to close it was felt that the two Tories would again be returned.
A little after nine the result was declared:-
Carpenter   668
H.C. Brown   565
Springall   421
J J Kidd   377

---

250 Copy of address inserted in minutes.
251 This was the title of chapter two of Nordau's work.
252 Copy inserted in minutes.
253 An official employed at an election to detect anyone trying to vote under a false name.

A number of friends at once made their way to the Socialist Hall where a meeting was held presided over by Comrade Dorer. Satisfaction was expressed at the amount of support given to our Candidate who fought for the first time, and on a straight Socialist ticket.[254]

Dec 4 Monthly General Meeting. Comrade Mills in the chair. In the absence of the secretary who was unwell Comrade Kidd read the minutes of last meeting which were confirmed.

It was agreed that the Executive be called to consider the question of our members giving papers to outside organisations.

Election Comrade Dorer stated that expenses were £3. 0s. 9d. and that all the special contributions had not yet been collected.

New member Mr Harry Jarvis Saddlebow Rd was proposed by Com Mills & seconded by Com Dorer and adopted as a member of the Party.[255]

The question of the Assistant Secretaryship was brought up and Com Francis said he had applied for work but none was given him so he considered the office had lapsed.

Agreed that Dorer & Francis compile program & issue it in monthly parts.

Dec 17th Special General Meeting Comrade Dorer in the chair. This meeting was called to consider certain reports having circulated in the town attributing to Com' Kidd misconduct ~~with a nurse~~ at the workhouse and that an apology had been made to the Guardians.

Com Mills proposed & W Jarvis seconded:- That all discussion be considered strictly private and not to be carried beyond the walls of the hall. Carried

At this juncture a letter from Com Kidd was received at the hall which was read by the Secretary.[256] The letter contained admissions which were discussed at some length. Com Triance then moved "that having considered the letter sent by Com' Kidd we ask him for the present not to identify himself with the Socialist Movement in Lynn.[257] W Jarvis sec'd. Carried

---

254 The *EDP* (3 Nov. 1902) noted that 'for a Socialist to receive nearly 300 [sic] votes in a Conservative stronghold is looked upon as a great performance' – but thought his candidature might have spoiled the chances of Springall (a Liberal) defeating Brown (a Conservative). Kidd received 91 plumpers, 241 voting for both him and Springall.

255 John H. 'Harry' Jarvis, born 1879, railway engine fireman of Saddlebow, South Lynn: a founder member of the Lynn ILP in 1906 but resigned a few months later.

256 See Appendix 1.

257 Kidd had been having an affair with a nurse at the Workhouse, as a result of which his wife had left him. He made several attempts to get himself reinstated and was eventually allowed back into the Party in late 1903. However, he was never again the force he had been in the Socialist cause in Lynn. See below, note 294 for his later career.

Com Bush moved an amendment "that we defer the matter for the present and that Com' Kidd be asked to meet the Party. Lost

Com Dexter moved:- "that in order that we may decide as to his position on the Board of Guardians we ask Com' Kidd to meet us on Sunday 21 at 7 pm. Com Mills sec'd. Com Shears prop'd that a deputation be sent to ascertain the facts. Com Lyon sec'd. Lost. The resolution was carried.

The Secretary reported that Com Mrs Kidd had gone away to her sisters at Manchester and had handed over books & monies to him. Com Francis proposed Com' Bush seco the appointment of Miss Burke in her place. Carried.

Comrade Triance moved & Com Bush seconded the following resolution which was carried unanimously:- Resolved "That this meeting tender to comrade Mrs Kidd our deep sympathy in her trouble & hopes that this expression of our feeling towards her may help to lessen the effects of the unhappy event.

The meeting then adjourned.

Dec 20th Comrade Bush in the Chair.

The minutes of the last meeting having been read Comrade Fraser proposed Com' Neave seconded "that Com' Kidd make a statement as to the scandalous reports current in the town. Carried

Com' Kidd at some length stated what had given rise to the reports, denying that anything had occurred beyond the exchange of silly correspondence with the nurse in question and that he wrote the chairman of the Board the night before the last meeting asking for the opportunity of making a personal statement to the whole of the Members of the Board which was granted. After admitting his fault the Guardians had stated he had acted very honourably in bringing the matter forward and each member shook him by the hand.

He hoped those members of our party would forgive him.

Several members complained that Com' Kidd should have made a statement to the Board before consulting his party and taken its members into his confidence.

It was resolved:- "that Comrade Kidd be asked to take no active part in the local Socialist movement until such time as he and ourselves confer as to the desirability of his re-entering". Carried

Comrade Kidd's position as a Guardian was discussed and as hints at resignation was dropped the Chairman stated that he should accept no resolution taking such drastic steps.

Com Neave then moved "that as Com Bush the Chairman appeared to be biased he be asked to leave the chair". Com Triance seconded. Carried

Com Dexter was proposed and it was carried. Com Bush then vacated the chair which was taken by Com' Dexter.

Comrade Kidd complained bitterly of the harsh treatment he was receiving and referred to a private letter which he had received from the Secretary. The Secretary stated that he would read the letter referred to which was written privately and in which he had stated that it was sent at the dictation of no one else.

Com Kidd again expressed himself strongly as to the strong measures some of the members were advocating &c &c

The following resolution was ultimately carried. Comrades Dorer & White dissenting "that Comrade Kidd still continues to sit as the representative of our Party on the Board of Guardians". Moved by Comrade Bush, seconded by E Lyon.

Dec 31 Social Evening a good company of members & friends met and indulged in games etc. During the evening the secretary sent a telegram to comrades F.R Turner & Miss Burke congratulating them on their marriage. At Midnight the company heralded in the year 1903 by joining hands and singing "Auld Lang Syne".

Jan 7th 1903 Annual Banquet.

Sunday Jan 11 Comrade Triance gave selections from Whittier the poet.[258]

Sunday 18th Mrs Frost read an interesting paper on "The Natural equality of Mankind".[259] Comrade Triance occupied the chair several visitors were present and a good discussion followed.

Sunday 25th Comrade White gave a paper on "Socialists and the unemployed question". Comrade Denny took the chair. A good muster of members were present and two or three friends including J.E. Dobson (organising secretary A.S.R.S London) and Mr Furbank (Local Sec of A.S.R.S) who both took part in the discussion following.[260]

---

258 John Greenleaf Whittier (1807–1892), American poet and Quaker, best known for his anti-slavery writing.

259 Mrs Frost not certainly identified, perhaps the wife of Thomas Asa Frost, or perhaps the Mrs Adelaide Frost recorded as joining the Lynn branch of the ILP in 1909 (see below, note 452).

260 An error, actually J. H. Dobson (see above, notes 57 and 61 for the two Dobsons). Press cutting describing the meeting inserted.

<u>1903</u> Jan 29 Annual Meeting Comrade Dorer in the chair.

Present Comrades Mrs Kidd, S Sporne, Mrs Turner, Bush, F.R. Turner, Denny, Francis, Mills, R. Drew, Dorer, White.

<u>New Member</u> Comrade Mills proposed Miss Kate Jex.[261] Miss Sporne seconded. <u>Adopted</u>

The minutes of last Annual Meeting were read and adopted on the motion of Mrs Kidd seconded Com Denny

<u>Secretary Report</u> was then read and Com Turner proposed & Francis seconded "that it be inscribed in the minute book of the party

<u>Financial report</u> Comrade Dorer read the report for Mrs Turner Comrades Bush moved Mills seconded its adoption subject to its being audited.

<u>Election of officers</u>. Comrade White was re-elected General Secretary.

<u>Assistant secretary</u> A discussion arose as to the necessity of appointing anyone to this office. It was decided to appoint an assistant and after Comrades Dorer & Francis had each refused this office <u>Comrade Mills</u> was adopted on the proposition of Com Denny seconded by E Lyons

<u>Financial secretary</u> Comrade Denny proposed Com' Lyons seconded Mrs F R Turner as Financial Secretary. <u>Carried</u>.

<u>Committee</u> Mrs J J Kidd, Dorer, R. Drew, Denny, Turner, J Neave were nominated (& the secretaries) as members of the Committee.

Comrade Mrs Kidd then made a suggestion that the party make a small present to Mrs Despard of London as a mark of our appreciation of services rendered from time to time. This proposal was agreed too [*sic*] and it was proposed that the present should take the form of a photograph (framed) of the "Greyfriars Tower",[262] the amount expended not to exceed 5/-. Mrs Kidd was deputed to make the purchase.

<u>Mrs Kidd</u> suggested that the secretaries of the various societies using the hall be ~~written~~ \notified/ that the practice of spitting on the floor by their members is detrimental to health and that the practice be stopped.

Comrade Dorer raised the question of the Handicraft Guild and proposed that the Secretary be asked to attend the next meeting. Comrade Denny seconded.

A letter was read from the Secretary of the I.L.P. Norwich stating that a demonstration was being arranged at Norwich which would be addressed by Keir Hardie M.P. and that G.H. Roberts would be put forward as the

---

261 Kate M Jex, born 1876. A draper's assistant, she lived in Wisbech with her mother and her sister (Ada, an elementary school teacher).

262 The tower of the thirteenth-century Franciscan friary in Lynn, preserved after the Dissolution because of its value as a sea mark.

proposed Labour candidate for Norwich. Lynn Comrades were invited to attend.

It was agreed that the Secretary write congratulating the I.L.P. on their decision to contest the seat and on their choice of Comrade Roberts as the candidate.[263]

Comrade Turner then briefly ~~acknowledged~~ \thanked/ the members for the wedding present. He said that Mrs Turner & himself greatly appreciated the kindness shown them. The congratulatory telegram received in London on the night of their wedding came as a surprise.

Report read by the secretary (Comrade White) at the Annual meeting Jan 29/03

Comrades. The year was opened in good style by a fine company attending a Banquet which was held in our hall on Jan 8. Comrade Belderson acted as chairman, Comrade Bush as vice chairman. The toasts of the evening were the International, national and local socialist organisations. The whole proceedings were highly successful and reflected great credit on those responsible for the arrangements.

During January several of the members kept up a recurring correspondence in the local press.

A meeting was held in our hall on the 22nd to protest against the increase of the Town Clerk's salary and reduction of corporation workmens wages, there was only a small attendance of the public.

A Programme of lectures etc was issued covering the months from Feb'y to end of April. Harry Lowerison, Rev Osborn, Mrs Despard (London) Mr Dines[264] Alderman R Green were amongst those who lectured, the attendance being good.

Meetings were continued in the hall throughout the month of May. An outing was arranged for the 19th Whit Monday to Ruskin School grounds Heacham but owing to boisterous weather a tea and social evening was held in our hall which was none the less a success for being hastily arranged.

---

263 Norwich was a two-member constituency, with two Conservative MPs at this time. In February 1903, Roberts was elected as Labour candidate at a meeting addressed by Keir Hardie. One of the Conservative MPs (Sir Harry Bullard) died on Boxing Day 1903, causing a by-election for his seat. In January 1904, there was a secret agreement between the Liberals and Labour to allow Labour to put up the second 'radical' candidate in such two member seats, but this did not cater for by-elections where there was only one seat to be won. Roberts stood, but many people were uneasy, thinking this went against the terms of the pact: the Liberal (Louis Tillett) won despite Roberts' intervention.

264 Dines had lectured on Vaccination. See press cutting (from *LN*, 21 Mar.) inserted after 9 Feb. minutes.

Members took part in organising a concert for the Bethesda Male Choir which was given in the Music Hall on behalf of the Penrhyn men. The proceeds amounted to over 20£.

On June 15 we received some of our Norwich Comrades and a good meeting was held on the Millfleet the principal speaker being G H Roberts. The Secretary (F W White) presided. In the evening an informal meeting was held in our hall presided over by Comrade Neave when the Lynn & Norwich comrades exchanged greetings and good wishes for the future of Socialism.

June 26th will be remembered by most folks as the day fixed for the Coronation of Teddy Wales,[265] (which did not come off) but it will be remembered by our Comrades for the enjoyable trip in the "Leader" to the Cockle sands. Ideal weather prevailed. On the Sands the party indulged in various games. The homeward journey was rendered pleasant by music & singing though a rival attraction in the person of the lady palmist from Spalding drew around of those curious to know their future fates. The outing was voted the best yet organised.

During the summer months readings from Shakespeare's Merchant of Venice & Twelfth Night were given by members. The parts were allotted out by Miss Green M.A.

On July 6th a visit was paid to Rising Castle where Harry Lowerison met us and lectured on the history of Castle & neighbourhood.

August 23 a party of our members met at the Labour Institute Norwich to join the Comrades there in welcoming Phillip Snowden who was conducting a weeks campaign there. On Sunday the day was commenced with a long drive in wagonettes which was enjoyed by a large party. In the afternoon & evening two splendid gatherings crowded round the wagonette in Norwich Market Place to listen to Phillip Snowden who lectured on "What Socialists Want" and "The Case for Labour Representation". At the evening a resolution was carried unanimously in favour of contesting Norwich at the next General Election in the Labour interest. A large quantity of literature was sold. After the evening meeting on the Market an adjournment was made to the Institute and a few speeches were made by the Lynn & Norwich comrades after which the party from Lynn left by the mail train.

With the first week of September meetings were commenced in the hall.

At the quarterly meeting held Oct 9th Comrade W. Dexter moved:- that we contest one of the Wards at the forthcoming November Municipal Elections." After a lengthy discussion it was decided to contest the South Ward Com' J J Kidd being adopted as the Candidate. Comrade Dorer undertook to act as Election Agent. From this date all the members [?worked] with a will. A

---

265 King Edward VII.

House to house distribution of addresses & leaflets was made. Beyond this the result was left entirely in the hands of the electorate. Our Candidate though not returned polled the respectable number of 377 votes. After the poll was declared a meeting was held in our hall.

During the year about seventy meetings of one kind or another have been held, few political organisations could show a better record of work done. On the last day of the year a Social was arranged and during the evening a telegram was dispatched congratulating Comrades F. R Turner & Miss Burke on their marriage. At midnight 1903 was heralded in by singing "Should Auld Acquaintance".

General Meeting March 5th
Minutes of meeting held Dec 4th read and adopted.
Minutes of the Special meetings held Dec 17th & 20th also read and adopted.
Secretary read a letter from Mrs Despard London in which she thanked the party for the framed view of the Grey Friars Tower sent her.
Comrade Dorer read a letter from G. N Barnes General Secy A.S.E. relating to his visit in connection with the Old Age Pension Meeting being organised by the Forward Association.[266]
Mrs Kidd & Turner, Mr Turner & Fraser were appointed to arrange programme for the Social to be held on the 25th.
Comrade Turner moved, Com' Denny seconded That a special meeting of members be called to consider our attitude towards Comrade Kidd. Comrade Lyon moved Comrade Dorer seconded an amendment that the matter be considered at the quarterly meeting to be held in April. Carried.
Comrade Dorer moved Comrade Francis seconded that portraits of prominent men in the Socialist Movement be framed and hung on the walls of the hall and that contributions be taken at future meetings towards the cost.

Quarterly General Meeting
April 16 Comrade Dorer in the chair.
Minutes of last meeting read and adopted. Some discussion then took place as to Comrade Kidd's position and the advisability of his re-entering the active work of the Party.

---

266 A Christian group, founded 1891, closely associated with the PSA, its meetings strictly temperance. Rarely mentioned in the Lynn newspapers but its Lynn meetings regularly reported in the *Downham Market Gazette*. Took an interest in the campaign for old age pensions, for example, holding a meeting on the subject in Lynn in 1907, with Revd Herbert Stead of Browning Hall, Walworth, as speaker (*EDP*, 12 Nov. 1907). For alterations to its premises in 1915, see NRO, KL/SE 2/2/2/415: the architect was William Jarvis and Son (see above, note 31).

Comrade Francis moved:- that the time has arrived when we should confer with Comrade Kidd. Comrade Fraser seconded. <u>Carried</u>.

Com Francis moved Com Turner seconded That the meeting for the purpose of conferring with Comrade Kidd be held the first Thursday in May. <u>Carried</u>.

Comrade Francis moved Comrade Mills seconded:- "that 4 doz copies of the Fabian pamphlet "How to make the best of the Education Act" be purchased and circulated amongst the members of the Town Council and educationalists of the town.[267] Carried.

May 7 General Meeting Comrade Dorer in the chair.

Minutes of the last meeting read and adopted. The secretary then read a letter from Comrade Denny resigning his membership.[268] Comrade Francis moved "that the Secretary write Comrade Denny regretting his resignation and expressing the hope that he would be found amongst us again in the near future. Com Turner seconded. Carried

Discussion then took place as to the advisability of forming a cycling club. Comrade Turner was asked to get the names of those of our members who cycled with a view to arranging runs out.

In accordance with a resolution passed at the quarterly meeting held in April Comrade J J Kidd was invited to confer with the members with a view to his re-entering the active work of the party. Comrade Kidd however sent a letter which was read by the Secretary in which he stated that the matter could be dealt with without his attendance.[269] Considerable discussion ensued in which all the members present took part it being agreed – Comrade Francis dissenting – that the Secretary write Comrade Kidd expressing the regret of the members that he had not attended which

---

267 Fabian tract 114, *The Education Act 1902; How to make the best of it* by Sidney Webb (1903).

268 Denny's letter survives but gives no reason why he has chosen to resign (NRO, SO 297/24). Denny is one of a group of six railwaymen listed separately in the subscription book for 1912–13, but he stopped subscribing before the end of the year as did two others (NRO, SO 297/6).

269 Kidd's letter reads: 'At its meeting of the Party which I attended December last it was agreed that I take no active part in the movement until invited to confer with the party. I have loyally adhered to the resolution. Now if the Party desires me to resume my former position there is no need to carry to its utmost literal limit such resolution. Its purpose has been served & the spirit of it can be fully carried into effect if the meeting tonight without further ado pass a resolution inviting me to attend in future the meetings of the organi-sation. This would show a sincere desire on the part of all to deal in the least unpleasant and least protracted way with the matter & can be done without any attendance, therefore you will not expect me to be there tonight.' (NRO, SO 297/24).

was necessary in accordance with the resolution passed in December last – before he re entered the active work of the Party, his non attendance leaving matters just as they were.

July 16 General Meeting Com Mills in Chair.
Minutes of May 7th read and adopted.
The Financial Secretary Mrs Turner gave a statement as to the position of the Party which was considered satisfactory.
The Secretary reported than in accordance with a resolution passed at a previous meeting 4 doz pamphlets issued by the Fabian Society entitled "How to make the best of the Education Act" had been circulated.
A letter was read from Mr Winch[270] acknowledging receipt of a copy and thanking the party for the same.
The members present then discussed considered arrangements to be made for the Annual Outing to Castleacre. Comrades Drew & Mills were appointed to arrange for a brake and Mrs Turner, Mills & White to provide the refreshments. Comrade Triance moved, Comrade Lyon seconded "that papers be read at the outing" and a program covering dates from July 26 to end of August was drawn up.

Annual Outing to Castleacre Sunday Aug 16
Owing to wet weather the outing could not take place on the original date (July 26) arranged. On this occasion however the conditions were all that could be desired.
The Brake left the Walks Gates just after nine leaving by Gaywood. Castleacre was reached in safety and the party explored the fine ruins. Dinner and tea were indulged in al fresco style on the green carpet, the good lady at the farm providing the necessary crockery & hot water. Visits were paid to the Castle and other interesting spots in the village. And a most enjoyable day came to an end all too soon. The return journey was made by East Winch and Middleton, Lynn being reached about nine.

Sep 13 Comrade Mrs Kidd read a paper in the hall, the first of the Autumn session. Comrade Fraser presided.

Wednesday

---

270 William Winch, (1861–1913), company secretary; treasurer of Lynn YMCA according to 1896 trade directory and one-time secretary of Rechabite Society. He and his wife were both on the Board of Guardians and Winch, a Liberal in politics, was a co-opted member of the Borough Education Committee. His daughter Mary Winch (born 1890) was a schoolteacher. See obituary, *LA*, 20 Jun. 1913.

Sunday 20 Comrade Mills read a pamphlet entitled "The Crime of Poverty".[271] Comrade Betts took the chair.

Wednesday 23 Special General Meeting. Comrade Dorer in the chair. It was decided that questions should be put to the Liberal candidate Lieutenant Bellairs[272] at the meeting on the following evening. After some discussion questions were allotted as follows:-

Comrade Dorer Free Trade & Poverty[273]
    ″   Kidd Trusts.[274] Mrs Kidd "Equal Adult Suffrage"
    ″   Francis Secular Education
              Dexter Old Age Pension
              Frost Taxation of Land Values

Municipal Elections

The meeting then discussed ~~the~~ what our attitude should be at the forthcoming November Election. The Secretary stated that delegates would be invited to attend a meeting of Trade Unionists to consider the question of Labour Representation and that we should be wise if we fostered this new departure.

Com' Kidd in the course of some remarks stated that unless some good reasons were shown why he should not fight it was his intention to come out ~~and~~ as a Candidate.

After some further discussion Comrade Francis moved Comrade Dexter seconded "that we nominate Comrade Kidd for the South Ward". Lost

Comrade Mills moved Comrade Drew seconded "that no action be taken until after the meeting of Trade Unionists". Carried

The Chairman pointed out that ~~to it was~~ the resolution of December last which debarred Com' Kidd from taking any active part in the work of

---

271 A pamphlet by Henry George, first published in 1885. George (1839–1897) was an American political economist and journalist, best known in England for his book *Progress and Poverty* (1879).

272 Carlyon Wilfroy Bellairs (1871–1955), a former naval officer, linked to reforming group The Co-efficients, who in Jan. 1906 defeated the sitting MP Bowles, standing as an Independent Conservative, and a second Conservative Burgoyne; crossed floor in Oct. 1906 to sit as Liberal Unionist until Jan. 1910; later Conservative MP, Maidstone, 1915–31.

273 The issue of free trade versus protection (tariffs) divided the Conservative government, leading to several resignations from the cabinet in September 1903. For Socialist responses, see F. Trentmann, 'Wealth versus Welfare: the British left between Free Trade and National Political Economy before the First World War', *Historical Research* 70 (1997), 70–98.

274 Trusts – large scale amalgamations – were a growing concern for the Labour movement at this time. See H. W. Macrosty, *The Trust Movement in British Industry: a Study of Business Organisation* (London, 1907). Macrosty was a Fabian.

the Party was still standing which placed upon him the responsibility of accepting and putting to the Meeting resolutions which meant Com' Kidd's re entry into active work. Comrade Francis then moved that the resolution of December last relating to Com' Kidd be rescinded". Comrade Dexter seconded. <u>Carried</u>

<u>Labour Representation</u> Comrade Mills moved & Comrade Shears seconded "that we send delegates to the forthcoming meeting of Trade Unionists. <u>Carried</u>

Comrade Frost was adopted as a member of the Party on the proposition seconded Com' Lyons.

<u>Delegates</u> to the Labour Representation meeting were then nominated – Comrades Frost, Francis, Kidd, Mills & White. On a ballot being taken Comrades Kidd, Frost, Francis & White were chosen.

It was agreed that at a future meeting the delegates be instructed what attitude they should take.

Oct 1 Monthly Business Meeting Com Fraser in Chair.

Minutes of meetings held July 16 and Sep 13 read and adopted.

Financial statement read by Mrs Turner showing a balance in both the general & election funds. Com Dexter moved Mrs Kidd second[ed] the adoption of the Report <u>carried</u>.

The Secretary read a letter from H Lowerison regretting that he could not give us a lecture this side of Christmas. Mrs Despard wrote offering to lecture for us in Nov. Com Mills moved Com Kidd seconded that this Lady's services be accepted, that the subject be "The New Order". Carried

The Secretary was instructed to try and arrange the date of Lecture for Nov 19th.

Discussion then took place on the condition of the Hall. On Mrs Kidds recommendation it was agreed that notices be hung on the Walls asking persons not to spit on the floor and that the Secretary act with Mrs Kidd in arranged [*sic*] for the thorough cleaning of the hall.

<u>Labour Representation Conference</u> – The Secretary read a letter from Mr Furbank Secretary A.S.R.S. inviting our Party to send delegates to consider the whole question of contesting seats at the forthcoming Nov' elections.[275] Com Bush moved that the invitation be accepted and that the appointment of the four delegates at the previous meeting be confirmed. <u>Carried</u>

Com Bush moved that the delegates be instructed to nominate Comrades Dexter & Kidd as candidates. <u>Carried</u>.

---

275 Inserted in the minute book.

LABOUR REPRESENTATION COMMITTEE CONFERENCE[276]
Copy of Minutes of Meeting held in the Socialist Hall Monday Oct 5 \1903/
Chairman Mr Jackson (A.S.R.S)[277]
Present Messrs Pooley, Bunnett, Furbank (A.S.R.S.), Dorer (Railway Clerks
Assoc), Fraser (Postmans Federation), Messrs Allen & Seaman (Operative
Bricklayers), Messrs Francis, Frost, Kidd, White (Socialist Party).[278]
The Chairman read resolution passed by the A.S.R.S convening the meeting
and then spoke as to the necessity of Labour entering the political field to
defend and watch over the interests of the workers.
Mr Bunnett followed in the same vein.
The Chairman then stated that having introduced the object for which they
were met it was open to them to appoint a chairman from amongst them to
preside over the meeting.
Mr White proposed that Mr Jackson keep the chair which was agreed too,
and thanked the A.S.R.S. for their invitation to the Socialist Party to send
delegates.
Mr Frost spoke as to the prospects of Labour in the three wards and gave
an opinion that candidates should be selected to fight at the forthcoming
elections.
Mr Dorer moved "that the time is ripe for contesting seats for Labour
Representatives on all our Public Bodies". Mr Bunnett seconded. <u>Carried
unanimously</u>.
Mr Frost move that "we contest the <u>North</u> & <u>South</u> Wards. Mr Dorer

---

276 These minutes have been loosely inserted at this point.
277 Miles John Jackson, (1869–1931), railway engine driver, member of ASRS from 1891;
on LRC 1903; founder member of Lynn ILP, October 1906; stood for Borough Council
as Socialist 1906, then for the ILP 1907, 1908, and 1909 without success (His obituary
in the local Liberal newspaper wrongly says that his 1906 campaign was as a Liberal, *LN*,
16 Jun. 1931). Resigned from ILP January 1910. Unsuccessfully stood for the Borough
Council as a Liberal in 1911 and 1912; finally elected 1913, when he was described in
the local press as 'the first representative of the industrial classes' on the council (*EDP*,
3 Nov. 1913). At that time, he was President of the Lynn branch of the NUR, and also
serving on the Board of Guardians. He was elected mayor 1916–17; lost his seat on the
Council 1920. Address: Checker Street, South Lynn, later moved to Epping, where he died.
A tall man, he was ironically nicknamed 'Tiny Jackson'.
278 Six of these men were already in the Socialist Party (the four indicated, together with
Dorer and Fraser), and four others later become members of Lynn ILP (Jackson, Pooley,
Bunnett, Allen). For Furbank, see above, note 79. George Allen, born 1882, a bricklayer:
founder member of the Lynn ILP in October 1906, recorded in subscription book as living
at Cambrai Terrace, Lynn. By 1911 had moved to Exton's Road, and is described as a coach
painter in the census of that year. James Seaman, William Street, South Lynn, born 1863
was also a bricklayer.

seconded. Mr Seaman supported. Mr Kidd moved as an amendment "that providing Candidates can be found all <u>three Wards</u> be contested. Mr White seconded but the amendment was withdrawn and the resolution <u>carried unanimously</u>.

Mr Seaman nominated Mr Fisher

Mr Allen	"	Mr White Wisbech Road
Mr Pooley	"	Mr Kidd
Mr Frost	"	Mr Walter Dexter junr.

Several speakers referred to the fact with regret that many qualified men amongst the workers were unable to take public positions owing to the fact that the meetings were held at such a time as debarred them from attending. The importance of <u>Evening Meetings</u> of the Town Council was urged.

On a ballot being taken for two candidates

Mr Walter Dexter gained 8 votes		Declared elected	
Mr J J Kidd	8 "	"	"
Mr Fisher	3 "		
Mr W White	2 "		

Mr Bunnett proposed that Mr Walter Dexter be asked to contest the South Ward. Mr Pooley seconded. Mr Furbank moved ~~as an amendment~~ that Mr Kidd be chosen to fight the South Ward and said that as Mr Kidd had already contested the seat once there was a better chance of success. Mr Francis seconded. The Amendment was carried. The Chairman then put the substantive motion which was carried. It was thus decided that Mr Kidd fight the South & Mr Walter Dexter the N. Wards.

Discussion then took place on the question of the payment of the <u>Election Expenses</u>. Mr Furbank stated that his Society had a rule which allowed them to vote sums for this purpose and they would bear a share of the cost. He moved "that the Committee defray the cost of the contests". Mr Bunnett seconded. <u>Carried</u>. Mr Allen on behalf of the Bricklayers stated that his Society had no rule which empowered them to vote a sum for the purpose named. Mr White proposed that those present be appointed as a Labour Representation Committee with power to add to their number. Mr Frost seconded. Carried.

After some discussion as to the necessity of getting to work at once Mr White proposed Mr A L Dorer as Organising Secretary to carry out the work of the Election. Mr Frost seconded. Carried.

After arranging for the next Meeting the Chairman declared the business at an end.[279]

---

279 End of inserted minutes. The *Labour Leader* noted how quickly the newly-formed Lynn LRC had got to work, and said of Kidd and Dexter 'they are fighting on a very

~~General Meeting Nov~~

<u>November Elections 1903</u> marked a new development in the history of the movement by the formation of a Labour Representation Committee which saw two candidates J.J. Kidd in the South & W Dexter in the N Wards.[280] A good deal of useful work was done in the contest which resulted as follows:[281]

North Ward 718 voted out of 1,086

Bristowe	Beloe Junr	W Dexter Junr[282]
57	17	185
387	387	
	20	20
51		51
---------	------------	-------------
495	424	256

South

Bardell (L)	Brown (C)	Kidd (S)
256	287	139
223		223
287	287	
	20	20
---------	------------	-------------
766	594	382

In this Ward Liberal & Tory worked together as the vote shows.[283]

Nov 6 General Meeting Comrade Kidd in the chair.
Minutes of last meeting read and adopted.
The Secretary gave a report of the result of the L.R.C. Conference

---

advanced programme, which includes a crusade against slums and the municipalisation of the docks'. (*Labour Leader*, 24 Oct. 1903).

280 For their election leaflets, see Appendix 2.

281 Two candidates were elected for each ward, and each voter could cast two votes (but need only cast one: this was called plumping). In these elections, the top row is the number plumping for each candidate, the next three rows are the votes of those casting two votes: for example, 387 people voted for both Bristowe and Beloe but just 20 went for Beloe and Dexter. Edward Beloe was a Lynn solicitor.

282 Walter Dexter sometimes called himself Junior, presumably to distinguish himself from his father Walter Sothern Dexter.

283 The figures do not entirely bear this out: 287 did vote for the Liberal/Conservative combination, but almost as many (223) voted Socialist and Liberal. The local Tory newspaper was dismissive: "the pretensions … of the 'Labour Party' … whose principal title to distinction was the peculiarity of printing its manifestoes on red paper instead of green, has been utterly defeated" (*LA*, 6 Nov. 1903).

<u>Mrs Despard's Lecture</u> It was agreed that 1000 handbills be printed & distributed & that an ad' be inserted in the Lynn News.[284]

Comrade Dorer read a letter from the Fabian Society London offering a course of lectures in January. Some discussion ensued as to the desirability or otherwise of our Party running the lectures. Comrade Triance moved:- "that failing any other organisation accepting them they be run under the auspices of our Party. Com' Frost seconded. Carried

Com' Dorer raised the question of the use of our hall being granted to the L.R.C and it was agreed that the meetings held during the Election be not charged for.

Municipal Elections. Discussion took place respecting the Election expenses and it was agreed that we share the cost with the A.S.R.S.

General Meeting Dec 3
Comrade Triance in the Chair.
The Secretary read the minutes of meeting Nov 6. Com' Turner Com' Dexter movd & secd adoption.

<u>Election expenses</u> Comrade Triance stated that he had collected about 3/15/0 on his subscription list. Comrade Dexter asked whether a branch of the S.D.F. existed in Lynn and if so would ~~they~~ it contribute. Comrade Kidd in reply said that a branch existed nominally in name only and that its members had contributed to the fund. Com' Triance stated that was so.

The Secretary state that the A.S.R.S had paid their share of the cost of election ~~3/17/6~~ \3/5/0/. Com Kidd moved, Comrade Francis seconded "that our share of the expenses be paid to the secretary L.R.C <u>Carried</u>.

<u>New Members</u> Com White proposed Com Mills secd Mr Anstey <u>Carried</u>.
                    Com Turner proposed Com Lyon secd Mr Petch <u>Carried</u>.[285]
The Secretary read the constitution of the L.R.C. which was adopted at the last meeting.

Com' Petch moved that "the word Parliamentary be included in ~~the~~ it and that our delegates be instructed to vote for this alteration" Comrade Dexter seconded. <u>Carried</u>

<u>Delegates to the L.R.C.</u> By the constitution of the L.R.C. four delegates can be chosen to represent affiliated organisations. The following names were nominated to represent our Party

---

284 The handbills described the speaker: 'Mrs Despard is a member of the Lambeth Board of Guardians, an earnest worker among the poor of London and an eloquent advocate of progressive principles'.

285 Anstey not identified; Petch, either James Henry Petch, born 1842 of Wisbech, tailor, or his son Arthur Petch, born 1880, also a tailor.

Dorer 12 ~~Francis~~ 2 Kidd 6 White 10 Dexter 8 ~~Frost~~ 6 ~~Mills~~ 4[286]

On a ballot being taken with the following \result/

Comrades Frost & Kidd receiving 6 votes each

A second ballot was taken when Com' Kidd received 7 & Com' Frost 6 votes.

~~The delegates~~

Hall caretaker. The Secretary suggested that someone be appointed to attend to the opening & cleaning of the hall up to March as several applications had been received for the hire and it was necessary for the place being kept in proper order. Comrade Dorer advised that the Secretary use his discretion and pay for any necessary labour required. Com' Lyon move that Com' Mills be appointed as caretaker and to charge for his time. Com' Kidd seconded. <u>Carried</u>.

Com' Dorer moved that the attention of the Landlord be called to the condition of stove & ventilator. <u>Carried</u>.

<u>Presentation of a screen by Com' Lyon</u>. Comrade Mills proposed Comrade Turner seconded "that the best thanks of the Party be given to Comrade Lyons for his handsome present of a screen for future use in the hall. <u>Carried</u>.

<u>Childrens Entertainments</u> Com' Mills proposed "that a Committee be appointed for the purpose of organising childrens entertainments during the winter. Com' Lyons seconded carried. Committee appointed as follows: Mrs & Mr Turner, Lyons & Mills with power to add.

<u>General Meeting Dec 20</u>

Comrade Neave in the chair.

Minutes of meeting held Dec 3 read & adopted.

The Secretary read a communication from the Kelmscott Club London inviting the opinion of our members \as/ to

The desirability of calling a conference of all socialist bodies in the country \to discuss the fiscal proposals of the Government/ with a view, if possible, to decide the attitude to be adopted by Socialists in regard thereto.

Holding a conference of the I.L.P. & S.D.F and other Socialist bodies in 1905 with a view to the formation of a united Socialist party.

Voting papers were ~~sent~~ enclosed to be filled in and returned. After some discussion it was agreed that our replies be unanimously in support of both proposals.

<u>Annual Supper</u> Com' Mills proposed Com' Lyons seconded that the Annual supper be held on Thursday Dec 31ˢᵗ. Carried.

---

286 The names of the unsuccessful candidates are struck through.

Mrs Turner Mrs Mills Mrs White was appointed to carry out the catering. The toasts were allotted out & Com Turner was appointed to arrange musical items.

Com' Triance brought forward the question of our late Comrade Rowe's Books & pamphlets and on the proposition of Com Drew it was agreed to purchase the pamphlets.

Annual Meeting Feby 3/04
Comrade Triance in the chair.
The Minutes of the last Annual Meeting were read & adopted.
New Member E Cremer[287] was adopted as a Member.
Secretary's Report was read and adopted
Treasurer's Report read by Mrs Turner showed a balance of about 6/0/0 in the general fund & the election fund also about 25/- in hand. The report was adopted and the thanks of the Party was awarded.
Election of Officers Comrade White was re-elected Secretary & Mrs Turner Treasurer. Com Mills was appointed Assist Sec'y. Bush Auditor
Committee elected Fraser, Francis, Dorer, Lyons, Anstey, Kidd
Cinderella[288] Committee Mrs Turner, Turner, Fraser, Cremer, Lyons, Mills, Mrs Kidd with power to add, reports of work to be rendered at the Quarterly Meetings.
Election of delegates to L.R.C Dorer, White, Kidd, Francis
Hardwick Road Encroachment: The Secretary reported that a piece of land \adjoining footpath/ had been fenced in just over the Hardwick Bridge and after some discussion it was agreed that the Town Clerk be written.
On the motion of Mrs Kidd the Secretary was instructed to address a letter of thanks to Mrs Despard (London) for her lecture.
Affiliation Motion Com' Lyons moved a motion that we affiliate with the S.D.F Bush seconded. Kidd moved amendment "that as the fusion of the two ILP & SDF seems very remote the members of our organisation join either the I.L.P or S.D.F if individually disposed, that the joint party continue to exist, that financial obligations be met by equal contributions from the ILP & SDF branches at the end of the quarter. Com Turner secd.
Withdrawn
For resolution 8 against 8 Chairman gave casting vote against

---

287 Cremer, see above, note 23.
288 Cinderella Clubs were social groups based around the *Clarion* newspaper, but intentionally non-political. Their concern was the support of underprivileged children. The first was founded in Bradford in 1890 and is the only Cinderella Club still in existence (Turner, 'Soul of Labour', 139–42). The Lynn club was formed in the first week of January 1904 (*Clarion*, 8 Jan. 1904).

General Meeting Feby 10
Comrade Dorer in the chair.
Minutes of Dec 20 read & adopted
New Members Com White proposed Mrs Mills secd Mrs Kidd Com Mills propd Com Neave secd Mrs White. Adopted.
Secretary intimated that Mrs Rowe wished to thank all those members who had purchased books & pamphlets from her.
Norwich Election Fund. Secretary read a letter from Bruce Glasier,[289] appealing for assistance. On the motion of Com Mills 1/0/0 was voted from the general fund.
Profits from Socials It was agreed on the proposal of Com' Dorer that profits from Socials should in future be paid into Election Fund
Lowerisons Lecture agreed that an advert' be inserted in Lynn News
L.R.C Lectures by Mr Sanders Fabian Lecturer.[290] Dorer (Sec'y) reported that the cost of these lectures would be about 4/-/- and there would probably be 2/-/- deficiency. After some discussion the matter was left over.

Feby 21 Special Meeting Chairman A L Dorer
This was a meeting to consider the following letter:-
(see copy).[291]
Mrs Kidd Secretary SDF was called on to submit her proposals which amounted to a joint tenancy of the hall and a share in the expenses & revenue. Bush moved adoption of the proposals Lyons seconded Lost
A warm discussion commenced, Comrade Mills asking whether the formation of the SDF active branch did not put us back into the same position previous of to our fusion.

---

289 John Bruce Glasier (1859–1920), Scottish socialist politician and one of the main leaders of the ILP (of which he became chairman in 1900) along with Keir Hardie, Philip Snowden and J Ramsay MacDonald: he is not so well known as he never became a Member of Parliament. The fund was for the Norwich by-election of January 1904: George Roberts stood for the ILP but came third, well behind the Liberal and Conservative candidates (Meeres *George Roberts MP*, 26)
290 William Stephen Sanders (1871–1941), appointed Fabian provincial organising secretary in July 1907; secretary of the Fabian Society 1913–20. Served on London County Council; stood unsuccessfully for Parliament at Portsmouth, 1906 and January 1910; MP for Battersea North, 1929–31 and 1935–40.
291 The letter is not included in the minute book, but the original survives. Signed Mrs Chrissie (J J) Kidd, it points out that the Lynn SDF had met on 9 Feb. and in view of 'the adverse vote' at the meeting on the previous Wednesday had decided that 'the Branch should cease to be merely nominal, but active.' She asked White to call a meeting to discuss proposals drawn up by the SDF.

~~Kidd~~ The Chairman read a letter from W Dexter urging on the necessity of unity being maintained.

JJ Kidd made a lengthy speech giving a history of the organisation but was corrected on several important points by the Sec'y

F White Sec'y spoke of the past good work of the Party and urged that the necessity for a united organisation was as needful today as in 1898 when we were approached by the SDF members re fusion. He then moved the following resolution:- That we regret to learn the S.D.F members have decided to form themselves into a separate organisation & thereby resume the position existing previous to the compact and on resuming the position as a Socialist Society we desire to place on record our regret that disunion should be brought about again". Com' Fraser seconded.

Com' Kidd moved as an amendment "that if the resolution aims at an alteration of name a special meeting of members be called to consider it. Com' Turner seconded.

Pressed for an answer Com' Kidd admitted that their decision to form an <u>active</u> branch of the SDF was a breach of the compact of 1898. The amendment <u>was lost</u>.

The resolution was carried.

The meeting of Feby 21 having decided that the action of certain members in forming an active branch of the S.D.F was a breach of our compact and that by so doing we resumed our old position

A <u>Special Meeting</u> was held on Feb 24th Comrade Fraser in the chair. The rules & constitution of the S.D.P were adopted the name being changed to "Socialist Society".[292]

<u>General Secretary</u> Comrade White was elected on the proposition of Comrades Drew & Frost.

<u>Treasurer</u> Comrade Frost was appointed <u>pro tem</u> on the proposition of Fraser & Mills

<u>Committee</u> elected Comrades Dorer, Fraser, Mills, Neave, Pooley & Secretaries

<u>Delegates to L.R.C.</u> Comrades Mills, Frost, Dorer, White

<u>Candidates for Guardians Election</u> delegates to L.R.C. were instructed to propose Comrades Mills & White for South Lynn parish.[293]

---

292 The page in the Minute book is stamped KL Soc'ist Soc'.

293 In the event, three men – White, Mills and Bunnett – stood under the label 'Labour', the local press commenting 'a new factor in the election will be candidates of the Independent Labour Party' (*EDP*, 11 Mar. 1904). However, none was elected (White 234 votes, Bunnett 221, Mills 180). Meanwhile Kidd himself successfully stood for re-election to the Board under the label 'Socialist', calling himself 'an ardent worker in the Trade

Special Meeting March 13th.
Comrade Mills in the Chair.
Minutes of Feb 24th read & adopted.
Discussion took place as to what attitude we should adopt to those members who had constituted themselves into an active branch of the S.D.F. It was decided that if the question of the funds be raised and any claims made we should be prepared to share the balance in proportion to the membership.

March 13th Comrade Dorer in the chair.
A meeting was held of members of the old S.D.P there was a large attendance.
Comrade Kidd refused to accept the position taken up by the majority of the old members. After a lengthy and heated discussion it was unanimously agreed that a ballot of members \be taken/ on four questions to be submitted and that the decision thereon be final.

Meeting Mar 17th
Comrade Neave in the chair
This was a meeting to receive the voting papers on the following questions
Question
The meeting held on 21st February 1904 was of the opinion that the formation of an active branch of the S.D.F. in Lynn was a violation of the compact of 1898. Do you concur in this? Answer 26 Yes
A resolution was passed by which the compact was dissolved & the Lynn Socialist Society resumed its old position. Do you approve of this? Answer No 2, Yes 24
Do you consider the local organisation should be affiliated with the S.D.F. or I.L.P.? Answer Yes 5, No 21
If you reply in the affirmative to Question No 3 state which you prefer Answer I.L.P. 3, S.D.F. 2
32 papers issued, 29 returned, 26 filled in 3 blank.
The ballot was treated as secret.

April 21 Quarterly General Meeting Comrade Frost in the chair.
Minutes read and adopted.
Secretary reported that the Rechabites had accepted Comrade J Neave as trustee in place of J.J. Kidd.[294]

Union, Labour and Socialist movements', but as *persona non grata* he is not mentioned in these minutes. (*LN*, 26 Mar. 1904; *EDP*, 29 Mar. 1904).
294 This is the last time Mr and/or Mrs Kidd are mentioned in the minutes: they remained with the SDF when the Socialist Society broke away from it, but did not remain long in Lynn; *EDP* (26 Mar. 1907) noted that Kidd was not standing for his place on the Board

Discussion took place as to the Financial Secretaryship and it was agreed that Comrades Dorer & White interview Mrs Turner and ascertain what her intentions were.

The Cinderella Secretary's report was held over to a future meeting.

It was decided to continue indoor meetings during May.

Hardwick Road Encroachment The Secretary reported that this matter had been discussed by the Norfolk Highways Committee & a sub-committee appointed to view the spot.

Special Meeting After disposing of the ordinary business the Special Meeting was held in accordance with notice "to consider the advisability of alteration of name. After the discussion. Com' Dorer proposed Com Mills seconded "that the word Party be inserted in our name instead of Society" Carried.

J. Neave

May 26 General Meeting J Neave in the chair.

Minutes read & adopted.

Appointment of Financial Secretary J Mills was unanimously appointed on the proposition of J Neave seconded by J Pooley.

A letter was read from the Secretary of the Lynn Branch of the S.D.F asking for terms for use of hall by them once a fortnight and the right to exhibit a board outside. After some discussion the following resolution was carried subject to its being submitted to members for their approval "That not being desirous of encouraging a second Socialist organisation in the town we are unable to grant the use of the hall to the S.DF branch our practice having been in the past to let it on such terms as to assist those using it."

Guardians Bye Election St Margarets Parish.

The Candidature of F W White was endorsed on the proposition of Comrade Mills secd by Com' Neave.[295]

---

of Guardians in that year as 'he had removed to Letchworth'. He appears in the register of electors for that town 1911–19, ran a flower nursery and served on the urban district council there. He died there (at his home in Baldock Road) 28 January 1920 (see obituaries in *LN*, 31 Jan. 1920, *LA*, 6 Feb. 1920). Probate was granted to his widow Christiana, who appears in the Lynn register of electors for 1923–25, having returned to the town: she died in Lynn on 23 July 1936 (*LN*, 28 Jul. 1936, death notice only).

295 The by-election took place on 9 June 1904, but White was unsuccessful, coming bottom of the poll with a mere 72 votes (the successful candidate polled 225). White's election leaflet is loosely inserted in the minutes before 21 April, noting that he is 'opposed to Compulsory Vaccination and a paid Chaplaincy. He will advocate fair Assessments all round and ECONOMY WITH EFFICIENCY'. There was more activity later in the year, not recorded in the minutes. In the municipal elections of 1 November 1904, White stood for the ILP in Middle Ward and Bunnett for South Ward (he was nominated not by the ILP but by ASRS, his union): both finished bottom of their respective polls.

[No meetings are recorded between 26 May 1904 and 5 March 1905][296]

March 5/05 Comrade Shears in the Chair.

Financial statement read and adopted accounts having been audited by Com' Frost.

J. Mills proposed W. Drew seconded "That subject to conditions being approved by the S.D.F the affairs of the Socialist Party be wound up from the 25th March, that the S.D.F take over sub-tenants & obtain the approval of the Rechabites for tenancy of the Hall".

From March 25th 1905 to Jan 14 1906 Socialist propaganda work was carried on by the S.D.F. Members of the old Party had hoped that unity would result from their fusion with the S.D.F. but unfortunately this effect was not obtained and a strong feeling manifested itself amongst the members to revert back to the old position by withdrawing from the S.D.F.

1906 Jan 14 Annual Meeting Lynn Branch S.D.F.

Comrade Neave in the chair.

Present Comrades Fraser, White, F Turner, Mrs Turner, Denny, Francis, Triance, Jordan, Drew, Pooley, Mills, Neave, Bridges, Dexter, Fox, Shears.[297]

After the Secretary's & Treasurer's report had been passed, it was moved by Com Drew sec by Com Mills that we cease to be a branch of the S.D.F. This was carried by 10 voting for 5 against

Com Mills moved Fraser sec that henceforth our name be King's Lynn Socialist Party

That Com Mills be Sec Pro Tem was Pro by White Sec by Pooley

It was decided that we send a telegram wishing success to Com Roberts at Norwich.[298]

---

296 On 23 November 1904, there was a by-election for the South Ward of the Borough Council. Kidd stood, nominated by the SDF (a fact not recorded in these minutes, he now being outside the Socialist Party). His proposers, seconders and assenters included J. T. Neave, Horace Lyon (brother of Ernest Lyon), J. W. Spurling, C. E. Cremer, R. J. Drew, G. Bocking, J. Pooley, J. Mills, R. Denny). However, he also came bottom of the poll, with 123 votes compared to 450 cast for the winner Alfred Jermyn (*EDP*, 11, 24 Nov. 1904; *LN*, 19 Nov. 1904 for list of names).

297 Jordan and Bridges not certainly identified and only mentioned this once: perhaps they had been – and remained – loyal to the SDF rather than the Socialist Party. Jordan probably John Jordan, born 1859, in 1911 an 'iron monger porter', living at 12, Priory Lane, Lynn. Bridges is probably George Matthew Bridges, born 1855, in 1901 'artist' at St James' Place, in 1911 scenic artist and decorator at County Court Road, in 1921 living at Goodwin's Road.

298 Roberts stood for Norwich in the 1906 general election and came top of the poll. He was one of the 29 LRC members elected who formed the Parliamentary Labour Party and

Next Meeting to be held on Sunday Jan 21 for election of Officers for coming year.

Jan 21st Special Meeting Kings Lynn Socialist party <u>F White in Chair</u>.
Minutes read and adopted
<u>New Members</u> Com White Pro Com Triance Sec
 F Piper, Miss E Sporne,[299] G Allen, Mrs Mills, Mrs White, Mrs Drew, C Lock,[300] T Frost,[301] Mrs Fraser.[302]

'

<u>Constitution & Rules</u> After some discussion we adopted the amended Constitution & Rules of the Old Social Democratic Party.
<u>Election of Officers</u> Comrade Mills was elected Secretary & Com White Treasurer. Com Allen was appointed Assist Sec'y & Triance <u>Auditor</u>
<u>Executive Committee</u> Comrades Frost, ~~Hall~~, Allen, Dorer, Triance, Drew, ~~Watts,~~ Fraser, Secretary & Treasurer.[303] <u>Quorum 4</u>

---

was soon appointed the party's Chief Whip. In Lynn, the Social Democratic Party had planned to put up a candidate in the 1906 general election, even naming him (William Gee (1869–1954), a prominent member of the SDF, but with no local connections). He addressed several meetings in the town, but in the end he did not stand. (*EDP*, 6 Oct. 1905).
299 Ethel Winifred Sporne (born 1888), a sister of the already mentioned Spornes. Ethel would have been only eighteen when she joined, and she resigned within a few months, reason not known. She joined the ILP in 1910, last paying her subscription April 1913. By 1911 she had followed in her sister's footsteps by becoming an elementary school teacher, living with her parents in South Street. In 1919 she married George Ridley. Ethel was a member of the local Gilbert and Sullivan Society (see e.g. *EDP*, 16 May 1907 when she was performing in 'Pirates of Penzance')
300 Correctly Charles Locke, born 1881. In 1901, a bricklayer's labourer living at his parents' house in Lynn; by 1911 a 'window cleaner publican', address *King George* Conduit Street, Lynn. Publican at the *King George* from 1908 to at least 1913 (in which year he was fined for allowing gaming). One of the founder members of the Lynn ILP in October 1906. His name is sometimes spelled without the final 'e' in the minutes, as here. Probably the Charles Robert Locke, described as a motor fitter, of Norfolk Street Lynn in 1921 census.
301 Thomas Asa Frost (1873–1958), draper and clothier; of 90 London Road (by 1911, had moved to Railway Road). Later references to Comrade Frost presumably refer to him rather than to Walter Frost. Thomas Asa Frost was a founder member of Lynn ILP in 1906: he and his wife were among the eleven people still members of Lynn ILP when it was dissolved in 1916. He served as councillor for North ward from 1929 to 1946, and as mayor in 1933–34 and 1937–38. In later life, lived at South Wootton and was a magistrate on the Grimston bench. He died in a nursing home in Gorleston. See Raby, *Allotted Span*, 54–5.
302 Jessie Susan Fraser, wife of Richard Fraser. They married in South Lynn in 1903: her maiden name was Hoare. The couple had moved to Mansfield by 1911, returning to Lynn in the 1930s; she was in their house at the time of his suicide in 1934.
303 Watts and Hall not further identified. Both are noted in minutes for 1 April 1906 as having resigned. Hall could be F. W. Hall, a founder member of Lynn ILP in October 1906,

<u>L.R.C. Delegates</u> It was agreed that the appointment of Delegates stand over till next meeting.

The Secretary was instructed to write to Fabian Society for a box of Books, the same to be left at Comrade Mills, & a list of books which members care to lend for Mutual Benefit

<u>Banquet</u> Com White pro Com Frost sec'd that we have a banquet on Jan'y 31. Coms Fraser & Triance to arrange programme & the lady members be asked to form a Committee to do the catering.

Next meeting to be held ~~Wed~~ Thur Jan'y 25ᵗʰ to arrange future work and draw up programme.

Signed FW White Chairman

Jan 25 Special K.L.S. Party Comrade in Chair (White)

Minutes read & adopted.

<u>Delegates to L R. C.</u> Comrades Allen, Fraser, White, Mills.

Agreed that we have the hall cleaned & the usual price be paid.

<u>Application from Good Templars for hall left in Com White hands</u>

Letter from Lynn Branch of S.D.F. asking for use of Hall one night per week. ~~The secretary was instructed to inform the S.D.F Branch that the hall was engaged every night therefore could not oblige~~ \The Secretary & Treasurer to draft letter to submit to a future Executive Meeting in reply./

Carried unanimously that Com White take the chair at the banquet.

Agreed that the hall be open on Thursday & Sundays for educational lectures & a programme be issued for February.

A proposition was moved by Com Watts & carried that the charge of 6d per year be made for the use of Fabian Books

The secretary to write to Com Lowerison asking if he could arrange to give us a lecture at a future date.

Cinderella Committee Comrades Frost, Drew, Fraser, Mills, Allen, Mrs Triance, Mrs Mills, Mrs White, Mrs Fraser with power to add.

Signed T Frost Chairman

Feb 4ᵗʰ 06 Executive Committee Meeting Com Frost in Chair

The Secretary read letter from H Lee Sec Social Democratic Federation asking for reasons why Lynn Comrades had left the Federation. It was decided that Sec & Turner draw up reply.[304]

---

but it is a very common name; Watts is once identified in the minutes as P.E. Watts but no one of that name appears in 1901 or 1911 censuses, nor in the ILP subscription book: perhaps Watts (and Hall?) went with the SDF rather than the ILP.

304 A draft copy of the reply to Lee has been inserted into the Subscription Book (SO 297/6). It reads:

Agreed that a subscription list be drawn up for clearing off debts of 1905
That the Executive meets once a week, next meeting to be on Feb 8th at
8 p.m.
Signed R Fraser Chairman

Thursday Feb 8th 1906.[305] Executive Meeting Com Fraser in Chair.
Minutes of last meeting read and confirmed.
That a copy of letter sent in reply to Lynn branch of S.D.F. be inserted in
minutes and approved.[306]
Comrades Allen & Dorer was appointed to get all information relating to
cost of newspaper
Decided on the motion of Comrade Allen that the "Labour Leader" be
offered to Public Library committee to be placed in News room.[307]
A special meeting to be held on Thursday Feb 15th to alter Rule relating to
Executive Committee, & any other business.
Moved by Comrade Mills seconded by Comrade White that Comrade Hall
purchase a neo-cyclo-style for the Party
Next Meeting of Executive Feb 14th at 7 o'clock.

With regard to our decision to withdraw from the S.D.F, the main reason is on account of
the attitude taken up by that body towards the L.R.C.
For years Socialists have agitated inside the Trade Unions urging upon them the necessity of
capturing the political machinery of this country and now that they have entered the field
of politics as an independent party their early efforts have been hindered rather than helped
by the ~~bickering~~ attitude taken up by the S.D.F towards them.
We have for our object the building up of a strong local Socialist party ~~and we have found
that the tactics of the S.D.F retarded us in our work~~ under whose auspices all Socialists can
work. J Mills (The words struck through were presumably not in the letter as actually sent.).
305 The minutes make no record of decisive events elsewhere. At the General Election
of 1906 (held 12 January to February, elections then not being confined to a single day),
'the Liberal Party scored its most decisive win at a general election in modern times.
Twenty-nine LRC MPs, soon to be 30, were returned to the Commons to form the new
Parliamentary Labour Party. During the 1906 Parliament the PLP – white males from
working-class origins and mainly trade union backgrounds, mostly religious, nearly half
teetotallers, with an average age of 46 – at first occupied the opposition benches, often
voting with the Liberal government. But this new collective group – roughly half of whom
saw themselves as socialists – also provided a distinctive voice to working-class demands for
old-age pensions, feeding poor children, a national minimum wage, tackling unemployment
and trade union legislation.' (Shepherd and Laybourn, *First Labour Government*, 9). Almost
all the MPs subsequently invited to speak at Lynn came from this group.
306 Letters relating to disputed use of the Hall are loosely inserted; see Appendix 3.
307 Lynn had finally adopted the Libraries Act on 17 January 1899. The Public Library
was built with the help of money from by American philanthropist Andrew Carnegie: he
gave £5,000 for the building on condition that the Council provided a site and agreed to
maintain the Library and was present at its formal opening, 18 May 1905.

New Members Mr A Dorer Mrs Dorer & Mrs Gittings were proposed & accepted.[308]

Signed P.E. Watts Chairman

Executive Meeting – Feb 14th 1906 Comrade Watts in chair.

Minutes of previous meeting read and confirmed.

Comrade Allen reported that they were making good progress with newspaper.

A Circular drawing attention to our Movement and its Literature, written by Com White, was accepted by the Meeting for distribution throughout the Town.

The Secretary was instructed to write to the national L.R.C. for Cartoons to be placed outside hall.

The Partys name to be put on Large Board and a small board be used for announcing lectures.

Agreed that a letter to the Town Clerk on the Housing question be submitted to general meeting for approval.

Signed J. Triance Chairman

Special Meeting Feb. 15th 1906

Comrade Pooley in the chair.

Comrade Hall moved that the word six in place of four be inserted in rule (5) so that it reads (There shall be an executive consisting of the General Secretary and six members).

Comrades Triance and Dorer was then proposed and carried as members of the executive.

The meeting decided the letter on the Housing Question should be submitted to a Sunday night meeting & then forwarded to the Town Clerk and the Press

Signed Thos A Frost Chairman

Executive Meeting March 26/1906.[309] Com Triance in the Chair

Minutes of last accepted as read.

Com White was instructed to get details & cost of circular for a house to house distribution throughout the town.

Com Triance was asked & consented to be responsible for the drawing up of future programmes.

Our Thursday night meetings be devoted to the study of Britain for the British & other Educational Books.

---

308 Frances Gittings, born Hodd 1882, wife of W. C. Gittings (see below, note 313). They married in Gaywood, 11 Feb. 1904.

309 An error: the correct date must be 26 February.

The next executive meeting to consider best means of drawing up a directory of the town.

Comrade Frost to act temporarily in place of Com Fraser until confirmed by \general meeting/ as delegate to the L.R.C.

Distribution of old Clarions, Opening of Hall. Cuttings from newspapers, to be brought up at next general business meeting.

Signed Geo. Allen Chairman

Mar 5th Executive Meeting 1906 Comrade Allen in Chair.

Minutes of last meeting read & confirmed.

The meeting decided that on account of our funds being low the circular drawing attention to our movement must stand over for a while.

The South ward to be divided into 14 districts small pockets books to be supplied to each person who has charge of district in which he \or she/ must write down all he or she can get to know of every voter living in the district.

Signed A.L. Dorer 12-3-06 Chairman

March 12 Executive Meeting 1906 Comrade in Chair (Dorer).

Minutes of last meeting read and confirmed.

Agreed that Comrade Frost's offer to pay the cost of the Labour Leader being sent to the Library weekly be accepted.

The letter from the Town Clerk re the Loke road Extension and building bye laws be entered in Minute Book.[310]

Signed F.W. White Chaiman

March 19 Executive Meeting 1906. Comrade White in the Chair.

Minutes of Previous read & confirmed.

Division of South into Districts as drawn up by Com Allen be submitted to Quarterly meeting for Approval.

Deputation from the Local Branch of the S.D.F. asking for our assistance in organising a meeting at which Sir John Gorst will speak on the Feeding of School Children. Resolved that as the S.D.F. asked for no financial support we assist them in every possible manner.[311]

Signed [*initials illegible, presumably those of Frost, as chairman of the next meeting*] Chairman

---

310 This has not been done.

311 Sir John Eldon Gorst (1835–1916), lawyer and politician. He served in several non-cabinet posts in Lord Salisbury's Conservative governments, and was Vice-President of the Committee on Education 1895–1902. The issue of infant welfare was highlighted by the Boer War and taken up by the Labour movement, especially Margaret McMillan (see below, note 344).

April 1ˢᵗ Quarterly Meeting 1906 Comrade Frost in Chair.

Minutes of last meeting read and confirmed.

The division of the North and South Wards into districts to be left untill district books are ready.

Decided that the Sec interview Com Fraser re the distribution of Britain for the British

That Comrades Drew & Allen be members of Executive Committee in place of Com Watts & Hall resigned.

Comrade Triance be asked to draw up programmes for Sunday nights only up to May.

Signed A.L. Dorer May 20/06 Chairman

Proposed by Com Drew Sec by Pooley that the Party meet on every Sunday at a given place outside, if wet in the Hall, & that a programme be drawn up for June & July.[312]

Business Meetings to be held once a month when convenient.

That Com Lowerison be asked if he could meet us Heacham to show us round his school on Whitmonday.

Outside propogander [sic] Meetings be held during Summer the Secretary to get the names of Speakers.

Signed C.W. Gittings Chairman[313]

May 20ᵗʰ Monthly Meeting, 1906 Comrade Dorer in Chair.[314]

Proposed by Com Dorer, Sec by Neave the Districts Books be left to the Election Committees of the L.R.C.

That Copys of "Britain for British" be left at Com Mills and a list of names be kept to whom they are lent.

 Com Frost was asked to act as Collector untill Annual Meeting.

Com Triance undertook to write to all sympathisers with the movement with a view of getting their Financial support.

The question of a Labor Institute was brought up decided it be left till a future meeting.

---

312 From the spacing and the fact that this is written in a different hand from the previous entry, this is clearly another meeting but it has no heading or date.

313 William Carter Gittings (1873–1918), piano tuner, Greyfriars Road, moving to Tennyson Avenue 1910. One of founder members of Lynn ILP, October 1906; last paid his subscription 6 Apr. 1914. Sometimes referred to as W. C. Gittings, sometimes as C. Gittings.

314 The minutes do not record a public meeting on 20 April at which newly-elected MP for Norwich George Roberts gave 'a splendid address'. The largest Hall in Lynn was hired by the Socialists for the first time, and almost a thousand people attended (*Labour Leader*, 27 Apr. 1906)

Members present: Comrades Triance, Drew, Lock, Gittings, Fraser, White, Mills.
Signed John Pooley Chairman[315]

Quarterly Meeting June 25/06. Com Fraser in the Chair.
Minutes of previous meeting read & adopted.
Agreed that Com Shears act as Collector in place of Comrade Frost till annual meeting.
The Secretary proposed Miss Clara Ducker & Mr E Ducker of Snettisham as members of our Party. Carried unanimously.[316]
The probable Formation of a Branch of the I LP in the town was discussed & our attitude towards it. It was decided that members could join it if they chose but the Socialist Party could not be dissolved until they were relieved of Financial obligations.
Members present Comrades Triance Drew Lock Gittings Fraser White Mills.
Signed desp John Pooley Chairman

Special Meeting Aug 2/06 Comrade Pooley in Chair
Present Comrades Shears Triance Neave Gittings Mrs Mills Drew Dorer Frost Pooley Fraser & Miss E Sporne
Minutes read and adopted
New Members Mr Frost Proposed Albert Ducker Ingoldisthorpe, the Secretary proposed Mr Allsopp of Tilney & Mr Sparks of Terrington as members.[317] Carried unanimously.
Comrades Dorer & Drew were appointed Treasurer & Collector in place of Com White & Shears resigned.
Municipal Elections The selection of candidates to be left to the Executive.
Our attitude to the formation of a Branch of the I.L.P was then discussed.

---

315 These two lines have been entered here by mistake and are repeated in their correct place at the end of the following meeting.

316 Clara Ducker, born 1863, and Albert E. Ducker, born 1874. They lived at Kingston House, Snettisham. Ducker was a cart and coach-builder and Clara is described in the 1901 census as his sister and housekeeper.

317 *Alfred* (according to the 1901 census and 1906 trade directory) Ducker, born 1870, wheelwright, presumably a relative, probably brother, of the before mentioned Duckers (the 1900 trade directory lists 'Ducker brothers, cart and van builders, Snettisham'); James Sparkes, born 1868, schoolmaster at Terrington St John; Frederick J. Allsopp, born 1872, schoolmaster at Tilney St Lawrence, later at Upwell. He wrote to Mills on 11 June 1906 saying that, as a reader of the *Clarion* for ten years, he was glad to hear of the movement locally. Mills clearly went to meet him as in a second letter, dated 19 June, Allsopp said that he had 'a neighbour in my profession of Socialistic opinions' who also wanted to meet Mills: this was probably Sparkes (NRO, 297/9).

A resolution was moved that we welcome the formation of a Branch of the ILP and as soon as such Branch is formed a meeting be called to consider dissolving our Party. Carried Unam.

Tenancy of Hall. Resolved that this question be left ~~untill~~ to the meeting called to discuss the last resolution.

The Secretary to write to the Rechabites asking for a new lock to be placed on the Hall Door.

That only business meetings be called as occasions arise during September

The Secretary report that Members of the Branch of Social Democratic [*sic*] had entered the Hall and taking a screen[318] and box banner etc with \out/ our consent. Resolved that report of their Action be entered in the Minutes. Signed F.W. White Chairman

---

318 The screen had been presented by Lyon in December 1903: see minutes of that date. As Lyon was now a member of the SDF, he presumably felt entitled to take 'his' property with him!

Minutes of the King's Lynn
Independent Labour Party, 1906–1916[319]

1906

Meeting held at the Rechabite Hall, Coronation Square, on Sunday September 16th, to take steps to form a branch of the Independent Labour Party in King's Lynn.

<u>Present</u> Messrs T.A. Frost, M.J. Jackson, J.H. Jarvis, J.W. Mills, H.C. Shears, J.W. Spurling,[320] R. Bunnett,[321] F.W. White

Mr F.W. White in the Chair

Letters were read from:-

Mr Philip Snowden M.P. expressing regret at not being able to take part in Inaugural Meeting of the New Branch but would be pleased to visit Lynn at a convenient date.[322]

Com. J. Parker M.P. of Halifax stating his willingness to speak at a Meeting on either 8th or 9th of October.[323]

---

319 NRO, SO 297/5.

320 John William Spurling: founder member of Lynn ILP October 1906, and one of the eleven members of the party at the time of its dissolution in 1916. Address in 1916: Queen's Avenue, Lynn. According to the 1911 census, he was a letter press printer.

321 Robert Bunnett (1870–1952), railway signalman: beginning as a lad porter in 1888, he was soon promoted to signalman and worked continuously for the MGN Joint Railway until his retirement in December 1935. Member of ASRS from 1892. He was on the LRC 1903. Founder member of Lynn ILP October 1906. He became one of Labour's earliest councillors in Lynn on his election to South Ward in 1919: at the time, he was secretary of Lynn Branch of NUR and involved in a railway strike, as was his fellow candidate, John Raby, then chairman of the Branch. Bunnett was deputy mayor in 1935–36, and mayor in 1945, serving for two successive years. He last attended a meeting of Lynn Borough Council on 11 December 1952, his 82nd birthday: he died on 30 December 1952. See Raby, *Allotted Span*, 55–7, 76–7.

322 Philip Snowden had been elected for Blackburn in the 1906 general election.

323 James Parker (1863–1948), secretary, Halifax branch of ILP from 1895, later member of ILP Administrative Council and of Labour Representation Committee. Elected to Halifax Council in 1897, and Labour MP for the town from 1906. Given special responsibility for

The Secretary of the Norwich I.L.P. to arrange for a Lantern lecture by Com. Gavan Duffy in connection with other towns in this District.[324] The Secretary was instructed to reply that at present the Branch could not entertain the offer.

It was proposed Comrade J. Mills seconded by Com. H. Shears that a Branch of the Independent Labour Party be formed in Lynn, and carried unanimous.[325]

Proposed by Com. Frost seconded by Com. Jarvis that J.W. Spurling be appointed Secretary (pro tem) and carried.

Proposed by Com. Bunnett seconded by Com Spurling that Com. M.J. Jackson be Chairman of the Branch, and carried.

Com. Mills stated that the Socialist party were desirous of joining the I.L.P. but could not do so until relieved of their liability respecting the Rechabites Hall, where after discussion thereon it was proposed by Com. Jackson seconded by Com. Shears and agreed "That the I.L.P. take over the Hall from September 29th next.

Proposed by Com. Jackson seconded by Com. Bunnett "That a Public Meeting to inaugurate the New Branch be held on October 8th providing the Central Hall is clear on that date, and that the Secretary make the necessary arrangements.

The Sec. was instructed to write Mr Will Thorn M.P.[326] and Com Withard of Norwich to assist at the Meeting.[327]

M. J. Jackson

---

the Eastern Counties by ILP in 1907. Like the Norwich MP George Roberts, he was forced to leave the ILP after taking a ministerial position in the coalition government, 1917.

324 Thomas Gavan-Duffy (1867–1932), general secretary of Cumberland Iron Miners' Association from 1907. Author of Socialist tracts such as *The Merchant Shipping Bill, a Liberal fraud* (ILP, not dated) and *The Labour Party in Parliament* (The National Labour Press, not dated); MP Whitehaven 1922–24.

325 The ILP branch in Yarmouth was founded at almost the same time, following a public meeting in the town on 18 August 1906. (The Norwich branch had been founded over a decade earlier, in 1894).

326 Correctly Will Thorne (1857–1946), founder of the Gasworkers' Union and MP for West Ham from 1906.

327 Correctly Herbert Witard (1873–1954), member of Socialist League, founder member of the Norwich ILP 1894, its first member on the City Council 1903, led the anti-war party in the city during First World War. Norwich Radical newspaper *Daylight* said of him: 'there is nothing of the fire-eater or anarchist about Mr Witard: he is a well-informed unassuming man of the better class artisan type' (*Daylight*, 28 Nov. 1903). Stood unsuccessfully for Parliament in Norwich 1918 and 1922 (defeated both times by former Labour M.P. George Roberts). The first Labour Lord Mayor of the City (in 1927). Created national headlines in 1936 for his claim to have seen a sea serpent while walking with friends on Eccles beach!

Meeting held Monday September 24th in the Rechabites Hall at 8.30 p.m. Com. M.J. Jackson in the chair.

Minutes of Meeting held Sunday Sept 16 were read and confirmed.

Letters were read from Mr W. Thorn M.P. regretting his inability to be present at Inaugural Meeting of the Branch, from Com. Harry Lowerison expressing his intention to be present, from Com Witard who is unable to be present and from Com. J. Parker fixing date of meeting.

Proposed by Com. Frost seconded by Com. White that the Secretary book the Central Hall for Tuesday October 9th.

The Secretary was instructed to have 50 posters, 5000 Handbills, and Reserved Seat tickets printed, wording to be decided by the Chairman & Secretary.

The Secretary was asked to write the Secretary of the I.L.P. (Mr Johnson) asking for aid from the Central Fund.[328]

Thos. A. Frost

Minutes of Meeting held Sunday Sept 30/06 at Rechabites hall. Com. Thos. A. Frost in the chair. Minutes of Meeting held Sept 24 read and confirmed.

Letters were read from Mr P Snowden, stating that it is impossible for him to give us a date at present, but will try to do so at a future time, from Mr Mould, Peterboro I.L.P. stating that they could not arrange a meeting on Monday October 7th for Mr Parker.

It was proposed by Com Allen and seconded by Com Lock, & carried that the Branch meet every Sunday Evening at 7 oclock and every Thursday evening at 8 oclock.

Com Frost offered to provide Hospitality to Com J Parker on the occasion of his visit to Lynn, which was accepted with thanks.

It was agreed that a Meeting be held on Sunday Evening next to make final arrangements for Inaugural Meeting.

Subscriptions received 4/- Sale of Cards 8d.

Thos. A. Frost

Meeting held Sunday October 8th 1906 at the Rechabites Hall. Com Thos. A. Frost in the Chair. Minutes of Meeting held Sept 30th Read and Confirmed.

Arrangements were made for Public Meeting and Collectors appointed.

Secretary was authorised to have 300 copies of Circular appealing for members printed.

---

328 Francis Johnson (1878–1970), general secretary of ILP, 1909–24.

Delegates for L.R.C. were appointed, Messrs White, Mills, Allen & Frost to act until December 31st 1906.

Com. Drew was appointed Collector

Com. Dorer was appointed Treasurer

It was agreed that a Programme for the winter Session be drawn up and Printed.

Cash received Subs 1/6 cards 3d.

M.J. Jackson

Meeting held Sunday October 14th 1906 at Rechabites Hall, Coronation Square. Com. M.J. Jackson in the Chair. Minutes of Meeting held October 8th read and adopted.

The Branch Secretary presented accounts of the Inaugural Meeting, which were passed and submitted to the Head Office.

Moved by Com. Dorer seconded by Com. Pooley, and carried, "that The Branch adopt no 1 to 15 of the Model Rules with the addition that the Lecture Secretary and *Collector* be ex-officio members of Committee.

The following Officers were elected to serve until the Annual Meeting in March 1907

    Chairman:- M.J. Jackson

    Treasurer:- A.L. Dorer

    Lecture Secretary:- J.C. Triance

    Collector:- R.G. Drew

    Auditors:- T.A. Frost and J.T. Neave

    Committee:- R Bunnett, T. Castleton, F.W. White, J. Pooley.[329]

    Trustees:- F.W. White and J.T. Neave

The Election of Secretary was postponed until next Meeting.

It was agreed that the Branch meet on Thursday evening next, October 18, to discuss November election and take steps to further the Candidature of Com. Jackson, Candidate for the North Ward.[330]

Cash received Subs 1/-. Cards 6d. Hire of Hall 5/-. Literature 2d. Tickets 2/6.

M.J. Jackson

---

329 Thomas Castleton, born 1876, a baker at Keppel Street in 1881, in 1921 an engine driver living in Beulah Street, Gaywood. A 'G Castleton' is recorded in the subscription book as a founder member of Lynn ILP but is noted as having resigned, and never in fact paid a subscription: Thomas had an elder brother George, born 1871, so perhaps both men were members of the party, even if briefly.

330 He did stand, the only Socialist candidate to fight in the 1906 municipal election: He came bottom of the poll with 206 votes, the local Liberal newspaper lamenting 'the split in the Progressive forces in the North Ward' (*LN*, 3 Nov. 1906).

Executive Meeting held Thursday November 15/06

Present Messrs Dorer, Drew & Spurling.

The Secretary read a letter from the General Secretary, stating that the Organising Comtee had agreed to contribute £2 towards cost of Inaugural Meeting.

Read a letter from the Norwich Branch asking this Branch to try and arrange for a Lantern Lecture by Com. Gavan Duffy in February next.

Read a letter from the Peterboro' Branch requesting this Branch to furnish them with a speaker for the first Sunday in December. It was agreed that Com. Allen be asked to take the appointment.

It was agreed that a Meeting of the Members of the Branch be called for Thursday November 22nd, and that the two first mentioned letters be brought up for consideration.

M.J. Jackson

Meeting of Members held Thursday November 22nd/06 at the Rechabites Hall, Coronation Square. M.J. Jackson Chairman.

Minutes of Meeting held October 14th read and adopted.

Minutes of Executive Meeting held November 15/06 read and adopted.

The Secretary explained the Financial position of the Branch, it was agreed that all members ~~be~~ as can be asked to pay for a years Subs in advance to meet present liabilities.

It was agreed on the motion of Com. Dorer seconded by Com ~~Mills~~ Neave that, commencing with the New Year, the Meetings of Branch be advertised on Handbills, 4 subjects on each.

Secretary read an offer from the Secretary of the Norwich I.L.P. of special terms for a Lantern Lecture by Com. Gavan Duffy. When, after discussion, it was proposed Com Neave seconded by Com Allen and carried that the offer be not entertained.

It was agreed that the stock of Pamphlets be brought to the Hall, and offered for sale at all Meetings of the Branch., Com Gittings consenting to take charge.

It was agreed that the hall be decorated with Texts and Mottoes, and that Com. C. Gittings be authorised to procure material for same.

The Secretary was instructed to write the owners of the Hall, asking them to undertake the re-colouring of the Walls.

Com. Mills proposed that a list of Names be drawn up of members to undertake the opening of the Hall, each one to take a week in rotation, when after considerable discussion the matter was left in abeyance.

W.C. Gittings

<u>Executive meeting</u> held December 2nd/06 at the Old Liberal Club, Windsor Road. Present: M.J. Jackson (Chairman) Com. Pooley, Drew, Spurling
The Secretary stated the terms on which Com White was prepared to let the Old Liberal club to the I.L.P. when after discussion it was moved by Com. Pooley seconded by Com Drew, and agreed that the Committee recommend the Branch to rent that Hall, it being better suited to the requirements of the Branch.
Moved by Com. Drew, seconded by Com. Pooley and agreed "That a 'Banquet' be held early in the New Year.

W.C. Gittings

Meeting of Members held at Rechabite Hall, Coronation Square, on Thursday December 15th 1906. Com Gittings in the Chair.
Minutes of Meetings held Nov 22nd & Dec 2nd read & signed.
The Secretary stated the terms on which Com. White was willing to let the Clubroom in Windsor Rd., when after discussion it was agreed that the Secretary meet Com White and offer to take the Room at £1 per quarter from Dec 25th next until September 1907 all time not occupied by the Shepherds Friendly Society after which date to become sole Tenants at £7 per annum, and subject to these terms being suitable, to give notice to terminate the tenancy of Rechabites Hall on March 25th next.
It was agreed that Com Drew, Spurling & Mills be a Sub Committee to carry out arrangements for Supper & Social to be held on New Years Eve and that the Lady Members be invited to co-operate.

M.J. Jackson

Meeting of Executive held at the Club Room Windsor Road on Wednesday January 16th 1907. Com. M.J. Jackson in the Chair.
The Secretary submitted Books showing the Financial state of the Branch, it was agreed that a statement of liabilities be presented to Meeting of Members.
It was agreed that Affiliation Fees be paid on 33 members for 3 months.
It was agreed that the question of Monthly Socials be submitted to Members.
Agreed that Meetings of the Executive be held every alternate Monday evening from January 7th.

M.J. Jackson

Meeting of Members held at the Clubroom Windsor Road, on Thursday January 17th 1907 at 8 p.m. M.J. Jackson (Chairman) in the Chair. The Minutes of meetings held December 13th and January 15th 1907 read and signed.
The Secretary read a Statement showing the Financial position of the Party, when after discussion it was agreed that the Collector approach members

with a view to inducing them to pay their subscriptions in advance to meet pressing liabilities.

The attached Resolution which had been sent to the various local papers and public men interested in the Loke Road sale of town land was read out and approved.

'That the Lynn Independent Labour Party views with great disfavour the proposal brought before the recent meeting of the Lynn Council for the selling of public land situated along the Loke Road extension, and pledges itself to exert all possible influence to prevent the ratepayer's property being handed over to a few speculators or other private persons.

The Party recognising with thousands of our fellow countrymen that the great obstacle to housing and other reforms is the private ownership of land an obstacle as keenly felt in Lynn as elsewhere.

The Party also affirms its desire for the Town Council to have houses erected on the land in question with large gardens attached, let at reasonable rents, and the present open space used as a public playground not be built upon, but laid out in a proper manner as a Recreation Ground, the crowded condition of the locality badly needs one.'[331]

The question of cleaning and opening the Club Room was discussed, when it was agreed that a list of Comrades willing to take weekly turns be drawn up, the following volunteering for the first month

Commencing Jan 20 – Com. Jackson
          ″   27 – Com Mills
      Feb 3 – Com White
      Feb 10 – Com Locke

Also that the Room be thoroughly cleaned at intervals, the Secretary and Com. White to engage a suitable person for that purpose to be paid from the funds of the Party.

It was agreed that Monthly Socials be held, and that Com Allen & Gittings be a Sub Committee to make necessary arrangements.

It was agreed that Com. G. Allen be Secretary of this Branch, with Com. J.W. Spurling Assistant Secretary.[332]

M.J. Jackson

---

331 The Council planned to extend Loke Road, North Lynn, and auction the adjacent open land as building plots (*LN*, 12, 19 Jan., 16 Feb. 1907). The *LN* (19 Jan.) published a letter by Jackson opposing the selling of public land on Loke Road.

332 The *Labour Leader* (26 Oct. 1906) listed Lynn ILP as a new branch, leaving the name of the Secretary blank. The Secretary's name was later given as G[eorge] Allen (*Labour Leader*, 25 Jan. 1907).

Meeting of Executive, held at the Labour Club Windsor road on Monday January 28th/07. Present M.J. Jackson (Chairman) Comrades Dorer, White, Allen, Drew & Spurling. Minutes of Executive meeting held Jan 16th were read.

The Secretary produced receipts for payment of Affiliation fees 8/5, Membership Cards 3/9

A letter was read from Com. Frost, Secretary of L.R.C. crediting the Branch with £1.

It was agreed that a Meeting of Members be held on Sunday February 3rd at 6.30

The Secretary reported that there were several vacancies of on the Executive, it was agreed that Com. Fox be nominated.[333]

Com. Dorer read a letter from Com. Day of Norwich, offering to come to Lynn and speak on Poor law work, it was agreed that it be left to Com. Dorer to fix suitable date, convenient to both parties.[334]

It was agreed that the following names be submitted to the next Meeting of members to be nominated as candidates for the forthcoming Election of Guardians.

South Ward:- J. Mills and F. White.

St Margarets:- M.J. Jackson & G. Allen

Recommended that a charge of 1d a week be made for all members using the Club.

Agreed that Handbills be printed announcing Public Meeting to be held during February

Com. G. Allen's offer of Hospitality to Mr White of Nottingham when visiting Lynn was accepted with thanks.[335]

M.J. Jackson

---

333 Percy Edward Fox, born 1877, coal merchant, 5 Diamond Street, Lynn. He joined Lynn ILP in 1906–07 (along with his brother Cecil, born 1878, of the same address, locomotive fireman, who, however, is not mentioned in these minutes).

334 H. A. Day, a Norwich manufacturer, stood for Norwich city council in Heigham ward as Fabian Society 'Progressive Working Man's Candidate' in 1897; elected to Norwich City Council as a Liberal in 1900, but moved to the ILP; supported Roberts as the Labour candidate in the 1904 Parliamentary by-election (Cherry, *Doing Different*, 47, 70, 80).

335 John Thomas White (1871–1932), railway engineer stoker, official of ASRS and ILP member of Sandiacre council. See Nottingham press, e.g. *Nottingham Journal*, 25 Nov. and 6 Dec. 1907. His talk at Lynn was entitled 'The English Revolution': during it he 'endeavoured to explain' the difference between the ILP and the SDF (*LN*, 23 Feb. 1907).

Meeting of Branch held Sunday February 3rd 1907 at the Labour Club, Windsor Road. Com. M.J. Jackson in the Chair. Minutes of Meeting held January 17th and Executive Meeting held January 28th/07 Read and confirmed.

The Secretary was instructed to write Com. Frost thanking him for contribution of £1 to the Branch. Com. P. Fox was elected a member of Executive.

Com. Dorer read a letter from Com. Day of Norwich offering to Address a Meeting in Lynn on March 4th next. Subject:- Board of Guardians, what they do and what they may do. It was agreed that the offer be accepted with thanks.

It was agreed that Comrades M.J. Jackson and G. Allen (St Margarets) J. Mills and F. White be the I.L.P. candidates for the ensuing Election of Guardians for King's Lynn and the Secretary was instructed to forward these names to the Secretary of the Labour Rept. Committee.[336]

The Sub-Committee reported that they had arranged for a Social to be held on Thursday evening February 7th.

It was agreed that Smoking be prohibited at all Public Meetings, and that members be requested to observe this Rule.

The Executive recommendation that 1d per week be charged all members using the Club was discussed, when it was agreed that:- "That all members using the Club be invited to pay 1d a week towards the heavy expenses of maintaining same, and that the Collector (Com. Drew) collect same.

The Secretary reported that he had remitted £1/1/0 to the Special Effort Fund.

J. Pooley

Meeting of the Executive held Monday Feb 11/07 at the Labour Club, Windsor Road. Com. M.J. Jackson in the Chair. Comrades Dorer, Allen, Drew & Spurling.

Minutes of Meeting held Monday January 28th were read.

Public Meeting to be held Sunday Feb. 17th, addressed by Mr J.T. White. Agreed that Advt be put in Lynn News. That Com. M.J. Jackson be Chairman.

Agreed that February 24th be fixed for Mr H. Lowerison's Lecture on the "Artist and the Workman."

---

336 In the event, the Committee put up three men for each ward under the label 'Labour', the four named here plus Furbank (St Margarets) and Bunnett (South): none was successful. Furbank was not a member of the ILP, but a leading light in the Co-operative Society: see above, notes 49 and 97.

The following Names of New Members were submitted and accepted
E Seamer. C. Ducker. J. Wells. Stewart. A. Sporne. G. Mann and W. Woods.[337]
G. Mann and W. Woods[*sic*]
The Secretary reported that he had paid the Rent of Rechabites Hall for the
Christmas Quarter £2/15/0
Com. P. Fox stated that he could not accept office on Executive.
Agreed that Weekly Lectures be held at the Club Room Windsor Road
every Wednesday evening commencing February 20th on Socialism. The
following preliminary programme was drawn up:

   Feb.   20th   Com. Mills:-   "Socialism, what it is and what it is not".
     "   27th   Com. White:-   "Some objections to Socialism answered".
   March 6th   Com. Spurling:- "The I.L.P. what it stands for".
     "   13   Com. Dorer:-   "Poverty, its cause and cure".
     "   20   Com. Allen:-

                                       A.L. Dorer Feb.25/07/ J. Pooley

Meeting of Executive held Monday February 25th at the Labour Club,
Windsor Road. Present:- Com. A.L. Dorer in the Chair, Pooley, White and
Spurling.
Minutes of Meeting held February 11th read and signed.
The following new members were accepted: Mr Raby,[338] Mr Barnard,
Mr W Collier, Mr R Fraser, Mr Wellsman.[339]

---

337 Ernest G. Seamer, born 1872, steam engine turner, in 1911 living at Cresswell Street,
Lynn; C. Ducker, see above, note 316; James Mactarlane Wells, born 1875, locomotive
engine driver, Bara Terrace, South Lynn; Stewart not identified: appears in 1908–9 list of
members, but with no further details; Arthur Raymond Sporne, youngest child of William
and Hannah Sporne, born 1890. He was a keen swimmer, often mentioned in the local
press for his part in swimming galas. In 1911, he was an education student boarding in
Sheffield by which date he was no longer paying his subscription; William George Mann,
born 1874, railway engine driver, Wisbech road, Lynn; Walter Woods, born 1881, schoolmaster at Terrington St John.
338 John William Raby (1879–1951), joined locomotive department of Great Eastern
Railway 1894: he worked on the railways for 50 years, a member of ASRS and later
chairman of the Lynn branch of the NUR for 27 years. In 1911, living at Exton's Road,
Lynn. Raby was co-opted to the Borough Council for South ward in 1917, was elected in
1919, and was a member until 1949. He became the first Labour mayor of Lynn in 1927–28,
and served again as mayor in 1935–36; his obituary calls him 'the chief architect of the
workers' political and trade union movement in the Lynn District' (*LA*, 26 Oct. 1951). In
late life, he wrote a series of reminiscences for *LN*, published as *King's Lynn Portraits* (King's
Lynn, 1949), and in expanded form as *The Allotted Span in King's Lynn* (King's Lynn, 1950).
339 Barnard not certainly identified and does not appear in 1908–09 list of members,
probably Ernest Barnard, born 1879, in 1911 living at 38, South Everard Street, no
occupation given, in 1921 described as 'invalid', his father John working as a scenic artist

Agreed that Affiliation Fees[340] for Jan & Feb be paid.

A letter was read from the secretary of the Norwich I.L.P. asking this Branch to send a Delegate to a Conference of Eastern Counties Branch with a view to forming an Eastern Counties Federation. It was agreed that the Branch be advised to send a Delegate with power to act.

It was agreed that the question of the Easter Conference of I.L.P.,[341] Ballot for the N.A.C., and attendant Business be submitted to a Special meeting of the Branch.

Agreed that Special Meeting of the Branch be summoned for Sunday March 3rd @ 7 p.m.

Agreed that 1000 Handbills be printed to Advertise Com. Day's Meeting on March 4th, and that no Advt. be sent to Local Newspapers.

The Secretary announced that the attached Resolution had been forwarded to Local Newspapers together with Lieut Bellairs' reply.

To the Editor of the Lynn News

Sir,

OLD AGE PENSIONS

The following Resolution was passed at a meeting of the above Branch and forwarded to Lieut. Bellairs. Resolution That the Member for the Borough (Mr C. Bellairs) be asked to work strenuously for the passing, during the coming session of Parliament, of a scheme of Old Age Pensions that will give adequate support, free from any taint of pauperism, to our Veterans of industry on their reaching the age of 60. Our country was never more wealthy and the nation's financial prospects have never, probably, been so rosy as now, hence there is no just cause, why the present state pension list of over £9,000,000 per annum should not be extended and Old Age pensions granted to ordinary workmen, whose needs are even more than those of the Statesmen, Civil Servants, or Naval or Military Officers, who now receive pensions from public funds.

House of Commons Feb 13

Dear Sir, I am much obliged for your resolution, which has my cordial support. It is a great misfortune that so rich a country should be behind Germany in respect of old age pensions. Yours faith'y Carlyon Bellairs.

J. Pooley

---

for G. M. Bridges; William Michael Collier, born 1874, railway engine driver, member of ASRS from 1902, address Kitchener St, Lynn; Fraser, see above, Introduction, p. 8; George Wellsmann, born 1852, labourer on fruit farm, lived at Saddlebow.

340 Fees for affiliation to the ILP.

341 The ILP held a Conference every Easter, to which branches sent delegates. The 1907 Conference was held at Derby, Mills attending as the delegate for King's Lynn.

Special Meeting held Sunday March 3, 1907, at the Club Room, Windsor Road. Com. Pooley in the Chair.

Minutes of Meetings held Feb 3 and Executive Meeting held Feb 11th read and signed.

Sub-committee of Members were appointed to act with L.R.C. in forthcoming election of Guardians.

A Ballot was taken for appointment of Eastern Counties Delegate of N.A.C. with the following results:-

Stanton Coit.[342]	1
Davis.[343]	0
McMillan, Miss.[344]	1
Sanders.[345]	1
Witard	12
Total	15

Members present 16.

Agreed that the Annual Meeting be held on March 17th next.

After discussion it was agreed that Com. Mills be the Branch Delegate to the Easter Conference at Derby, and that he be given a "free hand" in the matter of voting, that the Branch pay the Conference Fee of 5/- all other expenses to be defrayed by the delegate.

The Secretary read a letter from the Norwich Secretary re suggested Eastern Counties Federation, and the Executive recommendation thereon, when it was agreed that the Branch be represented by Com. M.J. Jackson and Com.

---

342 Stanton George Coit (1857–1944), founder of Union of Ethical Societies, a predecessor of the British Humanist Association. He stood for Parliament for the ILP in 1906 and 1910 but was unsuccessful on both occasions. Strong campaigner for women's suffrage, though his motives were questionable, early suffragist Elizabeth Wolstenholme Elmy writing 'I do not wish to be unfair, but I cannot trust him. He seems to me more anxious to found a new sect, of which he shall be pope, than to do real service to humanity.' (Elizabeth Crawford, *The Women's Suffrage Movement: A Reference Guide 1866–1928* (London, 2000), 136).

343 William John Davis (1848–1934), brassmaker; chairman of Labour Representation Committee, 1902 (see Haworth and Hayter, *Men who made Labour*, 19); treasurer of Trades Union Congress, 1902–10; its president, 1913.

344 Margaret McMillan (1860–1931), educationalist, speaker and lecturer for ILP from 1893, based in Bradford, where she was first ILP member of the Bradford School Board, serving 1894–1902; moved to London 1903. Southern Division representative on the ILP NAC, 1906–09: her campaigning was an important factor in the passing of the 1906 Provision of School Meals Act. Later served on London County Council. See Carolyn Steedman, *Childhood, Culture and Class in Britain: Margaret McMillan, 1860–1951* (London, 1990).

345 Sanders, see above, note 290.

A. Dorer, with power to act. A further letter stating that the correct date was March 23ʳᵈ was read.

It was decided that Nominations be received for the various officers of the Branch before the Annual Meeting.

J. Pooley

Executive Meeting, held Monday Mch 11/07 at Club Room Windsor Road Present M.J. Jackson (Chairman), Messrs Pooley, Dorer, Drew, White & Spurling.

Minutes of Executive Meeting held February 25 were read.

The Secretary reported that he had paid Conference Fees 5/- and 4/6 for pamphlets, also that he had returned half the stock.

William E. Pye was recommended for admission to the Branch.[346]

The Agenda for Annual Meeting to be held on Sunday March 17ᵗʰ was drawn up and agreed to. The Secretary reported that Com. H. Lowerison had returned Railway expenses forwarded.

J. Pooley

Annual Meeting held at the Labour Club Windsor Road Sunday March 17ᵗʰ 1907 at 7 oclock. M.J. Jackson (President) in the Chair.

Minutes of Meetings held March 3ʳᵈ and 11ᵗʰ were read and signed.

The Secretary presented a Statement of Accounts for the preceding Five Months showing the Income of the Branch to be £16-11-2 and the Expenditure £15-13-2 leaving a Balance in hand of 18/-. The total Membership being 44. The Balance was adopted as presented.

The following officers were elected for the ensuing year:-

Chairman: J. Pooley
Secretary: J. Mills

Assistant Secretary: J.W. Spurling

Treasurer: A.L. Dorer

Executive: T.A. Frost; M.J. Jackson; W. Russell;[347] F.W. White

Delegates to L.R.C.: G. Allen; A.L. Dorer; T.A. Frost; J. Mills

Auditors: J. Neave & H.C. Shears

Collector: R. Drew

The question of the Tenancy of Club Room Windsor Road was discussed when it was moved by Com. Jackson that the Minute of December 13ᵗʰ,

---

346 William Ernest Pye, born 1882, railway siding foreman, 21 Hockham Street, South Lynn.

347 William Russell, listed as a founder member of Lynn ILP in October 1906, but does not appear among the subscribers in 1908–09. Probably William Russell, born 1873, letterpress printer, living at Earlscliffe, Tennyson Avenue, Lynn.

providing that we become sole Tenants after September 29th, be rescinded, which on being put to the meeting was declared lost.

The second Ballot for a Delegate to the N.A.C. for the Eastern Counties was taken, the names of candidates were Com Witard and Miss McMillan when the voting was as follows:-

Witard   12

Miss McMillan   7

The Asst. Secy. reported that the proposed Conference of Eastern Counties Branches had been postponed until April 6th.

Com. Dorer gave notice that he would move the following motion at the next Branch Meeting "That we take in Associates, not to be Members of the party, but to use the Club only, at 1d a week.

J. Mills/FW White

Executive Meeting held Monday Mch 25th at Labour Club Windsor Road. Present:- Messrs Dorer, Drew, Frost, Russell and Spurling.

Minutes of Executive meeting held Mch 11th were read.

A letter was read from the Norwich Secy stating that Miss McMillan was about to visit the Branch with a proposal to contribute to the expenses of an Organizer for Eastern Counties when after discussion Agreed that the Secretary write Com Holmes asking for particulars and the Branch's share of the Expenses.[348]

Com. C. Gittings promised to give a paper on the "Ethics of Socialism" on Sunday March 31st.

J. Mills

Executive Meeting held Monday Apl 8 1907. Present:- Com. Pooley (Chairman) Messrs Dorer, White, Mills, Russell, Drew and Spurling.

Minutes of Meeting held March 25th were read.

Agreed that Sunday April 21st be set apart for Com. Mills Report of Easter Conference of I.L.P. held at Derby.

Com. Dorer reported that he had attended the Conference of Eastern Counties Delegates held at Norwich, and that it had been decided to form a Federation of the Eastern Counties Branches. It was agreed that Com Dorer be asked to report to a meeting of members.

---

348 William 'Billy' Holmes, 'a socialist, gas-worker and ex-labourer'; stood unsuccessfully twice for Norwich Board of Guardians; elected to Norwich City Council in 1905, second ILP member of the council (after Witard); Eastern Counties Organiser for ILP from 1908. (Alun Howkins, *Poor Labouring Men: rural radicalism in Norfolk 1872–1923* (London, 1985), 99.)

The Secretary was instructed to forward the names of Com. Mills, Dorer and White as additional Speakers, in connection with the movement to reach outlying Districts.

The Secretary reported on the Financial position of the Branch.

It was decided that a Letter be sent to the "Lynn News" in answer to the false accusation recently published concerning the Branch.[349]

J. Mills

Executive meeting held at the Club Windsor Road May 6th 1907.

Com. J. Pooley (Chairman). Comrades Dorer, Frost, Drew, Mills, White, Russell and Spurling present.

Minutes of Meeting held April 8th were read.

The Secretary read correspondence from Com ~~Witard~~ \Cadman/,[350] Secretary of Eastern Counties Federation, containing List of Speakers, Constitution etc of Federation. The Secretary was instructed to answer same, and suggest that Meetings be arranged for Whit Sunday at Swaffham, Dereham or other suitable place near Lynn. It was agreed that the Subscription to Federation (5/-) be paid.

Agreed that the Secretary obtain 1 dozen copies of the I.L.P. Annual Report. Labour Newspapers. The following Resolution was submitted by Com. Dorer:- "That a Sub Committee be formed to formulate a scheme for the production of a Socialist newspaper in Lynn". After discussion it was agreed that:- Comrades Dorer, Frost, Russell & Spurling be a Sub-Committee for considering same.

The following New Members were accepted:

James Thurston, Wisbech Road. Proposed by T.A. Frost seconded by J. Pooley.[351]

H.E.B. Green, Bridge Road, Sutton Bridge. Proposed by F.W. White seconded by R. Fraser.[352]

---

349 When the ILP took over the old South Lynn Liberal club, other organisations that had held meetings there were unhappy: Mills confirmed to the local press that as the ILP had hired the Club for daily use, previous tenants would no longer be able to use it (*LN*, 13 Apr. 1907).

350 Henry Cadman, bandmaster, former starch-packer at Colman's Norwich, won seat on Norwich City Council 1907, becoming ILP political agent same year. Died 1935, Dorothy Jewson writing to his (second) wife that Cadman 'had so much insight and understanding of the Labour movement, for which he did so much' (NRO MC 2959, cited in F. Meeres, *Dorothy Jewson, suffragette and socialist* (Cromer, 2014), 88. Member of the Gasworkers and General Labourers' Union.

351 John Thurstan, born 1870, 'skilled labourer', according to 1911 census.

352 Henry E.B. Green, born 1887, elementary school teacher.

Executive Committee held May 16th at Labour Club Windsor Road. Com. J. Pooley Chairman. Com. Dorer, Drew, Frost, Mills, Spurling, Russell and White present.

Minutes of Meeting held May 6th read.

Letter was read from Eastern Counties Federation stating that they proposed to engage a speaker for propaganda work in the District and asking if the Lynn Branch could do with him for a meeting. Agreed that the Secretary write and accept his services for a Weekend if possible.

The Secretary stated that he had arranged with Com Payne of Banbury to give an Address on Friday May 17th at the Walks Gate, subject "Would Socialism be Practicable".[353] Com. F.W. White was selected to ~~ack~~ act as Chairman. Agreed that 1000 Handbills be printed.

The Secretary was instructed to order Half dozen I.L.P. Reports, also supply of New Pamphlets.

J. Mills

Executive Meeting held Monday June 3/07 at Labour Club, Windsor Road. Present:- Com J. Pooley (Chairman), A.L. Dorer, R. Drew, J. Mills, Russell, White & Spurling.

The Secretary read a letter from the Labour Party with Resolution on Old Age pension. Agreed that same be brought up for consideration at Branch Meeting.

The Secretary was instructed to write Eastern Counties Federation, asking if that body could arrange for an Autumn Demonstration to be held at Lynn, also to write to Mr Hudson M.P.[354] asking him to speak at a Meeting in October next.

Agreed that Sunday Evening Meetings be continued during June, Com. Mills promising to arrange Programme.

It was decided that a Branch meeting be held on Friday evening, June 7th @ 8 oclock.

---

353 Herbert Payne, ILP councillor in Banbury, 1906–17; led a successful campaign for council housing in the town, 40 houses being built in 1913. Herbert Payne Day was celebrated in Banbury in 2023.

354 Walter Hudson (1852–1935), MP for Newcastle-upon-Tyne from 1906. He was a railwayman and a full-time official of the ASRS. His work in Parliament included speeches on behalf of railway workers: his Private Members' Bill in 1906 formed the basis of the later Trade Disputes Act that reversed the Taff Vale judgement (in which the railway company had successfully claimed damages against the railwaymen's union). In Parliament, Hudson and fellow-railwayman MP George Wardle frequently found themselves opposing Richard Bell: see Bagwell, *Railwaymen*, 173, 236–9; Haworth and Hayter, *Men who made Labour*, 99–106, 207–12.

The following new members were accepted:-
Mr Stebbing (Prop) Com. White (Sec) Com Pooley.[355]
E Wanford Proposed Com White (Sec) Com Russell.[356]

J. Mills

Meeting of Members held Friday June 7th at Labour Club, Windsor Road. Com. J. Mills in the Chair. Minutes of Meeting held March 17th read and confirmed.

Minutes of Executive Committee read and confirmed.

Resolution in the name of Com. Dorer:- "That we take in Associates, not to be members of the Party, but to use the Club only, at 1d per week". Proposed by Com. Gittings, seconded by Com. Drew. After discussion thereon it was agreed that the matter stand over.

The Secretary submitted a Resolution from the Labour Party on Old Age Pensions when it was unanimously agreed that it be slightly altered, and forwarded to the Prime Minister and the Chancellor of the Exchequer.

A Letter was read asking the I.L.P. to arrange for a Meeting to be addressed by the Official Lecturer on \Anti/ Vivisection, when it was decided that the offer be not entertained.[357]

Proposed by Com. Drew, and seconded that we hold Educational Meetings during July and August once a month, after fully discussing the proposition it was proposed as an Amendment "that we hold a series of Outdoor Meetings, every Sunday during July and August, and that the Secretary write the Eastern Counties Federation thereon". The amendment was carried.

J. Pooley

Meeting of Executive held Monday June 17th 1907 at Com White's.

Present Com Dorer in the Chair, Comrades Frost, Mills, Drew, Russell, Spurling & White.

Minutes of last Meeting were read.

Read a letter from Com Cadman, Secretary of Eastern Counties Federation, asking the Branch to engage Organizer for the Week during August, when

---

355 Walter Stebbings, born 1885, of Keppel Street, later Edward Street, South Lynn, railway engine fireman, member of ASRS from 1907.

356 Albert Edward Wanford, born 1866, joiner, of Hockham Terrace, South Lynn. His name is listed in the subscription book covering October 1907 to March 1908, but it is crossed through and there is no record of any payments being made by him.

357 The National Anti-Vivisection Society had been founded in 1875 (as the Victoria Street Society, changing its name in 1897): the Society still flourishes today. Concern over animal welfare led to the Cruelty to Animals Act, 1876, which remained in force for the next 110 years.

it was proposed by Com. Mills seconded by Com Russell, and carried that we offer to engage Organizer for one week on the terms mentioned in letter. It was decided that we invite Com. Holmes, Myall, Dunnett, & W.R. Smith of Norwich,[358]and Fletcher Dodd of Yarmouth to speak at Outdoor Meetings during July.[359]

It was reported that Com Robert Blatchford, with Com. H. Lowerison of Ruskin School, would visit the Branch on Wednesday June 19th 1907, and it was decided that steps be taken to give them a cordial reception.

New member accepted:- A.S. Turbett prop. by Com. Mills seconded by Com White.[360]

Agreed that in future Executive Meetings be held at 8 oclock, instead of 9 as at present.

Executive Meeting held July 1st 1907, at Labour Club, Windsor Road.
Present: Com. White (in the Chair), Messrs Frost, Mills, Drew, Russell & Spurling.

Letter was read from secretary of Eastern Counties Federation asking for Financial Return etc. Agreed that same be sent.

The Secretary reported that Com. Coun. Holmes of Norwich would address Meetings at Lynn on July 13 and 14th.

A letter was read from Com. W.R. Smith of Norwich stating that he was unable to visit Lynn on July 13 and 14th.

The Programme for Outdoor Meetings was discussed when it was agreed that the Secretary write Com Fletcher Dodd of Yarmouth inviting him to speak at Lynn on July 7th, also Com. Sanders of London asking him to give names of Speakers.

---

358 Holmes, see above, note 348; Smith, see above note 193. Charles H. Myall and Arthur Dunnett were also prominent members of Norwich ILP: Myall was secretary of the Norwich Labor Church from its inception in January 1907, Dunnett (a shoe finisher by trade) was on Norwich City Council. Both were present at celebrations to mark the twelfth anniversary of the Norwich branch, attended by Philip Snowden (*EDP*, 11 Feb. 1907).

359 John Fletcher Dodd (1862–1952), a grocer by profession and founder member of the Yarmouth branch of the ILP in 1906: see Michael Wadsworth, 'The Independent Labour Party in Great Yarmouth 1906–14' *Yarmouth Archaeology*, 2006, 21–7. Best known for founding a holiday camp at Caister-on-Sea in 1906 to allow Londoners an opportunity to enjoy a cheap seaside holiday, supposed to be the first holiday camp in Britain. Dodd was teetotal and no alcohol was allowed in the camp. He served on Flegg Rural District Council and Board of Guardians between 1911 and 1914, and unsuccessfully contested East Flegg division (Norfolk County Council) for Labour in 1910 and 1913. In 1952, he returned to the Camp to celebrate his 90th birthday, dying in Tunbridge Wells 21 November (*EDP*, 8 Aug. 1952; *Daily Herald*, 22 Nov. 1952).

360 Alexander Stewart Turbett, railway engineer stoker, of Checker Street, South Lynn.

It was agreed that Meetings be held on Saturday Market, on Saturday evenings @ 8 oclock, Sunday Afternoon & Evening at the Walks Gates at 3.30 and 7.30 p.m.

Agreed that 1000 Handbills be printed announcing the Meetings when two speakers have accepted.

New Members

Mrs Belderson prop. Com Dorer. Seconded Com Mills.[361]

Mr R Timbey Sutton Bridge Lighthouse. Prop. Com. Green. Seconded Com Mills.[362]

Mr Housten Friday Bridge. Prop. Com. Mills, Seconded Com. Frost.[363]

Executive Meeting held July 22nd at Club, Windsor Road.

Present:- Com. Dorer in the Chair, Comrades Drew, Frost, Mills, White & Spurling.

Minutes of last Meeting read.

The Secretary reported on Financial position of the Branch.

The arrangement of Outdoor Meetings was discussed, when it was decided that in future Meetings be held at 11.15 and 7.30.

It was decided that a Meeting of Members be called for Saturday evening July 20th, to take into consideration the mode of procedure etc at Outdoor Meetings.

Appointment of Chairman was deferred until General Meeting.

J. Pooley

Minutes of Executive held Monday July 29th 1907.

Present Com. J. Mills (in the Chair), Messrs Dorer, Frost, Drew & Spurling.

Minutes of last Meeting were read.

The Secretary submitted list of Speakers willing to visit Lynn, and the dates offered, when it was agreed that a Programme be drawn up for August & September. The following dates & Speakers were arranged:-

Aug   4th Com Ives (Norwich)[364] Cancelled
  ″   6th Mr Allen (Norwich)
  ″   11th Com Myall (Norwich)

---

361 Rose Belderson, born 1870, wife of William Belderson, above note 72.

362 Robert Timby (so spelled in census returns), born 1891, labourer. (The lighthouse was one of two towers erected in 1829 at the then mouth of the river Nene. Timby's father worked on the river.)

363 Thomas Housden, (so spelled in census returns) of Friday Bridge, Elm, born 1867, general labourer according to 1901 census, fruit farmer according to 1911 census.

364 Not identified, not mentioned in Cherry, *Doing Different* , several possibilities in trade directories, census returns.

       " 18[365] Com Tilley (Boston)[365]
       " 25th Com Perriman (Ipswich)
Sept 1st Com A Carlyle Tait (Ilford)[366]
It was agreed that 1000 Handbills be printed to announce same.

J. Pooley

Executive Meeting held Monday Sept 1st/07 at labour Club, Windsor Road.

Present: Com. N. Drew (in the Chair), J. Mills, A.L. Dorer, Fred. White, T. Frost, J. W. Spurling.

Minutes of Executive Meeting held July 22nd were read.

It was agreed that the Outdoor Meetings be continued until the end of October and the secretary was instructed to try and provide Speakers.

The Secretary reported that Mr N Sanders[367] of the Fabian Society had written offering the services of two Speakers, Mr Francis Hyndman,[368] on October 27th and Dr Haden Guest,[369] on November 10th.

Agreed that a Tea and Whist Drive be held at an early date and that the Lady Members be asked to organize the Tea.

J. Pooley

---

365 George Hedley Tilley (1871–1954), boot maker. In 1907, he was living in Boston and actively promoting the Socialist cause. Between July and October alone, he wrote three letters to the *Boston Guardian*, and gave at least three talks. At one of these, he claimed that 85% of boots and shoes sold as being leather actually contained paper, a claim which can hardly have endeared him to employers! By 1911, he was back in Kettering (*Boston Guardian*, 27 Jul.–26 Oct. 1907, esp. 5 Oct.). Several letters survive from him to the Lynn Socialist group, in one of which (8 June 1906) he announces that he has formed a Pioneer Cycling Club in Boston (NRO, SO 297/9). In later life emigrated to Australia, where he died.

366 Andrew Carlyle Tait (b. 1878), was *c.* 1893–94, a clerk in the City of London at James Spicer & Sons, wholesale and export stationers, and was the son of a City bookseller (see M.Hulme, 'London Clerical Workers, 1880–1914', UCL PhD, 2003.).

367 Probably an error for W Sanders, see above, note 290.

368 (Hugh Henry) Francis Hyndman, born Calcutta, India, 1873. A cousin of Henry Mayers Hyndman, but Francis found expression for his Radicalism within the Liberal Party. An important figure in the League of Young Liberals and later the National Liberal Club. For nine months in 1905, he was prospective Parliamentary candidate for the Liberals in the constituency of South Kensington, but eventually retired in favour of another candidate 'owing to divisions among the Radicals'. A scientist, he wrote treatises on the subject, such as *Radiation,* published 1898.

369 Leslie Haden-Guest (1877–1960), doctor and socialist. Later (after the First World War) a member of London County Council and then a Labour Member of Parliament 1923–27 and 1937–50. Created a peer, 1950.

Executive Meeting held Monday September 15th at Labour Club Windsor Road.

Present Com. T. Frost Chairman, Messrs Dorer, Mills, Drew & Spurling.

Minutes of Executive Meeting held Sept 1st were read.

The Secretary read Letters from Mr Hyndman and Russell Smart.

Affiliation Fees for June, July & August amounting to 11/10 were paid.

Com. Dorer read manuscript of proposed pamphlet when it was decided that same be printed and offered for sale at One Penny each, and that a levy of 6d per Member be made to defray cost.

The Secretary reported that the total Income from the Outdoor Meetings was £2-10-0 and the Expenditure £2-11-5, leaving an adverse balance of 1/5.

		Receipts			Expenditure	
July		Holmes	Meeting	0-5-6	Expenses	0-6-6
"	29	Henderson's	do	7-6	do	--------
Aug	6	Allen's	do	2-7	do	6-6
"	11	Myall's	do	5-0	do	4-0
"	18	Tilley's	do	5-6	do	4-0
"	25	Perriman's	do	5-10	do	8-4
Sept	1	Tate's	do	11-0½	do	--------
do	16	Cadman's	do	4-7½	do	8-0
do	22	Ives	do	2-5	do	4-1
					Printing	3-6
					Postages	4-6
					Telegram	2-0
				£2-10-0		£2-11-5

J. Pooley

Branch Meeting held October 6th 1907 at Labour Club, Windsor Road.

J. Pooley (President) in the Chair.

Minutes of Branch Meeting held June 7th read and confirmed.

Minutes of Executive Meetings read and confirmed.

It was decided that Mr Francis Hyndman's Meeting be held in the Blackfriars Hall providing it can be obtained at a reasonable rent, and Com Fraser undertook to obtain all particulars and report to Executive Meeting. The Executive to make the necessary arrangements.

A letter was read from Com Fletcher Dodd offering to speak at Lynn in November, when it was decided to invite him for the 17th or 24th inst.

A letter was read from the N.A.C. stating that they would provide a Speaker for Autumn Demonstration, if one good enough to make the Meeting a success can be obtained.

<u>Winter Programme</u>. It was decided that a Programme be drawn up for 3 months ending January 1908, and that outside speakers be invited for Thursday evenings.

It was decided that a Discussion on Local Topics be held on Sundays October 13ᵗʰ and 20ᵗʰ, to be opened by Comrades Frost, White or Jackson. Circular Letter re Colne Valley Election was read.[370]

Com. Frost reported that he had the offer of a Billiard Table, when after discussion he was requested to obtain all particulars and if suitable to purchase same, the money to be raised by loans from the Members.

It was decided that a Subscription be got up for Com. Hedley Tilley of Boston who has been victimised for hold [*sic*] Socialist opinion. Com Frost undertook same.

Chairman F.W. White

Executive Meeting held October 7ᵗʰ 1907 at Labour Club, Windsor Road.
Meeting adjourned owing to particulars relating to Hire of Blackfriars Hall not being available.

The Assistant Secy (J N Spurling) asked to be relieved of his office at the end of October.

The pamphlet "How the Ratepayers Money is spent" was approved.[371] And placed on sale.

Executive Meeting held October 21ˢᵗ 1907 at Labour Club, Windsor Road.
Present. Com. J. Pooley (Chairman), Messrs Dorer, Mills, Russell, Drew, Jackson, Spurling, White.

The Secretary reported that the Meetings arranged to be held in the Blackfriars Hall were cancelled.

---

370 In 1903, a pact had been agreed between the Liberal Party and the Labour Representation Committee that Labour would be allowed a free run in some seats and allow the Liberals a free run in other seats. In the 1906 general election, 29 Labour MPs were elected, no fewer than 24 not being opposed by Liberals: these 29 then met and decided to form an independent Labour group in Parliament. The Colne Valley by-election of 1907 tested the viability of the Lib-Lab pact. Labour had not contested the seat in the 1906 general election, so should have left the running to the Liberals; however, the local party went against the wishes of the national Executive Committee and put up a candidate not on the official ILP list of candidates – Victor Grayson. Whereas most Labour candidates tended to be middle-aged union officials, he was only twenty-five: 'the charismatic Grayson stirred the constituency and he was followed everywhere by admiring crowds especially of young mill girls' (Pugh, *Speak for Britain*, 69). Grayson won by 153 votes (the mill girls, of course, however enthusiastic, did not have the right to vote). See also note 433 below.
371 An eight-page booklet, published by Lynn Labour Party. The full title was *Record, mark, learn: How the ratepayers money is spent in Lynn* (King's Lynn, 1908). There is a copy in the reference department of King's Lynn Library.

Com. Frost reported that he had purchased a Billiard Table and Marker Complete, on behalf of the Party for the sum of £8-1-6, the money being raised by loans from Members repayable from proceeds of the Table. The following Sub-Committee was appointed to draw up Rules for the Management of the Billiard Table G. Mann, T.A. Frost, J. Mills, M.J. Jackson.

It was agreed that a reply be sent to the Local Press in answer to a letter appearing in the Lynn News on Friday October 18, criticising Pamphlet issued by the Branch on "How the Lynn Ratepayers money is spent", a draft of same was submitted and approved.[372]

One Quarters Rent of Club Room £1 paid.

Branch Sub to L.R.C. £1 paid.

Gas Bill 4/11 paid.

The Secy reported that the Net profit of Tea held October 16 was 18/2.

Chairman F.W. White

Executive Meeting held December 15 1907 at Labour Club Windsor Road.[373]

Present Com. Dorer Chairman. Messrs White, Drew, Mills, Frost, Spurling.

Minutes of Meeting held October 7th read.

It was proposed by Com. Mills and carried that 20% of the Gross takings of the Billiard Table be taken by the Branch to defray expenses of Club.

The Secretary reported that the Total Receipts of Levy for pamphlet was £1-19-0.

The following are names of members who advanced the Money to purchase Billiard Table

Com Dorer, Angell,[374] Pye, Mann, Fox, Shears £1 each; White, Frost 10/- each; Mills 8/6.

---

372 The *Lynn News* published a long article referring to the publication by 'a Lynn Socialist Handful posing grandiloquently as the 'Independent Labour Party'. It stated that 'its arguments seemed to us so crude, narrow and one-sided that we did not deem the pamphlet worthy of serious notice', went through the pamphlet commenting on each paragraph, and concluded 'Is this what Socialism means? If so we don't want it'. (*LN*, 19 Oct. 1907: the paper does not appear to have published White's letter in response).

373 The minutes do not record that, perhaps on the strength of their pamphlet, the ILP put up one candidate in the municipal elections in November, M. J. Jackson in South Ward: he came bottom of the poll with 275 votes, including 189 plumpers. The successful Liberal candidate in the ward, Richard Green, was said by the local Liberal newspaper to have 'done more good for local workingmen than all the Socialists put together' (*LN*, 2 Nov. 1907).

374 William Robert Angell (1869–1950), railway accountant's clerk. In 1901, was living in Wootton Road, Gaywood; moved to New Hunstanton, *c*. 1906, still there at time of death. One of founding members of Lynn ILP, 1906.

The following were admitted as Members of the Party: S. Rout;[375] T. Hunt; H. Newell.[376]

F.W. White Chairman

Executive meeting held Monday March 2nd [*1908*] at Labour Club, Windsor Road.
Com. A.L. Dorer in the Chair. Present Com. White, Frost, Mills, Drew & Spurling.
Minutes of Executive Meeting held Dec 15 were read.
Read a letter from the Secretary of L.R.C. asking the Branch to nominate candidates for Municipal Elections. Decided that same be referred to Annual Meeting.
It was decided that the question of Summer work be brought up at the Annual Meeting.
The Secretary was instructed to write Com. Cadman of Norwich a letter of sympathy on the loss of his wife.[377]

F.W. White Chairman

Annual Meeting held March 22nd 1908, at Labour Club, Windsor Road.
Com. Pooley (Chairman) in the Chair.
The Chairman briefly summarised the years work.
The Minutes of last Annual Meeting were read and confirmed.
Minutes of various Executive Meetings read & confirmed.
The Asst. Secretary (J.W. Spurling) presented a Statement of Accounts and Report of the years work, which showed that the Branch had made substantial progress. The Membership had increased from 44 to 64 Members.
The total receipts for the year amounted to £29-19-11½
And the expenditure to   £26-16-07½
Leaving a balance in hand of   £3-3-4
The Balance was adopted as presented on the Motion of Com. White.
It was agreed that a letter be sent to Comrades Fraser and Shears who have left the town, expressing the regret of the Branch at their loss, and good wishes for their future prosperity.

---

375 Sidney (sometimes spelled Sydney) Rout, born 1883. Listed in 1910–11 subscription list as living at 12, Gladstone Road, the same address as Percy Storer (see below, note 399); not listed in 1901 or 1911 censuses, so occupation not known. In 1912 he married Annie Elizabeth Skerrit in All Saints church, South Lynn. In the 1939 register his occupation is given as bookbinder.
376 Harry Newell, born 1872, railway engine driver, member of ASRS from 1896, address: Wisbech Road South Lynn.
377 Margaret Aileen Cadman (1860–Jan. 1908). Cadman later remarried.

Com. Mills presented a Statement of the Receipts of Billiard Table, which showed Receipts £5-4-0, Paid back to Subscribers £3-10-0, handed to Branch Secretary 13/-, leaving 19/- in hand.

Com. Dorer reported on the work of the Eastern Counties Federation, and stated that an Organizer for the Eastern Counties would be engaged for the following Summer, and the Annual Demonstration hel would be held at Lowestoft this year.

Election of Officers:- the following were elected for the various offices for the ensuing year:

President: F.W. White

Treasurer: A.L. Dorer

Secretary: J. Mills

Asst. Sec.: W.E. Pye

Collector: R. Drew

Executive: J.W. Spurling; M.J. Jackson; J. Pooley; Thos. A. Frost

Labour Representation Committee Delegates: G. Allen; A.L. Dorer; Thos. A. Frost; J. Mills.

Eastern Counties Federation Delegate: A.L. Dorer

Special Ladies Committee: [blank]

Auditors: J. Neave and F. Hall

A letter was read from the Secretary of the L.R.C. was read asking the Branch to submit names of candidates for future elections, when after discussion it was agreed that the names of Comrades F.W. White and J. Mills be submitted.

The Ballot was taken for Eastern Counties Representative on the N.A.C. when a unanimous vote was accorded to G.H. Roberts,[378] 20 in all.

Agreed that the question of a Delegate to the Easter Conference of the Independent Labour Party be left to the Executive.[379]

It was agreed that steps be taken to hold a Demonstration in Kings Lynn in the Autumn, with Com. Philip Snowden as the speaker if same can be arranged.

A letter was read from the I.L.P. asking the numbers of members who would be present at the great meeting to welcome home Com. Keir Hardie from his world tour at the Albert Hall, London.[380]

---

378 Roberts had been elected Labour MP for Norwich in 1906. As the only Labour Member of Parliament in East Anglia, it is perhaps surprising he is not mentioned more often.

379 The Conference was held at Huddersfield, 19–21 April: no delegate was sent from King's Lynn.

380 Keir Hardie's health broke down in 1907 and a long sea voyage was decided upon. He left Liverpool in July, visiting Canada, India, Australia, New Zealand and South Africa.

<u>New Member</u>, proposed by Com Allen, seconded by Com. Mills and accepted: Mr Ridley.[381]

F.W. White Chairman

Executive Meeting held at the Labour Club, Windsor Road, March 30th '08. Present Com F.W. White (Chairman) Comrades Frost, Mills and Pye.

The Secretary was instructed to write various speakers for summer outdoor meetings.

It was decided to have a "Social" on either April 8th or Good Friday date & programme to be arranged by Ladies' Committee.

New Members. 2 new members proposed by Comrade Mills & accepted. Mr & Mrs H Hall Broad Street.[382]

F.W. White Chairman

Branch Meeting held at the Labour Club Windsor Rd Sunday April 26th '08. Comrade F.W. White in the chair.

It was decided to form committees to watch local municipal affairs & also for propaganda. The committees formed as under:

Propaganda Committee, Comrades Jackson, White, Mills & Pye, Mills Convening Secretary

Poor Law Committee, Comrades White, Mills & Allen, Convening Secretary Comrade Allen.

Town Council, Comrades Frost, Jackson, Dorer, Allen & Spurling, Convening Secretary Dorer.

It was also decided that the first Thursday in each month be summoned Branch meeting.

F.W. White Chairman

Executive Meeting held on Monday 27/4/08 at Comrade White's house. Comrade White President. Present Comrades White, Frost, Dorer, Spurling, Drew, Mills & Pye.

He returned to England in March 1908 to a triumphant welcome – 'the meeting at the Albert Hall, London, was remarkable for size and enthusiasm, and the recipient of so much adulation might have been pardoned if he had succumbed, if only temporarily, to the disease known as "swelled head"' (Stewart, *Hardie*, 260).

381   George Ridley, born 1888, a railway clerk and union official: unlike most of the Lynn Party members he was not a member of ASRS but of the Railway Clerks' Association: Ridley was the Eastern Counties representative on their General Executive. He played an important role in the Party as shown by frequent references in the minutes. In a testimonial of 1912, he is described as 'a ready and effective speaker' (NRO, SO 297/24). In 1919, he married Ethel Sporne in King's Lynn St Margaret church.

382   William Henry Hall, born 1869, builder and contractor, and his wife Margaret, also born 1869. By the time of the 1911 census they had moved to Valinger's Place.

It was decided to have a Social in about a fortnight's time, the Secty to make necessary arrangements.

Outdoor Speaking. It was decided to engage speakers for June, & write Fletcher Dodd & Comrade Cadman to confirm dates for visiting Lynn.

The Secretary was instructed to write Comrade Cadman & suggest that the Eastern Counties organiser visit Lynn the last fortnight in July commencing July 19th.

National Speaker for the Autumn. The Secy was instructed to write Comrade Cadman & ask whether he will obtain same or leave it to us.

East Anglian Federation. It was proposed by Comrade Dorer & seconded by Comrade Frost that an amendment to Clauses 6 & 7 relating to Officers & Executive & Auditor be submitted from this branch, which was agreed to. It was proposed that Comrades Dorer & Pye be the representatives from this branch, with Comrades Frost & Spurling as reserve, which was agreed to.

Caister Camp.[383] A letter was read from Comrade Cadman suggesting an outing to the Camp from the branches on either Saturday August 15th or 22nd, the secretary was instructed to write favouring the idea but supporting one Sunday.

Branch Meetings. Proposed by Comrade Drew & seconded by Comrade Mills that subsequent meetings be held \recommended to be held/ on Mondays, this was agreed to.

It was decided that Comrade Dorer be a member of the Propaganda Committee.

25 posters "What is Socialism" have been purchased by the branch cost 4/- & are being posted on the different hoardings in the town, several members offering to defray the expenses of posting & renewing.

F.W. White Chairman

Executive meeting held on Monday May 11th at Comrade White's house.

Present Comrades Dorer, Spurling, Mills, Drew & Pye. Comrade Drew presided.

Minutes of last meeting read & confirmed.

The Secretary reported that the Social decided upon at the last executive meeting was abandoned due to lack of response from the members.

Comrade Dorer reported the annual demonstration of the East Anglian I.L.P. Federation was to be held on June 28th /08 on which date he would be unable to attend.

The Secretary read a later from Comrade Cadman offering the services of J. Parker M.P. in Oct, & was instructed to reply asking for a speaker who

---

383 See above, note 359.

had not previously visited Lynn, & also to say that we were unable to pay
the £2 per meeting required.

Letters were read from Comrades Dodd & Cadman confirming their visits
on May 31st & July 12th respectively, & also from the P'bro & Ipswich
Branches offering outdoor speakers for summer propaganda.

Fredk.Wm.White Chairman

Executive meeting held on Monday May 25th 08 at Comrade White's house.
Present Comrades White, Dorer, Pooley, Mills, Drew Spurling, Frost &
Pye. Comrade White presided.

Minutes of last executive meeting were read & confirmed.

It was decided to print 1,000 handbills advertising the June outdoor
meetings, Comrade Spurling to get the printing done.

Communications were read from Comrades Holmes & Henderson offering
to speak at Lynn later. It was decided that Comrade Pooley take the chair on
May 31st for the first outdoor meeting, or in his unavoidable absence either
Comrade Mills or White.

Arrangements were made with regard to the hospitality for the Speakers up
to & including July 12th /08. June 14 Hall or White; June 21 White; June
28 Mills; July 5 Frost; July 12 White.

Proposed by Comrade Frost & seconded by Comrade Drew that the club be
thoroughly cleaned, Comrade White to arrange for this to be done.

Comrade Dorer made a statement anent the constitution of the Eastern
Counties I.L.P. Federation, showing that the Norwich branch had 6
representatives on the executive which was unpopular as it gave them a
majority, & that there was a proposal to amend the constitution so that
not more than one member of a branch may have a seat on the executive
committee, total of which to be not more than 12, and that it was essential
that our two delegates go to Lowestoft on June 28th /08.

F.W. White Chairman

Branch meeting held on Sunday May 31st at the Labour Club, Windsor Road
to meet & welcome Comrade H.E. Witard, Eastern Counties Organiser.
Com. F.W. White presided, small attendance.

Comrade Witard gave some useful hints as to how our propaganda can be
made successful, inter alia he advised that we elect ladies to any committees
that are formed, give each member a street to keep well supplied with
literature, & have candidates before the public long before any election takes
place, & also that each member supplies him with the names & addresses of
any sympathisers with the view of them becoming paying members.

A Resolution was unanimously carried that the meeting protests against
the visit of the King to the Czar of Russia, at such a time when so many

\members/ of the late Duma are either exiles or incarcerated in fortresses, it was left to Comrades Dorer & Pye to draw the resolution up & forward it to the proper quarters, & to the press.[384]

F.W. White Chairman

Executive meeting held at Comrade White's house London Rd on June 9th /08.

Present Comrades White, Drew, Mills & Pye. Comrade White presided.

Minutes of last executive meeting & branch meeting of 31st ulto read & confirmed.

The \assistant/ Secretary read a letter from Comrade Cadman offering Alderman Sanders L.C.C. as an autumn speaker, & was instructed to decline as we have in view the organising of an Autumn demonstration with a prominent M.P. as speaker.

The secretary reported that he had had a visit from the Chief Constable with regard to our meetings at the Walks Gates as the Free Church council[385] were also desirous of holding open air meetings there, & it was decided to meet the F.C.C. with regard to dates & ask permission of the Chief Constable to meet on the Green in the Broad Walks.

Pro. Mills Sec. Drew that we purchase a portable platform for outdoor propaganda meetings & invite subscriptions to defray the cost & also make enquiries with regard to the cost of a small banner with "Socialism" diagonally, white letters on red. Carried.

It was unanimously decided that we recommend to the branch that members be invited to contribute a minimum of 1s per month to an election fund.

A.L. Dorer Chairman

Executive meeting held at Com. White's house on June 22nd /08.

Present Coms Dorer, Mills, Frost, Spurling, Drew & Pye. Comrade Dorer presided.

Minutes of last executive meeting read & confirmed.

Proposed by Comrade Dorer & seconded by Com. Spurling that the lady members of the branch make a banner. Carried. The Asst Secy read a letter from Comrade Witard, Eastern Counties organiser, asking for alternative dates to be sent to Lowestoft by our delegates. \Sent/. July 19th & following fortnight or last week in Aug & first in Sept, also last week in October.

---

384 On 9 June 1908, King Edward VII became the first-ever British monarch to visit Russia, meeting Tsar Nicholas II, to whom both he and his wife Alexandra were related.

385 Local branch of the Free Church Council, created to explore common ground amongst the various Nonconformist churches; see E. K. H. Jordan, *Free Church Unity: history of the Free Church Council Movement 1896–1941* (London, 1956).

New Members. Prop. Mills Sec. Drew that Henry Crowe be admitted a member.[386] Carried.

Comrade Dorer then gave our delegate a few suggestions with regard to the constitution of the Fed to come up at the conference at Lowestoft.

John Pooley Chairman

Branch meeting held at the Labour Club, Windsor Road July 6th /08, Comrade Pooley presiding.

Minutes of last branch meeting & executive meetings read & confirmed.

Proposed Com Dorer, Sec Com Mills That we confirm the action of calling the meeting of protest & passed a resolution That we protest against the Borough Surveyor's salary being increased seeing that the application of lowly paid workmen have been refused. Carried.

Comrade Frost gave his report of the Conference of the East Anglian Federation held at Lowestoft 27/6/08.

Organisers visit. Comrade Dorer suggested that a meeting be held on Sunday morning July 19th to meet the organiser at the club & also that we have a morning meeting at the North End, & that the Asst Secy write Comrades Green, Sutton Bridge, Fox, Downham, Walker, Wisbech, & Lowerison, Heacham with regard to the organisers visit to those places, that we have 6 meetings in Lynn & 4 out during the fortnight. Accommodation to be left to the E.C.

Outdoor Propaganda. Pro. Mills Sec. Frost that members meet at the Club ¼ hr before the meeting. Carried.

The Asst Secy asked for volunteers from the members who would make themselves responsible for at least one Sunday for certain duties with regard to the successful carrying out of our outdoor meetings, viz chairman, collector, & also someone to take the platform down to the pitch &c but met with no response. The Asst Secy & volunteered [sic] to take up the Sunday morning collection & the rest of the work was left to chance.

Sunday morning meetings. Proposed Com Mills Sec. Com Drew That Sunday morning meetings at the Walk's Gates be abandoned after next Sunday. Carried by 4 to 1, 7 members neutral.

It was decided that Comrade Jackson be the Chairman at the Protest meeting at Walks Gates on July 7th /08.

Fredk Wm White Chairman

Outdoor meeting held at Walk's Gates at 8 p.m. on Monday July 13th 08 when Comrades White, Mills & Allen the deputation appointed at a Public Meeting to attend the Town Council's meeting to oppose the Borough

---

386 Henry Crowe, see above, note 196.

Surveyor's increase in salary & also the proposed increase in allotment rents, gave their report to a large audience, collection 2/3 taken to help to defray the cost of printing & distributing handbills.

Executive meeting held at Comrade White's house London Road on Tuesday July 14th /08.
Present Comrades White, Drew, Mills & Pye.
Minutes of Branch meeting read & confirmed.
Organisers visit. Comrade Mills offered to take organiser for the first week, the second week was left for the Sec'y to arrange. Decided to hold meeting at Heacham on Wednesday 22/7/08 & one at Sutton Bridge the second week, handbills to be printed.[387]
The Asst Secy read a letter from Comrade Cadman asking for our opinion on the question of running a Fed. Paper & the prospects of a Bazaar during the winter, & also whether the Federation should engage Comrade Daisy Halling for a tour.[388] The Asst Secy was instructed to reply favouring the latter, but not to support the two former proposals.
Comrade Lowerison has offered the loan of several books on Political Economy etc for our Socialist Library & it was unanimously decided to accept with thanks.
New Members. It was unanimously decided to admitted the following as members of our branch C. Pattingale, Targett's Yard, High St;[389] J Bennett,[390] Clough Lane; W Cooper, Church St;[391] A Mace, c/o Mrs Kent, N. Everard St.[392]

---

387 The Heacham meeting is recorded in the local press: it was held at the Town Hall with White presiding and Witard and Lowerison among the speakers (*LA*, 24 Jul. 1908).

388 Daisy Halling, socialist campaigner: when she spoke at a Labour rally in Norwich, the local newspaper described her as a former actress 'who has recently left the stage to devote herself to Socialist propaganda'. (*EDP*, 23 Jun. 1908). She toured, mainly in the north, combining lectures with performances of Ibsen and Shaw. She also wrote several plays for Clarion Theatre groups such as 'Jumbo in Rumboland', 'Pinnacles of the Future' (praised by fellow socialist and playwright George Bernard Shaw) and 'The Setting and the Jewel', said in the *Clarion* to be 'very superior to the ordinary sketch' (Ros Merkin, 'The Theatre of the Organised Working Class', PhD thesis, University of Warwick Joint School of Theatre Studies 1993).

389 Charles John Pattingale, born 1882. In 1901, a dock labourer in Hull, his home town. Publican at Plough Inn, King Street, Lynn from 1908 until its closure in 1912.

390 According to the 1908 trade directory, James Bennett, a greengrocer. Subsequent minutes do not always distinguish him from S. Bennett, see below, note 491.

391 William Cooper, born 1851, hawker.

392 Albert Edward Mace, born 1883, described in 1911 census as 'tin smith, general work and brazier' of Hockham St; earlier (in 1909), he lived at 15 North Everard Street.

Proposed by Comrade Mills & Sec. Com Drew that we recommend to the Branch meeting that handbills be printed with place of meeting left blank & a rubber stamp be purchased to fill in particulars. Carried.

Proposed by Comrade Drew & Sec Com Mills that the Rev R.W. Cummings be communicated with, with a view to fixing date for an outdoor meeting one weeknight during Aug or Sept.[393] Carried.

John Mills Chairman

Special branch meeting held in the Labour Club, Windsor Road on Tuesday August 4th 08.[394] Comrade Mills presided.

Minutes of executive meeting read & confirmed.

The Federation have decided to engage Rev. R.W. Cummings for a week & Daisy Halling for fortnight next year. It was decided to have 2000 handbills printed as recommended by the executive.

H. Walker, T. Turnbull & Joplin were proposed & accepted as members of the Party.[395]

It was suggested by Comrade White & agreed to that letters be sent to new members informing them of their admission to the party & welcoming them to the club. It was suggested by Com. Dorer that we send particulars of what the I.L.P. is to Philip Green, Gaywood, Mr Whitmore, Gaywood, & R. Hall, Valingers Road.[396]

The Eastern Counties Organiser Comrade H.E. Witard then addressed the meeting at some length, giving useful hints with regard to our propaganda &

---

393 Revd Robert William Cummings, born Liverpool 1870, a Church of England clergyman, elected to Norwich Board of Guardians for the ILP in 1905, at which time he lived at Aylsham Road, Norwich. However, he left the city soon afterwards, being last recorded in the register of electors for 1904–05: he was at Withernsea, near Hull by 1909 and was there at time of 1911 census.

394 The minutes do not mention that the Clarion Cycle Summer Meeting was held at Lynn on 1–3 August. Blatchford was there, but disappointed the crowd by speaking for just 30 seconds, leaving the main speech to Henderson. White was probably there as a copy of the programme survives among his papers (NRO, 297/10). See LN, 8 Aug. 1908 for report of the meeting. The visitor's list survives, with 140 names including Blatchford (NRO, SO 297/8).

395 Walker is listed in subscription book as H. C. E. Walker of Strad House, presumably a relation of F. M. Walker, see above note 168, although there is nobody of those initials at that address in the 1911 census. A third Walker was also a member, though not mentioned in these minutes – Carl Weber Walker, a merchant's clerk, originally of Strad House, but listed in the subscription book as of Sutton Bridge 1910–11; Thomas Turnbull, born 1856, slater, Rosebery Avenue, later Priory Court, Lynn: Alfred Joplin, born 1870, railway engine stoker, in 1901 living at 2, Edward Street, South Lynn: he does not appear in subscription book for 1908–09.

396 The effort paid off in the cases of Green (see below, note 410) and Hall, who both joined and paid their subscriptions until March 1914. However, Whitmore's name is not in

the methods to adopt etc, suggested getting to work at once on the distribution of literature & that we get the register & mark out sheets for different members & check men delivering same, & also have our candidates before the public as soon & as often as possible. Get good deal in election \address/ 4 page leaflet & point out where our opponents have failed to carry out our principles, & that diseases are largely the result of slum life & also that the Town Council are acting contrary to Act of Parliament by not putting the Housing of the Working Classes Act into operation. Punctuality to be practised with regard to our meetings, the organiser suggested closing the meeting in the event of there not being a quorum at the time the meeting is called for. Comrade Witard coming back second week in October to take charge of Elections, in the meantime members to keep pegging away at propaganda. Comrade White supplemented the organiser's remarks & suggested that we start at once & pledged himself to work his hardest to get our men returned to the Council. Comrade Hartley[397] also followed on same lines as Comrade Witard.

F.W. White Chairman

Executive meeting held at Comrade White's house London Road Aug 10th /08.

Comrade White presided. Present White Drew Pooley Dorer Frost Mills & Pye.

Minutes of last meeting read & confirmed.

Propaganda arrangements, it was decided to recommend to the branch the appointment of 3 ward committees, minimum number 6 with Chairman and Secretary.

New Members. Pro. Mills Sec Frost that T.W. Edmunds be admitted a member of the party.[398] Carried.

A communication from Comrade Hunter of Peterboro was read by the Secy & dealt with.

F.W. White Chairman

---

the subscription book, so he presumably decided not to join the ILP (Robert Whitmore, born 1846, builder).

397 Edward Robertshaw Hartley (1855–1918), a Bradford butcher and early ILP activist, its candidate at Dewsbury in 1895, and 1902 before supporting Quelch of the SDF; served for ILP on Bradford Town Council but stood for SDF at Bradford East in 1906, gaining 23% of the vote; Socialist candidate at Newcastle-on-Tyne, 1908; secretary of Clarion Van movement, 1910–12; after 18 month visit to Australasia, stood for BSP at Leicester in 1914; pro-war views led him to British Workers League later. For his role in Yorkshire politics, see Martin Crick, 'To make twelve o'clock at eleven: the history of the social-democratic federation' (Huddersfield University, PhD. 1988).

398 Thomas Walter Edmunds, born 1873, brush and hardware salesman, Norfolk Street, Lynn.

Branch meeting held at the Labour Club Windsor Road Aug 11ᵗʰ 08 Comrade White presided.

Minutes of last meeting read & confirmed.

Proposed by Com. Mace Sec Com Drew that the following members constitute the 3 Ward Committees recommended by the Executive. Carried unanimously.

South Ward: Mills Chairman, Spurling Secty, White, Drew, Triance, Frost, Trowse & Storer.³⁹⁹

Middle Ward: Dorer Chairman, Allen Secty, Lewis,⁴⁰⁰ Ridley, Turnbull, Mace, Pattingale & Pye.

North Ward: Jackson Chairman, Gittings Secty, Edmunds, Joplin, Seamer, Cooper, Green & Russell.

Proposed by Comrade Mills & Sec Drew That the Committees formed on April 26ᵗʰ still remain. Carried.

Comrade Dorer accepted the responsibility of delivering notices to all Lynn members.

F.W. White Chairman

Executive meeting held at Comrade White's house London Road August 24ᵗʰ /08.

Present Comrades White, Dorer, Frost, Drew, Spurling, Pye, Comrade White presided.

Minutes of branch meeting held Aug 11ᵗʰ were read.

Minutes of Executive meeting held Aug 10ᵗʰ were read and confirmed.

Proposed by Comrade Dorer & sec Frost that Com. White be convening secretary for Poor Law Committee in place of Comrade Dorer. Carried.

The secretary reported that he had written to the Town Clerk to be supplied with Corporation minutes each month.

A letter was read by the secretary from the Grantham branch re Comrade Bolton, when it was agreed that the secretary send a testimonial as to Comrade Bolton's ability as a Socialist lecturer.⁴⁰¹

---

399 Subscription book has Percy Storer as a member from July 1907, A. Trowse as a member from January 1908. Percy Storer born 1883, in 1911 census described as assistant, music warehouse; lived at 12 Gladstone Road, Lynn. Trowse, in 1910–11 subscription book given as A Trowse, 44 Checker Street; not identifiable from 1911 census, probably the Arthur Trowse who married Alice Ward in Lynn in 1904: in 1939, the family were living in Norwich, his occupation then given as wireless mechanic (retired) and birthdate as 1880.

400 William Lewis, born 1860, lived at Goodwin's Road in 1901, described in census as 'railway canvasser'; same address in 1911 when described as 'a railway cattle canvasser'.

401 Harry Bolton, born 1866, engine fitter, ILP member of Grantham Town Council.

It was agreed that Comrade White take the measurement of Club room & see Trenowath with regard to the possibility of purchasing secondhand lino.[402]

A letter was read from Comrade Koch of Peterboro offering to give a lantern lecture, the secretary was instructed to reply referring him to the P.S.A. People's institute.[403]

The ~~question~~ possibility of organising a Labour Church was discussed at much length & Comrade Frost was instructed to make enquiries anent the Blackfriars Hall & the Unitarian Church & report next executive meeting.

F.W. White Chairman

Executive meeting held at the Labour Club, Windsor Road Sept 14th /08. Comrade White presided. Present White, Mills, Jackson, Spurling, Frost, Drew & Pye.

Minutes of last executive read & confirmed.

Comrade Frost reported that he had written & declined the room offered by Mr Perry in People's Institute.

A communication from the Woman's Committee of I.L.P. was read offering to assist in the forthcoming election campaign, the secy was instructed to reply accepting same.

Communications from the Right to Work National Council were read re Unemployed Campaign 1908, the secy was instructed to reply that we were willing to co-operate.[404]

F.W. White Chairman

Executive meeting held at Comrade White's house Sept 28th /08. Comrade White presided. Present Comrades White, Frost, Jackson, Dorer, Spurling, Mills, Drew & Pye.

Minutes of last meeting read & confirmed.

It \was/ decided that we do not accede to the request of the Women's League with respect to holding weekly meetings in the Labour Club.[405]

---

402 Trenowath Brothers, general drapers, and house furnishers, with two shops in the High Street, King's Lynn.

403 Koch not identified, no one of this name in Peterborough in 1901 or 1911 census. A 'Mons. Koch' took a Socialist line at Peterborough Debating Society in 1907 and 1908 (*Peterborough Express*, 27 Nov. 1907, 25 Mar. 1908).

404 'The 'Right to Work' was the most innovative feature of Labour's controversial Unemployed Workmen Bill of 1907. The Bill had been defeated 267 to 118 in March 1908. The Right to Work National Council founded 1908 jointly by ILP, SDF and Fabian Society. See Duncan Tanner, *Political Change and the Labour Party 1900–1918* (Cambridge, 1990), 53, and article criticising its manifesto in *The Spectator*, 10 October 1908.

405 Probably a local branch of the Women's Labour League, founded in 1906 to promote the representation of women in local and national politics. Women members of the ASRS

Decided that 200 6d tickets be printed for Snowden's meeting, the matter be left to Comrade Spurling.

A communication was read from Head Office re grants to Organisers, this matter was left to delegate.

It was resolved that the secy write Library Committee offering Socialist Review for Magazine room, free of cost.[406]

New pamphlet "Why Lynn rates are high" was read & unanimously accepted.

F.W. White Chairman

Branch meeting held at the Labour Club Windsor Road Oct 5th 08.
Comrade White presided.

Minutes of last Branch meeting read & confirmed.

Comrade Ridley's appointment as secretary of Middle Ward vice Allen endorsed, Allen to assist Gittings in the North Ward.

Executive minutes. Dorer moved, Green seconded. Adopted.

Pro Dorer Sec Gittings That Ward Committee's secretaries go thro list of members & invite those residing in each ward to assist in Election work. Carried.

Secretary to write Duncan for terms for this weekend or next week.

Mrs Reeve's[407] visit, secretary to write Mrs Reeve to speak in N Ward, also send her fare.

Clarion Election Number. Comrade Frost agreed to write for specimen copy & Executive to decide.

New Members H. Pooley W.R. Purchase proposed by Com Frost & Sec Ridley accepted.[408]

Pro Dorer, Sec Mace, That the Education Committee be written asking for use of British School for a Labour Church on Sunday evenings during the winter. Carried.[409]

---

had a major role in its formation. See Bagwell, *Railwaymen*, 228,229; Christine Collette, *For Labour and for women: the Women's Labour League, 1906–1918* (Manchester, 1989).

406 *The Socialist Review: a monthly review of modern thought*, pub by ILP, 1908–34; first number, March 1908.

407 Annie Reeves, ILP, ex-Salvationist, first Labour woman to hold political office in Norwich when she was elected to Board of Guardians 1894, stood unsuccessfully for Norwich City Council in 1907 and 1908. Member of WSPU, spoke at large rally in Norwich Market Place in July 1912, saying, 'we are tired of men thinking us angels. We want them to think us women' (Meeres, *Dorothy Jewson*, 17).

408 Herbert Pooley, born 1885, railway clerk, Diamond Street, South Lynn; William Richard Purchase, born 1886, schoolmaster, married Florence May Hall in Lynn, 28 Dec. 1909; in 1911 they were living in London.

409 The matter was discussed at the next meeting of the Borough Education Committee, which voted to respond that the building was not suitable (*LN*, 31 Oct. 1908).

Winter Programme. It was decided that meetings be arranged for winter in Club Room on Sunday evenings, programme to be arranged from first Sunday after elections.

Social for November 4th. Dorer moved Drew Seconded That the authorities be written for use of Assembly Rooms & terms, failing that St James' rooms. Carried.

New Pamphlet. Comrade Dorer moved Frost sec that levy of 1/- per member be made & that 12 copies be given in exchange for sale. Carried.

Comrades Spurling & Drew appointed as joint literature secretaries responsible for sale & purchase of new literature.

The following resolution was proposed by Com Ridley sec Drew. That a leaflet be distributed at Snowden's meeting setting forth on one side the basic elementary principles of Socialism, & on the other side allowing anyone who from any cause is afraid of taking an active part in the Socialist movement that they can become members & the matter be treated in confidence. Carried.

Fred^k.W^m.White Chairman

Executive meeting held at Labour Club Oct 19th.

Present Comrades White, Drew, Spurling, Mills, Frost, Dorer & Pye.

Minutes of last E.C. read & confirmed.

Communication from Head Office read intimating that P. Snowden M.P. was unable to visit Lynn as arranged, the cancellation of St James' Hall was left to Comrade White.

New member Phillip Green Pro Mills Sec. Frost unanimously accepted.[410]

Moved by Com Dorer & Sec. Frost That Comrade Triance be asked to take charge of Special subscription list.

Moved Dorer Sec Mills That all members be circularised with a view to getting as many workers as possible during the municipal elections.[411]

Fred^k.W^m.White Chairman

Executive meeting held at Comrade White's house November 9th /08.

Present Comrades White, Dorer, Drew, Spurling & Pye. Comrade White presided.

Minutes of last executive read & confirmed.

---

410 Philip Green, born 1863, plasterer, Wootton Road, Gaywood at time of 1911 census. His wife Frances Emily Green, born 1865, described as 'housekeeper' in the census, although not mentioned in the subscription book, was also a member: see minutes for 15 May 1910.

411 In November 1908, the ILP put up one candidate in each ward for the first time, although all were heavily defeated: Jackson in North Ward (215 votes), T. A. Frost in Middle Ward (224 votes), White in South Ward (372 votes)

It was decided that Comrades Dorer & Hall take subscription lists in hand. Programme for Sundays up to the end of the present year was arranged as follows: Nov 15 Dorer; Nov 22 Mills; Nov 29 White; Dec 6 Allen; Dec 13 Jackson; Dec 20 Frost; Dec 27 Spurling. Also write Messrs Henderson & Dodd & Mrs Reeves.

The secy was instructed to write Fed. re result of Miss McMillan's visit with regard to the financing of speakers & & also to Head Office for first speaker, Keir Hardie or another.

Financial statement was presented showing deficit £4.

It was decided Comrade Dorer write Mr Gemmell [412] with a view to discussing our latest pamphlet.

F.W. White Chairman

Executive meeting held at Comrade White's house on Nov 23rd /08.

Minutes of executive read & confirmed.

Agreed that Mrs Reeves be asked to visit Lynn on Dec. 6 in the Labour Club & that the meeting be advertised, also that Comrade Dodd's date in Jan be accepted. Comrade Frost to be chairman for Mrs Reeves.

Agreed that Com. Allen be asked to take the office of Lecture Secretary.

Collector to give list of members in arrears etc at the next executive meeting. As a result of the August Meet £4.4.0 was handed over to the I.L.P. with the proviso that any a/c from the "Clarion" be paid by I.L.P.

Comrade Dorer read a reply from Mr Gemmell.

F.W. White Chairman

Branch meeting held at Labour Club Windsor Road 8.0 pm sharp Dec 7th 08.

13 present. Comrade F. White presided.

Minutes of last branch meeting read & confirmed. Comrade Dorer moved, Woolway seconded.[413]

---

412 For George Gemmell senior, see above note 103. The reference here could possibly be to his son of the same name, born 1890, educated at King Edward VI Grammar School in Lynn, and in 1911 studying to be a schoolmaster: he might have offered advice as to the grammar of the pamphlet. (Relatively poorly educated socialists could be sensitive about this: the first editor of the *Railway Review* was mocked for his grammatical errors, Bagwell, *Railwaymen*, 87).

413 Woolway, not certainly identified: he had joined Lynn ILP in September 1908. His address is given in 1910–11 subscription book as 'WHS & Son': presumably W. H. Smith newsagents, which had a shop on High St and a bookstall at the railway station. A copy of a letter survives, dated 12 October 1910, saying that Woolway had not paid his subscription for six months (NRO, SO 297/11): his last mention in the minutes is 20 March 1910. The only Woolway named in the 1901 census is John Frankpitt Woolway, born Briningham in 1889, in 1901 living with his grandfather John Linder at Melton Constable: Linder is

An application from the Women's League re the use of Club for an hour on Thursday evenings was unanimously acceded to.

Soiree Committee. Moved by Comrade Dorer & seconded by Comrade Woolway that the following members constitute a committee to carry out all arrangements with regard to Soiree on Jany 5ᵗʰ 09: Spurling, Hall, Mills, Gittings & Ridley. Carried.

Proposed by Comrade Mills & seconded by Com. Trowse that piano be purchased & that Comrades Storer & Gittings be given a free hand. Carried. It was unanimously agreed to defer earmarking the £4.4.0 \from Clarion acct/ until financial statement presented.

The following comrades were elected as a Billiard table committee. Mace \secy/, Drew & Woolway.

Book case. Proposed by Comrade Mace & Sec Mills That Comrade Trowse put same in order. Carried.

National policy of I.L.P. Comrade Mace moved & Drew seconded that we now discuss the National policy of the I.L.P. Amendment to adjourn moved by Com. Pye & seconded by Com. Sporne. Resolution carried 8 to 7. Meeting subsequently decided to adjourn for a week, amendment for a month lost by 6 to 3.

F.W. White Chairman

Adjourned branch meeting held at the Labour Club Dec 14ᵗʰ 08.
Com. White presided.

Discussion on the National policy of the I.L.P. opened by Com. Frost. A resolution was proposed by Com. Ridley & Seconded by Com. Woolway as follows: "That this meeting of the ILP hereby expresses its continued confidence in its parliamentary representatives & believes that the best that the hampered circumstances permitted had been done by them, yet realise however the very unsatisfactory position in which the ILP now stands, and remembering that the object of the ILP is Socialism demands that an early opportunity be taken of severing our connection with the present Labour party thereby obviating the extremely difficult situations in which the party has found itself at recent bye elections & believes that the best method of propagating Socialism is by fighting for it & not for Labour representation". Amendment by Frost & Spurling "That this meeting expresses its entire approval of & confidence in the election & general policy of the N.A.C. & Labour party & places on record its appreciation of same". This was subsequently withdrawn after hearing Comrade Dorer's criticism & the

---

described as postmaster and railway ganger. This Woolway was buried in Briningham in 1918, having died aged 29.

following amendment by Dorer & Allen was carried by 14 to 4, "That we deplore the personalities which have been so rife of late in the movement & appeal for more fellowship & a more militant socialist propaganda".

Comrade Mills brought forward the question of associate members & on the motion of Comrade Allen & Pye it was decided to refer the matter to the next executive.

F.W. White Chairman

Executive meeting held at the Labour Club, Windsor Road, Jan 4th /09.

Com. White presided. Present: White, Dorer, Frost, Drew, Spurling, Allen, Mills & Pye.

Minutes of the Branch meetings held Dec 7th & 14th read.

Minutes of Executive meeting held Nov 23rd read & confirmed.

Moved by Comrades Mills & Drew, that we advertise in the "Lynn News" the meetings to be addressed by Comrades Dodd & Reeves. Carried.

The Club question was discussed & \it was/ decided to appoint Messrs Allen, Mills & Spurling to form a sub committee to go fully into the matter. Dates for Organiser's visit to be left to the Lecture Secretary.

A gift of books for the club library from Comrade Miss Britton was accepted, and the Secty was instructed to tender the best thanks of the Committee for the same.[414]

It was decided to recommend the following resolution to the next branch meeting on the motion of Comrades Spurling & Frost, "That no motion affecting the constitution or policy of this party be accepted except at a meeting of members specially summoned for that purpose. The terms of such resolution to be set out in full in the circular summoning the meeting".

F.W. White Chairman

Executive meeting held at Comrade White's house on Jany 18th /09.

Comrade White presided. Present Jackson, Drew, Frost, Mills, White, Dorer & Pye.

Comrade Hall presented the balance sheet of the Soiree which showed a balance in hand of 2/- but 6 packs of cards obtained from Com White were unsaleable & the committee decided to purchase for 5/-.

---

414 Not certainly identified: in the subscription books she is listed as Miss Britton from her first payment in November 1907 and for the next three years. Listed as Miss Brittain of 'The Chase' in 1910–11 (now Chase Avenue, off Goodwin's Road): she paid her subscription for the last time in January 1911. Probably Florence Gerty Britton (born 1886) or Lilian Emma Britton (born 1887), the two eldest daughters of Charles John Britton, a Lynn grocer involved in both the PSA and the YMCA. The whole family were living in Norwich at the time of the 1911 census, perhaps explaining why the subscription ended.

It was also decided to have another soiree & whist drive early in February, Comrade Hall undertaking to carry out all the arrangements excepting the refreshments, for which the following were appointed to form a committee, Comrades Rout, Woolway & Ridley, Mrs White, Mills & Drew.

The minutes of last executive meeting were then read & adopted.

The report of the Club Committee was not ready.

A short report of the E.C. of the E.A.F. was read by the Asst. Secty & supplemented by Com. Dorer, & matters dealt with as follows:- Com Rev. W.B. Graham is visiting the area in Decr. next, & we decided to have him for one night if fee not too much.[415] Decided on the motion of Dorer & Frost that we subscribe 5/- to help to liquidate a debt of £4 incurred by the Beccles branch now defunct. The Fed. are trying to get Com. W.C. Anderson for a mission before August next & it was agreed that we row in with Fed.[416] The Organiser is visiting the branch on Feb. 6th for a week & a series of meetings is suggested. Keir Hardie is visiting NOW on Friday March 12th.[417] The secty was instructed to write him with a view of having a meeting here on March 13th.

A financial statement was presented by Com. Dorer.

New Members. The following names were submitted & accepted: Messrs Bocking, Smythe, Watson, Waters & F. Bunkall.[418]

F.W. White Chairman

---

415 Revd Walter Burn Graham: of Askham, originally associated with agricultural labourers of Westmorland; later active in Bradford and Colne Valley where a supporter of Grayson. Author of *The Lord's Prayer: the aim and life-work of all true Christians* (Wakefield: Wakefield ILP, 1909).

416 William Crawford Anderson (1877–1918), ILP politician. On NAC from 1908, chair of ILP 1910–13. Married women trade unionist leader Mary Macarthur (see below, note 461) 1911. Elected an MP on his third attempt 1914 but defeated 1918 due to his anti-war opinions. Victim of influenza epidemic. A handbill for a meeting in 1912 calls him 'the orator of the Socialist Movement' (NRO, SO 297/4).

417 Norwich: the meeting was 'one of the largest political meetings ever held in the city'. (Cherry, *Doing Different*, 81).

418 Herbert Thomas Bocking (1860–1920), gilder and picture framer, Market Street. He put paintings by Walter Dexter in his shop window: see obituary in *LA*, 6 Aug. 1920 and Paton, *Walter Dexter*, 111. Frank Bunkall, New Conduit St, later Lynn High St (1910–11), then March, Cambs. (1911–12), a grocer: he was the younger son of John Bunkall, the former mayor (see above, note 114). Smythe is probably William Crosby Smythe, born 1850, market gardener, address in 1911 The Common, Outwell. Watson, A. J. Watson, Diamond Street, Lynn, according to the subscription book, not further identified: there is no A. Watson at this address, and no A. J. Watson anywhere in Lynn, in 1901 or 1911 census. Waters not identified.

Branch meeting held at the Labour Club Windsor Road Jany 25ᵗʰ /09.
Com. White presided.

Minutes of last branch meeting read & confirmed. & Executive minutes adopted on the motion of Comrades Allen & Mace.

New Members: A Seapy & J Skerritt were unanimously accepted as members of this branch.[419]

Refreshment committee for Soiree. The Asst Secy to be convenor.

Moved by Spurling & Allen, "That no motion affecting the constitution or policy of this party be accepted except at a meeting of members specially summoned for the purpose, the terms of such resolution to be set out in full in the circular summoning the meeting. Amendment by Ridley & Woolway That a 2/3ʳᵈ majority of the branch meeting be necessary pass such resolutions. Resolution carried with two dissentients. \Rule covers amendment/

It was unanimously agreed to hold a Branch meeting on Feb 1ˢᵗ to consider resolutions & nominations for the Edinboro' conference.[420] Comrade Ridley gave notice that he intended moving his resolution \again/. Com Mills & Allen also gave notice to move the following, "That we instruct the N.A.C. to alter our name to "The Socialist Party". Comrade Mace desires to move, "That means be taken to form a united party for local propaganda & Election work".

A communication from Federation was read re proposed newspaper. Moved by Drew & Spurling, That the Newspaper question be referred to the Executive Committee, that body to report to the branch. Carried.

Miss McMillan's letter to be brought up again.

Com Frost reported that he had not yet obtained any linoleum but hoped to do so early.

                                                                J. Pooley Chair

Branch meeting held at the Labour Club Windsor Road Feb 1ˢᵗ /09. Com J. Pooley (Chair).

Minutes of last meeting adopted on the motion of Comrade Mills & Mace. Resolution,

---

419 James Skerritt, born 1885, shoeing smith, Garden Row, Windsor Road, Lynn. A. Seapy given as *Thomas* Seapy in 1908–09 list of members, born 1836, a retired stevedore, lived at 10 Birkett's House, Queen Street, Lynn. He died in early 1912, buried in Lynn, 16 January (NRO, PD 39/48).

420 The Easter Conference for 1909 was at Edinburgh, 10, 12–13 April. No delegate was sent from King's Lynn. At the Conference, a proposal that the ILP should sever itself from the Labour Party received the support of just eight delegates, with 378 supporting the continuance of 'the alliance of Labour and Socialism' (Stewart, *Hardie*, 283).

Moved by Ridley & Woolway to be sent to N.A.C. for Conference Agenda, "That this Conference demands that an early opportunity be taken of severing our connection with the present Labour party". Carried by 11 to 6.

Moved for Conference Agenda by Allen & Mills, "That this Conference takes steps to at once alter our name from the ILP to the "Socialist Party". Carried.

Moved by Mace & Ridley, "That means be taken to form a united party for local propaganda & Election work". After discussing round the question for some time, the next business was moved by Comrade Dorer & carried.

It was agreed that the Organiser's meetings be advertised on the proposition of Dorer & Frost, the question of hospitality be left to the lecture Secretary. Moved by Ridley & Drew, That suitable hall be obtained for Comrade Lowerison's lecture. Carried.

F.W. White   Chairman

Executive meeting held at the Labour Club, Windsor Road, Feb 15th /09. Com. White presided. Present: White, Drew, Mills, Dorer, Frost & Pye.

Minutes of last executive meeting adopted on the motions of Comrade Drew & Mills. Minutes of the two branch meetings were also read.

No definite report from the Club Committee.

Newspaper question. Moved by Mills & Drew, That we recommend the branch to guarantee 500 copies per month. Carried.

Organisers pamphlet. It was decided to obtain 4 doz of same.

Financial statement by Comrade Dorer.

The Clarion a/c 15/- reported paid & approved

Liabilities:	s	d
Beccles deficit	5.	0
Cards (per Com White)	3.	0
Dues Head Office	12.	6
Gas Bill	10.	10
£ 1	11.	4

Cash in Hand   -18/10

The following a/c's were approved for payment:

Head Office	12.	6
Beccles deficit	5.	0
25% Organiser's collns		9
	18.	3

It was decided to obtain 100 Contribution Cards matter to be left to the Asst Secty.

It was agreed to advertise Com. Lowerison's meeting in the "Lynn News", the Hall to be left to Comrades White & Allen to arrange.

It was agreed that the Secty write Keir Hardie as to the accuracy of the report in the press re the agreement with Gibson Bowles that no Labour nominee should oppose him.[421]

Resolved that the next meeting of the executive be held on Monday Feb 22nd 09.

F.W. White Chairman

Executive meeting held at Comrade White's house, London Rd, Feby 22nd /09, Comrade White presiding. Present Comrades White, Spurling, Frost, Drew, Mills & Pye.

Minutes of last executive meeting read & confirmed.

Secty reported having received a negative reply from K Hardie.

In the absence of the Lecture Secty the questions of Summer Propaganda & Speaker's Class were left over until the next executive meeting.

Cummings' Meeting. Moved by Mills & Drew that 50 large posters & 200 6d tickets be printed, matter be left to Spurling & Allen, the question of Handbills was left over. Carried.

The question of a parliamentary candidate was discussed & the impression was that same is desirable & that we approach Comrade Witard with a view to adoption.

F.W. White Chairman

Branch meeting held at the Labour Club Windsor Road March 8th 09. Com. White presided.

Minutes of last Branch meeting read & confirmed & Executive minutes adopted on the motion of Comrades Frost & Drew.

Election of Divisional Representative for N.A.C.[422] 18 members present. Dodd 15 \votes/ Witard 1 Neutral 2

Cummings meeting. Proposed by Drew & Frost, That Com. Witard be one of the Speakers & that Com. White takes the Chair. Carried.

---

421 In theory, the Lib-Lab pact still held in 1910, but many ILP men wanted to oppose Liberal candidates. The situation was complicated as many union men still supported the Liberals rather than Labour. These issues lay behind the Lynn situation; no specific reference to Keir Hardie supporting Bowles has been found. In general, the pact still held: Labour fought only seventy-eight seats in January 1910 and only fifty-six in the second general election of the year in December. The importance of the pact for Labour is shown in the fact that they did not win a single seat out of the thirty-five constituencies where all three parties put up candidates in these elections.

422 The ILP Federation for the Eastern Counties was replaced by a Divisional Council in 1909: see Wadsworth, 'ILP in Great Yarmouth'.

1. Early Socialist outing: Frederick White is in the boat on the far right of the photograph and Walter Dexter is in the boat on the far left.
Source: Norfolk Record Office, (NRO, SO 297/22).

2. Frederick White and family outside his shop in King's Lynn. Source: Norfolk Record Office (NRO, SO 297/23).

3. Election leaflet for John J. Kidd standing for the King's Lynn Board of Guardians, 1901: the first socialist to run for office in the town. Source: Norfolk Record Office, (NRO, SO 297/3)

BOARD OF GUARDIANS ELECTION, 1901.

TO THE ELECTORS OF

SOUTH LYNN PARISH.

FELLOW ELECTORS,

Having consented to be a Candidate for the above Board, permit me to state that I am opposed to the appointment of a Chaplain for the Workhouse, accompanied as it must be, according to law, by a salary from the Rates.

Believing as I do, that Vaccination is not a preventative of Small-pox, I am opposed to the prosecution of anti-vaccinators.

Being a pronounced Democratic Socialist, (which does not imply a belief in the sharing out of wealth as so often stated), my sympathies are with the workers, and against all loafers and shirkers.

I am prepared to advocate and support the granting of adequate relief to the aged poor in their own homes, the boarding out of the children, when practicable, and the equitable adjustment of Assessments.

Yours faithfully,

JOHN J. KIDD.

Goodwin's Road,
March 16th, 1901.

DATE OF ELECTION, MONDAY, MARCH 25th.

Polling Station—Infants' Schoolroom, South Everard Street.

Your Number on the Register is

VOTE FOR

The Democratic Candidate.

Printed and Published by WATTS & ROWE, High Street, Lynn.

Mrs. Leach,
*Vice-Chairman Great Yarmouth
School Board.*

21

4. Ethel Leach,
Great Yarmouth suffragist.
Source: Norfolk Record
Office (NRO, SO 141/1).

5. The Society's stall on
Yarmouth Market Place.
Image courtesy of Norfolk
County Council at www.
picture.norfolk.gov.uk

6. Start of the Great Pilgrimage March in Yarmouth, 1913.
Image courtesy of Norfolk County Council at www.picture.norfolk.gov.uk

Russell Smart's meeting. Proposed by Jackson & Mace, That meeting be held in Blackfriars Hall & that subject be "Hell & the way out".[423] Carried. Delegate to Conference be left in abeyance.

Pro. Mills & Jackson, That the correspondence relating to the newspaper question be brought up at the Annual Meeting. Carried.

Parliamentary Candidate. Proposed by Comrades Frost & Trowse, "That considering the progress the I.L.P has made in Lynn during this last two years the time has come when a Socialist Parliamentary candidate could be run with success, & request the executive to do all in its power to obtain the consent of the N.A.C to use its financial guarantee. If the sanction of the N.A.C is given that we invite Comrade H.E. Witard to become our prospective candidate, & providing Comrade Witard accepts our invitation, our delegates to the L.R.C be instructed to submit his name as prospective parliamentary candidate to that committee".

Amendment by Ridley & Jackson, "That we defer the question until the Annual Meeting & that notice summoning the meeting" have the subject on the agenda. Amendment lost by 12 to 3. Second Amendment by Mace & Spurling, That Witard's name be deleted. Amendment lost by 6 to 5.

The resolution was then put to the meeting & lost by 6 to 4.

The resolution & both amendments being lost Comrades Spurling & Mace moved the first part of Comrade Frost's resolution leaving out all after "guarantee".

Amendment by Ridley & Lewis, "That a specially convened meeting be held to consider the matter". Amendment lost by 7 to 3.

Comrade Spurling's resolution was then carried by 6 to 3.

F.W. White   Chairman

Executive meeting held at Comrade White's house, London Rd, March 9th /09, Comrade White presided. Present Comrades Allen, Dorer, Spurling, Drew, Mills & Pye. Minutes of last executive meeting adopted on the motion of Comrades Spurling & Allen. Minutes of Branch meeting read.

Proposed by Spurling & Mills, That 2,000 circulars advertising both Comrade Cummings' & Smart's meeting be obtained, matter left to Allen & Spurling. Carried. Small folders "What ILP is" etc to be obtained from Head Office. Collections to be organised by Comrade Drew. Literature Spurling & Drew.

---

423 According to a local newspaper, about 250 people attended Smart's meeting, held at Central Hall (*LA*, 26 Mar. 1909).

Russell Smart's meeting. It was agreed to obtain 100 small posters, 50 6^d & 50 3^d tickets. Chairman Jackson or Mills.[424]

Financial statement by Com Dorer. a/c's paid 18/3 since last time, a/cs to be paid 6/- for Con. Cards.

It was decided to hold the Annual Meeting on Monday April 5th /-09, & the next E.C. March 22nd /-09, & special meeting to consider the agenda for Easter Conference as soon as rec'd.

Hospitality for Comrade Cummings was left to Comrade Allen to arrange.

Parliamentary Candidature. This matter was left to the next executive meeting.

Speaker's Class. Comrade Mills to arrange.

Summer Propaganda. Comrade Allen has matter in hand.

F.W. White   Chairman

Executive meeting held at Comrade White's house on Monday March 22nd /09. Com. White in the chair. Present White, Drew, Spurling, Mills, Allen & Pye.

A communication was read by the president from Comrade Dodd of Yarmouth offering Lansbury's services,[425] & the Secty wrote by the evening post to procure the same.

Minutes of last meeting were then read & confirmed.

Treasurer's report & balance sheet read & it was decided to submit same to the branch.

Club Committee reported further progress with regard to properties.

Summer Propaganda. Lecture Secty reported 14 week-ends booked up.

Russell Smart's Meeting. Hospitality & Chairman Comrade Mills. Resolution Allen & White.[426]

Parliamentary Candidate. Proposed by Comrades Frost & Mills, That the executive of the I.LP is of the opinion that considering the growing

---

424 Cummings' meeting was held at Central Hall 16 March 1909, and was a discussion about the possibility of a Socialist parliamentary candidate for Lynn: Russell Smart was suggested but nothing was decided. During the meeting, Cummings said that Lynn had become a 'sort of dumping ground for all sorts of Tory and Liberal candidates' and in a meeting at Norwich the following day he called Lynn 'that godforsaken toryridden district.' (*LN*, 20 Mar. 1909)

425 George Lansbury (1859–1940) fought elections for SDF before joining ILP in about 1903; elected as ILP MP for Bow and Bromley in December 1910 general election; resigned 1912 to fight by-election on behalf of women's suffrage but defeated. Returned to parliament 1922, served as leader of Labour Party 1931–35, forced to resign because of his pacifist ideas. Launched *Daily Herald* 1912, its editor from 1914.

426 The meeting was held at Central Hall on 23 March, with about 250 people present: Smart was described in the local press as Prospective Parliamentary for Elland, Yorkshire.

influence of the Labour party in Lynn the time has come when the L.R.C should endeavour a prospective parliamentary Socialist & Labour candidate for the borough & requests its delegates to invite the L.R.C to obtain one. Carried.[427]

Arrangements if Comrade Lansbury is secured.[428] Chairman Allen. Advertising, 2 adverts in Lynn News & 100 small posters. Comrade Drew to organise the collections.

Fred[k].W[m].White Chairman

Executive meeting held at Comrade Mills' house Windsor Rd March 29th /09. Comrade White presided. Present Comrades Allen, Drew, White, Frost, Mills & Pye.

It was decided that the Annual Meeting be held on Friday April 2nd 09.

It was proposed to have a Social on Good Friday providing enough support was forthcoming.

It was decided that the executive send a letter of thanks to the Forward Association for the use of the Central Hall at a nominal charge.

Collection at Lansbury's meeting £1.11.0

New Member. John Medlock, 4 Hospital Walk, was unanimously accepted as a member.[429]

Fred[k].W[m].White Chairman

Annual General Meeting held in the Labour Club, Windsor Rd, Friday April 2nd /09. Comrade White in the Chair.

Minutes of last annual meeting read & confirmed on the motion of Comrades Drew & Hall.

Minutes of last branch meeting read & confirmed.

The Secretary gave a report outlining the progress of the movement during the preceding year, which was accepted with congratulations.

Comrade Dorer presented the Balance Sheet & Report for the Year. This was also unanimously adopted.

G. Allen proposed the motion that the meeting welcomed the steps that the ILP were taking to put up a candidate for the next general election (*LN*, 20 Mar. 1909 for advertisement of meeting; *LA*, 26 Mar. 1909 for report).

427 The local press noted that the party would need to put up £100 to finance a Parliamentary candidate (*LA*, 19 Nov. 1909).

428 He *was* secured: the meeting was held at Central Hall on 29 March (announced in *LN*, 27 Mar. 1909).

429 John Medlock, born 1888, railway fireman. His father, Robert Medlock, born 1859, bricklayer, same address, was also a member according to the subscription book, although the minutes have no record of his application for membership.

Comrade White having briefly reviewed his Year of office, the election of Officers was preceded with. Results:

President	J.W. Spurling
Secretary	J. Mills
Asst Secy	G. Ridley
Lecture Organiser	G. Allen
Financial Secy	
to whom all money is to be paid	R. Drew
Treasurer	A.L. Dorer
Auditors	J. Neave & H. Pooley
Executive Officers	White, Lewis, Frost & Bunkall
L.R.C. delegates	Allen, Frost & Mills. & Ridley

Comrade Hall gave a report concerning the bagatelle table & the following were elected as a Committee for the ensuing year, Comrades A.J. Watson, R. Drew & Sec. Mace.[430]

Proposed by Comrade Mills, Sec Allen, "That this branch instructs the executive to continue their efforts to obtain a Parliamentary Candidate". Carried. Newspaper question. Proposed by Comrade Dorer, Sec Woolway, "That the Executive Committee's recommendation be acceded to". Carried unanimously. Old age Pensions. Proposed by Comrade Frost, Sec Mills, "That this branch respectfully requests Lieut Carlyon Bellairs to do all in his power to remove the poor law disqualifications for Old Age Pensions" to be sent to the Hon & Gallant member. Carried.

J.W. Spurling   Chairman

Executive meeting held at Com Mills house Tuesday April 15 09. Comrade Spurling presided. Also present Coms. Lewis, Dorer, Bunkall, Drew, Mills & Ridley. Minutes of last Executive meeting read & confirmed.

Parliamentary Candidature. Secretary read a letter which had been sent to N.A.C & the reply received. It was agreed that the matter be left in abeyance pending further reply from N.A.C

Visit of Comrade Witard E.C. organiser. Meetings to be arranged as under:
Monday Branch meeting

Tuesday	Hextable Rd
Wednesday	Walks Gates
Friday	Diamond St
Saturday	New Conduit St
Sunday	Walks Gates

1000 handbills to be printed advertising same.

---

430 Watson, see note 418 above.

Com Witard was also recommended to visit the Dock Gates during the morning & Savages etc at dinner times in view of the fact there are usually a quantity of men round these places. Hosp. Dorer & Frost.

It was mentioned that Com Lansbury would again speak on our behalf in Nov next.

Newspaper question. Com Dorer reported very poor prospects.

Executive meetings. Moved by Dorer & Mills, "That Executive meetings be held fortnightly on & from May 3 /-09 to commence at 8 pm".

Reported that Coms Gittings & Storer had been offered a piano, in good order, by Com Lowerison for £5. They were instructed to purchase on the motion of Coms Mills & Frost. Meeting closed at 11 pm.

J.W. Spurling Chairman

Branch Meeting held at Club Room London Rd, April 19 09.[431] Comrade Spurling presided.

Minutes of previous branch meeting read & confirmed on motions of Coms. Drew & White.

Minutes of previous Executive by Comrades Mace & Woolway.

Ass. Sec. asked for assistance for distribution of literature advertising Com Witard's meeting but met with no success.

Comrade Mace very kindly offered to again undertake distribution of branch notices & was thanked for past services.

Letter from Ruskin College was referred to Executive by Coms Dorer & Pye.

Com Witard then gave a very interesting & encouraging report of Edinboro Conference.[432]

J.M. Spurling Chairman

Branch Meeting held Sunday May 2. Comrade Spurling presided.

Nominations for N.A.C. Prop. Mills Sec. Frost that we nominate Witard & Dodd.

Comrade Witard then outlined an organisation scheme which he desired to see us adopt.

---

431 The minutes do not record an instance of practical socialism the previous weekend. Twelve unemployment marchers from London arrived in the town on Saturday 17 April, going to the mayor: he sent them on to the ILP who let them set up their beds in their Hall and provided food. A meeting was hastily organised, at which their leader said they were not loafers but in desperate need of work. The men set off back to London on Monday morning (*LA*, 23 Apr. 1909).

432 See above, note 420.

Executive meeting held Carmelite House London Rd May 3 09. Com Spurling presided. Also present Coms Lewis, Bunkall, Frost, White, Mills, Drew, Dorer & Ridley. Minutes of previous meeting read & confirmed on motion of Coms. White & Bunkall.

Appeal for funds for Ruskin College. Decided that we were unable to assist. Club room. Question deferred on motion of Comrade Lewis.

Organisation. Decided that we systematically organise South & Middle Wards as suggested by Com Witard. Each Ward to have a Secretary & subsequently small working ctee.

So Ward. Spurling Prop. Mills Sec. White.

Middle. Lewis Prop. White Sec. Drew.

The whole to be centrally controlled by Branch Secretary.

Moved by Mills Sec Frost, 'That the Secretaries be given discretionary purchasing power'

Comrade Allen reported that he had been unable to engage outdoor speakers for May.

In view of the success of Lowestoft branch in obtaining services of 4 prominent national speakers in less than 1 year, & our inability to get one it was decided that organising Secy write Cadman pointing this out & asking to be allowed to share in.

Comrade Dorer then gave financial report & stated it should greatly assist him if members would pay promptly & where possible in advance.

J.M. Spurling   Chairman

Executive meeting held Com Mills house May 17 09. Com. Spurling presided, also present Comrades White, Dorer, Lewis, Bunkall, Mills & Drew. Ridley

Minutes of previous \meeting/ adopted on motion of Comrades Mills & Drew.

Letter read from Pboro branch offering 80 pamphlets (Destiny of the Mob by Grayson) for 2/6.[433] Resolved that offer be declined.

Letter read from Com. G. Allen asked to be relieved of position of Lecture Secy. Resolved that letter be submitted to branch with recommendation

---

433 Victor Grayson (1881–?1920), M.P. for Colne Valley, elected in the by-election of 1907, but defeated in January 1910, by which time he had a well-publicised drinking problem. Regarded as a great speaker but disliked by the established figures in the ILP, whose continued adhesion to the Lib-Lab pact he deplored: during a debate on unemployment in the House of Commons, he called the other Labour MPs 'traitors to their class, who refuse to stand by their class'. Never returned to Parliament after 1910, and mysteriously disappeared in 1920, actual date of death uncertain. Author of *The Destiny of the Mob* (Huddersfield: Worker Press, 1908). See also note 370 above.

that Assis. Sec. be asked to undertake duties, that Comrade expressing his willingness to do so.

Club room. After discussion Coms Frost & Mills were appointed to go further into matter on proposition of Coms Dorer & Drew.

National levy for Parliamentary fund. Prop by Com Mills, Sec Bunkall that 3 receipt books be obtained.

Financial report given by Treasurer.

J.M. Spurling   Chairman

Branch meeting held Labour Club Windsor Rd 8 pm 19-5-09. Com Spurling presided.

Minutes of branch meeting held April 19th adopted on motion of Coms Mills & Drew.

Minutes of branch meeting held May 2 adopted on motion of Coms. White & Mace.

Letter was read from Com. G. Allen conveying his resignation as Assis. Sec.[434] Resignation accepted on motion of Comrades White & Mace & duties deputed to Assistant Secy.

Election of N.A.C. members was then proceeded with, with following results

Burgess[435] 3; Thomas[436] 3; Lansbury 18; Dodd 11; Witard 4; Cummings 4; Smith 5; Coit 3; Hartley 7; Anderson 6; Mcarthur 2; Henderson 1.

Several members accepted cards for districts for distribution of literature in accordance with previous resolutions.

J.M. Spurling   Chairman

Executive meeting held Com Whites house Tuesday June 1st. Comrade Spurling presided. Also present Coms. Lewis, White, Mills, Drew, Dorer & Ridley.

Minutes of previous meeting adopted on motion of Comrades Mills & White.

Letter was read from Secretary of Gilchrist lectures asking for 2 nominations

434 An error: Allen resigned as *Lecture* Secretary (see previous meeting).

435 Joseph Burgess (1853–1934), journalist and one of the leading founders of the ILP in 1893; served on NAC on several occasions; ILP candidate at Leicester (1894 and 1895) Glasgow Camlachie (1906) and Montrose (1908 and 1910). See K. McPhillips, *Joseph Burgess and the Founding of the ILP* (2005). Spoke in favour of the ILP seceding from the Labour Party at the Edinburgh Conference (see above, note 420).

436 James Henry ('Jimmy') Thomas (1874–1949), official of ASRS, MP Derby 1910–36, minister in Macdonald's Labour and coalition ministries. See G. Blaxland, *J.H.Thomas: a life for unity* (London, 1964), and a very different assessment in Andrew Thorpe, 'J.H. Thomas and the rise of Labour in Derby 1880–1945', *Midland History*, 15(1) (1990), 111–28.

for their Committee.[437] On motion of Coms Dorer & White – Ridley & Mills were nominated

Proposed establishment of a Divisional Council. Comrade Dorer elected as representative on motion of Spurling & Drew. Com Lewis promised to attend if Dorer unable to & this was agreed to on motion of Ridley & Mills. Club Room. Committee reported failure of projected scheme & after some discussion the following resolution was agreed on motion of Coms Dorer & Drew, "That directly the landlord of our present premises had had the necessary repairs executed, further renovations considered necessary by the Secy to be carried & a voluntary opened for purpose of defraying cost".

J.M. Spurling   Chairman

Executive meeting held June 15th Com. Whites house. Com Spurling presided, also present Lewis, Dorer, White, Bunkall, Ridley.

Minutes of previous meeting adopted on motion of Coms. White & Dorer.

Speakers. Secy reported & it was agreed that Com Witard conducts outdoor campaign as usual. Other bookings accepted.

Organisation. Agreed that an appeal be made at branch meeting for early return of block cards.

J.M. Spurling   Chairman

Branch meeting held Labour Club, Windsor Rd June 24 09. Comrade Spurling presided.

Organiser Witard's visit. Agreed that meetings be held as follows, Monday Walks Gates, Tuesday branch meeting, Wednesday Walks Gates, Friday Walks Gates, Saturday with W R Smith, Witard also to assist members in organising their blocks & agreed that 2000 leaflets be purchased for distribution.

Com Pointer's visit.[438] Estimate of Hall to be obtained & arrangements left to Executive.

"This branch meeting instructs the Executive to formulate & submit scheme for accommodation of speakers". Agreed to on proposition of Coms Mace & Lewis.

"The Kings Lynn branch of the I.L.P. protests against the official welcome about to be extended to the Csar of Russia by the Head of the State & the British \nation/ in view of the horrible atrocities which have been & are being perpetrated in Russia & desires that his Majesty the King should

---

437 Educational Trust founded under will of John Borthwick Gilchrist (1759–1841). Activities included an annual series of public lectures in British industrial centres.

438 Joseph Pointer (1875–1914), elected to Sheffield Council 1908, MP Sheffield Attercliffe from his victory in 1909 by-election until his early death 19 November 1914, aged just 39.

convey to the Csar the feeling of horror which is rife in England as a consequence of the tyranny & oppression which is being extended to our fellow workers in Russia".[439] Agreed to on motion of Com Dorer.

Secy. Resignation of Comrade Ridley accepted in mournful silence on motion of Coms Dorer & White, with whom, as a special case, brevity was a feature. Com W.L. Lewis appointed on motion of Coms. Pye & White.

Executive vacancy. Following 3 members went to ballot Pooley, Mace & Pye. Comrade Mace elected.

Notice was given of resolution to be moved at next branch meeting affecting the constitution.

Finis

F.W. White   Chairman

N.A.C. voting:
W.C. Anderson 6,
J. Burgess 6,
J.R. Clynes 4,[440]
E.R. Hartley 14
Connor Kessaak 2,[441]
G Lansbury 14,
McArthur 3,
Noel 5,[442]
Smith 5,[443]
Rose 1.[444]
Signed Geo Ridley June 24 09.

---

439 The Tsar of Russia visited England for Cowes Regatta, 2–6 August 1909, staying with his family on board the imperial yacht *Standart*. While in England he met with King Edward VII and with the Prime Minister (Asquith) and the Foreign Secretary (Grey).

440 John Robert Clynes (1869–1949), elected MP Manchester North East 1906. Served in Lloyd George's wartime coalition; leader of Parliamentary Labour Party, 1921, member of MacDonald's 1924 and 1929 cabinets.

441 James O'Connor Kessack (1879–1916), trade unionist; national organiser of National Union of Dock Labourers from 1909, unsuccessful parliamentary candidate for Glasgow Camlachie, January and December 1910; joined Army in 1914, killed at the Battle of the Ancre, November 1916.

442 Revd Conrad Noel (1869–1942), of the Church Socialist League. Assistant priest at Primrose Hill from 1904, vicar of Thaxted from 1910. Left ILP for British Socialist Party on its foundation in 1911.

443 Frank Smith (1854–1940), journalist and close friend of Keir Hardie; founder member of ILP and its first Parliamentary candidate at Sheffield Attercliffe, 1894; Secretary of Right to Work Council, 1908; MP Nuneaton, 1929–31.

444 Frank Herbert Rose (1857–1928), ILP and adult suffragist campaigner, originally an engineer, then a journalist; candidate at Stockton (1906 and Jan. 1910); MP Aberdeen East,

Branch Meeting held Thursday June 29ᵗʰ 09, Windsor Road. Com White in the chair.

Minutes of previous meeting read & confirmed on motion of Coms Mills & Frost.

Moved by Com Mills sec by Com Dorer that the \attention of/ Town Council be drawn to the promise made to the London police to grant them one days rest in seven and to urge that our local police be given the same opportunity forthwith. The resolution to be sent to the Town Clerk by the secretary.

Newspaper Cuttings: That cuttings be taken from the local press of all matters affecting the Municipality, & also other items of interest. Com White undertook to do this.

J.M. Spurling

Meeting of Executive Monday July 12ᵗʰ 09 Windsor Rd Com White's house. Present Drew, Dorer, Frost, Mace, White, Mills, Spurling, Bunkall, Lewis. Com Spurling presided.

Minutes of previous meeting read & adopted on motion Coms Drew & Dorer.

The Secretary reported that the resolution re visit of \Czar/ passed by the branch on June 24ᵗʰ 09 had been sent to the member for Kings Lynn, Lieut Carlyon Bellairs, with a request that that gentleman should lay it in the proper quarter but that a reply had been received from the member for Kings Lynn that he could not identify himself with the resolution nor did he approve of it & therefore declined to take any action in that matter. After discussion it was left for the Secretary to proceed with a view to the resolution being placed before the King.

The question of finance in connection with the maintenance of the Club Room was discussed at some length and eventually, on the proposal of Com Frost seconded by Com Mace, it was agreed to recommend to the Branch the desirability of increasing the subscription from 6d to 9d per month, the opinion being that such an advance was absolutely necessary in the interests of the party. It was also suggested that with the view of providing the Club with suitable furniture a [*deleted illegible word*] List, inviting subscriptions, be opened for that purpose.

The Secretary read the report of the formation of the Divisional Council.

J.M. Spurling

1918–28; publications included *The Machine Monster: A Warning to Skilled Workers* (ILP, 1909) and *The Coming Force: The Labour Movement* (ILP, 1909).

Executive Meeting Com White's house Thursday Aug 12ᵗʰ 09. Present White, Mace, Drew, Mills, Lewis. Com Drew in the Chair.

Previous minutes read & adopted on motion of Coms Mace & Drew.

The Secretary reported that Com Pointer's M.P. services had been secured for a meeting Thursday Oct 14ᵗʰ.

Com Mills undertook to prepare a report for ~~the~~ submission to the next Branch meeting, giving particulars of repairs re to Club room.

Next Branch Meeting Thursday Aug 19ᵗʰ.

Accommodation of speakers. The Executive recommend that at each Branch meeting members be detailed for the purpose of securing Chairman, collectors etc for the forthcoming meetings.

J.M. Spurling

Meeting of the Branch – Club Room, Thursday, August 19ᵗʰ, Com Neave in the chair.

Minutes of Branch meetings June 24ᵗʰ and 29ᵗʰ read and adopted on motion of Coms Drew and Frost.

Minutes of interim Executive Meetings also read.

The Secretary reported: the formation of Divisional Council No 5 – comprising Norfolk, Suffolk, Essex, Herts, Bedford & Hunts a copy of its constitutions being duly exhibited in the Club Room – and the dissolution of the East Anglian Federation, its organisation \duties/ being assumed by the foresaid Div Council. Reports re 'visit of Czar' and the resolution affecting Boro Police also read, the latter on motion of Coms Drew & Mills being referred back to Executive.

Com Pointer's visit Oct 14ᵗʰ. The feeling of the Branch was that a Hall and preferably the Central Hall be engaged for this meeting, Secretary to arrange. Moved ~~Drew~~ \Frost/, seconded Drew.

Moved by Com Frost, seconded Com Simpole that in the forthcoming Municipal Campaign that a supply of leaflets entitled "Statement of principles" be obtained for distribution.[445] The Secretary to proceed.

The recommendation re increase in subscription which the Executive consider necessary to successfully carry on the Club room was referred to the next Branch meeting, on the motion of Coms Drew & Mace – the Secretary to specially summon the Meeting for the purpose.

---

445 Jonathan Haygarth Simpole, born 1873, of Pleasant Row; a dock labourer, joined Lynn ILP in 1910–11, and also recorded as a new member in 1914–15: presumably had resigned in between, although there is no record of this in subscription book.

The following new members were made on the motion of Com Frost &
Simpole: Barrett, Pollentine, Kinderson.[446]
J.M. Spurling

Meeting of Executive Committee Monday Aug 30th 09, Club Room,
Windsor Rd. Present Coms Drew, White, Frost, Lewis & Spurling. Com
Spurling in the Chair.
The previous minutes were read & adopted on motion of Com Drew &
Spurling.
The Secretary reported that the Central Hall could be obtained on Thursday
Oct 14th for Com Pointers visit at a cost of 30/- and lighting.
Com Frost reported that he had a scheme for the employment of an
organiser, for at least 3 months, to assist & in other ways organise the
\autumn/ municipal campaign and the matters of the Branch generally,
details of which would be submitted to the next ~~branch~~ meeting for the
purpose of laying before the Branch.
J.M. Spurling

Meeting of Executive Committee Monday Sep 13th 09 Com Mills house.
Present Coms Mills, Drew, Spurling, Bunkall, Frost, Lewis. Spurling presided.
Minutes of last Exec Meeting read and adopted on motion of Com Mills
& Drew.
Com Frost again brought forward his scheme for the employment by the
Branch of an Organiser and after discussion it was unanimously decided
to recommend to the Branch that the scheme be given a trial, though the
Wage-fund necessary would amount to, for 3 months, £25.
That for the forthcoming Municipal Election the Executive unanimously
recommend that Coms White & Frost be asked to contest the South &
Middle Wards respectively.
J.M. Spurling

Branch Meeting held at Labour Club Windsor Rd 8 pm Thursday Sep 17
09. Com Spurling presided. Minutes of previous meeting read & adopted
on motion of Comrades Mills & Frost.
The resignation of Com Lewis was read & accepted on motion of Mills
& Drew branch desiring to place on record their thanks. Com Ridley
reappointed Assis Secy on motion of Coms Frost & Dorer.

---

446 H. Barrett of Wisbech; W. Polentine of Wisbech: despite the uncommon name, not
found in 1901 or 1911 census. Probably the William Polentine, born Cambridge 1861,
possibly the William Pollendine who served in the RAMC 1914–20. Kinderson is probably
a misspelling of a third member from Wisbech, Mordecai Kempston, a railway booking
clerk, born 1878. He soon left Wisbech: last paying a subscription in September 1909.

Com Dorer regretfully tendered his resignation as Treasurer. This accepted with much regret on motion of Coms Mills & Frost, the President ably voicing on behalf of the Branch their appreciation of his services. Com Lewis appointed Treasurer on motion of Coms Ridley & Drew.

The question of organiser was discussed at considerable length, the matter eventually being referred back to Executive with full power to deal, on motion of Coms Dorer & Drew.

Municipal Elections. Coms White & Mills were suggested to the LRC as suitable Candidates for the coming election.

Increase Sub. Was again discussed. Further consideration of the matter was deferred until the Annual General meeting March 1910 on motion of Coms Ridley & White both Comrades expressing the desire on behalf of the Executive that all those members who could should advance their Sub.

Com ~~Jones~~ \Jermy/ a member of Norwich Board of Guardians was cordially accepted as member on motion of Coms Drew & White.[447]

The following resolution to be forwarded to the usual quarters was Prop by Com Dorer Sec Drew.[448]

Last (Thursday) night the Lynn branch of the Independent Labour Party met and unanimously passed the following resolution: "That to show our contempt for the tactics adopted in the Town Council by which the ratepayers are being put to the expense of a poll in respect of the much-needed new elementary school, we abstain from voting and urge our fellow ratepayers to do the same". This is, of course, the policy of common-sense, and will be followed by all reasonable people. To vote either for or against Mr Brown's faddist policy is merely to stamp the voter as thoughtless and foolish.[449]

---

447 Arthur Reginald Jermy (1875–1962), elected as Poor Law Guardian for Mousehold Ward Norwich in March 1907. A letter by him in the *EDP*, 28 Feb. 1908 gives his address as Scoles Green, Norwich. The Lynn subscription book of 1908–09 gives his address as Wisbech, so he had presumably moved there. He served his full three years on the Norwich Board, but a letter to the same paper on 29 March 1910 complained of his poor attendance at Board meetings in the second half of his term of office – he had only attended four meetings in the previous year. He only appears in the Lynn subscription books once, in September 1909.

448 The words of the Resolution are inserted in the form of a press cutting.

449 The Board of Education wanted the borough to build a new elementary school in the town, but Councillor Thomas Brown, as chairman of the Education Committee, objected to the expense and ordered a referendum among ratepayers as to the necessity. The referendum asked the question 'Is the Council to resist demands of the Board of Education and decline to build a new elementary school?' and ratepayers agreed, by a vote of 631 to 257, not to build a new school (*LN*, 4 Sept. and 24 Sept. 1909).

Executive meeting held Com Mills house Friday Sep 17 09. Present Comrades Mills, White, Drew, Lewis, Ridley. Com White presided.
After prolonged discussion it was agreed to employ a full time organiser but final consideration of the matter was deferred to permit Secy to write to several possible applicants.
J.M. Spurling

Executive meeting held Com White's house Tuesday Sep 21ˢᵗ. Present Coms Lewis, Mills, Drew, Bunkall, Mace, Spurling, Ridley, Com White in Chair. Question of employment of Organiser was again discussed & on motion of Coms Frost & Bunkall the following resolution was unanimously agreed to, "That in view of recommendations from Snowden & Preston we employ Com J. Arnott for 2 months with a possibility of 3".[450]

Executive meeting held Com White's house Sept 27ᵗʰ 09. Present Coms Arnott, Lewis, Frost, White, Drew, Mills, Mace, Bunkall. Com Spurling presided.
Minutes of last meeting adopted on motion of Coms White & Mace.
After an address from Comrade Arnott on the Municipal Campaign Comrades Mills & Drew moved "That quotations as to cost of different methods outlined be submitted to next branch meeting".
The following meetings were arranged to be addressed by Organisers Witard & Arnott:

Monday   4 Oct Union Chapel Wisb. Rd
Tuesday   5 "   Highgate
Wednesday 6 "
Thursday   7 "   Loke Road
Friday   8 "   So Clough Lane
Saturday   9 "   Market Place
J.M. Spurling

Branch meeting held Labor Club Sep 30, Com Spurling presided.
Organiser Arnott addressed the branch on the Municipal Campaign at some length & it was agreed that we adopt Arnott's scheme for a complete canvas on motion of Coms ~~White~~ Lewis & Drew.
Printers meeting. Proposed Com Mills Sec Green that Com Fred Henderson be asked to take the Chair.[451]

450 John Arnott (1871–1942), blacksmith in shipbuilding, steel and engineering, member of ASE, Middlesborough; later prominent in Leeds city politics; Labour MP for Hull, 1929–31; Preston has not been identified.
451 The public meeting was held on 14 October, Henderson presiding and Labour's

New member. Mrs Frost was accepted on motion of Coms Mills & Ridley.[452]

Executive meeting held Labor Club Tuesday Nov 2nd 09. Present Coms Arnott, Frost, White, Mills, Ridley, Spurling in Chair.
The recent Municipal results were discussed at some length & it was agreed that we make an early consideration of the Campaigns for the future.[453]
Minutes of previous meeting read & confirmed on motion of Coms White & Mills.
Letter was read from Com Cadman asking for name of delegate to Council meeting at Norwich on Nov 6th when our Parliamentary Candidature would be considered. Com Frost appointed on motion of Coms White & Mills.
Speakers: Secy instructed to endeavour to procure speaker just prior to Guardians & Municipal elections 1910.
J.M. Spurling

Executive meeting held Com Mills house Tuesday Nov 9th 09 8 pm. Present Coms White, Mace, Lewis, Arnott, Bunkall, Frost, Ridley, Com Spurling presiding.
Minutes of previous meeting adopted on motion of Coms Mills & White.
Com Frost reported upon his visit to the Eastern Divisional Council & his report in connection with a Parliamentary Candidate for the Borough shewed that that [sic] the matter had reached a further & interesting stage.
It was agreed that the following be suggested as Election Officers for next branch meeting:

Election	Secy	T.A. Frost
Middle Ward	"	J Mills
South	"	"	J.W. Wand[454]
North	"	"	

The Executive to act as our Election Ctee.

---

three candidates for the forthcoming municipal elections – White, Mills and Jackson – all speaking (*EDP*, 16 Oct. 1909). This was Jackson's last campaign as a member of the ILP.
452 Not, as might be assumed, the wife of Thomas Asa Frost. The subscription books record her name as Mrs Adelaide Anne Frost, born 1884, of London Road. Her husband was Francis Frost, a bricklayer's labourer, whose name never occurs as a party member.
453 For the second year in a row, the ILP had put up one candidate in each ward and again all three were heavily defeated: Jackson, North Ward (226 votes), Mills, Middle Ward (125 votes), White (South Ward) 252 votes. Jackson was already seen in the local press as a prospective Liberal: 'it would seem questionable whether [Jackson] is powerful enough to win a municipal seat unless he should be officially taken up by the Liberal party.' (*LN*, 6 Nov. 1909).
454 John Wand, born 1874, bricklayer, living at 34, Checker Street, South Lynn at time of 1911 census.

Regular cleaning of Club Room was again discussed & on motion of Coms Mills & Bunkall, subject to sanction by Branch meeting to pay for it.
J.M. Spurling   Chairman

Branch meeting held Labour Club Windsor Ro 6 pm Sunday [*Nov.*] 21ˢᵗ 09. Com Spurling presided. The previous branch meeting minutes were read & confirmed on motion of Comrades Drew & Mace.

Comrade Frost reported that the E.D.C. required a contribution – weekly – to their Organisers fund. Proposed by Comrades Frost & Drew that we contribute 6d per week.

In response to the Council's offer it was agreed on motion of Coms Drew & Frost that we ask for 500 copies of Benson's pamphlet on Socialism,[455] to be distributed by Ward Workers.

Labour party delegate. Com Witard nominated by vote.

Offer of Womens League to contribute towards cleaning of Club room was accepted on motion of Coms Watson & Mace, several members present also agreeing to contribute.

Com Watson moved & Com Pooley seconded This branch endorses the actions of the Executive in relation to a Parliamentary Candidate.

Com Ridley moved a vote of thanks to Organiser Arnott for his services to the branch, Seconded by Frost & supported by Mills & Spurling.

On motion of Arnott & Mills the following new members were welcomed: Mr Snodgrass, London Rd;[456] Mr Cox, Sillfield Tce; Mrs Rayner, Gaywood; Mrs Green, Gaywood; Miss Green, Gaywood; Mr Bloy, Wellesley St.[457]
J.M. Spurling

---

455 Thomas Duckworth Benson (1857–1926); of Eccles, Manchester; accountant and later estate agent, as well as socialist activist; writer of ILP tracts including *Socialism* (London: ILP, 1907). Others included *The Workers Hell and the Way Out* (London: ILP, ?1905) and *Woman, the Communist* (London: ILP, ?1907). He was Treasurer of the ILP, 1901–20.

456 Burns Snodgrass, (1886–1954), elected 30 Sept. 1909 (Thomas Asa Frost had been a boarder in the Snodgrass household in 1901). Born Kings Lynn, 25 Jan. 1886; educated at the National School to Dec. 1898; Municipal Technical School, 1898–1901; apprentice A. Dodman & Co Ltd engineers, 1901–07; attended Technical Institute, 1902–07; scholarship to Royal College of Science, London, 1908–1911 (Whitworth exhibition, 1910); described as science student in 1911 census, when living at London Road, Lynn with his mother, and a live-in servant; Associate, Institute of Mechanical Engineers, 1911; instructor, Royal College of Science and Paddington Technical Institute, 1911–12; Assistant Lecturer in mechanical engineering, University of Hull, Sept. 1912– ; wartime assistant inspector of gun armaments, Ministry of Munitions; in 1920 pioneered a unique slide rule and combined its manufacture with teaching at the Brighton Technical College until 1935 when he became a full-time manufacturer with his son, with a booming business in wartime; author, *Teach Yourself the Slide Rule* (1955); left £18,449 in 1954. See https://sliderulemuseum.com/Unique.htm.

457 Cox not identified (according to subscription book lived at Silfield terrace, Lynn in

Executive meeting held Com Mills house Nov 23ʳᵈ 9.0 pm Present Coms Lewis, Frost, Mace, Mills, Ridley & White presiding.

Minutes of previous meeting adopted by motion of Comrades White & Mills. Cleaning of Club room. Moved by Comrade Frost Sec Mills "That a voluntary fund be started to defray cost", Comrade Mills agreeing to collect until Annual meeting. 3/- weekly to be paid.

Annual Soiree. Moved by Mills & Frost "That the Secy be instructed to engage St James Rooms for a suitable [?*fee*] & have power to co-opt Ctee to assist with arrangements"

Affiliation fees. Secy instructed to send 25/- to headquarters.

A financial statement was given.

Executive meeting held Com Mills house Wednesday Jany 5ᵗʰ 09.[458] Present Coms Lewis, Mace, Drew, White, Frost, Mills, Ridley & Spurling presiding. Minutes of previous meeting Drew & White.

The Parliamentary situation was again discussed & it was agreed that the branch be recommended to issue a Manifesto setting forth their position regarding the two Capitalistic Candidates.[459]

Com. Mace reported that he had a weekly deficiency 1s 1d in the Room Cleaning fund & it was agreed to recommend that the deficit be defrayed from branch funds.

The ~~Assis~~ Secy was instructed to write to Com. Jackson pointing out that his membership of Gibson Bowles Ctee was not in accordance with the constitution of the party, requesting him to state which he desired to retain membership of.

Nominations for National Officers, N.A.C. members & resolutions for Conference were also considered.

The following Sunday evening lectures were arranged:

Jan 6.   J. Mills –   Land taxation
  "   23   G Ridley   Socialism & Trade Unionism
  "   30   H Lowerison   Memoirs of an old Campaigner
Feby 6 J.W. Spalding
  "   13 F.W. White

1909–10, but no Cox recorded at the address in 1901 or 1911 census); Anna Elizabeth Rayner, born 1873, wife of William Rayner, railwayman, Gaywood Road, Lynn; Frances Green, born 1865, 'housekeeper'; Ethel Ada Green, born 1888, piano teacher, the wife and daughter of Philip Green (see above, note 410), Gaywood Road. Bloy could be either the William Bloy, an original signatory to the Socialist Society 18 August 1897, or the William E. Bloy who signed the Socialist Society's rules 3 January 1898 (NRO, SO 297/2).

458 An error: should be 1910.

459 Viz. Bowles, now a Liberal and Hon. E. Cadogan, a Unionist.

\Com Jackson replied to Secy stating that he would give his answer at branch meeting./

Branch meeting held Labor Club 8 pm Jany 9ᵗʰ 1910 Com Spurling presiding.
Minutes of previous meeting adopted motion Comrades Lewis & Drew.
Nominations for National Officers were:-
Chairman   Geo Lansbury
Treasurer   T. D. Benson
N.A.C.   Anderson, Jowett,⁴⁶⁰ Lansbury, & MacArthur⁴⁶¹
District N.A.C. Fletcher Dodd
Cleaning Room – Agreed on motion of Dorer that branch funds bear balance.
Parliamentary situation Moved by Mills & Frost supported by White & carried "That this branch declares its inability to support either of the Capitalistic Candidates now in the field & agrees to issue a manifesto to that effect". 4 against.
A manifesto prepared by the Executive was read & it was agreed to issue 3000 on motion of Coms White & Frost.
Resolution for Conference. Moved by Mills & Drew "That this party in future be known as the Socialist party instead of ILP". Carried by 10 votes to 8.
Com Jackson. Correspondence which had passed was read by Secy & technical position explained. Com Jackson declared his inability to resign from Bowles Ctee but after considerable discussion be [sic] persuaded to accept until the following – Monday – evening & let the Executive have his decision then.

Executive meeting held Club room Jany 24ᵗʰ. Present Comrades Mills Frost Bunkall Ridley & Spurling presiding.
Communication from Comrade Jackson was read & fully considered. Moved by Mills & Drew that it be further considered at next Executive.

---

460 Fred Jowett (1864–1944), ILP politician. Elected MP Bradford 1906, one of only two of the 29 Labour MPs to be elected in a three-way contest. Chairman of ILP, 1909–10 and 1914. Lost seat 1918, re-elected 1922, Minister of Works in Labour government of 1924 – 'a firebrand member of the ILP from Bradford' (Shepherd and Laybourn, *First Labour Government*, 59).
461 Mary Macarthur (1880–1921), founder of the National Federation of Women Workers 1906, served on NAC, 1909–1912. Member of Adult Suffrage League, campaigning for votes for all adults. Married W. C. Anderson (see above, note 416) in 1911. Defeated at Stourbridge in 1918 general election.

Executive meeting held Com Frosts house Feby 8th 09.[462] Present Comrades Lewis Bunkall Mace Mills Frost Ridley & Spurling presiding. Minutes of previous meeting adopted on motion of Coms Frost & Bunkall.

Com Witard. It was agreed to invite Witard for a week on & from Feby 14th on motion of Frost & Drew, Frost & Mills agreeing to share hospitality.

Mr Chatterton. Agreed that he be invited to address the party in the Club room on Wednesday Febry 14th & strong attempt be made to fill the room.

Com. Grayson. Secy was instructed to write for dates & make suitable arrangements.

Finances thoroughly considered.

Branch meeting held Labour Club Sunday Febry 27th 1910 8 pm, Com White presiding.

Minutes of previous meeting were read and confirmed on motion of Coms Drew & Frost.

A letter was read from the Women's Freedom League offering to send a speaker to address the branch.[463] On motion of Green & Mills the Secy was instructed to obtain information from them as to the kind of meeting they desired.

A letter was read from Com Dalton of London offering to speak on Oct 3 1910 for 10s /6d.[464] Moved by Drew & Gittens that we accept.

Question of delegate to Annual Conference[465] was discussed & the matter was referred to Executive on motion of Coms Drew & Fox.

Moved by Mrs Mills seconded by Mrs Frost that the clubroom be closed at 10 pm each evening except on special occasions. Amendment by Drew & Frost \Triance/ substituting 11pm. Carried.

Guardians Elections. Moved by Frost & Sec Drew "That we fight the whole town providing Candidates can be found who can command the confidence of this branch & for whom members of this branch are willing to work & do all possible to ensure their return to the Board of Guardians.

Executive meeting held Com Frosts house Feby 28 /1910. Present Coms Frost Drew Mills Mace & Spurling presiding.

Absence of Secy prevented adoption of previous minutes.

---

462 An error: should be 1910.

463 Suffragette group, founded 1907. See below, page 260.

464 Probably Arthur A[rchibald] Dalton, 49 Milner Sq, Barnsbury, who appears on a contemporary list of ILP speakers for London and the Eastern Counties.

465 The Annual Conference was held at Memorial Hall, London on 28 and 29 March. There was no King's Lynn delegate, in contrast with Ipswich who sent five (including Edith Fletcher Dodd, John Fletcher Dodd's wife). Norwich sent three and Lowestoft one (A. H. Bond).

Annual Conference business was discussed but no definite arrangements made.

The question of Guardians Election was discussed at great length and the following Comrades were recommended to the Branch as Candidates:
St Margarets Com Frost,
               "   Mills,
               "   Edmunds;
South Lynn Com White,
                      Bunnett.

Executive meeting held Labor Club Windsor Ro 9 pm Mar 8 /1910. Present Coms Drew Lewis Frost White Mills Bunkall Mace Ridley & Spurling presiding.

Minutes of previous meetings adopted on motion of Coms Drew & Frost.

Secy reported that owing to continued ill health of Grayson he had been unable to arrange anything definite.

Correspondence was read from Comrade Cadman E.D.C. Secy to say that the date upon which J. Parker M.P. can visit this area are not convenient. Also to ask for one of the following speakers for a Summer demonstration Coms Hardie, Barnes, Crooks,[466] McDonald, Snowden or Lansbury.

Also to state that this branch are not booking local speakers at present.

Guardians elections were again considered & White Frost & Mills agreed to draw up a joint address & present to next Executive meeting on March 14 /1910. In the meantime Secy to write Break up of Poor Law Ctee for samples of literature & enquire as to powers of Board of Guardians.[467]

Executive meeting held Comrade Mills house Mar 14 1910. Present Mace Drew Bunkall Frost Mills Ridley & White presiding.

Minutes adopted on motion of Mills & Frost.

---

466 Will Crooks (1852–1921), one of the first Labour members of the London County Council, 1892; elected to Poplar Board of Guardians, 1893; Mayor of Poplar, 1901, the first Labour mayor in London; MP Woolwich 1903–21.

467 A royal commission into the Poor Law produced two reports in 1909. Both thought that Boards of Guardians should be abolished and their responsibilities pass to local authorities. The Minority Report written by Beatrice Webb, with the support of Revd Russell Wakefield, Dean of Norwich, went much further, suggesting that the issue of employment was too great for local authorities and should be dealt with by central government. A National Committee to Promote the Break-up of the Poor Law was formed in 1909 to promote the Minority Report, which was debated in Parliament in April 1911. Nothing was done at the time, but the changes it recommended did finally become law in 1929 (Laybourn, *British Social Policy*, 166; Robert Ensor, *England 1870–1914* (1936), 517; *Hansard*, 8 Apr. 1911).

Mills promised to see Bunnett concerning Guardians elections.

Sanders meeting. Proposed by Mills & Bunkall that Central Hall be engaged for March 31st. Universal admission 1^d front seats 6^d. Mace & Mills proposed that the Dean of Norwich be invited to speak.[468]

Letter read from Com Dalton offering further dates which were accepted on motion of Coms Mills & Frost.

The Annual Meeting of the branch was held in the Club Room 7.30 pm Sunday March 20 1910. Minutes of last annual meeting read and confirmed on motion of White & Drew.

Minutes of previous branch meeting read and confirmed on motion of Mace & Lewis.

Com Mills reported that Bunnett declined to accept nomination to contest Board of Guardians.

The As[s]is Secy gave a brief report of the work of the branch during preceding year which was accepted on motion of Mills & Frost.

Treasurers report & Balance sheet was adopted on motion of White & Woolway.

Miss Green & Mrs Frost appointed Scrutineers. Election of Officers was then proceeded with & resulted as follows:

President	T.A. Frost
Secretary	J. Mills
Assis "	G. Ridley
Financial "	R. Drew
Treasurer	J.C. Triance
Librarian	Carter Gittens
Executive	White Bunkall Spurling Green
L.R.C.	Frost Bunkall Mills Ridley
Auditors	J. Neave & H. Pooley

Comrades Mace Jenkinson & Simpole offered to assist in distribution of branch notices for ensuing year.[469]

The retiring Chairman J.W. Spurling in an excellent address regretted the absence of loyalty & enthusiasm amongst the members adding a word of appreciation for the work of his Executive colleagues during his year of office.

The question of increased subscription was again discussed at some length & after various resolutions & amendments the following proposed by Com

---

468 Henry Russell Wakefield (1854–1933) Dean of Norwich Cathedral, 1909–1911, later Bishop of Birmingham.

469 Henry Jenkinson, born 1880, general labourer, lived in Windsor Road, Lynn.

Mace was agreed to unanimously, "That the subscription be raised to 8d extra 2d to be optional where more than one member in a family".

Ald. Sanders meeting. Chairman T.A. Frost on motion of Spurling & Bunkall. 50 posters White & Bunkall.

Assis Secy reported that Dr Russell Wakefield Dean of Norwich wrote regretting that another engagement prevented him from attending the meeting.

Com Spurling proposed Com White seconded "That this meeting supports the Minority report Bill (which is to come on for Second reading in the House of Commons on April 8th) and earnestly requests the Parliamentary representative for this Constituency to be in attendance on that day & to give his vote for the second reading of the Bill".

On motion of Coms Drew & Mace Mrs Triance & W. Stevens were accepted as members.[470]

The meeting was informed that the Guardians election addresses and notices of Sanders meeting would be ready for distribution on Easter Tuesday evening.

Continuance of Cleaning Clubroom was left to consideration of Executive on motion of Coms Spurling & White.

Com H Pooley suggested that Socialist weekly papers should be placed on Club table.

Com Gittens agreed to give Justice
  ″   Mills   ″   ″   ″   Clarion
  ″   Ridley   ″   ″   ″   Labour Leader

Executive meeting held Com Mills house 9 pm April 11 1910. Present Coms Drew Green Triance Mills Bunkall Ridley & Frost presiding. Minutes of previous meetings adopted on motion of Bunkall & Green.

Agreed that future Exec meetings be held on alternative Monday evenings at 8 pm on motion of Drew & Bunkall.

Cleaning of Clubroom. Agreed that Caretaker be paid 1/6 per week from Mar 1st to Novr 1st.

Summer meetings. Assis Secy to secure services of Coms Leonard Hall Pickles Stott & Higgenbottom.

Branch meeting held Labor Club Tuesday April 19th 8 pm, Com Frost presiding. Minutes of previous meeting adopted on motion of Drew & Bunkall.

Following nominations were made for E.D.C.

---

470 Mrs Triance, see above, notes 76, 225. William Stevens, born 1863, a fisherman, lived at 2 Market Lane, Chapel Street, with his father (born 1842) of same name and occupation.

Chairman Fletcher Dodd Yarmouth
Treasurer J.C. Triance Lynn
Executive T.A. Frost   "

Letter from Cadman answered which contained invitations to branch members to make application for position of Organising Secy. Chairman announced that it was Com Ridley's intention to apply. Com White proposed & Drew seconded "That the Executive make best endeavours to secure his appointment".

Owing to his leaving the town Com Ridley regretted his resignation as Assis Secy. Frost expressed mutual regrets on behalf of branch.

Com Frost proposed White seconded that in the event of Billiard table being sold for £5 that amount to be earmarked to assist in purchasing a better one.

Executive Meeting held in Club Room April 24. Com Frost presiding. Com Triance, Mills, Drew, Bunkall, Ridley & Snodgrass, Phillip Green being present. The minutes of previous meeting were adopted upon the motion of Com. Mills & Drew.

It was decided to forward to the Parliamentary ~~Candidate~~ Member the Resolution received from the W.F.L. urging his support of same. It was decided after discussion, that in order to support Com Ridley's application to E.D.C. Com Mills should write Com Fletcher Dodd & Henderson, & Com Frost should write Com Miss Pounder[471] & Whittard urging their personall support of his application.

Executive Meeting held in Club Room Monday May 9th, the following Com were present Triance, Drew, Mills, Snodgrass, Com. Spurling presiding. The previous minutes having been read were adopted upon the motion of Com Mills & seconded by Com Triance.

Upon the motion of Coms Triance & Drew it was decided after discussion to reduce by 10 the number of affiliations to E.D.C.

Com Triance proposed & Com Drew seconded that a Branch Meeting be called for Sunday May 15th, & that a Whist Drive be held on Whit Monday commencing at 7.20 pm.

Branch Meeting held in the Club Room Sunday May 15 8 pm, Com Spurling presiding. The minutes of previous meeting having been read, were adopted upon the motion of Com. Mills & White.

---

471 Correctly, Mrs Alice Ponder of 'Waldo', Oulton Broad, member of Lowestoft branch of ILP. Accepted nomination for a place on the Mutford and Lothingland Board of Guardians 1913, but withdrew before the election took place (*Lowestoft Journal*, 15 March 1913). Also a suffragist: see below, page 292, note 67.

Upon the motion of Com Mills & Drew supported by Com White it was decided to endeavour to arrange for August Clarion Cycle Meet to be held at Lynn, all the necessary arrangements to be left to the Executive. Com White to write as secretary to Clarion Club to Lowerison to endeavour to obtain his support in conjunction with that of Com Blatchford.

The ballot for the executive Committee of E.D.C. was the next business. The ~~votes~~ following votes were cast & counted under the scrutiny of Coms Mrs Mills & Mrs Phillip Green: Witard 18, Henderson & Dodd 17, Reeves 15, Ponder & Rowntree[472] 10, Morley 9, Elliott 7,[473] Kerry 4,[474] & Bates 2.[475]

It was proposed by Com White & seconded by Com Triance, that it be left to executive to engage speakers in connection with our summer propaganda. On the motion of Coms Triance & Mills, Miss Ethel Sporne was accepted as member of the Branch.

Executive Meeting held in the Club Room Friday May 27 ins. Com Triance, Mills, Spurling, Drew & Snodgrass being present, Com Frost presiding. The previous minutes been read were adopted upon the motion of Coms Spurling & Mills.

Com Mills was elected to attend the 1st Annual Conference of the E.D.C. to be held at Ipswich, upon the proposition of Com Frost & Seconded by Com Spurling.

It was decided to decline the offer of Com Pickles of Bradford to speak ~~at the~~ during the summer propaganda, owing to rather heavy expenditure incurred in Travelling expenses etc.[476]

Com Mills proposed & Com Frost seconded that if the surport of Com Lowerison & Blatchford could be obtained, all efforts to \be/ used to hold the annual August Bank Holiday meet of the Clarion Cycle Club at Lynn.

472 John William Rowntree, born 1865, in 1911 a factory foreman living at Stafford Road, Gorleston. On committee of Great Yarmouth Industrial Co-operative Society 1907, chairman of Yarmouth ILP 1909 (*Yarmouth Independent*, 9 Feb. 1907, 27 May 1909). By 1921, living in Hull, where he had been born.
473 Frederick George Elliott of Ipswich, born 1878, bricklayer: in 1911, living at 19 Alan Road, Ipswich.
474 George William Kerry of Colchester, born 1882, carman. In 1911, living at 19, Victor Road, Colchester.
475 George Bates, born 1869, shop manager, in 1911 living at 223, Nevells Road, Letchworth.
476 Alfred Pickles (1875–1936), insurance agent and prominent member of Bradford ILP. Later served on Bradford City Council, from *c.* 1919, becoming lord mayor, 1930–31.

Executive Meeting held in the Club Room Friday June 6 1910, at 9.30 pm. Com Triance, Drew, White & Snodgrass being present, Com Frost presiding. Minutes of previous meeting, having been read was adopted upon the motion of Coms Drew & White.

Com Frost proposed & Com White seconded that a branch Meeting be held on Saturday June 12th to consider proposal of Kings Lynn S.D.P. the appointment of speakers for summer propaganda & the voting for election of members for E.D.C a second Ballot being found necessary.

Regret was expressed upon the abandonment of efforts which were being made by Com White to arrange for the August Bank Holiday meet of Clarion Cycle Club to be held at Lynn. Com Lowerison having intimated that it was impossible as both he & Com Blatchford would be away at that time.

Branch meeting held in the Club Room June 11 1910 @ 8.30 pm, Com Frost presiding. Minutes of previous meetings having been read were adopted upon the motion of Coms Spurling & Pye.

The voting for E.D.C (a second Ballot having been found necessary) was carried out, the following votes being cast. Elliott, F.G. Ipswich 19. Bates G. Letchworth 8. Rowntree Yarmouth 4. & Kerry G. Colchester 1.

Com Triance proposed & Com Drew seconded, that in view of the fact that we have already arranged 2 meetings for Sept & Oct, & bearing in mind the financial position of the party funds, that we decline the offer of the Local Branch of S.D.P to jointly hold 2 meetings, but at the same time assure them of any & all assistance & support that lies in our power.

The appointment of speakers for the summer propaganda was the next business. Com Mills promised 1 meeting a suitable date to be arranged. Com Mills proposed that the secretary approach the Federation to obtain names of any speakers in the area who would be willing to pay a visit to Lynn & speak & to fill up all dates from local supplies with a view to minimising all expenses incurred, this was seconded by Com Triance. Com Spurling further proposed & Com Drew seconded, that resolution giving Secretary full power to engage 4 speakers be rescinded. Both resolutions were carried.

Executive Meeting held in Club Room Friday June 20th @ 9.30 pm. Present Coms Mills Drew Spurling Snodgrass and Frost presiding. Previous meetings minutes were adopted upon motion of Coms Mills & Drew.

It was decided to leave the appointment of speakers for Summer program to the Delegates of the branch visiting Ipswich Conference of E.D.C.

The proposal of the Local F.C.C to hold meetings alternate Saturdays at the

Walks Gate during July & August was discussed, & it was agreed to fix our meetings as far as possible so as not to clash with those of the F.C.C.[477]
It was also agreed after discussion to make a special effort, as suggested by the I.L.P, throughout the branch, to help them with their appeal.

Executive Meeting held in Club Room Friday July 4. Present Coms Mills, Drew, Triance, Spurling, White, Snodgrass and Frost presiding. The adoption of minutes of previous meeting was proposed by Com Mills seconded by Com White & carried unanimously.
The secretary was requested to write Com Witard & endeavour to book July 24, also write Com Henderson Norwich, requesting him to give us a date when he would be able to to speak at Lynn. These dates being filled in then write Com G Bates Letchworth offering him remaining vacant dates. It was also proposed that secretary write Com Ducker of Snettisham requesting him to inform to the secretary if at any time he should have staying with him any speaker who would care to visit Lynn & propagate socialism.[478]
Proposal to Form Club Committee – After a lengthy discussion Com Mills was delegated to propose the suggestion at Branch meeting.
Com Frost gave notice of a proposal made by N.A.C & R.C.A to employ part time organiser. This was deferred until next executive meeting when Com Frost hoped to be able to give more definite & reliable information.

Branch Meeting held in Club Room Sunday July 10. Com Triance presiding. Minutes of previous meeting's were adopted upon motion of Coms Mills & Stevens.
It was agreed upon the suggestion of Com Mills, that owing to financial position of Branch, to [*illegible deletion*] gather (if any) by voluntary contributions any financial assistance from our comrades connected with the \Abercynon Branch/ South Wales I.L.P.[479] The secretary being requested to place on notice board a subscription list for that purpose.
It was proposed by Com Mills "That a Club Committee be formed, this committee to endeavour to raise sufficient revenue apart from subscriptions to defray expenses other than rent incurred in maintaining the Club, to organize socials, entertainments, Whist Drives, Outings Etc for the members". This was seconded by Com Snodgrass & carried unanimously.

---

477 Free Church Council, see above, note 385.
478 Albert Ducker, cart and van builder (1908 trade directory).
479 In 1909 the Abercynon branch of the ILP alleged the local district council was employing labour at less than union rates. Sued for libel, the branch lost the case and had to pay costs of £200. The Abercynon Libel Fund was promoted by the *Labour Leader*, see for example *Labour Leader*, 4 Feb. 1910 and 28 Oct. 1910.

The following Com were elected for the Committee Com Mrs Green Mrs White Mrs Triance Storer Mills & Hull with power to add.[480]
The Annual Outing was next discussed. ~~The~~ July 31ˢᵗ being the probable date. Castleacre, Snettisham Beach & Ringland Downs being mentioned as suitable places. The arrangements being left to the Club Committee.
Com Mills gave a very clear, concise & lengthy report of the Ipswich Conference of E.D.C.
A letter was read from Com Frost requesting his release, owing to pressure of business, from his position of Chairman of the branch. Regrets were expressed on all sides, but it was agreed to ask him to retain his office, the vice-chairman acting in all ways for him, till such a time as he would be able to renew his duties.
J.W. Spurling

Executive Meeting held in Club Room Friday July 22. Present Com's White, Drew, Triance, Mills, Snodgrass & Spurling presiding. Minutes were adopted upon the motion of Com's Mills & Drew.
It was decided to offer Com Bates of Letchworth Sept 4ᵗʰ ~~as date~~ to speak at Lynn. Com Faulkner's of Southport application for a fixture was declined owing to absence of vacant dates.[481] The secretary was requested to write Com Dalton & state, with regrets, that we are unable to arrange any other date, other than Oct 1-2-3 already booked.
Letter from Divisional Committee was deferred till next Branch meeting.
J.W. Spurling

Executive Meeting held Com Mills' house Aug 4ᵗʰ. Present Com Mills, Drew, Snodgrass & Spurling presiding.
The adoption of minutes of previous executive meeting was moved by Com Mills & carried.
It was decided to book Com Bates of Letchworth on Sept 11 as requested. The secretary to write & confirm same.
Com Faulkner, Southport, request to speak at Lynn in November ~~was~~ on Minority Report was reluctantly refused owing to no suitable vacant date.
The Assit Secretary gave in his resignation owing to his leaving town.[482]

---

480 Edward Williams Hull, born 1880, railway ticket collector, in 1911 living at Victoria Street, Lynn.
481 William Faulkner, born 1881, described in 1911 census as writer on sociology, living at 54, Warren Road, Southport. Faulkner was Southport representative at the Edinburgh ILP Conference 1909: it was he who proposed the amendment that the Independent Labour Party secede from the Labour Representation Committee. See above, note 420.
482 Snodgrass, see above, note 456.

This was accepted by the executive on behalf of the branch, Com Mills undertaking his duties till such time as a successor could be appointed.
J.W. Spurling

Executive Meeting held at Club Room Windsor Road August 25th 1910. Present Comrades Spurling (Chair), Mills, Drew and Triance. Minutes adopted on the motion of Com Drew & Triance.
Letter was read from Com Bates of Letchworth stating he could not fulfil his engagement to speak on Sept 11th, and offering Sept 17th & 24 and, as neither dates were suitable, it was resolved to cancel the engagement.
The organisation of Russell Williams Meeting was discussed and it was agreed that an Advt be placed in "Lynn Opinion" Com Mills undertaking to arrange matter.[483]
New Member Miss Lila Wright prop. Com Drew Sec. Com Mills.[484]
Com Mills reported that the Club Committee had sold the Billiard table for £2-10-0, whole amount would be utilized for purchase of New Table.

Executive Meeting held at Com Mills House Sept 11th 1910. Present: Com. P. Green Chair Mills, Drew, White & Spurling.
Com Mills announced that Victor Grayson would be at Heacham shortly, and suggested that steps be taken to try and secure his services for a Big Demonstration. It was decided that Com Mills see Harry Lowerison and enlist his services for this object.
The ensuing Municipal Elections were discussed at some length, and it was decided to advise the Party to contest the South Ward, provided suitable candidate could be obtained, and that the question of the other Wards be deferred. It was agreed to recommend that Com Mills and White contest the South Ward.

---

483 Local newspaper, running from 1909 to 1912 only. Copies in British Library (NEWS 13999), lacking 1911, no copies in Norfolk Libraries. J. Russell Williams (1869–1926), of Huddersfield: member of NAC of ILP; LRC candidate for Huddersfield in general election of 1906 and in by-election of that year; candidate for Spen valley in general election of Jan. 1910.
484 Lila Wright occurs frequently as a singer in local newspaper reports between January 1907 and May 1911. In 1908, she is recorded as bridesmaid to her sister May, the eldest daughter of Jasper J. Wright (*LN*, 8 Aug. 1908). This enables identification: Lila's baptismal name was Eliza Wright, born in Lynn in 1893. Her father was a photographer. By the time of the 1911 census, the family had moved to North Runcton: Eliza is recorded as a photographer's assistant, presumably working in her father's studio. Several of the reports of her musical activities show members of the Sporne family as fellow musicians: for example, Lila was a member of the King's Lynn and Hunstanton Operatic Society along with Ethel Sporne (*EDP*, 16 May 1907), while she and Arthur Sporne took part in a concert together in 1909 (*LA*, 23 Apr. 1909).

It was decided that a Branch Meeting be held for Thursday Sept 15.
New Member Mr Frank Knowles prop by Mills, seconded Drew.[485] Carried.
J.W. Spurling

Branch Meeting held at Labour Club, Thursday Sept 15. Com W Spurling
in the Chair. Minutes of previous Meetings were adopted on the motion of
Drew & Gittings.
The Minute of the Executive relating to Municipal Elections was considered
and it was Prop by Com F. Hall & Seconded by C. Gittings that the matter
be left to the Executive, and carried.
It was agreed that a night be set apart to discuss the Minority Manifesto.
Several questions were asked relating to the Club Committee, but as no
satisfactory answer was forthcoming, it was agreed that the Committee be
asked to report to the Branch at an early date.

Executive Meeting held in Comrade Mills' house Sept 26th/10. Present Com
Spurling (Chair), Mills, White, Triance & Drew.
Moved by Com Mills & seconded by Com Triance minutes be adopted as
read.
Moved by Com Drew & seconded by Com Triance that the Club Committee
be asked to report to the Executive at least once a month.
Proposed by Com White & seconded Com Triance Com Pooley be ~~asked~~
appointed Assist Secy \vice Com Snodgrass/ until a suitable applicant turns up.
Com Mills proposed each Thursday commencing at 8 pm after Nov local
elections be set apart for discussion of various phases of Socialism for
education of branch members, & suggested the Fabian essays be taken
first.[486] Carried.
Municipal elections. Com Mills was proposed, on motion of Com Drew, as
candidate for South Ward. Seconded by Com Triance & carried.
It was decided to go fully into the Candidature on Oct 9th at the Special
Branch Meeting.
J.W. Spurling

Special Branch Meeting held at Labor Club Sunday 9th Oct/10. Comrade
White in chair.
Minutes of previous meeting were adopted on motion of Comrade Mills &
Gittings.

---

485 Not certainly identified, no one of this name within twenty miles of Lynn in 1901
or 1911 census. Perhaps *Frederick* Henry Knowles, born 1877, assistant school master at
Heacham in 1911: he was a master at Lowerison's school in the village.
486 *Fabian Essays in Socialism* (London, 1889).

<u>Club Committee's report</u>. Comrade Hall moved & Simpole seconded that minutes of previous meeting be altered so as to read after Committee "but they were not in a position to report".

Municipal Elections. Comrade Mills was adopted as Candidate for South Ward on motion of Comrade Gittings & seconded by Comrade Simpole. It was agreed that the Executive be given the full power to control the work of Election Address, canvassing etc on suggestion of Comrades Hall & Gittings.

Wallheads Meeting.[487] Com Mills was elected to chair on motion of Comrades Drew & Bunkall. It was decided to advertise the meeting in the Local press.

<u>Winter Propaganda</u>. Several suggestions were made & the branch decided that the Secretary be asked to provide speakers for Winter Months.

<u>Grayson's Meeting</u>. Com Mills reported a p.c. had been received ~~stating~~ from \Com/ Lowerison & a promise given, date to be left open.

<u>10/10/10 Executive Meeting held Com White's house.</u> Com Spurling in Chair. Present also Com White Mills & Drew. ~~Report~~ Minutes of previous meeting adopted on motion of Coms Drew & White.

Club Ctees' rpts. Com Mills gave a satisfactory report which was accepted.

Municipal Election. It was agreed after some discussion on motion of Coms White & Mills a notice be sent to the local press advertising Com Mills candidature for the South Ward, & that a preliminary leaflet be issued at the earliest possible moment.[488]

Executive meeting held Com Mills house Sunday Nov 20th 1910 11 am. Present:- Comrades Bunkall, Green, Triance, Drew, Mills & Spurling presiding. Minutes of previous meeting were adopted on motion of Triance & Drew.

Correspondence was read re National Policy, Daily newspaper & from Com Simpole re appointment of Election agent. It was agreed to lay these before the next branch meeting.

Offer of James Thornes services for lecture via Fletcher Dodd was declined on motion of Triance and Bunkall.

Com Mills introduced the question of a ~~Daily~~ Local paper & it was decided after discussion to refer the matter to the branch meeting.

---

487 Richard Collingham Wallhead (1869–1934); originally a decorator before becoming an ILP journalist and lecturer; opponent of First World War; served on Manchester City Council, 1919–22: MP Merthyr Tydfil, 1922–34.

488 In the event, no candidates were put forward for any ward, the local press commenting, 'the Socialists, it is to be noted, gave their usual generous assistance to the Liberal party' (*LN*, 7 Nov. 1910).

Branch Meeting held at Labor Club Sunday Nov 20/10. Minutes of previous meeting read & confirmed on motion of Com Hall & Simpole.

The following new members were proposed: J Purchas J Hall & F Beales.[489] Prop by Com Mills Sec by Com Neave that an Organising Secretary be appointed. Carried. Com Mills was proposed by Mills [*sic*] Sec by Triance & carried unanimously.

After discussing for some time Re a Socialist Daily Paper it was decided that the newly appointed Organiser get to know how many Comrades & Sympathisers ~~whould~~ would be prepared to buy it and give those names to Com White so that he could order the number required.

Com Mills introduced the question of a Local Monthly Paper after much discussion it was proposed by Com Drew Sec by Com Neave that a committee be elected at this meeting. Com Hall then proposed & Com White Sec that the committee consists of 3 members Comrades Spurling White & Dorer & that they present a report to the next Branch Meeting.

Graysons Visit it was proposed by Com F Hall Sec by Com Triance that we write Com Grayson asking him if can give us dates for a meeting in Lynn some time in January as we find it impossible owing to the general election to hold a meeting on the 27th 28th or 30th December the last dates sent to him.[490] Moved by Com Ridley Sec by Com Triance that Miss E Green be Assit Secretary Carried Unam It was decided that Com Pointer M.P. be paid 30/- owing to him as soon as possible.

11/12/10 Executive Meeting held at Labour Club, Com. Frost in chair. Present also Coms. Mills Drew White Simpole ~~Ridley~~ Green & Triance. Minutes of previous meeting adopted on motion of Coms Mills & Drew. Meeting was then adjourned to following Tues. Even.

11/12/10 Branch Meeting held at Labour Club, Com. Frost in chair. Comrade F. Hall move that we hold a Soiree this season. Sec. by Com D. Hall & carried.

Pro. By Com Mills we hold a supper & social in Labour Club Jan 4th/11 Tickets 1/- each. Sec by Com. Triance & carried.

The following new members were proposed & accepted. S.S. Bennett & F. Barton.[491]

---

489 John Alfred Purchase, born 1894, (brother of W. R. Purchase) a railway clerk, lived at Coronation Square, Lynn; Hall either Joseph Hey Hall born 1879, coal agent, St John's Terrace, Lynn; or James Hall, born 1886, printer, Norfolk Street, Lynn; Frederick Beales, born 1861, labourer at manure works, All Saints Street, South Lynn.

490 The second general election of 1910 was held in December.

491 S. Bennett, of Railway Road, Lynn, according to the subscription book. Not further identified: no one of this name at Railway Road in 1901 or 1911 census, perhaps Sidney

14/12/10 Executive Meeting resumed from 11ᵗʰ, Com. Mills house, Com Frost in Chair. Also present Coms. Mills Green Simpole Triance Drew & Spurling.

Com. Mills moved that we write Com. Grayson asking if he will speak to us on some date about the end of Jan. or beginning of Feb. as it is imperative that we hold a demonstration about that time. Com Spurling Sec. Carried.

Moved by Com Spurling Sec. Com Drew that Com. Ridley be written to asking him to hold in abeyance the matter re. Com Roberts, until a reply is received from Com. Grayson. Carried.

Jan 20ᵗʰ/11 Executive Meeting held Com Mills house.
Minutes of previous meeting read & confirmed.
Proposed by Com Spurling that Com Ridley be written to Re. Com Roberts' Meeting. Carried.
Thos. A. Frost

Jan. 22ⁿᵈ/11 Branch Meeting held at Labour Club, Com. Frost in Chair.
<u>Minutes</u> of previous meeting read & confirmed on motion of Coms. Drew & White.

Report of <u>Sub-committee</u> re <u>monthly</u> paper, Com. White proposed that the Executive be asked to deal with the matter Com. Gittings sec. All agreed.

Correspondence & Nom. Papers for N.A.C. Proposed by Com. White sec. Com. Drew that N.A.C. proposal respecting procedure re conference resolutions be agreed to. Carried.

Com Frost moved sec. \by/ Com Triance that Peter Jackson of Ipswich be nom. for Divisional Representation. Com Mills proposed H. Snell to be nom as Chairman sec. by Com Drew.[492] Coms Spurling & White moved that T.D. Benson of Manchester be nom for Treasurer. Proposed by Com. Mills & sec by Com. Hall that F. Dodd of Yarmouth be National Council. All carried.[493]

Bennett, born 1891, in 1911 a commercial traveller living at 3, Carmelite Terrace, South Lynn. Subsequent minutes do not always distinguish him from J. Bennett, see above, note 390. Fred Barton, not certainly identified, only man of this name in Lynn in 1911 census is a ladies' tailor, born Morley, Yorks 1885, living at 7, Victoria Street, Lynn: however, subscription book gives address as 'Fleet', either an abbreviation for Millfleet or the Lincolnshire village 20 miles west of Lynn, connected to it by railway. No person called Barton occurs there in 1901 or 1911 census.

492 For Snell, see above, note 42. 'Chairman', means of the ILP.

493 In the event, Snell did not stand and the chairman W. C. Anderson was re-elected; Benson was re-elected unopposed as Treasurer.

Jan. 31st/11 Executive held at Com Mills' house. Com. Frost in Chair.

1/ Minutes of previous meeting read & confirmed of Coms Drew & Simpole.

2/ A letter was read from Com. Jackson of Ipswich declining to accept nomination to N.A.C. as he objects to paid officials of the party becoming members of that council.

3/ Com. Roberts is unable to give us a meeting as his time is fully occupied owing to the Printers Strike.[494] Therefore it was proposed that we write Com Ridley asking him to inform Com. Walkden that the Branch is prepared to run a meeting provided he finds an M.P. to speak with him.[495]

4/ Local paper. It was decided that we have 2000 copies published for May 1st. Proposed that Coms. Spurling & Mills be appointed to collect money & adverts to pay for same. Also the Organiser was asked to introduce a scheme at next meeting whereby subscribers could be put on a weekly basis & to start at once.

5/ New members. Mr Slack Goodwins Rd. Proposed Com Mills sec. Com Spurling.[496] Accepted.

Executive Meeting held at Com Mills' house Feb 28th/11. Com. Frost in Chair. Members present Coms. Mills, Drew, Spurling & White.

Re Public Meeting. It was reported that Com. Ridley has seen Com Walkden who is negotiating with several M.Ps. with the object of arranging a meeting for us as early as possible.

A scheme for the distribution of Local paper, arranged by the Organiser, Com. Simpole, was received with approval by the members, who desire to thank Com. Simpole for the very valuable assistance he has rendered in fulfilling so troublesome a task.

Meeting was then adjourned to Mon. March 6th.

Executive Meeting resumed Com. Mills house March 6th 1911. Com. Frost in Chair. Also present Coms. Drew, Green, Mills, Triance and Spurling. Minutes of previous meeting read and confirmed on motion of Coms. Drew & Green.

The Treasurer presented his report which showed a balance in hand of 12/6.

---

494 Printers in London struck for a 48-hour week, a national agreement for a 51-hour week being reached on 6 May after intervention by the Board of Trade: see A. E. Musson, *The Typographical Association, origins and history up to 1949* (London, 1954). Musson is not enthusiastic about Roberts's contribution, noting that after he had been elected an MP in 1906 'henceforth he did little organising' (112).

495 Alexander Walkden (1873–1957), general secretary Railway Clerks' Association, 1906–36; MP Bristol South 1923–31 and 1935–45 when created first Baron Walkden.

496 Harold Slack, born 1880, assurance superintendent.

It was suggested that we enlarge the Executive Committee for the purpose of electing a certain number of Executive members to Club committee, thus bringing about a connection between the two bodies.
New members proposed & accepted Mr. & Mrs. D. Batterbee.[497]

The Annual meeting of branch held in Club-room 7.30 P.M. March 12th 1911. Minutes of last Annual Meeting read and confirmed on motion of Coms. White & Drew. Minutes of previous Branch meeting read & confirmed on motion of Coms. Ridley & Neave. Minutes of Executive Meetings since last Branch meeting read & confirmed on motion of Coms. Drew & Hall.
The Sec. Cm. Mills gave a brief report of the work of Branch during previous year, which was adopted on motion of Coms. Hall & White.
The Treasurer's report & balance sheet was accepted on motion of Coms. White & Ridley.
Report of work of Club Committee given by Com. Hall Sec. was accepted on motion of Coms. Spurling & Mann.
Coms. Frost & Spurling being appointed scrutineers, the election of officers was then proceeded with, it resulted as follows:

President	Com. Green
Secretary	″ Mills
Assis Sec	E Green
Treasurer	Com. Triance
Collector	″ Drew
Librarian, Organiser	″ Simpole
Auditors	″ Neave & Poley
L.R.C.	Coms. Frost, Bunkall, Mills & Ridley.

Com. Hall proposed & Com. Watson sec. that the minimum subscription be reduced to 6[d] a month. \Carried/. It was also agreed that each member must have a sub. card.
It was here pro by Com. Mills & sec. Com. Neave that the Executive council be enlarged for the purpose of electing a certain number of Executive members to Club Committee thus bringing about a connection between the two committees. This was agreed to & the following executive appointed Coms Pye, Skerrit, Spurling, Ridley & Mrs Frost.
Ballot was taken in conjunction with E.D.C. Election, Coms ~~Ridley~~ \Frost/ & Spurling being appointed scrutineers. The result was found to be unanimously in favour of Com. Henderson.

---

497 Daniel and Harriet Batterbee, lived at 11 South Street. Daniel was a stationary-engine driver, born Terrington St John 1878; his wife Harriet was born in Somerset in 1879.

Resolution for one days rest in seven for Policemen pro Com. Mills & sec Com Frost. Carried.

Socialist papers for the use of the Club were promised as follows:

Com Frost   to give   Socialist Review
  ″   Triance   ″   ″   Labour Leader
  ″   Green   ″   ″   Clarion

Com Green proposed that Sun Even meetings commence at 6.30 prompt. Com. Hall sec. Carried.

It was agreed that the Executive be empowered to elect full Club Committee at their next meeting.

Local papers. Com. Mills reported that every effort is being made by the committee to insure the success of the proposed paper and that there is still much to do in collecting funds etc. for same. The meeting expressed approval & hoped the efforts of the committee would meet with the entire success they deserve.

Com. Ridley moved, sec. by Com. Frost that the following resolution opposing the Increased Naval Estimates Bill then before Parliament be passed, That this meeting of the King's Lynn I.L.P. protests against the swollen naval estimates in the mad race for armaments, and calls upon the representative of the borough to support the Labour Party in their Parliamentary action. Carried.[498]

Copies to be sent to Messrs. Ingleby,[499] Macdonald[500] & McKenna.[501]

Com. Mills promised to arrange programme of Sun. Even. Meetings for remainder of the season.

Meeting of Executive Council March 13th 1911. Com. Green presiding.

Club Committee. It was agreed that the C.C. should consist of six members, two ~~three~~ from the Executive Mrs. Frost & Mr. White & four others namely Mrs. Mills, Mrs. Green, Mr. Bennett & Mr. Skerritt.

---

498 See Martin Daunton, 'The Greatest and Richest Sacrifice Ever Made on the Altar of Militarism: The Finance of Naval Expansion, c. 1890–1914' in: *The Dreadnought and the Edwardian age*, ed. by Robert J. Blyth, Andrew D. Lambert and Jan Rüger (Farnham, 2011), 31–50.

499 Holcombe Ingleby (1854–1926), of Sedgeford Hall, Norfolk; London solicitor who became deeply involved in Kings Lynn following his marriage to Harriett Neville Rolfe, of Heacham Hall; mayor of King's Lynn in 1909 and 1918–22; stood as Conservative in Dec. 1910 election, defeating Gibson Bowles; survived as MP after an election petition alleging bribery and corruption.

500 James Ramsay MacDonald (1866–1937), leader of Parliamentary Labour Party, 1911–14, when he resigned because of his opposition to the war; later became the first Labour Party Prime Minister.

501 Reginald McKenna (1863–1943), First Lord of the Admiralty Apr. 1908 to Oct. 1911, Home Secretary Oct. 1911 to May 1915.

Com. White pro & Com Triance sec that the C.C. ask Com. Hall to conduct the repayment of Billiard table. Carried.

Com. Spurling moved, sec by Com Drew that the duties of the C.C. shall consist in organising Whist Drives, Outings, Socials, Billiard tournaments etc. & also present the Executive with report & financial statement from time to time as requested. Carried unanimously.

It was decided on motion of Coms. Spurling and Simpole that henceforth executive meetings shall be held every alternate Monday at 8 oclock P.M.

Meeting of Executive Committee Mar 27th 11. Com. Green presiding. Also present Coms Mills, White, Skerrit & E. Green.

Minutes of previous meeting adopted on motion of Coms White & Skerrit. Correspondence for Com. Holmes of Norwich re Divisional Representation was read, which, after some discussion, it was decided to ignore.

Meeting of Executive Committee April 10th 11. Com. Green presiding. Also present Coms. Skerrit, White, Drew, Spurling, Mills, Triance & E. Green.

Minutes read & confirmed on motion of Coms. White & Spurling.

Correspondence was read from Com. Cadman re. Summer campaign.

Resolution pro. & sec. by Coms. Spurling & Drew that we apply to the E.D.C. for a speaker for Autumn demonstration. Carried. Com Spurling pro & Com Skerrit sec. that Com Cadman be given week-end covering June 10th. Com Drew pro that the branch engage one speaker per month, in addition to those supplied by E.D.C. from June to Oct. Com Mills sec. It was agreed that the Secretary engage Speakers whose expenses would not exceed 10/-.

Local paper. Com Mills reported on behalf of the paper committee that they have 30/- in hand & also an assured income of 30/- per month. That their next business is to apply for Printers' Estimates in order to ascertain what will be the exact cost of publication having decided to start in July.

~~Owing to the resignation of Com. F. Hall~~ Com Triance was appointed Treasurer of the Club Committee, it being felt advisable that the funds of the Club Committee and those of the branch should be in the same hands.

Meeting of Executive Committee April 24th/11 Com. Green in Chair. Also present Coms. Spurling, Simpole, Drew, Mills & White.

Com Mills reported that the Local paper funds now in hand amounted to £7.0.0. On motion of Coms. Spurling & Green it was agreed to hold a special meeting May 1st at 7.30 P.M. to fully discuss business connected with the paper. Com Drew moved that Com Mills be authorised to make arrangements with Mr Lowerison for Aug. Meet. Agreed.

Com White proposed & Com. Green sec. that we continue to hold Sun. Evening meetings in the Club through May, but to start at 8 oclock. Carried. New members Miss White pro by Com. Drew sec.by Com. Mills.[502]

Special executive Meeting May 1st 1911. Com. Green presiding. Also present Coms. White, Dorer, Drew, Mills & Spurling.
Re Monthly Local paper. The estimated income for first year dating from first issue £25.0.0. Estimated cost £30.0.0. It was recommended that the Club Committee be asked to make special efforts to raise £5.0.0 yearly towards the expenses of the paper. All branch advertisements re meetings etc must be paid for at the usual rates. It was suggested that the first issue takes place on July 1st.
The August Meet. Sec. reported that Com. Grayson promised to speak for us either at Aug. Meet or Autumn demonstration. The\n/ it was decided to write Com. Blatchford asking for his aid in the matter. Therefore until we receive his reply we cannot make any definite arrangement with Mr. Grayson. Agreed that we hold a Branch meeting on Sunday 7th at 7.30 P.M.

Branch Meeting held in Labour Club at 7th 11 at 7.30 P.M. Com Green in Chair. Minutes read and confirmed on motion of Coms. Drew & Frost.
Local Paper. The scheme prepared by the Executive for the publication of a Socialist Monthly Paper was laid before the meeting by Com. Mills. It was received with approval & the following resolution was passed on the motion of Coms Frost & Gittings, That this meeting endorses the action of the Executive to bring out a Local Paper & pledges itself to do all in its power to make it successful.
Correspondence from the E.D.C. asking for nominations was then dealt with and it was decided to offer the following:
Treasurer Com. Mills
Chairman Com. Dodd
The speakers for Autumn demonstration. The Sec. reported that he had been negotiating with Messrs Snowden, Macdonald, Hardie & Landsbury but was unsuccessful in securing either, and it was also decided that we do not engage Comrade Wallhead, his open dates not being suitable. After some discussion it was agreed that the matter be referred to the Executive. Com. White pro. Com Frost sec. that we write Com. Richardson member for Whitehaven asking if he will speak for us as we understand he will be in the district about that time.[503] Carried.

---

502 Frederick's daughter Annie, born 1879. According to the 1911 census she worked as assistant in his shop.
503 Thomas Richardson (1868–1928), Labour M.P. Whitehaven from December 1910–1918.

Re Outings. It was agreed that we go on Whit Monday to Snettisham & on Coronation day to Middleton Woods.
(Signed) J.W. Spurling

Executive Meeting May 8ᵗʰ 1911. Com Green presiding. Also present Coms Drew, Miles, Spurling, Skerrit, Triance & E. Green.
Com \Spurling/ pro the adoption of the minutes & Com. Drew sec. Carried.
Having been so far unsuccessful in obtaining a speaker for Autumn Demonstration, Com Miles pro & Com. Skerrit sec that we try to engage either Landsbury or Will Crooks or failing both Rev Cummings. Agreed.
For outdoor meetings the Sec. was asked to obtain dates from Coms. Withard, W.R. Smith, J.J. Kidd, Bolton, Henderson, & Mrs Reeves.

Executive Meeting May 22ⁿᵈ 1911. Com. Green in Chair, also present Coms. Skerrit, Spurling, Drew, White, Mills & Pye. Minutes read & confirmed on motion of Coms White & Green.
A letter from Com. Ridley re Autumn Demonstration was read informing the meeting that Com. Goldstone M.P. National Union of Teachers has offered to speak for us with Com Walkden on some date before the Nov. elections.[504]
Re August Meet. A letter from Com. Tom Groom favouring the suggestion was read by Com. White.[505]
Com Spurling moved that Com Ridley be asked to engage Com Goldstone on the best terms possible for some date before Nov. Elections. Sec. by Com. White.
J.W. Spurling

Executive Meeting June 12ᵗʰ 1911. Members present Coms. White, Simpole, Drew, Spurling & Mills.
Correspondence was read from Com. Ridley stating that he has booked Goldstone for Oct. 23ʳᵈ. Moved that the Central Hall be booked on a definite reply being received from Goldstone himself.
Com. White moved & Com. Drew sec. that a Branch Meeting be held on Thur 15ᵗʰ inst. at 8.30 P.M.
Re Local Newspaper. The Sub Committee reported that the paper will be published in July and that the title will be "The King's Lynn Socialist

---

504 Frank Goldstone (1870–1955), of the National Union of Teachers, Labour M.P. Sunderland from January 1910–1918.
505 Thomas W. Groom, born 1874, described as 'general labourer, chemical works' in 1901, 'mixing manures' 1911, general labourer for a shipping company 1921. All censuses give his address as Southgate Street, South Lynn.

Herald".[506] On motion of Com. Drew & Simpole the report & title were accepted.

J.W. Spurling

Branch Meeting in Labour Club June 15th. Com. Spurling presiding.

Minutes read & confirmed on motion of Coms. Mrs Green & Mrs Mills.

Voting for officers for E.D.C. was then proceeded with Coms. Hall & Storer being appointed scrutineers, results as follows:

Chairman Dodd 13 Withard 1

Executive Members Bates 13. Mrs Ponder 14. Rowntree 14. Henderson 14. Morley 10.[507] Kerry 7. Dodd 14. Savage 5.[508] Smith 7.

It was agreed on motion of Coms. White & Gittings that Com. Mills be instructed to support on our behalf Resolution No. 1 to come before the E.D.C. Conference.

The Local Paper. Executive was instructed to divide town into districts for the convenient distribution of same.

Previous minute re outing to Mid. Wood on Coro day being rescinded, it was decided on motion of Coms. Drew & Simpole that we go to W. Winch Common instead & the C. Committee be asked to arrange all details.

Meeting of Executive Meeting June 19th 11. Com [*blank*] in chair. Also present Coms Drew, Triance, Skerrit, Spurling, Mills & White.

Minutes of previous meeting adopted on motion of Coms. Drew & Skerrit. After some discussion as to the best method to adopt for distributing the paper, it was agreed on motion of Com. White sec by Com Drew that the districts as drawn up by the Organiser be made use of, and that all members be written to and asked to take a share of the work of distribution.

(Signed) J.W. Spurling

Executive meeting July 10th/11. Com. Spurling presiding.

Minutes read & confirmed on motion of Coms Triance & Drew.

A letter from Mrs. Reeves in which she offered to speak to us on Aug 27th was read but the proposal was not accepted as the date is not suitable.

---

506 There is no copy in the Norfolk Libraries catalogue, nor in the British Newspaper Library. Circulars survive asking members to contribute at least 3d. a week to the paper, which would cost £36 a year to produce (1 Feb. 1911), and asking for members willing to distribute it as only ten people out of a local membership of 40 had volunteered to do so (29 Jun. 1911) (NRO, SO 297/11).

507 Not identified.

508 William Savage, born 1870, leading figure in Norwich branch of NUBSO, contested Catton ward for Norwich Board of Guardians May 1908, and city council elections for same ward November 1908: unsuccessful but became both ILP councillor and member of Board of Guardians before the First World War.

It was suggested that a Branch meeting be held on Friday 14th inst at
8.30 P.M.
(Signed) J.W. Spurling

Branch Meeting July 14th/11 8.30 P.M. \Com Spur. Presiding/. Minutes of
\last Branch &/ all Meetings since read & confirmed on motion of Coms
Watson & Jenkinson.
A report of the Annual Conference of E.D.C. at Caister Camp June 24th &
25th/11 was read by Com. Mills. It was therein stated that Coms. Henderson
& Savage of Norwich both obtained sufficient votes for election to the
Committee for 1911 to 12 but belonging to the same branch it was decided
by the Conference to take a vote throughout the area between these two
coms. and ask for nominations for the vacant seat. Votes for same were
therefore taken the result was as follows:-
Henderson 14 Savage none
Com Spurling was nominated for the vacant seat.
Coms. Hall & Batterbee being appointed scrutineers, ballot for election of
available Parliamentary Candidates was then proceeded with.
It was agreed on motion of Coms Watson & Hall that the Sec write Com
Landsbury asking on what date he will address a meeting on behalf of the
Branch.
As Com Keir Hardie is to be in Castle Rising on Sun July 30th it was
suggested that we write him asking if he could arrange to address a meeting
in Lynn on Sat 29th.
Re engaging Local speakers. After some consideration this business was
relegated to the Executive.
(Signed) J.W. Spurling

Executive Meeting July 25th 11. Com. Spurling presiding, also present Coms
Mills, Drew, White & Skerrit.
Minutes of previous meeting read and confirmed on motion of Coms White
& Drew.
A letter was read from Mr Landsbury offering Nov. 4th for a meeting, it was
decided that we write accepting that date providing a hall can be engaged.
Also a letter from Mr Kidd offering either Aug 13th 20th or 27th. Agreed that
we write him that either will suit.[509]

---

509 The Kidds were visiting Lynn: in the 1911 census they are recorded as visitors staying
with a relative of Christiana's, James Plowright, at Greyfriars House, Tower Place. There is
no further mention of Kidd in the minutes, so the proposed talk presumably never took
place.

Keir Hardie is unable to speak to us on 29th owing to previous engagement. It was suggested that we raise a subscription on behalf of Com Gittings in order to render him some assistance in this time of his trouble.
J.W. Spurling

Executive Meeting Aug. 8th. Com. Green presiding also present Coms Mills, Spurling, Drew & Skerrit. \Minutes read & adopted on motion of Drew & Spurling./
Re Com. Landsbury's meeting, as nothing further has been heard, it was suggested that we write to him asking him if his engagement to speak to us Nov. 4th still holds good.
The Financial position being discussed it was decided that the Sec. should see Com. Bennett & explain that the Executive desires Com. Triance to have sole control of the finances.
Com. Spurling moved & Com. Drew sec. that the question of the Nov elections be discussed at the next Executive Meeting. Carried.
J.W. Spurling

Executive Meeting Aug. 29th. Com. Spurling presiding.
Minutes read & confirmed on motion of Coms. Drew & Triance.
A letter was read from Com. Landsbury stating that he is unable to speak for us on Nov. 4th owing to there being no train service to Lowestoft on the 5th. Agreed that we write him again asking for a date in next year.
Re Nov. Elections. Mov. By Com Drew and sec by Com Triance that we fight the Sth. Ward only and that Coms. Mills & White be asked to come forward as candidates for same.
It was decided that the C.C. Sec[510] be asked to write Com. Simpole inquiring what are his intentions with regard to his position as caretaker.
Com. Drew moved & Com Triance sec. that every member be requested to contribute 1d monthly to Local Paper fund.

Executive Meeting Sep. 12th. Com Spurling presiding.
Minutes read and confirmed on motion of Coms Drew & Skerrit.
The Sec. was asked to arrange for hospitality for speakers Walkden and Goldstone.
Moved that we write the Secs. of N.U.T. and R.C.A. asking for their support on Oct. 23rd when Com. Walkden R.C.A. and Com. Goldstone (M.P.) N.U.T. will address a Meeting in Central Hall.
Re Advertising Meeting. Moved that we have 50 double den [sic] placed on hoardings & Sandwich Men. Bills to be printed in black or green, and also

---

510 Club Committee Secretary.

50 tickets of admission @ 3^d each. Moved that we invite Com Allsopp to take the chair.[511]

Re proposed Labour daily. Moved that the Branch be recommended to take shares in it & the members be asked to obtained the names of sympathizers for the Sec. to forward to the proper quarter.[512]

Re C.C.'s letter to Com. Simpole. A reply to same from Com. Simpole was read after which it was decided that he should \continue/ to hold the position of Caretaker.

Branch Meeting Oct 1st 1911. Com. White in chair.

Minutes of previous meeting read and confirmed on motion of Coms. Drew and Skerrit.

A letter was read from Com. Landsbury saying that he is sorry that he cannot fix a date for us at present.

A letter from Com. F. Henderson was also read re. his book "The Case for Socialism".[513] Moved we buy one copy for Branch purposes and pay for it out of branch funds. Carried.

Winter Programme. On motion of Coms. Gittings and Hall it was decided that we hold the Students Class on Thur. evenings as heretofore. Also Com. Gittings promised to do his best to arrange for speakers for Sun. Even. Meetings throughout the season commencing Sun. Oct. 8th meetings to start 7 oclock prompt.

Municipal Elections moved that we proceed to the next business. Agreed.

Local Newspaper. A desire was expressed that the Organiser be asked to see that the distribution be more effectively accomplished.

National Labour Newspaper moved that the branch acquire two £1 shares in same. Carried.

Voting for Parliamentary Candidates resulted as follows.[514]

Re Coms. Goldstone & Walkden's meeting proposed that we ask Com. Ridley to take the chair. Coms. Bennett, Gittings, Mrs Batterbee & Mrs White promising to act as collectors.

---

511 Frederick Allsopp, see above, note 317.

512 The *Daily Citizen*, launched in October 1912, in effect the official newspaper of the Labour Party, organised as a limited company and issuing a share prospectus. For the contrast between the 'rebel' *Daily Herald* (first issued in January 1911 as newsletter of the London printing unions, reissued as a national labour daily in April 1912) and the 'official' *Daily Citizen*, see R. J. Holton '*Daily Herald* versus *Daily Citizen*', *International Review of Social History* 19 (1974), 347–76.

513 Fred Henderson, see above, note 215. *The Case for Socialism* (London: Jarrold, 1911), much reprinted thereafter.

514 This is the text as given, there is no further information.

<u>Com Bennett</u> proposed & Com. Drew sec. that we approach the S.D.F. with a view to joining the B.S.P.[515] <u>Lost</u>

Special Executive Meeting 5/10/11. Com. Spurling in the Chair. Also present Coms. Simpole, Drew, White, Triance, Skerritt & Mills.
Re Municipal Elections. On motion of Coms. Spurling & Drew Com. White was invited to come forward as candidate for the Sth. Ward. Com. White agreed to do so, at the same time asking for the loyal support of all the members. Moved that we hold a Branch Meeting on Sunday 8th to consider arrangements for Com. White's candidature.

Special Branch Meeting Oct. 8th 1911. Com. Green presiding. Minutes of previous meetings read and confirmed on motion of Coms Gittings and Simpole.
This meeting having been called for the purpose of considering arrangements for Com. White's Candidature it was agreed to appoint Com. Spurling Election Agent, the members unanimously promising to render all possible assistance.[516]
J.W. Spurling

Meeting of Executive Committee held the Club Room, Windsor Road, Novr 14th 1911. Com. W. Spurling in the Chair. Present: Com. White, Drew, Skerrit, Simpole & Triance.
An expression of regret at the illness of our Secretary Com. Mills was raised & the hope was expressed that he would soon be able to take his place amongst us again. Owing to her husband's illness Mrs Mills had asked to be relieved of her position as a member of the Club Committee to the end of our financial year, February. Com D Batterbee was elected in her place on the motion of Com. Drew seconded by Com Triance.

---

515 The British Socialist Party, founded in 1911 by those who thought the ILP insuffi-
ciently socialist in its approach: at its inception it was made up of 77 branches of the SDF,
30 Clarion Clubs – and 36 ILP branches. A minority within the Lynn ILP clearly wished
to join. It never became a political force, however: 'the attempt to form the British Socialist
Party as an effective alternative to the ILP flickered briefly and failed miserably between
1911 and 1914.' Keith Laybourn and Jack Reynolds, *Liberalism and the rise of Labour,
1890–1918* (London, 1984), 159.
516 White's election manifesto was uncompromising: 'The Labour Party are fighting for
your rights to choose and send your own representatives to the Council. Both Parties are
determined to prevent this, and unfortunately a candidate has been found from your own
class willing to assist them … . You are defeating your own ends by voting for any candidate
put forward by the Capitalist parties, whose interest is to keep you divided' (NRO, SO
297/24).

It was mentioned that Com Harry Lowerison had sent us some 18 volumes which had been added to the Party's Library. Com White had already sent a letter of thanks for the generous gift. Com Simpole was asked to produce a scheme \of rules/ for loaning the books to members & to ensure their prompt return to be submitted for the approval of the Executive.

Com Drew promised in cooperation with Com Frost to see each member of the Club personally to induce them to take a closer interest in the work of the Party both in its social side & its propaganda.

It was proposed by Com Drew & seconded by Com Triance that the Club Committee be asked to meet as soon as possible to arrange for the running of Billiard Tournaments, to promote a Social this month & to arrange for sundry repairs needed in the Club.

A financial statement was presented by the ~~Secretary~~ Treasurer.

Com Drew proposed that a program be at once drawn up for the Winter Session seconded by Com Triance.

It was suggested that a record of \the result/ of the recent South Ward Election be entered here

Nov 1st 1911[517]

Brown	70	63	523	8				664
Smithard	35		523		20		10	588
Jackson	332	63			20	98		513
White	46			8		98	10	162

Branch Meeting held in Club Room Sunday Nov 19th 1911. 19 present. Com. White in the Chair.

Minutes of previous Meetings adopted on motion of Com. Watson, seconded by Com Gittings.

A letter from Com. Dorer was read & commented upon by the Chairman. Proposed by Com. Frost, seconded by Com. Drew that we discontinue the issue of the Socialist Herald owing to the hampered circumstances of getting what material we would desire to publish, printed. Carried.[518]

---

517 The format is the same as described in note 281 above, with the top two candidates elected and voters casting up to two votes: this time the figures are written out horizontally rather than vertically. The left-hand column records the number of plumpers for each candidate; the next six columns are the votes cast by people voting for two candidates; the right-hand column the total votes cast for each candidate. So, White, the Socialist candidate, finished bottom of the poll with 162 votes, well below Jackson, campaigning for the first time as a Liberal, who received 513 votes but was also unsuccessful. Note the very high numbers plumping for Jackson at this poll.

518 The paper had run to only three monthly issues. A circular suggested that members take shares in *the Daily Citizen* instead but only four did so: Ridley bought two shares (at

Organiser to arrange for Students' Class to commence ~~at~~ from Thursday next. Proposed by Com. Hall, seconded by Com. Batterbee that the book for study be the "Fabian Essays". Agreed.

Suggested that Com. Triance should reply to Com. Dorer's letter informing him of the Party's activities & Winter Program.

Minutes of Executive held in Club Room Monday Jan 1/1912. Com. W. Spurling in the Chair. Present: Coms Drew, Skerrit, Simpole, Triance & White.

Minutes of previous Meeting adopted.

Notice from Secretary of N.A.C. re Adult Suffrage read. Suggested resolution to be submitted to next Branch Meeting.[519]

Notice from Planet Friendly Society re working of National Insurance Act discussed.[520] Question affects our members very little.

Handbill \read/ re issue of photo of Margaret Macdonald.[521]

Circular from Eastern Divisional Council considered respecting resolutions for the Party's Annual Conference at Merthyr to be first submitted to the Divisional Conference at Romford on Feby 4th next.[522] No resolutions.

Circ from E.D.C. read advising the names of delegates ~~sugg~~ elected to represent the area at the Labour Party Conference at Birmingham in January.[523]

Letter from Organising Secretary of Labour Daily Paper read. To be considered by Members.

Several little matters needing to be settled by Club Committee referred to (Billiard tournament, supply of coke & fixing of lino. on stairs)

2/6 a share), and W. R. Angell, H. Pooley and J. W. Spurling one share each (NRO, SO 297/11).

519 The resolution called on the Government not to introduce a bill extending male suffrage but instead introduce 'a genuine measure of adult suffrage, establishing political equality between the sexes' (*LA*, 19 Jan. 1912).

520 Planet Friendly Assurance Society was founded and managed by the ILP, frequently advertised in its annual reports: based in Birmingham. For the National Insurance Act of 1911 see Laybourn, *Social Policy*, 170–6. Many socialists opposed the Act because it was contributory.

521 Margaret MacDonald (1870–1911), wife of James Ramsay MacDonald, had died from blood poisoning on 8 September 1911. 'Her early death was a tragedy not only for MacDonald personally, but indirectly for the Labour Party since it removed one whose character complemented his and gave it a stability the lack of which was in the end to bring tragedy' (Stewart, *Hardie*, 29). Margaret was actively involved in the National Union of Women Workers, the NUWSS, and the Women's Labour League. Ramsay MacDonald was chairman of the Parliamentary Labour Party at the time of her death.

522 The 1912 Annual Conference was held at Merthyr Tydfil 27, 28 May.

523 Held 24–26 January.

Offer of stock of Whist Drive Score cards for 5/- made by Messrs. Bolton & Co. Accepted.

Branch Meeting held in Club Room, Windsor Road, Sunday Jany 14th 1912. Com. W. Spurling in the Chair.
Minutes of previous Executive Meeting adopted on motion of Com White, seconded by Com. Frost.
Resolution of N.A.C. re Adult Suffrage proposed by Com. White, seconded by Com. Frost. Carried.
Eastern Divisional Conference at Romford, Feby 4th 1912. Election of Officers considered.
Comrade Mills   nominated ~~at~~ as Treasurer. Carried
    "   Spurling nominated for Executive
    "   Ridley   "   " Parliamentary Committee
    "   Spurling proposed as Delegate to the Conference on motion of Com. Ridley, seconded by Com. Frost. Chairman desired it to be faithfully recorded that this nomination was carried unanimously.
Resolutions to be discussed at Romford Conference were then submitted & our Delegate instructed what & what not to support.
Daily Labor Paper. Resolution submitted that Com. Triance sees Members with a view to getting their support as Shareholders in this venture on the lines suggested by the Organising Secretary of the Committee promoting the paper.
Moved by Com. Spurling that the hearty thanks of the Party be accorded the ladies who so ably assisted in making the Supper held on Jany 3rd a success. Seconded by Com. Ridley & approved by members present with tumultuous applause.
Balance in hand from King's Lynn Socialist Herald Fund. Proposed by Com Spurling that this be allocated to the purchase of Shares in the Labour Daily, one share for each level £ in hand. Seconded by Com. Ridley.
Letter Com Portass,[524] Brightlingsea, read re Mr W.C. Anderson's proposed visit to the District. Left with Com Ridley to see Mr Anderson at the Labour Party's Conference at Birmingham this month, & get particulars of dates & terms, to be submitted to the Executive for approval.
Resolution passed that no Franchise Reform should be complete or acceptable which did not include both men & women.
\Com Ridley moved, Com Frost seconded the following resolution – "This Branch is of opinion that the policy of the Foreign Office constitutes a perpetual menace to the peace of Europe & demands the immediate

---

524 Not identified, not in 1901 or 1911 census, or in trade directories.

resignation of Sir Ed Grey".[525] Copies of the resolution to be sent to the Premier,[526] Sir Ed Grey, Bonar Law,[527] Mr Macdonald, Mr H Ingleby and the local Papers./[528]

Special Branch Meeting held Jany 28th 1912. Com. Spurling in the Chair – 15 present.
Election of Executive of E.D.C.

Com Dodd   unanimously voted upon as Chairman   27 votes
   ″ Spurling   ″   ″   ″ to Executive   37 ″
   ″ Ridley   ″   ″   ″ ″ Parliamentary Committee 37 ″

Com. Hall proposed & Com Watson seconded That an official invitation be sent to all old members of the Party, still holding the same views, to return to the Party, also any ~~one~~ in accord with our views to be invited to become members. Carried unanimously. To be left with Executive to decide to whom applications should be sent.

Executive Meeting held in Club Room, Sunday Feby 11th. Com. Spurling in the Chair, 5 present. Minutes of previous ordinary & special Branch Meetings adopted on proposal of Com. White, seconded by Com. Drew.
Form of letter to be sent to old & prospective members submitted & discussed & names to whom it should be addressed decided upon.
Issue of Daily Citizen discussed. Agreed that we wait receipt of proposals which N.A.C. are making to Branches to take shares.
Date of Annual Meeting chosen as March 10th.

Executive Meeting held in Club Room Tuesday, March 5th. Com White presided. 4 present.
Minutes of previous meeting adopted.
Matters discussed:- Letter of invitation to old members to rejoin us. Daily Citizen shares & preliminary business of Annual Meeting.

---

525 Sir Edward Grey (1862–1933), Foreign Secretary Dec. 1905–Dec. 1916.
526 Herbert Henry Asquith (1852–1928), Prime Minister 1908–16.
527 Andrew Bonar Law (1858–1923), leader of Unionist (Conservative) Party from 1911; Prime Minister 1922–23.
528 This resolution and the suffrage resolution were announced by Mills in a letter to the press (*LN*, 20 Jan. 1912). At the 1912 Labour Party conference, Keir Hardie moved a similar resolution 'That this Conference, believing the anti-German policy pursued in the name of the British Government by Sir Edward Grey to be a cause of increasing armaments, international ill-will, and the betrayal of oppressed nationalities, protests in the strongest terms against it'. It was carried unanimously. (Vickers, *The Labour Party and the World*, 45).

Annual Meeting of Branch held at the Club Room, Sunday March 10th 1912. 24 present. Com. W. Spurling presided.

Minutes of last Annual Meeting read & adopted on motion of Com Ridley, seconded by Com. Drew.

Last Branch Meeting Minutes read & adopted on the condition that the mo-\resolu/tion of Com Ridley censuring Sir Edward Grey & calling for his resignation be inserted. The omission from the records was quite an oversight on the part of the assistant Secretary.

Secretarys report read & adopted with the exception of that part where his resignation was tendered.[529] It was proposed by Com Frost, seconded by Com Neave that we ask Com. Mills to retain the post of Secretary & this was found to be the unanimous desire of the party present.

Financial Report read by the Treasurer & adopted on the motion of Com. Ridley seconded by Com White.

Election of Chairman:- Com Mann proposed by Com Drew, seconded by Com. Gittings.

Election of Secretary:- proposed that Com Mills be asked to accept re-election. Com Frost sec Com Neave.

Election of Asst Secretary. Com J. Purchase proposed by Com Drew, seconded by Com. Watson.

Treasurer – Re-election of Com. Triance proposed by Com. Neave, seconded by Com Drew.

Collector – Com Drew unanimously re-elected.

Librarian & Organiser Com Simpole do

Auditors – Coms. Neave & H. Pooley do

Nominations were then taken for the Executive Committee & a ballot of members present resulted in the following being elected – F.W. White. W. Snodgrass.[530] R. Hall. W. Spurling. D. Batterbee & H. Gilden.[531]

Nominations for Club Committee, after it had been decided that the Treasurer should be an ex officio member of the Committee. Com. Hall moved that this Committee should consist of eight instead of six as heretofore, \four ladies & four gentlemen/, which was carried. As the

---

529 Mills had written on 9 March 1912 resigning his post. His letter reflected his disappointment at the state of the party; 'it seems to me the worst year of our existence … . I am not in the habit of looking on the dark side of anything as you know but I cannot see much brightness in our last year's work' (NRO, SO 297/24).

530 (John) William Snodgrass, born 1889, younger brother of Burns Snodgrass.

531 Harry Gilden, born 1878, living in Cambridge at time of 1911 census, occupation shop assistant, moved to Union Street, Lynn in 1912. Last paid subscription in June 1914. Served in Army Service Corps in First World War. Described as grocer and provision merchant in 1939 register, at which time he was living in Norwich.

Executive nominate two of their body upon this Committee, six were chosen by a ballot of members present, as follows: Mrs Batterbee, Miss White, Mrs Frost, Mrs Gilden, Mr Watson & Mr Bennett.[532]

Propaganda for the year – Com Ridley stated that he had seen Mr C W Perry & arranged for him to book the services of W.C. Anderson on Sunday afternoon April 21st, in return for which he would let us have the Central Hall at night for an inclusive fee of 10s/6d, subject to the Party's approval. Com. White proposed & Com. Gilden seconded that we accept these terms & that the Party proceeds to make the visit of our \National/ Chairman a success. Com. White suggested that we have a tea in the Club Room on Sunday at which the members could meet & fraternise with Mr Anderson.

Com Ridley also suggested that if we were to have any national speakers of reputation we must get to work at once to book dates. Keir Hardie would probably be conducting a week's propaganda for the Agricultural Labourer's Union in the Summer, when he had practically promised to give us an address in Lynn on a Sunday night. The name of F. Richardson M.P.[533] was also mentioned as an attractive speaker.

Sunday Program – Com. Simpole was proceeding to book speakers for Sunday evening meetings.

Com Ridley offered to speak next Sunday night on The Socialist Movement, its cause & its effect.

Com White suggested that to dispel prevalent ignorance among our ancient & loyal townsfolk that we purchase & distribute pamphlets dealing with the Nationalization of the Mines as the moment when the Miners were striking for a minimum wage was an opportunity to push such propaganda.[534] Referred to Executive Committee.

Com White also suggested that now that we had the Dockers & Transport Workers organising in our midst we should back their efforts by helping them in every way. Com. Ridley said that he had been booked to give the Dockers an address.

---

532 Elizabeth Kate Gilden, born 1875, maiden name Gotobed, married Harry Gilden in Cambridge 23 August 1908. Dressmaker in 1911 census. Living with her husband in Norwich in 1939.

533 A confused reference. T. 'Freddie' Richards (1863–1942), MP Wolverhampton West was a popular speaker, but had lost his seat in January 1910; alternatively, Tom Richardson MP may be intended, see above, note 503.

534 The first national coal strike by miners began on 28 February 1912: the aim was to secure a minimum wage. The strike ended on 6 April after the Government extended minimum wages to the mining industry: see B. R. Mitchell, *Economic development of the British coal mining industry 1800–1914* (Cambridge, 1984).

Following proposed as Members. H R Hammond,[535] & C.A. Parker,[536] by Com Bennett seconded by H. Pooley
H. Proctor by Com Drew, seconded by [blank].[537]
Carried unanimously.

Executive Meeting held in Club Room on Tuesday March 12th 1912 at 8.30 pm. Com. Spurling presided. 6 present.
Minutes of previous Executive Meeting read & adopted.
Minutes of Annual Branch Meeting read.
Election of Secretary & another member for Executive in place of Com. Mills who declined to accept re-election as Secretary, & Com Snodgrass who would not be able to attend Executive Meetings – Referred to next Branch Meeting.
Moved that Coms Hall & Batterbee represent the Executive on the Club Committee. Carried. Prop by Com Spurling sec. by C. Triance.
Mr W.C. Anderson's visit. Advertising. It was suggested that Secy of Forward Association be seen as to the cost of advertising the evening visit in the weekly program. Com Triance to see Mr Riley.
The ventilation of the Club was also discussed – Deferred.

Branch Meeting held March 24th 1912. Com. Mann presided.
Minutes of previous Executive Meeting adopted.
Election of Secretary – proposed by Com Frost that Com White be appointed Secretary, seconded by Com. Hall. Carried unanimously. Com. White remarked that he would only take the position temporarily.
Question of Collector raised by Com Triance. Com White proposed & Com Watson seconded motion that this matter be referred back, as it was hoped that there would be no difficulty arise needing any further action.
New member. Chas. Bishop proposed by Com Batterbee, seconded by Com White.[538]

---

535 Horace Reginald Hammond, born 1886, lived in Saddlebow Road, South Lynn with his parents; 'clerk' in the 1911 census; his father described as 'blacksmith'.
536 Charles A. Parker, born in 1886, in 1911 lived in Heacham, a telegraph clerk for the M & GN Railway. Lived with his widowed mother: the family were residents of High Street, Lynn at the time of the 1901 census.
537 Horace Edward Proctor, born 1892, newsagent's assistant living with father at Wellington Street, Lynn, in 1911 census.
538 Not certainly identified, probably the Charles Bishop listed in 1901 census as printer's apprentice, born 1884, living in Tennyson Avenue, Lynn.

Executive Committee Club Room April 15th. Comrade Spurling in Chair. Minutes read and adopted.

Resolution from Club Committee re billiard takings. Moved by Com Batterbee sec'd by Com Gilden that this matter be brought up at next meeting.

Anderson's Visit. Letter read from Wisbech Branch inviting our Members to attend & assist at their meeting to be addressed by W.C. Anderson on Saturday evening April 20th. Comrades Hall & Batterbee agreed to arrange for a wagonette to run.

Anderson's Meeting Central Hall April 21. It was agreed that 50 large posters be printed & posted on hoardings, also 2000 handbills for distribution and an advertisement inserted in Lynn News. Comrade Ridley be invited to take the Chair. Comrade Frost be invited to entertain Anderson.[539]

Executive Meeting April 20. Chairman Comrade Spurling. Present Comrades Hall, Triance, Batterbee, White. Minutes read and adopted.

Letter read from Pollard Sec'y Colchester Branch re Chairmanship of Party inviting our support of Lansbury. Agreed that no action be taken in the matter.

Re billiard takings. Comrade Drew having sent key of box to the Club Committee their resolution on the matter fell through.

Collectorship Comrade Drew having expressed a wish to give up the post the Secretary agreed to see him and get his definite decision.

Andersons' Meeting The Secretary gave a financial statement that showed a possible deficiency of about 35/-.

The Committee placed on record their thanks to those members responsible for making whist drive tables.

Secretary was instructed to write Comrade Ridley re visit of Keir Hardie asking that anything in the way of arranging a meeting be done by the branch.

Executive Meeting May 15 Comrade Batterbee in the Chair present also Comrades Simpole Triance & White. Minutes read & adopted.

Comrade Drew having announced his decision to give up the Collectorship Comrade Triance agreed to collect until the vacancy was filled.

Letter read from Cadman giving result of voting for E.C & Parliamentary Committees.

---

539 One of the handbills is pasted into the minute book.

Com' Simpole reported that several books borrowed from the library were out and had not been renewed. Executive authorised the Librarian Com Simpole to call the attention of members in question to rule regarding same.

<u>Branch Meeting</u> May 19
Comrade Mann in Chair.
Minutes of last branch meeting & Executive meetings read and adopted on the motion of Comrades ~~Batterbee~~ Hall & Simpole.
Letter read from Cadman Secretary E Divisional Council giving results of voting for Committees.
Comrades Savage of Norwich & Kirkham, Letchworth to be reballoted on.[540] Also asking for any scheme for claim to grants from the Division to be sent by June 1st.
After some discussion it was agreed on the motion of Comrades Hall & Gilden that the secretary get into communication with the Agricultural Labourers and try and arrange for a visit from Keir Hardie and approach the Eastern Divl Council for a grant towards the expense of meetings etc.
<u>Collectorship</u>. Proposed by Com Hall seconded by Com' Batterbee that Comrade Watson be appointed Collector. Carried.
Discussion of summer program. Secretary reported that Higginbottom[541] & Councillor Gutteridge of Nottingham[542] had through Comrade Ridley offered to speak at Lynn. It was agreed that meetings be arranged during June, July & August.
Re Anderson's return visit. On motion of Com Batterbee it was decided to approach Mr Perry and endeavour to hire hall on same terms as last occasion.
Members present gave their votes (18) for Kirkham of Letchworth for E.D Council.
Letter read from Holmes Norwich re J Russell Williams visit to district after some discussion it was agreed that as the branch was already committed to several meetings no action be taken.[543]

---

540 Savage and Kirkham each received 142 votes. The seats on the Parliamentary Committee were won by Mrs Reeves (Norwich) 153; Com Dodd (Yarmouth) 151. The unsuccessful candidates were Ridley (Lynn) 66; Pope (Colchester) 62 (NRO, SO 297/24)
541 Sam Higginbottom, originally from Blackburn, full-time organiser of Nottingham ILP, 1906–12. He then moved to Liverpool, Ridley applying to fill his Nottingham post (for testimonial, NRO, SO 297/24).
542 G. Gutteridge, Nottingham city councillor: he also spoke at a meeting at Sutton Bridge on 13 July 1912 (NRO, SO 297/24).
543 See above, note 483.

Branch Meeting July 7th.

Minutes read and adopted.

Letter read from Mr Perry intimating that arrangements was already booked for the date of W C Andersons visit on Sep 29 and it was agreed that the meeting be held at the Walks Gates. Agreed that Com Ridley be invited to take the Chair for the meeting on the 14th and that an advertisement be inserted in Lynn News.

Parliamentary Levy Comrade Watson volunteered the sale of the 1/- Levy stamps.

The Secretary raised the question of G Edwards' action in supporting the Liberal Candidate at the N W Norfolk bye election.[544] Com Gittings proposed and Triance seconded "that our representation on the E.D.C bring the matter before that body. On the motion of Comrades Spurling & Pooley it was agreed to purchase 2000 Leaflets @ 1/3 1000 for distribution.

Comrade Spurling raised the question of whether the Branch intended putting forward Candidates at the Nov elections. Referred to Executive.

Executive Aug 16 Comrade Triance in chair.

Owing to small attendance the question of fighting Municipal elections was further deferred. Comrades Triance Spurling and White to interview J Neave in meantime.

Arrangements was then made for the visits of Comrades Higginbotham (of Nottingham) & Thatcher (of Sheffield)[545] and it was agreed to ask Com Ridley to preside.

Daily Citizen. Comrade Triance reported receipt of share certificates for the four fully paid shares held in trust by the N.A.C. for the Branch.

Executive Meeting Sep 12 Com Spurling in chair. Minutes adopted.

Com Triance reported result of interview with Com' Neave ~~and reports~~ \who/ stated that he must decline to stand as a Candidate.

Com' Spurling that the branch dissolve the old Club Committee and re-appoint a new one.

Agreed that Branch Meeting be called for Sep 15.

---

544 George Edwards (1850–1933), son of a farm labourer, founder of the Eastern Counties Agricultural Labourers and Small Holders' Union. Elected to Norfolk County Council in 1906 as a Liberal: supported the Liberal candidate Edward Hemmerde at the 1912 N.W. Norfolk by-election (there was no Labour candidate). Moved to Labour after the First World War, serving as a Labour Councillor from 1918. Labour M.P. for South Norfolk 1920–22 and 1923–24. See *ODNB*, the article being written by Alun Howkins.

545 A. J. Thatcher, originally from South Wales ILP, secretary of Sheffield ILP 1912–24. He also spoke at a meeting at Sutton Bridge on 31 August 1912 (NRO, SO 297/24).

Branch Meeting Sept 15. Com' Triance took the chair.

Minutes adopted.

Com' Triance reported to branch the result of interview with Com Neave and his refusal to stand as a candidate at the forthcoming Municipal Elections.

The Treasurer (Triance) called attention to the Party's Election Fund and appealed for support from Members. He then gave a statement as to the finances of the billiard table which showed it was now paid for and should prove a source of revenue.

Arrangements was made for Andersons visit the question of his entertainment being left to the Secretary.

A long discussion then took place as to the future of the Club Com Triance agreeing to see the Secretary of the Club Committee and get a meeting arranged.

Com' Simpole was appointed to get together a winter program.

Letter read from Com' Ridley offering to arrange a meeting to be addressed by G. Roberts M.P. but the meeting decided the matter stand over.

On the proposition of Com Simpole it was agreed to hold meetings on Thursday evenings.

Com Drew proposed & Com Maud seconded that that the Branch pay Com' Ridley's out of pocket expenses in connection with Sutton Bridge & Lynn Meetings. Carried.

Oct 27th Branch Meeting Comrade Spurling Chairman

Minutes Read and adopted.

Comrade Triance reported that he had forwarded 14/- to the I.L.P Parliamentary Fund as a result of Levy Appeal. Secretary read correspondence from Labour Leader regarding its position now that the Daily Citizen has appeared and appealing for the support of all members to both papers. Com Triance moved & Com H Pooley seconded a resolution that handbills as circulars be written for and distributed by Members of the branch". Carried. Municipal Elections. Comrade Frost proposed & Comrade Snodgrass seconded a resolution "that as a party we support M.J Jackson at the forthcoming municipal elections". Discussion of a lengthy nature followed nearly all members present taking part. On being put to meeting the motion found only 3 supporters it was therefore defeated.[546]

Comrade Simpole reported the loss of a book from the Library entitled

---

546 Frost's original letter survives (NRO, SO 297/24). Jackson, standing again in the South Ward but now as the second Liberal candidate, was unsuccessful: he received 539 votes, 69 plumpers and 409 voting both for him and for the other Liberal, Bardell, who was elected.

"Todays Work".[547] Members were reminded of the rule that names of members taking out books should enter same in the book kept on the shelves for this purpose.

Nov 24 Branch meeting 16 Members present Comrade Frost in chair.
Minutes read & adopted.
Correspondence. Letter from Gravesend Parliamentary Committee enclosing draw tickets for fund – Comrade Simpole undertook sale. Letter from Daily Citizen announcing opening of London Publishing offices inviting our assistance. Members agreed to distribute circulars.
Letter from Holmes Norwich.
Resignation. Com' G Mann wrote tendering his resignation, after lengthy discussion it was agreed on motion of White & Gittings that he be invited to reconsider same.[548]
Comrade Ridley asked for the endorsement of the Branch of a resolution he intended submitting to the E.D.C in favour of Public Farming as opposed to the creation of Small holdings. Agreed.
Secretary announced messages of greetings & good wishes to members from H.B. Craven & Mrs & Mr Dawson Large Clarion Vanners of Bury.

Branch Meeting Dec 22 Comrade Spurling in Chair.
Minutes read and adopted.
Secretary reported that he had not received any reply to his letter to G. Mann inviting him to reconsider resignation.
Letter from F Henderson announcing publication of 6th edition of the "Case for Socialism" and the Branch decided on the motion of Spurling & Watson to purchase a dozen copies.
Correspondence read from "Prevention of Destitution Committee and handed to Comrade Triance.[549]
Com' Triance reported on work of Club Committee and Whist Drives and raised the question as to the position of the Party thereto being of the opinion it would not be desirable to continue them.

---

547 G. Haw, *Today's Work: municipal government: the hope of democracy* (London: Clarion, 1901).
548 Like Mills earlier in the year, Mann commented on the poor state of the Party, writing of 'the general apathy of the members'. He cited the fact that only two of the six proposed winter talks were actually held, and that the attendances at the two were only 11 and 8 members. Mann went further than Mills: he resigned not just from the Executive but from the Party itself.
549 The National Committee for the Prevention of Destitution, active 1911–13, set up by the Webbs and the Fabian Society in support of the Minority Report on the Poor Laws: see above, note 467.

Executive meeting Jan 27 J Spurling in Chair

Minutes read and confirmed.

Correspondence read from Head Office of the E.D.C at Norwich. Decided
that as the Branch would be represented by Com' Spurling as a Member
of the Council not to send a delegate. Resolution for Conference Agenda
moved by Com' Spurling seconded by Com' Gilden "that a full time
organiser for the Division be appointed". Carried.

The following nominations were agreed too:

   Fletcher Dodd for Divisional Representative on N.A.C. & for Chairman
   of Divisional Council.

   J. Mills Treasurer. J Spurling as a Member. Agreed.

Letter from Councillor Jackson (Ipswich) offering to arrange a free supply
of Citizens for distribution. This was left over for the consideration of the
Branch.

Branch Meeting Feby 16th Comrade Spurling Chairman 14 Members
present.

Minutes read and adopted.

Secretary read correspondence from Head Office re Annual Conference, a
suggestion for re-enrolling lapsed members, and from Secy Divisl Council.

Com Ridley had attended as a delegate to the ED.C.

Comrade Spurling gave a lengthy report as to the Divisional Conference at
Norwich announcing that Com' Mills had been re-elected Treasurer and
himself as a member.

Balloting took place for election of divisional representative to N.A.C,
Comrades Triance & Pooley acting as scrutineers. Result Holmes 11,
Pollard 2, Saul 1

Guardians Elections Comrade Neave moved & Gittings seconded that the
Branch contest at the forthcoming Election, providing candidates can be
found and that the Executive take steps in the matter. Carried.

Com Triance announced that the Annual Supper was a success.

Re Citizen offer of copies for free distribution it was decided that the matter
stand over with a view to being worked with a distribution of Guardian
literature

Agreed that the Annual Meeting be held March 16.

Secretary announced receipt of report & findings of N.A.C on enquiry held
into expulsion of Fletcher Dodd from Yarmouth Branch, and that Members
wishing could read same.[550]

---

550 This does not appear to be reported in the Socialist press, nor to have resulted in
Dodd's expulsion: he stood for the ILP in the county council election of March 1913, and

Executive Committee Mar 2 Comrade Triance in chair
Minutes read and adopted.
Correspondence re Yarmouth Branch and Com' Dodd, decided to ignore the matter.
Lengthy communication from Pollard Secretary E.D.C. suggested Federation of Branches, decided to bring up later at Branch meeting.
Annual Conference Decided to appoint Com' Ridley as delegate.[551]
Guardians election. Gilden moved Watson seconded that Comrades Mills & White contest South Lynn Parish.

Annual Meeting March 16 1913. Chairman Comrade Spurling.
Secretary read minutes of last Annual Meeting & last Branch Meeting. Adopted.
Treasurers report showed a balance in hand of two pounds. But that subscriptions from members had fallen by 4/6/6. Comrade Frost moved the adoption Com' Bennett seconded. Carried.
Secretary then read his report which showed that taking into consideration the loss the Branch had sustained by removal of members and the resignation of others a fair amount of good work had been done.
Chairman of Branch Comrade J Neave having refused to accept office Comrade Spurling was elected unanimously.
Secretary Comrade White re-elected
Treasurer Comrade Triance stating he would be unable to accept nomination Miss White was elected unanimously.
Collectors Comrades Watson & H Pooley elected
Librarian & Organiser Comrade Simpole
Executive Committee Comrades H Pooley, Bennett, Frost, Mr Gilden & J Mills (with Treasurer, Organiser, Collector, Secretary & Chairman)
Club Committee Comrades Mrs White, Mrs Gilden, Gittings, Triance, Hammond, Bennett (& 2 from Executive later)
Candidature of F W White for Guardians South Lynn Parish endorsed by Members.
Correspondence read from Com' Pollard Secretary E.D.C. was read and the Secretary was left to reply to same.

---

unsuccessfully stood for re-election to the Board of Guardians and Rural District Council in the following year (*Yarmouth Independent*, 15 Mar. 1913, 11 Apr. 1914). The matter is not mentioned in Wadsworth, 'Yarmouth ILP'.
551 The Annual Conference of the ILP was held in Manchester on 24 and 25 March, with Ridley as the King's Lynn delegate: he reported back on 20 April.

April 20 Branch Meeting Comrade Spurling in chair.

Minutes read and adopted.

Letter read from Secretary A.S.R.S with resolution passed by the Branch "That in the interest of working class local organisations Trade Unions, Co op, I.L.P. & Friendly societies some scheme of united action is most desirable for Municipal Elections & other matters. This Branch hereby considers the present time most opportune for each section to appoint a small sub-committee with a view of meeting together to formulate some plan for the future & report to this Branch". After discussion Comrade Ridley moved and White seconded "that Comrades Frost & Spurling be appointed to represent the I.L.P. with instructions that \the/ formation of any local organisation be on the lines of the National Labour Party". Carried.

Letter read from Sydney [*sic*] Webb offering "The New Statesman"[552] to the branch for 10/- a year post free. No decision.

Comrade Ridley stated he had arranged a tour for Joseph Rule,[553] and Com' Frost proposed we accept his services two nights (Thursday & Friday) in June. Agreed.

Comrade Ridley gave a report of his visit to the Manchester I.L.P. Conference and was awarded the thanks of the members for his services.

Executive Meeting May 22 Comrade Mills in chair.

Minutes adopted.

Letter from W Holmes summoning a meeting at Norwich Sunday May 25 for the purpose of forming a federation of I.L.P Branches in the Norfolk area. Meeting decided our Branch was not in a position to send a delegate.

Lengthy communication from Secretary Pollard calling attention to the I.L.P Coming of Age campaign[554] & Meeting at Norwich May 25 & Peterboro June 8 for the purpose of forming federation of branches in their respective areas. After some discussion it was felt that it might be an advantage to join the Peterboro federation.

---

552 *The New Statesman*, a weekly political and literary magazine, first issued 12 April 1913. It was founded by members of the Fabian Society, including Sidney Webb (1859–1947), his wife Beatrice, and the playwright George Bernard Shaw.

553 Member of ILP (Stockport branch), with a very high reputation for his oratory. Mentioned many times in the *Labour Leader*, for example, 'made a big impression by his forcible speeches on the 'New Politics' and 'The Charge of Immorality' (in Nottingham, June 1910); 'has proved to be by far the best propagandist we have had in Bermondsey' (August 1913). Also wrote pamphlets for ILP, such as *100 Pills for Tariff Reformers* (1909).

554 The ILP celebrated its 21st anniversary in 1914.

Branch Meeting May 25. 15 present. Comrade Ridley in Chair.

Minutes of previous meeting read and adopted on the Motion of Comrades Gilden & Pooley. Mrs & Mr Evans[555] were proposed as New Members and adopted.

Joseph Rule's Visit. It was agreed to produce 3000 Handbills advertising these meetings and also to insert announcement in Lynn News.[556] Comrade Evans agreed to entertain Mr Rule. Comrade Duberry of the N.A.C offered to speak for the Branch as a wind up to Rule's meetings.[557] It was decided to accept his services and Comrade Spurling offered to entertain him.

Executive Meeting Club Room Sepr' 18th[558] Comrade Spurling (in chair) Watson, H. Pooley & Secretary. Minutes read and adopted.

Arising out of minutes the Secretary reported he had ~~had~~ no settlement yet with Com' Ridley as to our proportion of Joseph Rule's expenses.

Secretary gave a rough Financial statement (in absence of Treasurer) showing a balance in hand of 10/6½

Fees to N.A.C were paid up to August on 28 Members.

Secretary stated that Snowden was visiting ~~Norwich~~ Colchester & Ipswich during December and it was agreed that the Head Office be written reminding them of Snowden's promise that Lynn should have first claim to his services.

A general discussion then took place as to weakened position of the Branch and lack of interest by members. Comrade White reminded Executive that he had only accepted office as Secretary temporarily and that someone

---

555 Mr and Mrs Evans of Goodwin's Road, Lynn. Although their names are in the subscription book for 1913–14, no payments are entered against their names and their names are crossed through in the 1914–15 list.

556 A draft of the handbill survives, announcing two meeting to be held at the Walks Gates on 19 and 20 June. The titles were originally printed as 'Who are the Atheists?' and 'The Cry of Immorality', the latter being altered in the final text to 'The Minimum Wage' (NRO, SO 297/24).

557 Harry Duberry, postman and Labour activist; edited Post Office Union journal *The Post*, 1911–18; prominent in ILP – London District representative on ILP *c.* 1908–12; opposed conscription in First World War.

558 This is four months after the previous meeting, an indication of the decline of enthusiasm among members. Events passing unnoticed included the meetings by Rule and also Lynn's part in the NUWSS 'Pilgrimage'. A group of suffragists left Hunstanton on 11 July, arriving in Lynn 'escorted by local suffragists': a meeting held on 12 July at the Walks Gates was described as 'most successful' in *The Common Cause*. The women then marched to Wisbech and eventually to London. Helen Chadwick provides a link between the suffragists and the Socialists: she was at one time secretary of the King's Lynn Suffrage movement, was a fellow member, with Walter Dexter and others, of the local Rationalist Society, and married Dexter in Lynn on 4 October 1915.

should be appointed who could spare more time to attend to the work. The Committee were in agreement that the revival of interest in Trade Unionism in the town offered splendid opportunities for good work being done by the Branch if its activities could be aroused. Comrade Spurling stated it was time some definite decision of the future of the Branch was decided on and gave notice to move that the party be disbanded. It was decided to summon a Branch Meeting for Sunday Sepr 28th.

Branch Meeting Sepr 28. 16 members present. Comrade Spurling in Chair. Minutes read and adopted.
Letter was read from General Secretary announcing that Snowden would be unable to visit Lynn this year.
Letter from Organising Secretary Suffrage Societies (Norwich) offering speakers.
Comrade Spurling moved resolution to disband Party notice of which had been given. Comrade Spurling stated that he had taken that step in order that the whole business of the Branch might be gone into and not with any serious intention of disbanding but he had felt for some time that something must be done to arouse interest on part of members. Comrade Neave was voted to the Chair. Comrade S Bennett seconded resolution, H. Pooley supporting it. Secretary read letters from G. Ridley, T.A Frost & Mrs & Mr Dorer opposing resolution. A lengthy discussion followed in which nearly all joined. H. Pooley and S Bennett announced their intention to resign there [sic] membership. Comrade Spurling in reply said he had felt it necessary to speak out straight but he had not intended to cast any reflection on any individual members, if any remarks of his had been taken in that light he would apologise. The resolution on being put found only one supporter.
After deciding that the Executive meet at once to go into the affairs of the Branch the Meeting closed.

Executive Meeting Comrade Whites House Oct 2nd Comrades Mills, Watson, Spurling, Miss White & Secretary present.
Minutes read and adopted.
Secretary stated there were vacancies on the Committees and it was decided to call a Branch Meeting for Oct 5th at which these should be filled also to appoint an Assistant Secretary.
Discussion took place on the forthcoming elections and of the importance that the people should have an opportunity of voting Labour. Comrade Mills stated that in the event of no one else accepting he would contest the South Ward. It was therefore decided to recommend the branch to Contest this Ward.

Branch Meeting Oct 5th Minutes read and adopted.

New members H Proctor,[559] J Proctor,[560] P Allen,[561] & Hammond.[562] Proposed by F White secd by Spurling.

Vacancies on Executive Comrades J Pooley ~~Watson~~ \Gittings/ & Mr Evans. Proposed by Frost seconded Triance carried.

Vacancies Club Committee Mrs Evans & Watson

<u>Assistant Secretary</u> Comrade Spurling was unanimously elected on the proposition of Comrades Gittings & Evans

<u>The Chairmanship</u> being vacant Comrade J Neave was proposed by T A Frost seconded by J Mills and agreed to. Comrade J Neave then took the chair vacated by J Spurling.

<u>Municipal Elections</u> Comrade Watson moved that we Contest the South Ward, this was seconded by C. Fox and carried unanimously.[563] Comrade Spurling proposed that J Mills be the Candidate and Comrade Gittings seconded. Carried. Comrade Mills said that he had agreed to stand only after it was found no one else would come forward as he felt that in the best interests of the party at least one seat should be contested.[564]

<u>Election Agent</u> Comrade J Spurling was proposed by F White & seconded by T A Frost, J Mills supporting. Carried

It was agreed that the Press be notified of decision to contest South Ward.

Com Watson proposed & T. A Frost seconded that the Agent (J Spurling) be empowered to arrange for speakers to meet the Chemical Workers & other Unions. Agreed.

Secretary read offers of speakers for "No Conscription" Campaign[565] and

---

559 Horace Edward Proctor, born in Lynn 1892, a newsagent's assistant (perhaps worked with Frederick White, his proposer). Address in subscription book: Wellington Street, Lynn. Last paid subscription in May 1914.

560 Joseph Proctor, born in Lynn 1848, father of the above, a widower at the time of the 1911 census. A grain warehouse foreman. The Proctors lived in Wellington Street, Lynn in 1911, but the 1914–15 subscription book gives J. Proctor's address as 'Seeche' (presumably Setch or Setchey, a village four miles south of Lynn). He last paid his subscription in March 1914.

561 Subscription book lists P. Allen, Wood Street Lynn. He last paid his subscription in March 1914.

562 The lack of initial suggests that he has been referred to previously, so presumably H. R. Hammond, see above note 525.

563 Cecil Fox, born 1878, fireman, Diamond Street, Lynn.

564 Mills stood in South Ward, coming bottom of the poll, but with 473 votes, the highest ever received by an ILP candidate in any pre-war municipal election in Lynn. However, the ward poll was topped by Jackson for the Liberals, with 770 votes. The election saw a swing to the left, with the Liberals gaining control of the council for the first time for many years. (*LN*, 8 Nov. 1913).

565 The beginning of a campaign which would grow with the outbreak of war in August

Comrade Evans proposed that J. Pointer M.P. be invited to address a meeting on Nov 23rd. J Mills seconded. Carried.

Winter Program Agreed that this be left to the Executive

Old Members Comrade Mills that old Members be invited to rejoin the Party by a letter signed by the Executive that in the event of no reply being received they would be treated as Members.

Executive Committee Oct 13 Held at Comrade Mills' house. Minutes read and adopted.

No Conscription Demonstration. Letters read from Divisl Sec'y Pollard stating that Pointer M.P was booked for Luton on the 23rd. it was decided that we approach the Friends society & other organisation inviting their support and in the event of favourable replys Pointer should be booked for the 24th.[566]

Re Wallhead & Russell's visit to area in January this was left over.

Suffrage Societies offer of speaker also left over.

Winter Program. Comrade Spurling agreed to undertake the work.

Executive Committee Comrade Mills House Oct 30.

Minutes read and adopted.

No Conscription Demonstration. Comrades Spurling & White were appointed to act with two representatives of the Friends to carry out arrangements.

Comrade Lowerison's offer to give a lantern lecture on Greek art was left over for further consideration

Application from Clarion Cycle Club for use of Club Room for Whist Drive \ in aid of Van Fund/ in November & December after discussion it was agreed to let them have the use of our Room for one Drive at at [sic] a nominal charge of 2/6/, the other date to be decided at next meeting of Branch as it was felt that the Room could not be closed without permission of Members.

Branch Meeting Club Room Nov 16 Chairman Com Neave.

Minutes read & adopted.

New Members. Mr W Bracey & H Watson were proposed and adopted as Members.[567]

Arising out of a discussion on the circular issued Comrades Triance & Watson agreed to see Old Members.

1914. One of the ILP's Coming-of-Age leaflets by Bruce Glasier was entitled *Resist the Foreign Yoke of Conscription! Now urged under the name of compulsory military service.*

566 Society of Friends, for whom pacifism was a tenet of their beliefs. See Martin Ceadel, *Pacifism in Britain, 1914–1945: the defining of a faith* (Oxford, 1980), esp. 23–7.

567 H. Watson, Graham Street, Lynn; Bracey unidentified.

No Conscription Meeting Comrades Evans agreed to entertain Mr Pointer M.P. if necessary. Collectors were appointed for the Meeting.[568]

The Municipal Election. The Members discussed the attitude of of [*sic*] the Party in the election and endorsed the action taken. Comrade Triance moved & R Hall seconded "that the Party appreciates the action of Comrade Mills in undertaking the contest and awards him the best thanks for the work put in and their great satisfaction at the fine poll. Carried.

Program Comrade Spurling announced that he had booked the services of R. Wallhead and Russell Williams for Feby & March, and Comrade Evans moved & H Watson seconded that a speaker be booked for a date in Jan if possible. Carried.

Clarion Cycle Club application for use of Club Room for Whist Drives it was decided that as the Branch would be holding Drives during December we could not well grant its use.

Comrade Spurling raised the question of a Class for Study and agreed to try and form one.

Executive Meting Club Room Dec 4th Comrade Frost in chair.
Minutes read and adopted.

Comrade Spurling election agent stated that the total expense amounted to 3/0/3 that bills had been paid and forwarded to Town Clerk.

Secretary stated that the Collection at Anti-Conscription Meeting amounted to 2/-/- and that expenses would total to about 3/-/-, that as a result of the interest shown in the subject he expected to be approached by the local Sec'y of the National Service League as to the possibility of a Public Debate being arranged on the subject.[569]

Proposed New Club. Members discussed the proposals of the Clarion Cycle Club and it was agreed that our Committee meet them to go into the matter.

Branch Meeting Dec 21 Comrade Neave Chairman.
Minutes read and adopted.

Secretary read a letter for the Local secretary of the National Service League suggesting a Public Debate and it was agreed that the Executive be empowered to negotiate providing no heavy financial liability be undertaken.

Club Committee Vacancy Comrade R Hall was elected

---

568 The meeting was held at Central Hall, Lynn. George Ridley took the standard Socialist line: 'the workers of the world had nothing to fight each other about' (*LA*, 28 Nov. 1913).

569 National Service League, founded 1902 to draw attention to England's unpreparedness for war and to campaign for compulsory military training. Its 1913 annual report claimed 96,526 members and 163,746 'adherents'.

<u>Annual Supper</u> It was agreed that the Club Committee be recommended to arrange for this Annual event.

<u>Programme</u> Comrade Watson proposed & R Hall seconded that F Henderson of Norwich be booked for January.

<u>Proposed New Club Premises</u> Comrade Spurling gave a report of the Joint Committee called on the initiative of the Clarion Cycle Club to consider proposals for securing a building in a central position. A lengthy discussion took place and on the proposition of Comrade Spurling a resolution was carried "that at the present juncture we cannot see our way to proceed further with the matter".

Executive Meeting Club Room Jan 9 Comrade Frost in Chair.
Minutes read and adopted.

Comrade Spurling announced that a meeting of delegates representing over 1000 Trade Unionists had been held at the Bank Room on Jan 7 with G. Ridley in the Chair and that as a result the King's Lynn & District Trades & Labour Council had been established. Further that it had been unanimously been decided to invite the I.L.P. to send Delegates to the next meeting. Comrade Frost moved and Com' Evans seconded that J. Mills & F W White be delegated to attend.

Agreed that the Secretary put forward a strong claim to the N.A.C. for the services of Phillip Snowden during 1914.

Agreed that meetings be arranged for Wallhead & Williams on Feby 20 & March 27 respectively and that the Blackfriars Hall be booked.

Secretary reported that the Friends through Councillor Errington had paid half the deficit on Anti Conscription Meeting 11ˢ/8ᵈ.[570]

Jan 30ᵗʰ Executive Committee. Comrade Neave in the Chair. Present Comrades Mills, Evans, Spurling, Gittings, Frost, White.

<u>Trades Council</u> Comrade White gave account of last meeting held at the Coffee Tavern. And it was decided to recommend to the Branch that Comrade Mills be the the Delegate to Represent the Branch at the next Meeting on Feby 11ᵗʰ.

<u>Proposed Public Debate</u> on Militarism. Further correspondence was read from the Secretary of the National Service League and it was agreed that the Secretary write that the I.L.P. are prepared to go forward with arrangements providing a guarantee be given against any serious financial loss. Comrades

---

570 Robert George Errington (1874–1959), tailor, with shop (Burlingham and Errington) at 105, High Street, 1901–1919, then a shop (in his own name) in St James Street; mayor in 1943.

Spurling & the Secretary with Councillor Errington co-opted to form sub-Committee to make arrangements.

The Housing Question. Following the action of the Town Council it was agreed that a resolution be sent to the Town Clerk "urging the Council to put into operation the full powers they possess under the Housing Act in meeting the demand for houses".

E.D.C. It was agreed on the motion of Comrade Evans that as Comrades Spurling & Mills were members of the Executive we do not send any further Delegates to the Divisional Conference at Ipswich on Feby 8th.

Letter read from the National Secretary re proposed visit of Phillip Snowden. Secretary read a letter from Divisional Secretary Pollard announcing that Walter Hampson ("Casey") the Popular Lecturer, Violinist & writer of the Labour Leader would be visiting this division and it was decided that we try and fix Wednesday April 1st for a visit to Lynn.[571]

Advertising Wallhead's meeting decided this be left to the Secretary.[572]

Branch Meeting Club Room Feby 8th.

Minutes read and adopted.

Comrades Frost & White gave a report of the Housing Conference at the Peoples Institute.

Trades Council members endorsed appointment of Comrade Mills as the I.L.P Delegate.

Wallhead's Meeting Comrade White was appointed as Chairman, Comrade Triance agreeing to write G. Ridley to act as second speaker. Comrade Watson to be responsible for collectors.

Branch Meeting March 8 Comrade Neave in chair

Minutes read & adopted.

Comrade Spurling gave a report of the E.D. Conference at Ipswich.

Ballot for Divisional Representation on N.A.C Comrades Bracy & Evans acted as scrutineers. The result showed 17 members present had voted for Pollard.

National Conference at Bradford.[573] Comrade Gilden moved Comrade Evans seconded that the Branch send a Delegate, and that G. Ridley be

---

571 Walter Hampson, wrote as 'Casey' (1864–1932); born Dublin: boy chimney-sweep in Stockport; self-educated; talented violinist; well-known Socialist propagandist. At the Lynn meeting, he began his recital with a talk on art and Socialism (*LA*, 3 Apr. 1914).

572 A handbill for the meeting *is* pasted into the minute book.

573 The 1914 Annual Conference was held at Bradford, (as had been the first in 1893): it ran from 11–14 April. Keir Hardie gave a rousing speech: 'The past twenty-one years have been years of continuous progress, but we are only at the beginning. The emancipation of the worker still has to be achieved, and just as the I.L.P.in the past has given a good straight

asked whether he would be able to arrange matters, the Branch paying the fee of 7/6. In the event of his not accepting the Secretary to deal with matter.

<u>Debate arrangements</u> Comrades Watson, Jenkinson, Gilden, Neave, Spurling & White agreed to act as stewards.[574]

Russell Williams visit Comrade Gilden move that four members act as sub-committee to carry out advertising. Agreed. Comrades Evans, Gilden, Spurling & White appointed.

<u>Casey's Visit</u> Comrade Gilden proposed & Spurling seconded that the Club Committee try and arrange a tea in the Club on the occasion.

The Annual Meeting was fixed for Sunday March 22 Comrades Gilden & Evans being appointed to audit Accounts in the meantime.

Annual Meeting Club Room March 22 1914. Comrade J Neave in the Chair

Minutes of last Annual & Branch Meetings read & adopted.

Secretarys report showing work done by the Branch adopted.

Treasurer's report and Balance passed

Election of President J. Neave was proposed by Comrade Frost seconded by Com Evans

The following was agreed to unanimously

Secretary F. W White

<u>Assistant</u> J W Spurling

<u>Treasurer</u> Miss White <u>Collector</u> Com' Watson

<u>Executive</u> Comrades Evans, Gilden, Frost, Mills, Triance

Appointment of Organiser & Librarian left to future meeting

Club Committee. Mrs Gilden, Mrs Evans, Mrs White, Miss White, Mr Gilden, Watson & Triance

Russell Williams meeting F.W White was appointed to take the chair and agreed to entertain the speaker.[575]

---

lead, so shall the I.L.P. in the future, through good report and ill, pursue the even tenor of its way, until the sunshine of Socialism and human freedom breaks forth upon the land.' (Stewart, *Hardie*, 336). Ridley is not listed as a delegate.

574 A public debate on conscription organised by the ILP was held at St James Hall on 18 March 1914: J Bruce Glasier was the anti-conscription speaker. The debate was given lengthy coverage in the local press (*LA*, 20 Mar. 1914; *LN*, 21 Mar. 1914). The minute book contains a handbill for the event: G. G. Coulton, NSL, vs Bruce Glasier, 'Is compulsory military training and service necessary and desirable?' also inserted loosely a subscription card for the ILP Anti-Conscription Campaign Fund.

575 For Williams, see above, note 483. The meeting was held at the Walks Gates on Monday 12 September: 'there was a good attendance' (*LN*, 16 Sept. 1910).

Arrangements were made for Casey's visit and Comrade Gilden agreed to take money at the entrance.[576]

October [*date left blank*] Meeting in Club Room Comrade Neave in the chair

Discussing the Municipal situation Comrade Spurling stated that the Trades Council was endeavouring representation on the Town Council but the general feeling was that owing to the public attention being diverted by the war, contests at the Municipal election would be avoided.[577]

The general position of the Branch and the Club \room/ was discussed and it was agreed that the present membership did not warrant it being kept open.

Comrad Mills moved and Comrade Spurling seconded "that from and after Dec 25 we cease to be tenants of the club room". Carried.

Billiard table. It was agreed that in the event of no reasonable offer being received for his, that it be stored at Comrade Mills'.

Piano. Comrade Triance moved that this be offered to Comrade Spurling for 5/1/1 with the option of the Branch being allowed to repurchase same at the expiration of two years. Comrade Frost seconded. Carried.

It was agreed that Comrade White should have the first option of purchase of the floor covering.

Comrades Neave Spurling and Triance were appointed to arrange for disposal of any other property of the Branch.

---

576 A handbill advertising the event (a 'Grand musical Lecture' at St James' Hall on 1 April) is pasted into the minute book.

577 The First World War had broken out on 4 August 1914: elections were indeed suspended for its duration. The war split the Labour movement: many of its members opposed it, including the leader Ramsay MacDonald and also Keir Hardie. However, the greater part of the Parliamentary Labour Party supported the war, and MacDonald resigned as its leader. The majority of members of the ILP were opposed to the war, and this was reaffirmed at its Annual Conference at Norwich at Easter 1915: Keir Hardie was ill but rose from his sickbed to condemn the alliance with Russia: 'the alliance with Russia is not to help Belgium. It is to open up fresh fields for exploitation by capitalists. We register our protest against all the infamies of the bloody cruelty of Russia.' This was his last public speech: he died in September.

For the drama of the announcement of war, see the note in the front cover of SO 297/1. White and the ILP were opposed to the war, but Lowerison was keen to play his part. He donated his field glasses in response to an appeal in September 1914, offered the use of his shooting range to troops and obtained special permission to visit the (normally prohibited) beaches to watch for invading Germans (NRO, MS 21382; Frank Meeres, *Norfolk's War* (Stroud, 2016), 13–14; Frank Meeres, *Norfolk in the First World War* (Chichester, 2004), 96).

December 13th 1914 Meeting in Club Room. Com. Neave in the Chair.
Minutes of last meeting read and confirmed.

Letter was read from Com. White, dealing with the position of the Branch, and offering the Party the use of the Club Room for the Nominal Sum of 12/- per quarter to enable the Party to have full use of the Room, and to help the Party to successfully negotiate the exceptional circumstances resulting from the War. Com Mills moved & Com Frost seconded that the Minutes referring to the Tenancy of the Club Room be rescinded. Carried. Com Mills moved & Com Gittings seconded "that the offer of Com White be accepted subject to the offer being for at least 12 months". Carried unanimously.

A Letter from the Trades Council was read, asking for terms for use of the Club Room for at least 13 meetings. It was decided to offer the use of the Room for 1/6 per meeting.

Annual Meeting held March 14, 1915 at Labour Club, Windsor road. Prest: Com Mills, White, Neave, Frost & Spurling.
Minutes were read & confirmed.

Com White presented a Statement of Accounts for the past year which were passed subject to Auditors approval.

All officers were re-elected

It was felt that nothing could be done while the War continues, but every effort should be made to preserve the nucleus of a Party to take action when things resume a more normal condition.

Annual Meeting held at Labour Club Windsor Road Sunday March 5th 1916. Present: Com. White, Neave & Spurling.
Minutes read & confirmed.

Com White presented a Statement of Accounts showing a Balance in hand of £2-13-10½

It was decided that it is impossible to continue the Party, and that the Property of the Party be sold, and after defraying all outstanding accounts the balance be banked in the names of three Members.

Books, Pictures & Platform to be stored and be handed over to any party having Socialism for its object that may start in the town in the future.

Floor Cloth to be left to Landlord in remuneration for various breakages.

The Secretary was instructed to negotiate with Padmore Bros, Birmingham, for sale of Billiard Table.

Appendix 1: John J. Kidd to Frederick White, 17 December 1902

NRO SO297/ 3

Dear Comrade White, It will be more conducive to free discussion if I do not attend tonight.

No one regrets more than I, in fact no one has more cause for regret than myself, that this unfortunate affair has happened, but it <u>has</u> happened & now it is everyone's duty to try & counteract the harm that follows, & let me ask the comrades not to talk or act as though one person were indispensable to the Socialist movement in this town.

It is not my intention here to state what I have done; suffice it to say that reports have greatly exaggerated everything & what has been readily seized on by opponents as a plausible excuse for damaging my character could at proper time & place be explained if I thought it necessary. Not that I wish for one moment to excuse the folly I have been guilty of; I <u>have</u> been foolish and I admit it willingly. Last Thursday evening I sent a letter to the Chairman of the Board of Guardians telling him I desired to speak before the Board, at what time he thought best on Friday, upon a personal matter. I made this voluntary statement making a clean breast of the whole matter & the Board acted in a most generous & kindly manner, in fact my most bitter opponents said some of the kindest things.

I now come to the most sorrowful part of it all.

Of course my wife has been keenly hurt, but being a good brave & generous woman as you know her to be she forgave me & a reconciliation followed. That is why we attended the meeting on Sunday evening.

We both of us thought if the air had been cleared both at home & at the Board the main difficulties had been removed.

But since that time slander & calumny has been so rife that my wife felt she must get away from it for a time, so now the situation is changed & I do not feel desirous of attending further meetings until her return so please omit my name from programme & appoint pro-tem a comrade in my wife's place as Treasurer etc. I can hand over books & money any evening.

Now as to the effect of my importunate wrong doing, excuse me if I indulge a bit; but is it not a revelation to us all that the public should expect so high a standard from its Socialists? It augurs well for our cause I think. The unfortunate thing about it is that we Socialists are human after all & to quote a familiarism 'to err is human'.

Not that I really think the people of Lynn are so outrageously shocked I would I could think so of the majority.

With many it is a passing opportunity for gossip & vulgar talk & were it not for the harm done & the pain caused to those near & dear to me I would take a delight in shocking the prurient morals of the prigs & prudes of our conventional & hypocritical present-day society, but this is by the way & ill befits the present crisis, therefore pardon the diversion.

Of the future I cannot speak. If my work for Socialism in Lynn is done, Lynn will not hold me much longer. For me to live, is to work & strive for the cause. This in Lynn has been my life in spite of shortcomings & personal failings, & since Socialism is neither local nor national in its expression, the future will find me while health & strength lasts contributing my small quota of service for its realisation.

I hope my comrades will forgive me for causing the personal pain which all of them must have felt, & hope they will forgive me the harm I may have caused the movement, or the temporary check it may suffer. These requests I feel sure are granted, before they are asked. Yours most fraternally J J Kidd.'

Appendix 2: King's Lynn Borough Election Leaflets, November 1903

NRO SO 297/4

Walter Dexter, North Ward

Electors of the North Ward Be PROGRESSIVE AND VOTE FOR
DEXTER
HE WILL directly represent the Workers.
HE WILL advocate the Workers' interests irrespective of their Politics.
HE WILL oppose all waste of Public Money.
HE WILL not tolerate Jobbery or Favoritism.
HE IS OPPOSED to Sectarian Education.
Workers Unite And PLUMP for the Nominee of the Labor Representation
Committee.
Poll Early, remember the Ballot is secret. No one knows how you Vote.

John J. Kidd, South Ward

Over **100** summonses for **Rates**
At the Lynn Police Court, Oct 22nd, and more to follow!!
Is this surprising? But GRUMBLING is no use, you must ACT
If you continue to vote as before, High Rates will continue.
Try a change and get NEW BLOOD upon the COUNCIL.
If the Council can make HIGH RATES it can LOWER RATES
ELECTORS We want to WIN We CAN WIN We MUST WIN
KIDD has a definite program.
KIDD'S program represents your welfare
KIDD will advocate his program, will not be silent when he should speak.
And remember KIDD is a pronounced opponent to the Education Act.
GIVE THE LABOUR REPRESENTATION COMMITTEE YOUR
SUPPORT AND VOTE FOR KIDD!

Appendix 3: Three Letters concerning the disputed use of the Rechabites Hall, 1906

NRO SO 297/4
Edward Denny,[1] secretary SDF Branch Lynn to John Mills, Secretary LSP, Jan 24th [1906]

Dear Comrade, the S.D.F Members met on Monday night Jan 22 and have directed me to write and say that they would be glad to hear whether you are prepared to let us have the Hall one night a week, and at what charge, we think there is a question whether you are entitled to the Hall or whether the S.D.F are not entitled to the same. But if you allow us to have the Hall one night a week the matter can be arranged amicably, of course you will understand that you cannot take over the Hall and brick up the S.D.F without taking over all liabilities and if your society is not prepared to do this the S.D.F will consider themselves the tenants and take over the liabilities. An early reply will oblige, yours E Denny

Copy, John Mills to SDF Branch, Feb 8th 1906

Dear Comrade, Re your application for our hall I have placed the matter before our members who have given it their most careful consideration, & as they are desirous of avoiding any possibility of complications in the future and having other applications for the hall they have decided not to accede to your request.

With respect to the liabilities which was about 6/- per member those who have resigned may not be legally responsible but they having helped to contract the same are therefore morally responsible, which responsibility

---

1 Edward Denny, b. 1867, greengrocer, living at Baxter's Plain in 1901. He became secretary of the SDF sometime between February and August 1905: *LN* mentions Francis as Secretary 28 Jan. 1905, Denny as secretary 26 Aug. 1905. He does not appear to be closely related to Robert Denny (for whom, see note 68 in main text).

we trust you will acknowledge by remitting your shares. Yours fraternally J Mills Hon Sec

Edward Denny to John Mills, Feb 12th 06

Dear Comrade, I read your letter to my Branch, and they request me to write and say, that as your society were responsible for breaking up the old party, they consider that you are both legally & morally responsible for the debt especially on your taking over the Hall & assets, they are surprised that you should talk about moral responsibility seeing that you fail to recognise any on your part.

We consider that we have a moral claim as socialists on our part to have the use of the hall, especially as we were prepared to pay, we fail to comprehend you talking about morality when you prefer to let the hall to outsiders, rather than fellow socialists if you are not prepared to take over the debts our last letter holds good & we shall not trouble you about the moral obligations on your side. Yours fraternally E Denny, Sec S.D.F

Appendix 4: Socialist Candidates in Elections in King's Lynn, 1901–1913

Municipal Elections

1902: South Ward, J. J. Kidd (377 votes)

1903: Middle Ward, W. Dexter (256 votes); South Ward, Kidd (382 votes)

1904: Middle Ward, W. White (123 votes); South Ward, Bunnett, standing for ASRS rather than the ILP, (151 votes)

[1904: By-election, Kidd stood for SDF, not supported by Socialist party]

1905: South Ward, F. W. White (235 votes)

1906: North Ward, M. J. Jackson (206 votes)

1907: South Ward, Jackson (275 votes)

1908: North Ward, Jackson (205 votes); Middle Ward, T. A. Frost (224 votes); South Ward, White (372 votes)

1909: North Ward, Jackson (226 votes); Middle Ward, Mills (125 votes); South Ward, White (252 votes)

1910: No Socialist candidates

1911: South Ward, White (162 votes)

1912: No Socialist candidates

1913: South Ward, Mills (473 votes)

Board of Guardians elections

1901: All Saints, KIDD (213 votes)

1904: All Saints, White (234 votes), Bunnett (221 votes), Mills (180 votes). Kidd re-elected but without support of Socialist party

1904: By-election, All Saints, White (72 votes)

1907: St Margaret, Jackson (366 votes), A. Furbank (319 votes), G. Allen (271 votes); All Saints, R. Bunnett (228 votes), White (217 votes), Mills (63 votes)

1910: St Margaret, Mills (200 votes), T. A. Frost (177 votes); All Saints, White (201 votes)

1913: All Saints, White (248 votes)

Only those names in capitals were elected, i.e. Kidd in 1901 Board of Guardians (re-elected, without Socialist support, 1904)

General elections were fought in 1900, 1906, January 1910 and December 1910. No Socialist candidates were put forward in King's Lynn.

The Minute Book
of the
Executive Committee
of the Great Yarmouth
Women's Suffrage Society,
1909–1915

Figure 4. Great Yarmouth and surrounding villages, 1900.
Source: *Kelly's Trade Directory.*

Introduction

The Minute Book of the
Executive Committee of the Great Yarmouth
Women's Suffrage Society, 1909–1915

The minutes of the Executive Committee of the Great Yarmouth Suffrage Society are recorded in a single volume, beginning on 10 May 1909 and ending 22 October 1915. The provenance of this manuscript is not fully known. It was at some time given to the Yarmouth Library and was passed by the Library (with a great many other unrelated documents) to the Norfolk Record Office at an unknown date. Its reference number is NRO, Y/L 16/32.

The Historical Background

The movement for the right of women to vote in Parliamentary elections is often dated from the late 1860s when petitions to that effect were submitted to Parliament: one from Great Yarmouth, dated 18 June 1869, had thirty-eight signatures. A meeting in support of women's suffrage was held at Yarmouth Town Hall on 8 October 1874, its supporters including a borough councillor, J. F. Neave, a Yarmouth fish merchant.[1] On 12 March 1880, forty to fifty people, mainly men, attended a meeting held by Ethel Leach, the leading light of women's politics in Edwardian Yarmouth, in the drawing room of her house in the Market Place.[2]

---

1 Joseph Fleming Neave (1817–1875), ropemaker, borough councillor, member of Board of Guardians, Primitive Methodist and property owner – his many houses and other properties produced rents of £335. 6s. a year (*Yarmouth Independent*, 19 Mar. 1892). Two daughters-in-law served on the executive council of the Suffrage Society: see Appendix.

2 Elizabeth Crawford, *The Women's Suffrage Movement in Britain and Ireland, a Regional Survey* (London, 2006), 83; Patricia Hollis, *Ladies Elect: Women in English Local Government, 1865–1914* (Oxford, 1987), esp. 160–6.

By the early years of the twentieth century, there were a very large number of societies promoting women's suffrage nationally, of which three were of the greatest significance, their differing approaches reflecting tensions within the movement as to how far women should go in their struggle for the vote.

The National Union of Women's Suffrage Societies (NUWSS). Founded in 1897 by Millicent Fawcett, this, as its name suggests, was originally intended to co-ordinate the activities of the many suffrage groups that had been set up in cities and towns throughout Britain. Gradually it became an organising society in its own right. It always insisted on the need to promote the cause by means that were within the law, – demonstrations, petitions, marches. The last began with the 'Mud March' of 1907 and culminated in the 'Great Pilgrimage' of 1913. In 1909, it set up its own newspaper, *The Common Cause*. A Norwich branch of the NUWSS was founded in 1909, with Mrs James Stuart as president, Edith Willis as secretary.

The Women's Social and Political Union (WSPU). Founded by Emmeline Pankhurst in 1903 to employ confrontational or militant tactics to obtain the vote – these led to members being called suffragettes to distinguish them from the law-abiding suffragists. The tactics became increasingly aggressive over the years and resulted in many members being sent to prison, and there going on hunger strikes. Its newspaper was *Votes for Women*, run by Frederick and Emmeline Pethick-Lawrence. In 1912, the Pethick-Lawrences split with the Pankhursts, and the WSPU established a new newspaper, *The Suffragette*. The WSPU founded an East Anglian branch based in Ipswich in 1910, organiser Grace Roe, and a Norwich branch was set up in 1911 with Margaret West as organiser.

The Women's Freedom League (WFL). In 1907, a group of women broke away from the WSPU to form this: its leader was Charlotte Despard.[3] This was a much smaller group which specialised in 'stunts' to obtain publicity rather than 'outrages' that involved the destruction of property. Activities included the refusal to pay taxes and to be enrolled on the 1911 census: the latter was an idea adopted by members of all the societies, and one in which several members of the Yarmouth group seem to have taken part. The WFL was known for its caravan tours, members like Violet Tilliard and Muriel Matters travelling through towns and villages, including many in East Anglia, to promote the cause. Its newspaper was called *The Vote*. A Norwich

---

3 Mrs Despard, see above, page 98, note 224. She was principal speaker at a meeting at Yarmouth Town Hall just a fortnight after the foundation of the Suffrage Society. This is passed over in the minutes, probably because it was organised the Yarmouth Independent Labour Party and did not meet the women's 'Non-Party' criterion (*Yarmouth Independent*, 29 May 1909).

branch was set up in 1909 with Margaret Jewson as secretary; she was the sister of the better-known Dorothy Jewson, who was an early member of the Norwich WSPU.

The question of how far women should go to promote the cause was divisive. Emmeline Pankhurst liked to refer to her supporters as 'her army' and in 1913 Christabel said: 'if men use explosives and bombs for their own purpose they call it war … why should a woman not make use of the same weapons as men.' Some writers have even seen the WSPU protesters as 'terrorists' and the forerunner of later violent groups.[4] However, the suffragette leaders did not want to hurt anyone, however much they might damage property: reminiscing in the 1970s, leading suffragette Mary Leigh recalled that Emmeline 'gave us strict orders … there was not a cat or a canary to be killed, no life.' At the height of the campaign in 1913 and the first seven months of 1914, there were more than 300 incidents of arson or bombing (according to *The Suffragette*): not a single person was killed or injured.

Tensions between the groups are reflected in the Yarmouth minutes.[5] The Yarmouth society was not founded as part of any of these national groups, but its rules stressed that it was a constitutional society. Many of the speakers whom it invited came from the WFL, such as Muriel Matters and Alice Abadam. The minutes show a consistent interest in, and support for, the WSPU among a minority of members. This came to a climax in 1912–13, when a number of members, led by Kate Guthrie,[6] left in order to form a separate WSPU society in the town. It is not known how many others followed her. Four people were specifically crossed off the list of members soon afterwards; they include Daisy Allen, the youngest member whose age is known (but no details are known for most members). Executive member Emma Barrow is not said to have been crossed off the membership list, but is no longer mentioned, so she too may have moved to the WSPU.

The members who remained were, naturally. those who supported constitutional methods, and speakers no longer came from the WSPU, but were

---

4 This view is most cogently expressed in Simon Webb, *The Suffragette Bombers: Britain's Forgotten Terrorists* (Barnsley, 2014)

5 Similar tensions occurred elsewhere. King's Lynn also had a suffrage society originally unaffiliated to any of the main groups. When it finally decided to affiliate to the NUWSS, the same splits arose; 'a number of members have withdrawn from the Society, some in horror and disgust at the destructive tactics of the militant party, and others in disgust at the active condemnation which these tactics have met with at the hand of the National Union.' (Annual report of ECF of NUWSS 1913)

6 Miss K.M. Guthrie appears in the WSPU annual report for 1913 as having collected £1/11/– for the Cause and as contributing 19/– in her own right.

invited both from the WFL and the NUWSS. The group formally affiliated
to the NUWSS in June 1913, and thereafter only speakers from that Society
were invited.

Because the minutes are those of the Executive Committee, the names
of ordinary members (apart from the twenty or so founding members listed
at the back of the book) only occur incidentally. It is noted that there were
34 members in April 1910. 35 new members were enrolled at one meeting
in February 1911, and in May 1912 there were 124 members. This may well
represent the peak of the membership, with the rival WSPU being formed
that month, and the Society, having lost its 'radical' members, becoming
part of the NUWSS. The Annual Report of the Eastern Counties Federation
of the NUWSS covering the year Jan.–Dec. 1912 noted that 'at present the
membership is small, as the society has only recently been formed'.[7]

Peaceful Protest and 'Outrages'

Great Yarmouth played its part in the 'Great Pilgrimage' of 1913. *The
Common Cause* reported: 'On Thursday July 9th the Yarmouth Society had a
meeting with two platforms in the Market Square and large audiences came
to hear the Suffrage speakers. On the following morning we assembled in
front of the town Hall and set off, about sixty strong, on the first stage of
our journey, our forces being swelled by a group of men from the Caister
Socialist camp. On leaving the outskirts of the town we were given a rousing
cheer. The weather was glorious and the interest of the event was heightened
by an aeroplane circling above us…. We entered Lowestoft about thirty
strong, including those who came to meet us'.[8] The group travelled slowly,
reaching Woodbridge on 16 July and Ipswich on the following day, where
Miss Waring gave a rousing speech. London was finally reached on 25 July.

In addition to its home-grown activists, the town attracted many suffragettes who liked to campaign there in the summer months. It was also the
scene of several 'outrages'. These would not have been perpetrated by this
group, who were entirely constitutional, and may not have been committed
by local people at all.

On 27 September 1913, the timber yard of Palgrave Brown, between the
Southtown Road and the river Yare was set alight. Anonymous postcards
were sent to the police, the town clerk and to local newspapers claiming
that suffragettes were responsible. The local press reported; 'The origin

---

7 The annual report lists the officers of the society: Secretary: Miss Teasdel; Committee:
Mrs Rogers, Miss ALS Brown, Mrs Turton, Mrs Palmer.
8 *The Common Cause* (8 Jul. 1913).

of the fire is unknown and considerable mystery is attached to it as the outbreak originated in the very centre of the yard'. On the following night, three greens at the Golf Club were damaged: suffragette newspapers were left there together with seven postcards with messages like 'No vote, no sport, no peace, no property is safe. Give women the vote' and 'the timber yard was fired by us. There is no mystery about it. Oil was poured over the planks and a candle left burning in a celluloid soap-box.' This led the local newspaper to comment: 'This is the first occasion Yarmouth has suffered any damage at the hands of the militant suffragettes and the incident has evoked considerable indignation. The cards were evidently written by some educated person, judging by the writing, grammar and punctuation.'

In October 1913, *The Suffragette* reported an attempt on the Scenic Railway on Yarmouth Beach, a structure made entirely of wood: at 5 a.m. a night watchman found firelighters and cotton under the rails. It was thought that a high wind had blown the fire out.[9] On 17 April 1914, the pavilion on Britannia Pier was burnt down. According to the local newspaper, a postcard bearing a slogan was found on the beach. *The Suffragette* carried photographs of the blazing building, and claimed that notes were found reading: 'Votes for women. Mr McKenna has nearly killed Mrs Pankhurst we can show no mercy until women are enfranchised'.[10] *The Times* noted that the militant suffragettes were meeting in Lowestoft at the time, and that 'inflammatory speeches' there had 'all but advocated' a renewal of the arson campaign.

No one was ever charged with these attacks. Were they by members of the local WSPU? There is no way of knowing. Damage to golf courses had been commended to her 'Army' by Emmeline Pankhurst as early as February 1913: they were seen as bastions of male privilege. However, the balance is against their involvement in the 1914 attack on the pier. A few days after it, the Bath Hotel in Felixstowe was set on fire. Two women – Hilda Burkitt and Florence Tunks – were arrested. A coded diary by Hilda was found, which suggested that not only were the pair in Yarmouth at the time of the Britannia pier fire, but that other entries might match up with other attacks in the first four months of 1914 in Scotland, Somerset, Birmingham and

---

9   *The Suffragette* (10 Oct. 1913).
10   Reginald McKenna (1863–1943), Liberal Party politician. As Home Secretary he introduced the Prisoners (Temporary Discharge for Health Act) in March 1913. Known as the Cat and Mouse Act, suffragettes on hunger strike in prison were released when they became sick but re-arrested on recovery. Emmeline Pankhurst was released and then re-arrested many times under the Act; see Antonia Raeburn, *Militant Suffragettes* (London, 1972), 267 for a full list.

Belfast: they appear to have been busy in the suffragette cause. However, they were charged only with the Felixstowe fire.[11]

Suffragette Visits to Great Yarmouth

Yarmouth was a popular place for summer visits by suffragettes, combining a holiday with propagandism. Elizabeth Crawford notes; 'Yarmouth was a popular venue for the WSPU's holiday campaigns, which combined the raising of public awareness with the raising of funds by selling Votes for Women.'[12]

The summer in which the Yarmouth group was founded, 1909, was an active one for the WFL in the town. It was announced that it was to be a 'summer centre': women were encouraged to go on holiday there, report themselves to the organiser in charge and give at least an hour or two a day 'towards educating the British public in the demands and policy of the WFL'. Muriel Matters was to be the organiser at Yarmouth. In August 1909, it was announced that Violet Tilliard's suffragette caravan was about to visit the town.[13]

In the summer of 1910, the WSPU organised a summer campaign in the town. This ran from 22 August and leaders of the campaign, organised from London by Grace Roe, included local women Mrs Leach and Miss Bond as well as visiting suffragette personalities like Leonora Tyson and Kathleen Jarvis. Several meetings were held in the Market Place, and the campaign climaxed in a meeting at the Town Hall on 8 September headed by one of the WSPU leaders, Emmeline Pethick Lawrence. This is not mentioned in the minutes, perhaps because it was organised by the WSPU: as a constitutional society, the Yarmouth women may not have wished to publicly support a 'militant' speaker: however, the Misses Bond, Miss Brown, Mrs Turton, Mrs Quigley and Miss Palmer, all mentioned many times in the minutes, are recorded in *Votes for Women* as contributing to the WSPU 'Hundred Thousand Fund' in September 1910.

The 1911 Census

The idea that women should boycott the 1911 census was first suggested by the WFL and taken up by the WSPU, some of whose members spent the

---

11 *The Times*, 18 Apr. 1914; Frank Meeres, *Suffragettes* (Stroud, 2013) 157–9.
12 Crawford, *Women's Suffrage*, 84.
13 *Women's Franchise*, 27 May and 26 Aug. 1909.

night in Aldwych skating rink or in caravans on Putney Common.[14] There is no documentary evidence of such activity by members of the Yarmouth society, but the absence of several leading members from the census returns very strongly suggests that such a boycott was put in place by some women. These members include Alice Turton and her two daughters at Southtown vicarage, Maria Wenn, Mrs McLuckie (wife of the Congregational pastor at Middlegate chapel, Yarmouth) and schoolteachers Emma Barrow and Helen Narburgh.

Ethel Leach

Ethel Leach, the founder of the Society, was born Mary Ethel Johnson in Yarmouth in 1851. In 1869, she married John Leach, an ironmonger: his store on the Market Place opened in 1868 and continued to trade until 1995. They had one child, a son Bruce, who died in 1905. John Leach died in 1902, so that Ethel was a widow during her time as a Yarmouth suffragist.

Ethel represents one side of the women's movement: women being elected to local organisations and earning respect by the way in which they handled their responsibilities there. This aspect of the suffrage campaign has been thoroughly examined by Patricia Hollis, whose work includes much information about Ethel.[15]

At least eight of the women appearing in the minutes were on the registers of electors as ratepayers in the early years of the twentieth century, and were able to vote in local elections. Five were single women, each qualifying as joint-occupier of a property with other women. Three (Sarah Aldred, Hannah Cooper and Kate Guthrie) were joint-occupiers with one or more sisters. The other two, Margaret St John and Kate Peace, were joint-occupiers with each other, clearly a long-term arrangement as they are first co-registered at St Peter's Plain, later at Marine Parade, Gorleston. The other three women registered to vote were widows: Mary Rogers, Catherine Stacy-Watson, and Ethel Leach.

With the right to vote came the right to stand for office, and in Yarmouth Ethel Leach led the way. **School Boards** had been set up under the Education act of 1870 and women ratepayers could both vote and stand as candidates: nationwide, seven women were elected at the first elections in

---

14 J. Liddington, *Vanishing for the Vote: Suffrage, citizenship and the battle for the census, with a Gazetteer of Campaigners*, compiled by Elizabeth Crawford and Jill Liddington (Manchester, 2014).

15 Hollis, *Ladies Elect*, 160–6. See also *The Vote*, 16 Jan. 1925, for biography of Ethel Leach in a series of articles about female mayors.

1870 and others soon followed. Ethel's political career began in 1881, when she stood as the first female candidate for the Yarmouth School Board and was successful. She continued to be elected to the Board at every election until the Board was abolished and its responsibilities taken over the local authority. Ethel had become the Board's vice-president in 1895: her contribution was so highly valued that she was co-opted onto the Education Committee on its establishment in 1903.

Boards of Poor Law Guardians were elected under the 1834 Poor Law Reform Act. For three decades it was assumed that only men could be elected: the mould was broken in 1875 when Martha Merington was elected in Kensington. Others soon followed, many more after a property qualification was abolished in 1894. In that year, Ethel became the first woman to be elected to the Great Yarmouth Board of Guardians.

Under an Act of 1907, it became possible for women to stand for **borough and county councils** for the first time. Ethel stood for Yarmouth Borough Council in 1908: this was such a rare event that her photograph appeared on the front page of the *Daily Mirror*. However, she was not elected. After the First World War, Ethel achieved many firsts in Great Yarmouth – first female Justice of the Peace in the borough in 1920, first female mayor (1924–25), first female alderman by 1933. She continued as a co-opted member of the Education Committee (but was not the first elected woman councillor, this honour falling to Mrs Ada Perrett and suffragist Charlotte Harbord, both in 1920). Ethel had cultural interests too – she was a member of the Norwich 'Woodpecker Club', an arts club in which many talented women were involved, but which was not exclusively female – Walter Dexter, the King's Lynn socialist and artist, was also a member, thus linking the two groups featuring in this volume. Ethel also played a role in the national suffrage movement. In 1885, she acted as election agent when her friend Helen Taylor tried to stand for Parliament at Camberwell: however, the returning officer refused to accept Helen's nomination. Ethel Leach died in 1936: she is buried in Gorleston cemetery.[16]

The Members of The Society

As noted above, the minute book is that of the Executive Committee, individual members being only mentioned occasionally. Nevertheless, it has been possible, by using census materials and other sources, to build up a picture of known members. Thirty women who were at one time on the Executive have been identified, as have another fifteen 'ordinary' members.

---

16 Frank Meeres, *A History of Great Yarmouth* (Chichester, 2007), 130–1.

In terms of occupation, the largest group was made up of teachers, some in local authority schools, others in the private sector. Six committee members and six ordinary members are known to have been teachers (or the wives of teachers). The next largest group represented a kind of individual perhaps not found in other suffragette societies – the boarding-house keeper or 'seaside landlady'. Seven committee members and two ordinary members were boarding-house keepers or their wives. Of the other Executive committee members, four are described as 'of private means', two as the wives of fish merchants, one a timber merchant's wife, one the wife of a newspaperman and one the wife of a rate collector. One woman was a laundry proprietor. Another woman described herself as a boot retailers' assistant in the 1911 census – but her father owned the business.

As this suggests, few of the suffragists came from the working class, although this could be a slanted picture as the Executive might well be of a higher social status than the general membership, of whom much less is known. Non-executive members included a purveyor of meat on the market (but her daughter was a violin teacher), and the wife of a 'tailor maker'. Most intriguing is a member called Mrs Woods or Woodes: her address is given as 6 Row 21. The Rows were the overcrowded slums within the old town walls of Yarmouth, where the poorest people lived, and had numbers rather than names: it is significant that just one member is known to have lived in this part of town. Unfortunately, nothing more is known about her: she does not appear at this address in the censuses of 1901 or 1911, and no Woods is recorded in the rate books there for 1909 or 1910.

In terms of age, few women were below thirty, although, again, the Executive might well be made up of older women than the general membership was. Of those whose ages are known, just two of the Executive were under thirty, and they were both the daughters of women who were themselves members of the Executive. Four were between 30 and 39, six between 40 and 49, 11 between 50 and 59, and three over sixty (including Hannah Cooper, well into her seventies). Ages are only known for nine ordinary members, and they included two more women under thirty, one of whom, Marie Quigley, had a baby in 1907, the only woman in the society known to have a very young child to look after (others had children who were teenagers or older). Marie and her husband were born in Ireland: the only other member known to have been born overseas was Mrs Charlotte Harbord, born in Australia.

The marital status of thirty-one of the Executive is known: fourteen single, nine married and eight widows. It is also known for fourteen ordinary members: eight single, three married and one widow: the differences may reflect the fact that members of the Executive tended to be older than

Figure 5. Yarmouth OS Map six-inch to one mile, 1906. Most suffragists lived in
the streets on or near the sea front – Wellesley Road, Marine Parade etc. (Others
lived across the river, on the Southtown Road and in Gorleston.) The narrow
streets of the Rows, the poorest part of the borough, held almost no members of
the society. Source: Norfolk Heritage Library.

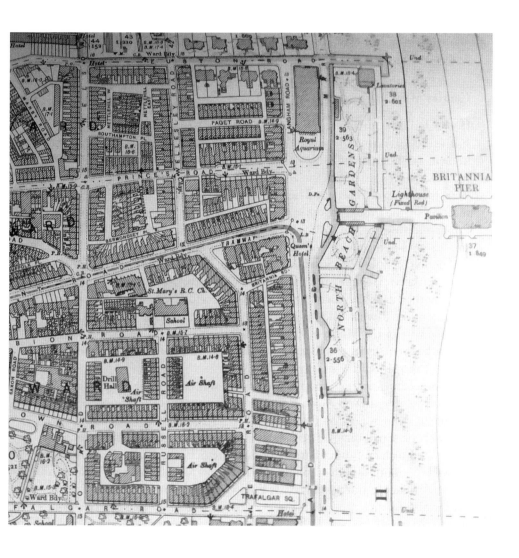

ordinary members. The number of single women also reflects the number of schoolteachers; in the local authority sector, women were normally required to give up teaching when they married.[17]

Centres of Suffrage

If one building in Great Yarmouth could be described as the centre of suffragism in Yarmouth, it would be 4 Wellesley Road, a boarding-house known as 'Edgbaston'. The house was run by Mary Rogers, residents included Mary's sister Anastacia Brown, and Miss Lilian Armitage: all three were founding members and served on the Executive, and the very first meeting of the group, together with many later meetings were held there. Public meetings of the suffrage society were held at the Town Hall, with smaller ones at the Savoy and Criterion hotels, both on Regent Road.

Another centre was Southtown Vicarage (256 Southtown Rd): Alice Turton (the vicar's wife) and her daughter Dorothy were on the Executive, and another daughter, Beryl, was also a supporter. Several other members were connected with Middlegate Congregational Church: Mrs McLuckie was the wife of the Minister, Leah Hurrell the wife of the church secretary, and at least one other member of the Church, Catharine Stacy-Watson, was on the Executive of the suffrage society.

Another interlocking group of suffragists was among the female school-teachers of the town. Most prominent was the above-mentioned Miss Armitage, who was head of the Pupil Teachers Centre on South Quay, and who personally invited several teachers into the group. Other teachers mentioned include Emma Barrow (Northgate School), Clara Westgate and Miss H. Narburgh (both Cobholm School), and Miss E. Brown (Yarmouth Vauxhall School), and possibly Miss E. Holmes (Edward Worlledge School): Frances Bunn, an Executive member, was the wife of an elementary school master. All these were part of the borough education system. The Education Committee itself had many supporters of women's suffrage. Ethel Leach and Sarah Aldred were co-opted members of the Committee (the only two women on it at the time of these minutes), as were Canon Willink, Revd M. Cullen and Revd W. T. Goodrich, all of whom participated in meetings in support of the 'Cause', as did Alderman Worlledge, the chairman of the Committee. Other members taught within the private sector, like Violet

---

17 This is clearly stated in the Education Committee Minutes for 1908: 'No married woman (except widows) will in future be appointed on the Teaching Staff, except under special circumstances. Existing Female Teachers on their marriage will not be retained on the Staff'. (NRO, Y/ED 478)

Alston of Great Yarmouth High School for Girls, Miss Georgina Harriss who ran a private school, and Miss Alice Bell, described in the 1911 census as a 'music teacher (violin)'.

The last entry in the volume is for 22 October 1915. Just over two years later, in February 1918, the vote was given to women who were over thirty, householders or the wives of householders, occupiers of property with an annual rent of at least £5, and graduates of British universities: about 8.4 million women were now able to vote. The first general election at which women could vote was held on 14 December 1918. The final victory came in 1928 when the vote was extended to women on the same terms as men, at that time everyone aged twenty-one or over.

From November 1918, women were also allowed to stand for Parliament. The first female MP in East Anglia was Dorothy Jewson, elected in Norwich in 1923. Yarmouth was slow in this field: the first woman to stand for Parliament there was Joan Knott for the Liberal Party in 1970, followed by Patricia Hollis who stood for Labour three times in general elections in 1974 (twice) and 1979. There have been several other female candidates since, but as of 2024 Yarmouth is still awaiting its first woman Member of Parliament.

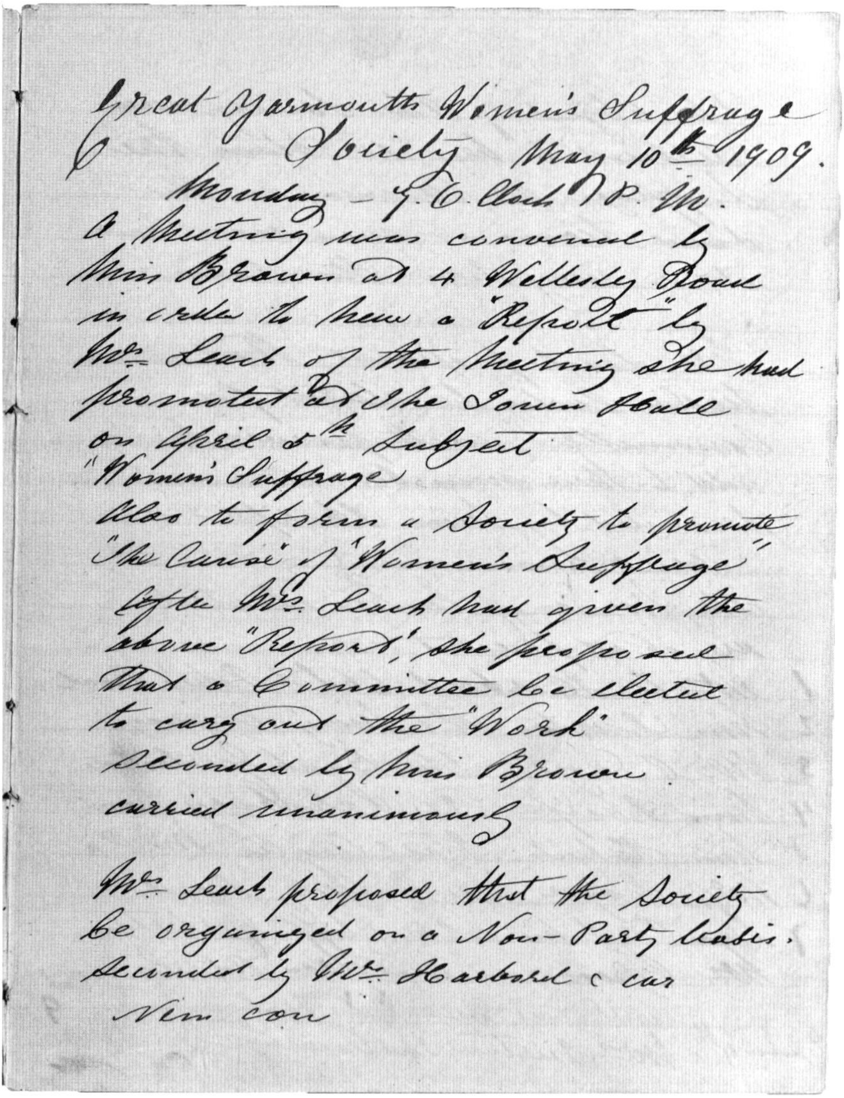

Figure 6. First entry in the Great Yarmouth Suffrage Society's minute book.
Source: Norfolk Record Office (NRO, Y/L 16/32).

Minutes of the Executive Committee
of the Great Yarmouth
Women's Suffrage Society[1]

Great Yarmouth Women's Suffrage Society May 10th 1909. Monday 7 o'clock PM.

A Meeting was convened by Miss Brown[2] at 4 Wellesley Road in order to hear a 'Report' by Mrs Leach of the Meeting she had promoted at the Town Hall on April 5th Subject 'Women's Suffrage'.[3]

Also to form a Society to promote 'The Cause' of 'Women's Suffrage'

After Mrs Leach had given the above 'Report' she proposed that a Committee be elected to carry out the 'Work'. Seconded by Miss Brown. Carried unanimously.

Mrs Leach proposed that the Society be organised on a Non-Party basis. Seconded by Mrs Harbord and car[ried] Nem con.

The object of the Society was declared to be 'to obtain the Suffrage for Women, on the same terms as men now have it, or may have the same.[4]

---

1 NRO, Y/L 16/32.

2 The names of members with brief biographical details, where known, are given in the Appendix.

3 The meeting received good coverage in the local press. The President was Dr Elizabeth Garrett Anderson, lady mayor of Aldeburgh, Suffolk; the main speaker was Miss Abadam from London (see note 69): Mrs Leach (who recalled that she had spoken at a meeting on the same site (the 'old' Town Hall) thirty-six years earlier) and Miss Armitage also spoke. It was held in the new Town Hall: 'The Assembly Room, in which the gathering was held, was crowded to the doors, the audience consisting about equally of both sexes, and many had to be refused admission … Some men at the back of the hall manifested the presence of an unsympathetic element by rather unmannerly requests.' (*Eastern Daily Press* (hereafter *EDP*), 6 Apr. 1909).

4 Not all men were yet able to vote, so it would clearly be illogical to expect all women to be able to do so. There were some supporters of women's suffrage who did not like the

Mrs Leach proposed that twelve ladies be elected for Committee, with power to add to their number. Seconded by Miss Thorpe, carried unanimously. The Names of ladies elected are as at present:

1. Mrs A Harbord 60 St Peter's Road
2. Miss Turton St Mary's Vicarage
3. Mrs C Dye The Bank Gorleston
4. Miss Thorpe 24 Salisbury Road
5. Miss Holmes 'East Anglia' M. Pa.[5]
6. Mrs Rogers 4 Wellesley Road
7. Miss St John The Cliffs Gorleston
8. ~~Mrs Cross~~[6] ~~44 Nelson Rd So.~~ \will not serve/ \Miss H Cooper instead/[7]
9. June 4th Mrs Turton The Vicarage So Town.[8]

The President of the Meeting, Miss Armitage, proposed that Mrs Leach should become the President of the Society, seconded by Miss Brown and carried, but Mrs Leach thought it would be better to try and obtain the service of another lady for that Office – she was then appointed Chairman of Committees, which she herself accepted pro tem.

Miss Armitage was then asked to become Hony Treasurer, which \Office/ she consented to fill.

Mrs Leach then proposed Miss Brown as the Secretary, seconded by Mrs C Dye. Miss B consented pro tem who also herself proposed that the title of the Society shall be 'The Great Yarmouth Women's Suffrage Society'. Seconded by Mrs Harbord.

Proposed by [blank] that the annual subscription be s1/- per annum. Seconded by Mrs Dye and carried unanimously.

The following ladies paid the same, viz

Miss Seymour 33 Wellesley Road

"   Thorpe,

---

idea of only some categories of women getting the vote: they formed the Adult Suffrage League (or Society). Orthodox suffragists were scornful of their efforts, Sylvia Pankhurst recalling Adult Suffragists 'who did virtually no work for suffrage of any sort' and quoting a comment by Keir Hardie 'it holds no meetings, issues no literature, carries on no agitation' (Sylvia Pankhurst, *The Suffragette Movement* (London, 1977), 245, 338). However, one of the leaders of the League, Margaret Bondfield, later became Britain's first female cabinet minister.

5 Abbreviation for Marine Parade.

6 Mrs Clara Cross, no occupation in 1901 or 1911 census, her husband Benjamin Cross ran a drapers' shop; their daughter Constance born 1888.

7 The deletion and the first insertion are in red ink, the second insertion in black.

8 South Town.

"   Turton,
"   Brown,
"   Holmes
Mrs Rogers,
"   Harbord,
"   Leach,
"   C Dye,
"   Armitage,
    "   ~~Seymour~~

Present at the meeting besides these ladies were Mrs Clayton, Mrs Brathwaite, Miss Chapman, Miss St John and Miss [*blank*].[9]
Mrs Harbord gave the names of Mrs J G Neave 53 Victoria Road, also of Mrs Woodes No. 6 Row 21. The Sec that of Mrs White 3 Apsley Road. The Committee thought it advisable that another Meeting C.[10] should be convened before the Season (in about three weeks or a month).

Ethel Leach C C[11]

A Committee was held at 4 Wellesley Road on Friday evening June 4th. Time 7 o'clock.

After the minutes of the previous C Meeting had been duly read and confirmed, Mrs Harbord proposed that Mrs Turton be elected a Mem[r] of Committee. Sec the Secretary and carried unanimously. Mrs Turton consented that her name should be added to M of C.
The Committee next discussed the Rules, when the following were agreed to, viz
Rule 1: Title to be 'The Great Yarmouth Women's Suffrage Society'.
2. Object: To obtain the Parliamentary Franchise, on the same terms as it is, or may be granted to men.
3. Methods: The promotion of united action in Parliament, and in the County B.[12] By means of large & small Meetings, distribution of literature,

---

9 The first three ladies presumably decided against joining as they are not mentioned again: they are Mrs Pattie Clayton, born 1874, boarding-house keeper and sister of Florence Seymour (see Appendix), living with her at 57, Marine Parade; Hannah Maria Braithwaite (spelled Brathwaite in the minutes), born 1847, 119 Nelson Road, widow, of private means; Celia Elizabeth Chapman, born 1845, unmarried sister of Hannah Braithwaite and living at the same address. Margaret St John did join, the unnamed lady could be Miss St John's friend, Kate Peace: see Appendix for these two.
10 Committee.
11 Chairwoman/chairman of Committees.
12 Borough (Great Yarmouth was a County Borough).

canvassing friends, and educating Women on the Subject by speeches etc, Socials etc.

4. Membership: That the Society shall be founded on a Non-Party basis, and have for its sole object Women's Suffrage.

5. Subscription: members shall pay not less than 1/- per annum.

6. The Affairs of the Society shall be managed by an Executive Committee, consisting of President Chairwoman of Committees, a Treas'r and Honorary Secretary, and not more than twelve other members – four of these last members to form a Quorum.

7. The Executive Committee shall have power to fill up any vacancies that may occur.

8. An Annual Meeting shall be held, at which the Accounts for the year shall be presented and the officials elected for the ensuing year.

9. The Committee will meet as occasion may require.

10. [blank]

Mrs Leach proposed that these be adopted. Sec by Miss Armitage, carried unanimously

Proposed by Miss Armitage that 200 copies of the Rules etc be printed for circulation together with other literature. Seconded by Mrs C Dye. Carried nem con.

The Secretary was then asked to write for specimen copies of literature from the Central Society, Women's Suffrage.[13]

Miss Turton reported that Miss Muriel Matters was coming in July to G Yarmouth to work for the 'Cause'.[14] The Secretary was asked to write and ascertain something about the visit – time etc. *Office* Address given as 1 Robert Street, Adelphi, Strand, London.[15] The Secretary reported that from private information received The Women's Defence League[16]

---

13 This organisation (the name of which had in fact been changed to the London Society for Women's Suffrage in 1907) was part of the NUWSS, in effect its London branch – it was responsible for events like the 'Mud March' and the demonstration at the end of the National Pilgrimage.

14 Muriel Matters (1877–1969), Australian-born, resident in England from 1905. A leading member of the WFL, she took part in two of their best-known 'stunts'. On 28 October 1908. she and another woman chained themselves to the metal grille of the Ladies' Gallery in the House of Commons. On 16 February 1909, the day of the formal opening of Parliament, she flew over London in a balloon, scattering leaflets promoting the suffrage cause. After these stunts she was much in demand as a speaker.

15 This was the office address of the Women's Freedom League from 1908.

16 Mrs Despard's organisation was in fact called the Women's Freedom League. The writer may be confusing it with the Women's Employment Defence League, founded in London in 1891 to protect women's employment rights (see Gerry Holloway, *Women and work in Britain since 1840* (London, 2005), 98.

– President Mrs Despard[17] – were about to send an organiser and two workers down to Yarmouth in July.

The expences of the Society 5/10 and the Postage up to this date were declared by Secy as paid by her leaving the H Treas Bal intact.

Present

Mrs Leach	Miss Holmes
″ Turton	″ Turton
″ Harbord	″ Thorpe
″ C Dye	″ Brown
″ Rogers.	″ Armitage.

The Committee wished to meet again before Miss M Matters' visit.

A Committee Meeting was held at 'The Criterion' 90 Regent Road, on Tuesday August 24th '09.[18]

To meet Dr Rosa Ford,[19] Miss Tyson and Miss Leonora Tyson,[20] Suffrage delegates from the W.S.P.U. London.

Mrs Leach in the Chair.

———————

17 Charlotte Despard (1844–1939), suffragette and pacifist. She joined the NUWSS in 1906, moving to the WSPU later in the same year. In 1907, she was one of a group of women to break away from the WSPU and form the Women's Freedom League. An advocate of 'passive resistance', such as refusal to pay taxes and to take part in the 1911 census. In 1908, she met Indian passive resister Mahatma Gandhi in London (both were members of the London Vegetarian Society). She was the sister of Sir John French, leader of the British Expeditionary Force in the First World War. According to Crawford, 'Charlotte Despard advocated, within the structure of a democratic organization, civil disobedience, militancy that broke no 'moral law', and a need for an awareness of the reality of the social and economic ills that could be remedied if women were enfranchised'. Elizabeth Crawford, *The Women's Suffrage Movement; A Reference Guide 1866–1928* (London, 2000), 167. See also above, page 98, note 224, and page 260, note 3.

18 A hotel at the sea end of Regent Road.

19 (Harriet) Rosa Delo Ford, London doctor and suffragette. M.B. University of London 1900. Various addresses in south-east London: 105 Pomeroy St, New Cross (1908 TD); 25 Queen's Rd Peckham (1911 TD), 30 Pepys Rd New Cross Gate (1913 *Medical Directory*). Listed as a WSPU subscriber in their 1913 *Annual Report*.

20 Leonora Tyson (1883–1959) is the most well-known member of the suffragette Tyson family, but her sister Diana and their mother Helen were all members of the WSPU, and all three went to prison for their activities. Leonora and Helen were arrested after a protest at the House of Commons in February 1908. A year later, Diana and Helen were among 25 suffragettes arrested as part of another WSPU demonstration at the House. Diana was sentenced to a month in prison: her 'prison medal' is now at the Museum of London. Leonora went on to commit further 'outrages', her activities culminating in prison and hunger strike in 1912.

When the scheme of propaganda by them for a week in Gt Yarmouth was laid before the Meeting,[21] also the Misses Tyson gave them an account of experiences in prison and in court. It was decided that the Gt Y WSS would render what assistance they could. A meeting was arranged for 'The Brush Quay' Gorleston Wednesday evening 7.15.

Guarantees were solicited by the delegates for expenses. Mrs Wenn promised 10/-; Mrs Leach ditto. Many copies of 'The Vote for Women' were disposed of.[22] Mrs Wenn promised also to see Mrs Arthur Johnson[23] about Friendly Societies Hall and Mr Aldred Gymnasium for Meetings.[24]

Present at the Meeting:

Dr Rose Ford	Miss Friend
Miss Tyson	Mrs W Harbord[25]
Miss Leonora Tyson	Mrs C Dye
Miss Hannah Cooper	Mrs Wenn
Miss Holmes	Mrs [blank]
The Misses Turton	
Miss Elliott	
Mr Petersen[26]	

With the Chairman and the Hony Sec, 17 attended.

Ethel Leach

---

21 The WSPU held a 'Votes for Women' campaign in Yarmouth, Gorleston and Caister in the week 24–31 August. An advertisement in the local newspaper announced that 'Members of the WSPU will work in conjunction with the Local Suffrage Society'. (*Yarmouth Independent*, 21 Aug. 1909).

22 Probably the WSPU newspaper *Votes for Women*, possibly, an otherwise unidentified pamphlet.

23 Arthur Herbert Johnson (1849–1917), clothing manufacturer, magistrate, borough councillor from 1901, member of the Education Committee from its inception in 1903. The family lived at 23, Euston Road. Arthur is described as a widower in the 1911 census, and his obituary in 1917 says 'his wife died several years since' (*Yarmouth Independent,* 3 Nov. 1917).

24 A 1909 trade advertisement refers to 'gymnastics and drilling' under the tuition of Miss Winifred Aldred at the Gymnasium, Middle Market Rd (reproduced in Paul P. Davies, *Stories behind the Stones* (Great Yarmouth, 2008).

25 Eleanor Harbord, born 1866, wife of William J. Harbord, corn merchant. The family lived at 65, King Street in 1901, at 96, North Denes Road in 1911.

26 Not identified. There are three people named Petersen in Yarmouth in 1911 census, all members of the crew of a Swedish vessel in harbour. Other possibilities include Aron Peterson, Danish-born upholsterer of St Margaret's Road, Lowestoft, and Bertie Petterson, newsagent and stationer, of Northgate Street, Yarmouth.

A Committee Meeting was held at 'The Criterion' 90 Regent Road on Tuesday evening October 19th '09. Time 6.30 pm.

Mrs Leach in the Chair.

\The minutes being duly read and signed./[27]

The Secretary gave some particulars as to the assistance rendered to the delegates of the W.S.P.U. and also to those of the Women's Defence League by different members of the Gt Yarmouth W.S. Society. The Chairman also gave important information on several points – one, as to the treatment of the ladies in Prison, another as to the formation of a Men's and Women's Suffrage Association[28] – at this time the circular of 'The Conservative & Unionist Association for promoting the Parliamentary Franchise for women' was laid on the table by the Sec.[29]

Following, a Resolution was put from the 'Chair', and carried nem con, protesting against the treatment by the Government of its political prisoners – this resolution to be forwarded to The Rgt Hon'able H Gladstone Home Secretary.[30]

It was proposed by the Sec that a communication be sent to the local N Papers announcing that a Women's Suffrage Society had been formed in Gt Yarmouth, seconded by Mrs Leach and carried.

Mrs Turton was asked by Mrs Leach to write to Mrs Worlledge to enquire whether that lady would consent to hold a Drawing Room Meeting on behalf of 'The Cause'.[31] Mrs Turton consented to write.

The next item on the agenda as to the best means of promoting Women's Suffrage in Gt Yarmouth.

Some members of the Committee thought a House to house 'Canvass' would be good, Miss St John offered to do this in Gorleston. Other

---

27 This sentence is inserted in the left-hand margin.

28 For Adult Suffrage Society see above, note 4. In October 1909, a society on the same lines was founded by Margaret Llewelyn Davies (1861–1944), the general secretary of the Co-operative Women's Guild. Named the People's Suffrage Federation, the new society was promoted in *The Common Cause*, 21 Oct. 1909.

29 Correct title *Conservative and Unionist Women's Franchise Review*, first published in 1909.

30 Herbert Gladstone (1854–1930, youngest son of the former Prime Minister William Gladstone) was Home Secretary between 1905 and 1910. His department was responsible for prisons, and the treatment of suffragette prisoners made him a special target of anger. His successor as Home Secretary, Reginald McKenna, attracted even greater opprobrium as the promoter of the 'Cat and Mouse Act of 1913, whereby women on hunger strike were released on licence and re-arrested once they were well enough to serve the rest of their sentence.

31 Edith Georgina Worlledge, born 1852. Her husband, Edward William Worlledge, was a borough alderman and chairman of the Education Committee. He was also a Yarmouth magistrate. The family lived at 10 Albert Square.

Yarmouth Members thought that small Meetings held in different parts of the Town would be more effective and prepare in some measure for a large Public Meeting. – the matter was left in abeyance.

As regards the date of the Public Meeting at To. Hall for the Municipal Election now at hand – then it was thought the time would be too short to work up a big Meeting before Christmas and after that there was the possibility of a General Election early in the New Year.[32]

The Members of Committee were then asked to take one of [or] the other of the Organs either Votes for Women,[33] or The Women's Franchise,[34]

 this concluded the business. Present Madames Wenn, Cooper, Armitage, Rogers, White, C Dye, Currington, St John, <Friend> *Mrs Peace*,[35] Mrs Turton, Miss Turton, Madam Leach, Harbord and the Sec

Ethel Leach

A Committee Meeting was held at 4 Wellesley Road on Monday evening Jan 31ˢᵗ. [*1910*]

When the minutes of the former C meeting had been duly signed, the first item of agenda being the consideration of whether it was desirable to continue the Society on its present lines, as Non-Party, or introduce separate sides of the same. After some discussion it was resolved that we continue on the same lines, but if possible to get up small Meetings in Cottages for the instruction of the people.

The Committee also declared that considering the Society was only founded in May 1909, that that was at the commencement of the busy time in Yarmouth, and succeeding to the Summer was a General Election, that we had had five Committee Meetings, assisted the Visitors from the Women's Defence League and the Women's Political & Social Union also corresponded with Offices at 4 Clement's Inn,[36] and dispatched a Protest

32 Municipal elections were held each year at the beginning of November. A General Election was held in January 1910.

33 Founded and edited by Emmeline and Frederick Pethick-Lawrence, first published in 1907. Originally issued monthly, after April 1908 weekly. At the time of this Committee meeting it was the official organ of the WSPU, a position it held until the Pethick-Lawrences split with the Pankhursts in 1912, after which the Pethick-Lawrences continued to edit it, while the WSPU brought out a new official newspaper, *The Suffragette*.

34 Published from 1907 by John E. Francis, deliberately intended to represent all strands within the suffrage movement. As each group published its own newspaper, sales declined: it ceased publication in 1911.

35 She was in fact **Miss** Peace, see Appendix.

36 London offices of the WSPU, often called simply 'Headquarters' by society members. According to Crawford, the organisation had a staff of 45 working there in February 1909. (Crawford, *Women's Suffrage,* 740–1).

to Mr Gladstone in regard to treatment of prisoners, also secured the attendance of about [*blank*] Members, that there was great encouragement to persevere with the Work (Women's Suffrage).

The next item was regarding the relinquishing the Office of Sec. by ~~its~~ Miss Brown declared that she did not consider her health allowed her to do all that ought to be done in the way of propaganda for the Society, and she would be glad to retire. As however only a few of the Committee were present, at the instance of these ladies she consented to hold Office for a time, hoping that soon some lady would come forward to take up the work. A letter was read from Mrs M Tuke,[37] also from Miss C Pankhurst,[38] and from Miss Armitage Treas'r who could not be present on account of cold but who forwarded the accounts – it was not thought necessary to peruse those at that time, all accounts were paid and a balance of 5/1 to the Cr of the Society.

The Sec announced that she had written to the newly elected MP Mr A Fell,[39] asking him to Ballot for place for 'Women's Enfranchisement Bill'.

This concluded the business. Present Madames Leach, St John, C Dye, Rogers, Brown.

Ethel Leach

A Committee Meeting was held at the Savoy Hotel,[40] Regent Road on Wednesday evening Mar 2nd. Time 7 o'clock The minutes of the last meeting having been duly read, and signed. The Committee proceeded to discuss at the instance of Mrs Leach, the advisability of holding a Public Meeting on the question of 'Women's Suffrage' at the end of March or beginning of April.

It was decided to organise a Meeting for Wednesday 30th Inst if possible, if not possible then during the week afterwards.

Miss Muriel Matters to be the 'Speaker', but the speech to be preceded by

37 Mabel Tuke (1871–1962), joint honorary secretary of the national WSPU. Sylvia Pankhurst wrote that everyone called her 'Pansy' and described her as 'pale and melancholy in appearance with large, mournful brown eyes'. (Sylvia Pankhurst, *Suffragette Movement*, 267).

38 Christabel Harriette Pankhurst (1880–1958), daughter of WSPU founder Emmeline and its effective leader. According to Antonia Raeburn, '[Emmeline] had complete confidence in Christabel's judgement and left her to make decisions on policy' (Raeburn, *The militant suffragettes* (London, 1973), 55).

39 Arthur Fell (1850–1934), Conservative M.P. for Great Yarmouth 1906–1922. A solicitor by profession. Strictly, the words should be 'newly re-elected' referring to his success in retaining his seat in the January 1910 general election.

40 A hotel on Regent Road, immediately west of the Roman Catholic church.

the performance of a Piece entitled 'How the vote was won' which would take about thirty minutes to perform.[41]

The Affair to be held at the 'Town Hall'.

In regard to a Chairman for the evening, and also the charge for admission, these subjects were left for further consideration.

Present

Madam Leach 'in the Chair'
    "   Armitage, Wenn, Harbord, C Dye,
    "   White, Turton, Neave.

Misses Turton, Crown, H Cooper, St John, Rose & Brown.

It was thought that friends from Norwich might assist with the performance of 'How the Vote was Won'.

Ethel Leach

A Committee Meeting was held at 4 Wellesley Road on Wednesday March 23ʳᵈ – Time 7 o'clock

To consider the best way of carrying out the Public Meeting arranged to take place at the Town Hall on April 1ˢᵗ (Friday)

The minutes of the last meeting being duly read and signed.

Mrs Leach informed the Committee that she had been successful in inducing the Revd Canon Tupper-Carey,[42] Rector of Lowestoft to take the Chair, and also the support of Gen'l and Mrs Upcher,[43] Col and Mrs Coombe,[44]

---

41 Play by Cicely Hamilton and Christopher St John, published by the Woman's Press in 1909 and first performed at the Royalty Theatre, London, on 13 April 1909. Frequently performed by local suffragette groups.

42 Canon A D Tupper-Carey, rector of Lowestoft 1901–1910. His character was summed up by the *EDP* on the occasion of his promotion to canon: 'He came from Christ Church Mission, Poplar, of which he had been head from 1898 to 1901, bringing with him a reputation for zeal, energy and earnest effort, and since he has been in Lowestoft these qualities have been noticeable in a marked degree and he has been exceedingly active.' (*EDP*, 12 Mar. 1910).

43 Russell Upcher (1844–1937), son of Henry and Caroline Upcher of Sheringham Hall, Norfolk. Distinguished army career included service in South Africa and Burma. Retired from the Army in 1902. At the time of the 1911 census, lived at The Warren, Fritton, Suffolk , a few miles south of Great Yarmouth.

44 Colonel Edward Henry Harvey Combe (the surname is wrongly spelled in the minutes), born 1846, a maltster; mayor of Great Yarmouth 1878–79 (the youngest to hold this office), colonel of 2ⁿᵈ volunteer battalion Norfolk Regiment 1892–96. Lived for many years at Ferryside in Gorleston. At the time of the 1904 Trade Directory, he lived at The Old House, Geldeston near Beccles. By 1916, he lived in Ipswich and was a Suffolk Justice of the Peace. He died there in 1920, aged 73. He married Caroline Elizabeth Laura Brown in Great Yarmouth parish church in 1869. Caroline died on Christmas Day 1909:

Mrs Buxton,[45] the Rev Thorpe Goodrich,[46] – Norfolk Esq,[47] the Rev'd G McLuckie,[48] and other distinguished persons on the occasion of the visit of Miss Muriel Matters to Yarmouth to speak on 'The Parliamentary Enfranchisement of Women'.

Regarding the distribution of literature, handbills & posters it was decided as follows:

The literature belonging to the Society to be placed in the seats in the Hall

Handbills to be delivered about two or three days previous to the meeting

Mrs Wenn would distribute over the N Quay

Mrs Leach & Mrs C Dye Gorleston and S town to the 'Half Way House',
Misses Turton as far as So To Bridge.[49]

Mrs Hull – Market Road

Miss Armitage – So Quay

Miss H. Cooper – Market Place,

Ditto – N Gate St

Mrs Harbord – St Peter's Road

Miss Brown – Regent Road,
ditto   "   – Euston Road,
  "   "   – Wellesley Road.

Some of these ladies also volunteered to place Posters.

Phamphlets for sale outside the Hall in the corridor.

Mrs C Dye assisted by Miss Turton & others.

Mrs May kindly volunteered to see to the Seating of the Company, assisted by some of the Committee

Mrs Tho [*full word illegible*] would see to the sale tickets at the door.[50]

a window was erected in Gorleston church in her honour in 1910 (*Yarmouth Independent*, 7 May 1910). Their son, Mr Edward Combe is also mentioned in the minutes: see note 87.

45 Mary Rosalind Buxton (born Upcher) of Fritton Hall, the wife of Henry Edmund Buxton, banker and J.P. The bank was at 15, Hall Quay, Yarmouth.

46 Incumbent of St Peter's Church Great Yarmouth.

47 Walter Norfolk of Cliff Road, Gorleston, a former borough councillor and at one time a member of the Borough Education Committee.

48 George McLuckie, BA, and his wife moved to Great Yarmouth when he was appointed pastor of Middlegate Congregational Chapel in November. He had previously worked in the east end of London, at Bow and later at Plaistow. He was clearly a popular figure: in June 1911, when he was considering a move to Carr's Lane Chapel in Birmingham, a resolution by the Yarmouth congregation, urging him to stay, received 662 signatures: he stayed. (NRO, FC 31/6). His wife became a member of the Society and is mentioned several times in these minutes.

49 South Town Bridge.

50 One name has been written over another, so strongly as to render both illegible: both names begin 'Tho'.

The Mayor kindly lends his parlour for the reception of Speakers and Officials – he would also be present & receive them. Mrs Leach kindly entertains Miss Muriel Matters, & the Revd Canon Willink will entertain the Revd Canon Tupper Carey.[51]

Several members of Committee undertook to interview the local Clergy & other Ministers.

Present at C Meeting: Madames Wenn, Leach, Brown, Hull, Harbord, H Cooper, Turton, H Turton jr,[52] G J Neave, C Dye, Armitage.

1910

A meeting at the Town Hall on Friday evening April 1st.

Chairman the Rev'd Canon Tupper-Carey Rector of Lowestoft who was supported by the Rev'd Thorpe Goodrich,[53] incumbent of St Peter, the Rev'd G McLuckie B A, Minister of King St, and the Rev'd E Hall,[54] Minister at Gorleston, \Mrs Leach/ [*added in footnote*], also the following ladies and gentlemen were amongst them Mrs Harbord, Mrs Norfolk, Col Bulmer,[55] Col and Mrs Combe, Mrs Worthington,[56] Mrs McLuckie, Mrs Hall, and the Committee

---

51 Revd Canon John Wakefield Willink MA, vicar of Yarmouth: the Vicarage is on Church Plain and is an enormous house with plenty of space for entertaining.

52 H Turton jr: this is probably (Neville) Harry Turton, Mrs Turton's teenage son: he would be called H Turton junior because his father's name was (Zouch) Horace Turton. Both probably used their second names, a very common practice among middle class families. He would not, of course, be a member, but present as a guest.

53 At the meeting, Goodrich strongly endorsed the NUWSS line: he stated that he held women to be as loyal and as intelligent as men, but he believed that some women who had adopted extreme measures did their cause great harm. This was Goodrich's last public meeting. Two days later he occupied the pulpit at St Peter's for the last time, after thirty years of public service. (*EDP*, 4 Apr. 1910). He moved to Potter Hanworth, Lincolnshire (NRO, Y/ED 17).

54 Revd Enoch Hall, Minister at Gorleston Congregational Church.

55 Edward Sewell Bulmer, born 1836, a timber merchant. At the age of sixty he married for the first time (to Mary Ann Holliman, widow, in St Martin-in-the-Fields London, 1895), but he was a widower by 1901, still living in London. He was in Gorleston by 1909: in that year, as treasurer of Gorleston Church Tower Restoration Fund, he was involved in a dispute with the vicar of Gorleston which was heard at the County Court: Bulmer won but was rebuked for poor record-keeping. (*Yarmouth Independent,* 19 Jun. and 10 Jul. 1909). At the time of the 1911 census, he was living as a boarder at 6 Marine Parade, Gorleston, the house of which Margaret St John and Kate Peace, two staunch suffragists mentioned frequently in these minutes, were described as joint heads. Bulmer died in Great Yarmouth in 1915, aged 79.

56 Mrs Worthington was Vice President of the Lowestoft Branch of the NUWSS. She was the wife of Dr Richard Worthington, referred to later in the minutes, a doctor in Lowestoft: they lived at 1 Wellington Esplanade. Mrs Worthington was closely associated with Alice

The Chairman after a brief opening speech proposed the Resolution, That in the opinion of this Meeting the time has arrived for "The parliamentary Enfranchisement of Women, on the same terms as men ["]. This was ably seconded by the Revd G McLuckie, and supported by Miss Muriel Matters,[57] in an eloquent and stirring speech, which was loudly applauded at the conclusion. Questions were invited from anyone in the audience, a few were asked and incisively answered, after which a vote of thanks to the Chairman concluded the Meeting.

The Mayor Councillor Swindell kindly lent his parlour for the platform company,[58] and was there to receive them and the Executive. The literature belonging to the Society was placed in the chairs before the Hall was opened to the public. The literature sold outside in Corridor belonged to the Chairman of Committees.

These ladies have signified their wish to be enrolled as members of our S.S. – Mrs G McLuckie, Miss Alston of 3 Marine Parade, and Miss Bond 56 Southtown.

(Hannah Cooper Chair)

A Committee Meeting was held at 4 Wellesley Road on Friday evening April 22nd. Time 7 o'clock

To receive the account of the Chairman's Public Meeting also Annual Accounts etc.

Mrs Leach not being present Miss H Cooper was asked to take the 'Chair'. The Minutes of the last Com Meeting being read & signed (also an account of Public Meeting received) the Annual Accounts of the Society were read by the H. Treasr. when the Subscriptions were declared to have been £2 6s 8d, and the disbursements £2 1s 8d leaving a balance from last year in Treasrs hand of 5/-.

The Sec then gave her Report for the year. Items from the same: Committee Meetings 7, Public Meetings at T.H. 2, Meetings in the open air by Speakers from the W D league, also from the WSPU. The sum of 17/6 was sent up to the WSPU for and towards expenses of "Demonstration Issues". A Protest was sent to Mr Gladstone against the treatment meted out to the political prisoners.

Ponder (*q.v.*), standing, like her, for the Board of Guardians in 1913 but withdrawing before the election, and supporting Belgian refugees after the outbreak of the war.

57   The meeting drew a large crowd thanks to Miss Matters' reputation as an activist. The *EDP* headlined its report 'Women's suffrage: Holloway Prisoner at Yarmouth' and described the event as 'a well-attended meeting'. (*EDP*, 4 Apr. 1910).

58   Theodore W. Swindell, 46 Wellesley Rd, town councillor (Market Ward) and borough magistrate.

Letters of thanks were sent to the Revd Tupper Carey Canon & Rector of Lowestoft the Revd Thorpe Goodrich, and the Revd G McLuckie – a few other particulars were given. The Chairman of Committees having sent the accounts of P.M. April 1ˢᵗ, T Hall, for perusal of Committee the following was ascertained to be correct.

Auditor Mrs C Dye
Expences of Meeting £12 ″ 19 ″ 6
By sale of tickets   £8 ″ 19 ″ 6
Deficit   £4 ″ 0 ″ 0

Mrs Leach generously subscribed the amount of the deficit so that the Society funds should not lose thereby. Whereupon Miss Armitage proposed Mrs Dye seconded, car unanimously That the best thanks of the Committee be given to Mrs Leach for the splendid organization of the Meeting, and the powerful social influence she was able to enlist for the "Cause of Women's Suffrage" also for her kind subscription.

The Names of Committee were next called over, when it was thought desirable to seek some new members on Committee as it had been signified by one or two that business matters kept them from attending their duties, ten members out of twelve being appointed.

In regard to the May demonstration,[59] it was decided that the Society could not afford to assist the funds of the W.S.P.U. at this time although they might do so later on.

Item of agenda Procedure during Summer, it was thought by the Committee to hold a Garden Party with a Speaker if possible during the Summer.

Suggested alteration of Rule 4 "That the Members of the Society are not expected to support any P Candidate unless he declare himself in his election address in favour of Women's Suffrage". Proposed by Miss Armitage, sec by Mrs Hull. Also that the subscriptions be paid on joining the Society.

Proposed from the Chair that Mrs A Ward be accepted as a member, sec by the Sec car nem con. Sub paid 1/-. Likewise the Name of Mrs Quigley 6 Churchill Road was proposed for Membership, also, Miss Cooper. Miss Armitage proposed Miss E B Brown and Miss Barrow for Membership,

---

59 A major march and demonstration was planned in London by the WSPU for May 1910. In fact, due to the death of King Edward VIII in that month, it was postponed, taking place instead on 18 June. On 14 June, a Conciliation Bill had been introduced by Labour MP David Shackleton which would enfranchise women who held property. Many people saw this as the beginning of the enfranchisement of women, and the 18 June demonstration was seen as a triumphal march. Emmeline Pankhurst pronounced at a rally in the Albert Hall: 'Victory! The bill will go through.' However, others, including Christabel Pankhurst, were less optimistic.

secd by the Sec. Miss Cooper from the Chair for Mrs Leach proposed the election of Mrs Stacy Watson as a Member sec by Mrs Hull, car nem con. Forwarded to the H. Treasr on behalf of Miss Cooper 2/-, Mrs Quigley 1/-, Mrs A Ward 1/-.

The \names of/ New Committee are

1	Madame	Turton Southtown 256
2	"	A Harbord St Peter's Road 60
3	"	J Rogers Wellesley Road 4
4	"	C Dye High St Gorleston (Bank)
5	"	Hull The Granville
6	"	Wenn "Milmont" N Quay
7	"	Armitage \Hon Trea'r/ Edgbaston Wellesley Road
8	"	C Turton Southtown 256
9	"	H Cooper Salisbury Road N 9
10	"	St John Fair Haven, The Cliffs, Gorleston

\Hon Sec/ Miss A L S Brown Wellesley Rd 4

\Chairman of Committees/ Mrs Leach "Stradbroke" Gorleston

Proposed from the Chair that a Vote of thanks be given to Miss Armitage Hon Trear and to Miss Brown Hon Sec. The Membership was declared to be 34.

Present Mrs J Rogers, Mrs C Dye, Miss Hull, Miss H Cooper, Miss Armitage, Miss Brown.

Ethel Leach

Committee Me Aug 24th

Present – Mrs Leach in Chair

Mrs Turton, Mrs Rogers, Mrs Dye, Miss Brown

The minutes of the last Meeting were taken as read & confirmed.

The Chairman read a letter that she had received from Miss Brown the Secretary announcing her resignation as sec, and that of the Treasurer Miss Armitage who is leaving the town to take up another appointment. The Comtte expressed their best thanks for the past service of the two ladies, & regret at having to lose them. It was proposed & seconded that Miss Bond be invited to act as Secretary & that Mrs Turton be asked to take the Treasurership, both of whom were kind to undertake the positions.[60] The Comtte expressed the hope that the friends & members would do all in their power to assist the W.S.P. Union to make the forthcoming meetings in Yarmouth and neighbourhood a success.[61]

---

60 The word 'enough' has clearly been accidentally omitted from this sentence.

61 The 'holiday campaign' described in the Introduction. It included a meeting held

At the close of the Comtt meeting Mrs Turton was kind enough to entertain the friends of the Association to tea and thus give them the opportunity of meeting and conferring with the two lady organizers of the WSPU the Misses Leonora Tyson & Miss Grace Roe.[62]

Ethel Leach

Committee Oct 11th 1910

Chair Mrs Leach, Miss Brown, Miss Cooper, Mrs Turton, Miss Turton, Mrs Wenn, Miss St John, Miss Guthrie (by invitation). Miss Bond Hon. Sec.
The minutes of the last meeting were read & signed.
The Chairman stated she had received a letter from Miss Roe W.S.P.U. saying if a meeting could be arranged for Oct 21st she would come over from Lowestoft with Miss Brackenbury,[63] & give an address. After some discussion it was decided that time was too short in which to work up a meeting and very little help could be given by the committee members. The Hon. Sec. was asked to write to Miss Roe and explain that it was impossible to hold a meeting at present.
Some discussion followed as to forming a W.S.P.U. branch in Yarmouth but no final decision was made.

A L S Brown

Members Meeting Monday October 31st 1910
Miss Brown in the chair
Present Mrs Rogers, Mrs Dye, Miss Bunn, Miss Cooper, Miss Alston, Mrs Palmer, Miss Guthrie, Mrs Stacy-Watson, Miss St John, Mrs Wenn, Mrs Harbord, Mrs Turton, Miss Turton.

---

at Fletcher Dodd's Socialist holiday camp in Caister (at which Leonora Tyson was the speaker), illustrating the links between the women's suffrage campaign and socialism.

62 Grace Roe (1885–1979), the first WSPU organiser in East Anglia. The branch was formed in 1910 and based in Ipswich: when Grace arrived, there was apparently only one WSPU member in the town! (Crawford, *Women's Suffrage*, 86). According to Sylvia Pankhurst, Grace Roe was a 'young Irishwoman'. She and fellow-prisoner Nellie Hall caused a commotion in court when they were arrested in 1913 for conspiracy to cause criminal damage: 'they struggled and refused to walk, flung themselves to the ground, fought to get out of the dock, and shouted at the top of their voices as continuously as they could.' (*Suffragette Movement*, 556).

63 Marie Brackenbury (1866–1946) of the WSPU, imprisoned for her suffragette activities, as were her sister Georgina and their mother Hilda, the last being well into her seventies at the time. Marie was imprisoned in 1908 and again in 1912: at her trial she said 'I am a soldier in this great Cause'. The Brackenbury house in Campden Hill Square London was known as 'Mouse Castle' because many women released under the Cat and Mouse Act stayed there while recuperating. (Crawford, *Women's Suffrage*, 76).

A letter was read by the Chairman from Miss Bond, & several letters were read by Mrs Turton from speakers willing to speak in December.

Miss Cooper proposed & Mrs Turton seconded that a suffrage meeting should be held. This was carried.

Some discussion followed as to when the meeting should be held & who should be the speaker.

Mrs Harbord proposed & Mrs Wenn seconded that Miss Jewson[64] be asked to speak at the meeting. This was carried.

It was finally decided that the Sec should write to Miss Roe & ask for a speaker, & that if by Novr 9th Miss Roe had not provided a speaker, Miss M Jewson should be asked to speak.

Nov 25th was the date fixed for the meeting.

A C Turton (Chair)

Members Meeting Wednesday Nov 9th 1910

Mrs Turton in the Chair. Present Miss Cooper, Miss Brown, Mrs Rogers, Mrs Harbord, Miss Guthrie, Mrs Dye, Miss St John, Miss Turton, Mrs Stacy-Watson.

The acting Sec stated that she had written to Miss Roe but had received no reply, & that she had wired to Miss Jewson but had not yet had an answer.

The minutes of the last meeting were read & confirmed, the minutes of the meeting before the last were taken as read & confirmed.

It was proposed by Miss Cooper & seconded by Miss Brown that a Suffrage meting [sic] be held on the evening of Friday Nov 25th in the Savoy Hotel. Carried.

Miss Cooper proposed & Miss Brown seconded that the meeting should begin at 7.45. An amendment was proposed by Mrs Harbord & seconded by Miss Guthrie that the meeting should begin at 8 o'clock. The amendment was carried.

---

64 Member of the Jewson family of Norwich: John Wilson Jewson, the head of the firm of timber merchants (later do-it-yourself stores) moved to Norwich in 1868. He had several sons who had families. Members of the family known to be in the suffrage movement include Mrs Mary Jewson, wife of John's eldest son George and a leading member of the Norwich NUWSS; Dorothy Jewson, Mary's daughter and later a leading light in the WSPU; Violet Jewson, daughter of John's youngest son Richard, and among England's earliest female doctors. Given the prefix 'Miss M' clearly none of these is meant: the reference is presumably to Dorothy's sister Margaret Jewson, who was secretary to the Norwich branch of the Women's Freedom League from its foundation in 1909 (Crawford, *Suffrage Movement*, 83).

Miss St John proposed & Miss Turton seconded that the meeting should be entirely free. Carried.

Miss Brown & Mrs Rogers very kindly offered to entertain the speaker.

It was proposed by Miss Cooper & seconded by Mrs Rogers that 3/- be voted for the Sec to lay out in Suffrage literature for distribution at the meeting. Carried.

Miss Cooper, Miss St John, Miss Guthrie & Mrs Dye were appointed to act as stewards at the meeting.

Miss St John proposed & Mrs Stacy-Watson seconded that Mrs Leach be asked to take the chair on Nov 25th. Carried.

Miss St John proposed & Miss Brown seconded that Mrs Turton should be asked to take the chair on Nov 25th if Mrs Leach were unable to do so. Carried.

Miss Brown proposed & Miss Cooper seconded that the Treasurer be authorised to take 10/- from the funds of the Society to help defray the expenses of the meeting on Nov 25th. Carried.

Miss Cooper proposed & Mrs Dye seconded that the meeting should consist of women only. Carried.

The Sec was instructed to write to Miss Cicely Corbett[65] & ask her to come & speak on Friday Nov 25th.

Hannah Cooper (Chair)

Committee Meeting Tuesday Nov 29th 1910.[66] Miss Cooper in the chair.

Present Mrs Rogers, Miss Brown, Mrs Wenn, Miss Turton.

The minutes of the last meeting were read & confirmed.

The expenses of the Suffrage meeting held in the Savoy Hotel on Friday Nov 25 were then posted.

Miss Brown proposed & Mrs Wenn seconded that the Sec be empowered to procure some ~~stamped~~ note paper stamped "Gt Yarmouth Women's Suffrage Society".

---

65 Cicely Corbett (1885–1959), suffragist and campaigner for rights of women and children. First involved with NUWSS when she was at Somerville College, Oxford, later a founder of the Liberal Women's Suffrage Group. Worked for Women's Industrial Council and campaigned against sweated labour for children. In 1913, she married journalist Chalmers Fisher.

66 One of the most horrific events of the suffrage campaign had occurred on 18 November; a group of 300 women marching towards Parliament were met by a large force of policemen and subjected to the most brutal treatment: the subsequent deaths of two women, one of them Emmeline Pankhurst's sister, were attributed to the treatment they received on 'Black Friday' as the day has become known. (Jane Robinson, *Hearts and Minds: the untold story of the great pilgrimage and how women won the vote* (London, 2018), 108–13).

A vote of thanks was passed to Mrs Rogers & Miss Brown for so kindly entertaining Miss Corbett, & for allowing the Society to hold its Committee & members meetings at their house; also to Mrs Leach for kindly consenting to take the Chair at the meeting on Nov 25th, also to Mrs Turton for paying Miss Corbett's fee.

A C Turton (Chair)

Committee Meeting Thursday Jan 5th 1911. Mrs Turton in the Chair

Present Miss Brown, Miss St John, Miss Cooper, Miss Bond, Miss Guthrie, Mrs Dye, Mrs Rogers, Miss Turton.

The minutes of the last meeting were read & confirmed.

~~A discussion was held as t~~

Miss St John proposed & Miss Guthrie seconded that a \suffrage/ meeting should be held in the Savoy Hotel at 8 pm on Friday Jan 27th as a speaker belonging to the W.S.P.U. was to be in Yarmouth on that day. Carried.

A discussion was held as to how the expenses were to be met.

Miss Guthrie proposed & Miss Bond seconded that a collection should be taken at the meeting. Carried.

Mrs Dye proposed & Miss St John seconded that both men & women should be admitted to the meeting. Carried.

Miss Bond proposed & Miss Guthrie seconded that any balance from the collection, after the expenses of the meeting had been paid, should be handed to the funds of the W.S.P.U. Carried

Miss St John proposed & Miss Guthrie seconded that the whole of the collection should be given to the funds of the W.S.P.U., & that the expenses of the meeting should be defrayed by subscription among the members. Not carried.

Mrs Dye proposed & Miss Cooper seconded that Mrs Turton be in the chair at the meeting. Carried.

Miss Bond resigned her post as Hon Secretary of the G.Y.W.S.S. & was accorded a vote of thanks for her past services.

Miss Cooper proposed & Miss Brown seconded that Miss Turton be asked to act as Hon Sec of the GYWSS, which she consented to do. Carried.

Ethel Leach

Committee Meeting held Wednesday Feb 1st 1911

Mrs Leach in the Chair.

Present: Miss St John; Mrs Turton; Miss K Guthrie; Miss Cooper; Miss Brown; Mrs Dye; Mrs Rogers; Miss Turton.

The Minutes of the last meeting were read and confirmed.

The accounts of the Suffrage meeting held at the Savoy Hotel, Jan 27th were passed. They were:

Receipts   £2-2-6
Expenses   £1-3-0
Balance   19-6

A discussion ensued on the alteration of Rule 4 proposed by Miss Brown, but it was decided to do nothing just then.

Miss Brown suggested that a Suffrage paper or papers should be taken each week by the Society & handed on to other members &/or to outsiders. After some discussion, Miss Guthrie proposed each member of the Committee should try & get members to take 'Votes for Women' & report at the next Committee meeting & this was agreed upon.

It was decided that the Sec should write to Mrs Ponder Sec of the Lowestoft WSS,[67] & to Miss Willis of Norwich,[68] with a view to co-operation in future meetings.

Miss Brown suggested that a Members Social should be held, but the details were not settled.

Mrs Turton proposed & Miss St John seconded that a public meeting be held. This was carried, 5 voting for it and 4 remaining neutral.

Mrs Leach proposed that Dr Ryley should take the Chair at the public meeting & it was decided that the Sec should write and & Dr Ryley to do so.[69]

---

67 A Suffolk branch of the Norfolk Committee for Women's Suffrage had been formed in Lowestoft as early as 1879: Ethel Leach was one of the speakers at a meeting there on 21 February 1879. In 1913, the NUWSS had 45 members in Lowestoft. Mrs Ponder is Alice, the wife of Horace Ponder, piano tuner, Waldo Cottage, Cotmer Rd, Oulton Broad: she was the Honorary General Secretary of the Lowestoft branch, and also involved with the ILP: see above, page 203, note 471. She was involved with aid for Belgian refugees in Lowestoft Oct. 1914 (*Lowestoft Journal*, 31 Oct. 1914).

68 Miss Edith L Willis, born 1876, Hon. Sec. of the Norwich branch of the NUWSS: her address was Southwell Lodge, Ipswich Rd, Norwich. As might be expected, the NUWSS branch in Norwich was the largest in Norfolk: the 1913 annual report stated that it had 'over 280 members'. At the time of the 1911 census, Edith was a visitor at the Carrow House, home of sisters Ethel and Helen Colman. They were leading members of the Norwich branch of the NUWSS and Edith's occupation in the census return is given as 'Hon Sec Women's Suffrage Society'. Ethel Colman later (1923) became the first female Lord Mayor of Norwich, and thus the first female Lord Mayor in England: Helen acted as her consort.

69 Dr James Ryley, Ferryside, High Road, Southtown and 15 Theatre Plain Yarmouth. He gained his medical degree in 1881. Came to Yarmouth in 1879 to serve as medical officer for the southern district of the Poor Law Union, later resigning to concentrate on private practice. He was a Liberal councillor from 1897 and served as mayor 1898/9. (Paul Davies *History of Medicine in Great Yarmouth* (Great Yarmouth, 2003), 138–9).

The Sec was also instructed to write to Miss Abadam & ask her to come & speak at the meeting, and also to write for lists of speakers from the National Union WSS & from the Women's Freedom League.[70]
Miss St John proposed and Miss ~~Brown~~ Cooper seconded that Miss Matters be asked to speak at the meeting if Miss Abadam could not come. Carried. The Sec was instructed to write to Mr Fell Member for Gt Yarmouth on behalf of the Committee, to ask him to press forward the cause of Women's Enfranchisement as much as possible.

A C Turton, Chair

Special Committee Meeting held at 4 Wellesley Road on Thursday Feb 9th 1911, 3.30
Chair Mrs Leach
Present Miss Brown; Mrs Rogers; Mrs Wenn; Miss Cooper; Mrs Turton; Mrs Dye
The Minutes of the last meeting were read.
It was proposed by Mrs Turton and seconded by Miss Cooper that a Social Meeting be held on Friday evening Feb 24th at the Savoy Hotel, from 7.30 to 9. Carried.
It was decided that the tickets were to be distributed by the Committee, replies to be sent to the Sec.
A speaker was to be procured from either Norwich or Lowestoft, whom Mrs Leach kindly offered to entertain.
From 150 to 200 people were to be invited to the Social Meeting.
Miss Brown kindly undertook to make all arrangements.
Committee to be stewards.
The proposed Committee meeting for Feb 15th was postponed, but the Committee decided to meet after the Social Meeting.

A C Turton, Chair

Committee Meeting held at 4 Wellesley Road on ~~Thur~~ Monday Feb 20th 1911, 3.30 pm
Chair Mrs Turton
Present Mrs Wenn; Mrs Rogers; Miss St John; Miss Cooper; Miss Brown.
The minutes of the two previous meetings were read and signed.
Letters were then read from the Women's Freedom League and from the National Union of WSS giving names of speakers who were disengaged for the end of April.

---

70 Alice Abadam (c. 1856–1940), one of the women who left the WSPU in 1907 to become a committee member of the WFL. 'Alice Abadam was a peripatetic speaker to a variety of suffrage societies' (Crawford, *Women's Suffrage*, 1).

After discussion it was proposed by Miss Cooper and seconded by Mrs Wenn that Miss Abadam be engaged to speak at the Town Hall on Thursday April 20th. Carried nem con.

Miss St John proposed to hold the Town Hall meeting on Tuesday April 18th. This was not seconded.

It was decided that the Treasurer should engage the Town Hall for Thursday April 20th.

It was also decided that Mr Lynde,[71] and Mr and Mrs Worthington, should be asked to support Dr Ryley who was to be offered the Chair for the Town Hall meeting.

Cards were read from Miss Mabel Hunt and Miss Willis re the 'At Home' on Friday Feb 24th 1911.

Ethel Leach

Suffrage 'At Home' at the Savoy Hotel, held on Friday February 24th 1911.

On Friday Feb 24th the Committee held an 'At Home' at the Savoy Hotel from 7.30 to 9 pm. Mrs Turton occupied the Chair and Miss Mabel Hunt of the Norwich Women's Suffrage Society very kindly came over from Norwich and gave a good address. Miss Hurrell sang three songs which were much enjoyed and Mrs Leach gave an account of the constitution and aims of the GYWSS. At the close of the meeting thirty five new members were enrolled. Many thanks are due to Miss Brown who kindly undertook all the arrangements.

Committee Meeting held at 4 Wellesley Road on Wednesday March 8th 1911 3.30 pm.

The minutes of the last meeting were read and confirmed.

The time of the Town Hall Meeting to be held on March 30th was agreed with no dissentients to be 8 pm.

Miss Brown very kindly again offered to entertain the speaker (Miss Abadam).

Miss Guthrie stated that she had written to Mrs Ryley who could not say whether Dr Ryley would take the Chair. Sec was instructed to write and ask Dr Ryley to take the Chair. The following ladies and gentlemen to be asked to take seats on the platform:
Dr and Mrs Dix;[72]

---

71 Humphrey Dela Lynde, 4 Trafalgar Rd, Yarmouth: he was a solicitor.

72 Dr William Ralph Dix, had a medical practice in Great Yarmouth, and was later medical officer and public vaccinator for the south district; lived at 43, King St.

Mr and Mrs Williams;[73]
Gen and Mrs Upcher;
Mrs Buxton;
The Rev Hare Patterson[74];
The Rev G McLuckie;
Mr and Mrs Coombe;[75]
The Rev A Banham;[76]
Mrs Swindell;
Dr and Mrs Worthington
Rev Father Stanley;[77]
Rev Father Cullen.[78]

The following ladies to be stewards:
Mrs C Dye,
Mrs J Rogers;
Miss Cooper;
Miss Brown;
Miss Turton;
Miss B Turton;
with power to add to their number. The stewards to wear white rosettes.
Proposed by Mrs Turton and seconded by Mrs Wenn that a leaflet be published giving a short account of the GYWSS and given away at the Meeting. Carried. The rest of the literature on hand to be distributed.
Mrs Leach proposed and Miss Guthrie seconded that Mr Buckle[79] do the printing. Sec to draw out the cards. Carried nem con.
Sub Com was formed to carry out the advertising. The Meeting to be announced in the Eastern Daily Press the day before and in the local papers the previous week.
Proposed by Mrs Rogers & seconded by Mrs Turton that the price of seats be 1/-. 6d. &, for women only, the Gallery 3d. Carried.

---

73 Walter George Williams, born 1871, a schoolmaster at Yarmouth Grammar School, and his wife Edith, born 1866. In 1911, they were living in Paget Road, Yarmouth.

74 Revd G Hare Patterson, Unitarian minister at the Old Meeting House, Middlegate St, Great Yarmouth.

75 Either Colonel and Mrs Combe or Mr Edward Combe and his wife: the surname is spelled wrongly in the minutes.

76 Revd Arthur Banham, a Primitive Methodist minister in Great Yarmouth.

77 Revd Henry Stanley, priest at St Peter's Roman Catholic Church, Gorleston.

78 Revd Michael Cullen, SJ, of the Presbytery, Regent Road, Great Yarmouth; another Roman Catholic priest supporting the suffrage cause.

79 John Buckle, printer, bookbinder and stationer, Theatre Plain, Great Yarmouth.

The discussion on cards of membership was left over to another Committee meeting.

It was not decided whether a printed report of the GYWSS up to May was to be published.

~~The subscription to be asked from Vice & President was left open~~

The subscription to be asked from President & Vice was left open

Chair Mrs Leach

Present Mrs Turton; Mrs Wenn; Mrs C Dye; Mrs Rogers; Miss Brown; Miss Guthrie; Miss Cooper.

AC Turton (Chair)

Town Hall Public Meeting March 30th 1911[80]

A public meeting was organised in the Town Hall for Thursday March 30th. Admission was free but seats were reserved at 1/- & 6 & the gallery was set aside for women, admission 3d. Dr Ryley MD was in the Chair & made some excellent remarks, followed by a short speech from the Rev G McLuckie who moved the Resolution, 'That this meeting is of opinion that the Parliamentary Franchise should be extended to women on the terms as it may be <granted> given to men'. Miss Abadam seconded the Resolution & was ~~loudly~~ much applauded on rising to speak & she kept the attention of her audience throughout a splendid well-reasoned speech. Many questions followed which were ably dealt with & then the Resolution was put, & carried with one dissentient. A vote of thanks to the speaker & chairman was moved by Father Stanley & seconded by Mrs Leach. Two new members joined at the close of the meeting.

Dr Ryley was supported on the platform by the following ladies & gentlemen: Major-General Upcher CB DSO, Mrs Upcher, Mrs EA Combe, Mrs W Wylley, Mrs W G Williams, Councillor Harbord JP,[81] Mrs Harbord, Rev G McLuckie BA, Mrs McLuckie, Father Stanley, Mrs Neave, Mrs Leach, Miss Brown, Mrs Wenn, Mrs Turton.

In addition to the appointed stewards the following very kindly stewarded: Miss K Guthrie, Miss St John, Miss H Leach, Mrs Arthur Ward, Mrs Wilson, Miss M Read.

---

80 Although nothing is said here, this meeting was just two days before the 1911 census, which a number of Yarmouth suffragists seem to have boycotted, including Alice Turton and her two daughters, Mrs McLuckie, Maria Wenn and Emma Barrow. The *EDP* (3 and 4 April) described boycotts in London under the auspices of both the WFL and the WSPU, but does not mention any local involvement in a boycott.

81 Arthur T. Harbord, solicitor, borough magistrate, borough councillor for St Peter's Ward, the husband of the Mrs Harbord mentioned frequently within these minutes. Mayor three times and later MP for Great Yarmouth (1922–24, 1929–41).

Committee Meeting held at 4 Wellesley Road on Thursday April 13th 1911 at 3.30 pm.

Chair Mrs Turton
Present Mrs Wenn, Miss K Guthrie, Miss Cooper, Mrs Rogers, Miss Brown, Miss Turton.
The minutes of the last meeting were read & confirmed.
The accounts of the Suffrage meeting in the Town Hall were then read & passed.
Miss Cooper proposed & Mrs Rogers seconded that they were
Receipts £10-8-6
Expenses £10-17-9
Deficit 9/3
Miss Cooper proposed & Mrs Rogers seconded that the deficit should be paid out of the general funds. Carried.
Miss Turton proposed & Mrs Rogers seconded that ladies who joined the WSPU one of the other Societies under a misapprehension should be admitted as members without further subscription to the GYWSS.[82] Carried.
A discussion ensued as to the arrangements for the Annual Meeting & Miss Cooper proposed & Miss Brown seconded that the Annual Meeting should be held on Tuesday May 9th or if the room were engaged on that night on Tuesday May 16th. Carried. The Meeting to be held in the Savoy Hotel.
Miss Brown proposed & Miss Guthrie seconded that each member should be asked to bring a lady friend. Carried.
Miss Cooper proposed & Miss Brown seconded that the meeting begin at 7pm. Carried.
The Annual Meeting to be a business meeting for members only, followed by a Social beginning at 8.30, with refreshments & music & a short speech.
A Subcommittee was formed of Mrs Wenn & Miss Turton to arrange the music.
The Sec was instructed to select a speaker.
The question of circulating a journal by the Society was left over to another meeting.

Annual Meeting of Members held at the Savoy Hotel on Tuesday May 9th 1911 at 7 pm.

Chair Mrs Leach
The Annual Report was read by the Sec & Mrs Rogers moved that it be adopted, Mrs Turton seconded, & it was carried.

---

82 It is not clear who these women were, or when they had joined, perhaps during the WSPU's campaign in Yarmouth the previous summer (see Introduction).

The following \14/ladies offered themselves for election to the Committee for the ensuing year, & as no other names were proposed ~~they~~ Miss Jarrett moved that they be elected & Miss B Bond seconded. Carried.

Mrs Leach; Miss Brown; Mrs Rogers; Mrs Wenn; Miss Cooper; Mrs Harbord; Miss K Guthrie; Mrs Joseph Neave; Miss Hetty Teasdel; Mrs Stacy-Watson; Mrs John Neave; Miss Bond; Mrs Turton; Miss Turton.

Miss Cooper proposed that the latter part of Rule 4 be amended to run ~~to~~ as follows – 'The members are not expected to support any Parliamentary Candidate who does not declare himself in favour of Women's Suffrage, until Women have obtained the Parliamentary Franchise.' Miss ~~Turton~~ Brown seconded. Carried nem con.

The Accounts for the year were then presented showing receipts £20-3-0; expenditure £16-11-6; balance in hand £3-11-6. Miss Harbord proposed that the accounts be passed, Miss Brown seconded. Carried.

A discussion followed on whether the Society should send a delegate to walk in the Suffrage procession in London on June 17th.[83] It was finally decided that the Society could not send a delegate, but Mrs Leach very kindly offered to represent the Society, if she were going to walk in the procession.

Miss Cooper proposed that if members of Committee failed to attend three consecutive Committee meetings, without giving a satisfactory reason, they should forfeit their places thereon. Miss Turton seconded. Carried.

Mrs Rogers proposed & Mrs Leach seconded that a vote of thanks be passed to the Treas & Sec. Carried.

ALS Brown (in the Chair)

Social Meeting held after the Annual Meeting at the Savoy Hotel on Tuesday May 9th at 8.30

After the Annual Meeting on May 9th a Social gathering was held \presided over by Miss Brown/ to which each member invited a friend. A pleasant evening was passed with vocal & instrumental music, to which the following ladies very kindly contributed. Miss Lilian Neave, Miss Ethel Bishop, Miss Daisy Allen, Miss Dora Johnson, Miss Hetty Leach.[84] Miss

---

83 The procession was a joint one by all suffrage groups: an estimated 40,000 women marched through London to Trafalgar Square. A Japanese visitor watched from a nearby window: 'I have never seen the crowd from such a height! Nothing but hats and hats, which were waving like the oatfields on a breezy day.' (Raeburn, *Militant Suffragettes*, 178–9).

84 Young members and/or supporters. Daisy Allen was certainly a member: see Appendix. The others are: (Sarah) Lilian Neave, born 1881, daughter of Joseph Samuel Neave and his wife Sarah; Ethel Mary Bishop born 1878, living in 1911 with her mother Mary Bishop at 88 Regent Road (in 1939 she was assistant matron at Great Yarmouth Training School for girls); Dora Johnson, born 1888, daughter of Robert Johnson, gasfitter and his wife Fanny,

Mabel Hunt came over from Norwich & gave a well-reasoned address which was much appreciated. This is the second time Miss Hunt has given up her time to come to Yarmouth & speak for our Society. Miss Parry-Evans very kindly designed some beautiful programmes which were much admired.[85] A Vote of thanks moved by Mrs Leach & seconded by Miss Cooper, to Miss Brown \Miss Hunt/ & to the ladies who took part in the programme concluded the proceedings.

Committee Meeting held at Wellesley Road on Monday October 2nd 1911 at 3.30 p.m.

Chair Miss Brown
Present Mrs Rogers, Miss Bond, Miss Teasdel, Mrs Turton, Mrs Joseph Neave, Mrs Stacy-Watson, Miss Turton.
The minutes of the last meeting were read & confirmed.
Mrs Stacy-Watson proposed & Miss Bond seconded that Miss Cooper be asked to act as Hon secretary. Carried unam.
Miss Brown proposed & Mrs Stacy-Watson seconded that Mrs Turton be re-elected Hon Treasurer. Carried. Mrs Turton proposed & Mrs Neave seconded that Mrs Leach be re-elected chairman of committee. Carried unam.
Mrs Turton proposed & Miss Turton seconded that a drawing \room/ meeting be held \in October/ at the house of Mrs Neave who \had/ kindly offered her room for the purpose. Carried. Mrs Turton proposed & Mrs Rogers seconded that the details of the meeting \were/ to be settled between Mrs Neave & the Secretary. Carried
The Secretary was instructed to ask Dr Mary Bell[86] to speak at the meeting, & failing her to try & secure a speaker from the Norwich Suffrage Society.

---

in 1911 barmaid at the Norfolk Hotel, Marine Parade; Hetty Leach born 1892, the niece of Ethel Leach.

85 Gwladys Mary Parry-Evans, born 1894, still at school at time of 1911 census. Her father was John Parry-Evans, manager of National Bank, Hall Quay. The family is recorded in the 1904 and 1908 trade directories as living at 58 Wellesley Road Yarmouth, in 1911 census at 48 Wellesley Road.

86 Dr Mary Cecilia Bell, M.B.; B.Sc. University of London 1903. Address in 1911 and 1913 directories 29 Unthank Road, Norwich. One of the first women doctors in Norwich (she is the only female among 63 names in the 'medical list' in *Jarrold's Directory for Norwich*, 1911). She was a member of the Norwich Woman's Suffrage Society, which, unlike the Yarmouth Society, accepted men: Dr Bell spoke at a meeting in Norwich in 1911 urging that *more* men be encouraged to join. In 1913, she was chosen to represent Norwich at the British Medical Association meeting at Brighton, a noteworthy achievement: 'we congratulate Norwich on its unprejudiced action and Dr Bell on the honour done her by the old city' (*The Common Cause*, 18 Jul. 1913).

Mrs Turton proposed & Miss Teasdel seconded that a public meeting be held in the Savoy Hotel in November. Carried.

The Secretary announced that the Secretary of the Lowestoft Suffrage Society (Mrs Ponder) had written, with a view to obtaining a speaker who could speak for the Lowestoft & Yarmouth Societies on consecutive days & so save expenses. The Sec was instructed to try & arrange with the Lowestoft Society for a joint speaker, for a \public/ meeting either in October or November.

Mrs Neave very kindly offered to postpone her drawing-room meeting till November if it were found more convenient to have the public meeting in October.

[signed] Ethel Leach

Committee Meeting held at 4 Wellesley Road on Wednesday Oct 25th 1911 at 3.30 pm.

Chair – Mrs Leach

Present Miss Brown, Miss K Guthrie, Miss Bond, Miss Teasdel, Miss Cooper, Mrs Turton, Mrs Wenn, Mrs Stacy-Watson, Mrs Rogers, Miss Turton.

The minutes of the previous meeting were read & confirmed.

The Secretary \made/ the following announcements

1. That Miss Cooper owing to pressure of work was unable to take the Secretaryship.
2. That Dr Mary Bell was unable to speak at Mrs Neave's drawing room meeting, but had very kindly offered to speak for the Society after Xmas.
3. That Mrs Hazard of Harleston[87] had kindly consented to speak at the drawing room meeting on Tuesday Oct 31st.
4. That Miss Muriel Matters had been engaged to speak at the public meeting on November 21st.
5. That Miss Brown had very kindly offered to entertain Miss Matters.

A discussion ensued on whether the meeting should be changed from the Savoy Hotel, but it was finally decided to hold it at the Savoy.

The Secretary was instructed to have 400 tickets printed, & sent out to the members of Committee for distribution. Each member of the Society to have two.

It was decided to announce the meeting in the local papers.

---

87 The wife of William Henry Hazard, solicitor, of the Harleston firm of Hazard and Pratt, and secretary of the Harleston NUWSS, founded in 1909. (Crawford, *Women's Suffrage*, 84).

It was also decided that the meeting be free, for men & women, but that a box be held at the door for contributions towards the expenses, that the meeting begin at 8 p.m, doors open at 7.30, & that the usual resolution in favour of Women's Suffrage be put to the meeting.

The question of chairmanship was discussed & it was decided to ask the Rev G McLuckie to take the Chair, failing him, Mr Arthur Johnson, & failing him Mr Edward Combe.[88] ~~Mr~~ The Rev Banham be asked to support Mr McLuckie if he consented to act as Chairman.

~~The S~~ Miss Turton consented to act as Secretary pro tem until another could be found.

A C Turton (Chair)

Public Meeting held on Tuesday Nov 21ˢᵗ 1911 at the Savoy Hotel at 8 p.m.

A public meeting was held in the Savoy Hotel on Tuesday Nov 2st at 8 p.m. Admission was free, by ticket only. The Rev G Hare-Patterson presided, & an address was given by Miss Muriel Matters. Questions were then invited & answered, after ~~this~~ \which/ the following resolution was passed with one dissentient "That this meeting records its opinion that no measure of electoral reform will be satisfactory, unless women are included in it".[89]

A vote of thanks to the chairman & speaker, proposed by Mrs Leach & seconded by Miss Teasdel concluded the proceedings. A box held at the door to receive contributions towards the expenses of the meeting obtained £1-18-10½.

Committee meeting held at 4 Wellesley Rd on Monday Nov 27ᵗʰ 1911 at 3.30 p.m.

Chair – Mrs Turton
Present Mrs Harbord, Miss Teasdel, Miss Brown, Mrs John Neave, Miss K Guthrie, Mrs Rogers, Miss Turton, Miss Waterson (by invitation)
The minutes of the last meeting were read & confirmed.

---

88 Mr Edward Albert Combe, born 1871, son of Colonel Combe, see note 43. Scholar at Haileybury School. A maltster by profession. Married Grace Kathleen Bosville in August 1894. They were living at 1 Beccles Rd, Great Yarmouth in 1901, later at Heather Cottage, St Olave's (1915 trade directory).

89 On 7 November 1911, Prime Minister Herbert Henry Asquith (1852–1928, PM 1908–1916) announced a bill to give the vote to all adult men; this effectively torpedoed (Lloyd George's word) the second Conciliation Bill, which was before Parliament, and which was based on extending existing franchise laws to women householders. The Memorial by the Yarmouth group referred to here was 'signed by about 100 influential and prominent electors of the Borough and presented [to Mr Fell] by a deputation'. (*Annual Report of the Eastern Counties Federation of the NUWSS*, 1913).

Notes were then read from Mrs Leach & Mrs Wenn expressing regret at inability to be present, & a letter of thanks from Miss Muriel Matters to Miss Brown.

The accounts for the ~~the~~ last public meeting on Nov 21st were then presented & Miss Brown proposed that they be accepted. Carried.

Mrs Harbord proposed & Miss Turton seconded that a vote of thanks be passed to Miss Brown & Mrs Rogers for entertaining Miss Matters. Carried unam.

Miss Turton proposed & Miss Brown seconded that Miss Annie Waterson be elected Hon Sec of the Society. Carried.

The question of forwarding the Resolution passed on Nov 21st to the Prime Minister (Mr Asquith)[90] and to Mr Fell was raised & Miss Guthrie ~~& Mrs~~ proposed & Mrs Rogers seconded that it should be sent. Carried.

Discussion ensued on a choice of a speaker for the drawing room meeting that Mrs Waterson had very kindly offered for December. It was decided to leave the choice to the Secretary.

Miss Brown proposed that new copies of rules be printed (300 to 500), the form the copies should take being left to the Sec. Mrs Harbord seconded. Carried.

Mrs Rogers proposed & Mrs Neave seconded that a letter of thanks be sent to the Rev G Hare-Patterson for presiding at the meeting on Nov 21st.

Hannah Cooper Jany 3rd 1912.

Drawing Room Meeting at Moat House Northgate Street on October 31st 1911 at 3 p.m.

By the kindness of Mrs Joseph Neave a drawing room meeting was held at her house on Tuesday Oct 31 when an address ~~to~~ was given by Mrs Hazard of Harleston which was listened to with much interest. A vote of thanks was passed to the speaker.

Drawing Room Meeting held at 3 Albert Sqre on Tuesday Dec 12th 1911 at 3 p.m.

On Tuesday Dec 12th Mrs Waterson kindly gave her drawing room for a meeting at which Mrs Worthington of Lowestoft gave an address, which was much appreciated. Mrs Turton presided & Miss Teasdel proposed a vote of thanks to the speaker.

---

90 See previous note and minutes for 21 November.

Committee Meeting held at 4 Wellesley Road on Wednesday Jan 3rd 1912 at 3.30 p.m.

Chair – Miss Cooper

Present Miss Brown, Mrs Rogers, Miss Bond, Miss Guthrie, Mrs Turton, Miss Turton.

The minutes of the last meeting were read & confirmed.

Notes were read from Mrs Leach & Mrs Joseph Neave regretting inability to be present owing to previous engagements & Miss Brown stated that Mrs Watson had told her she was unable to come. ~~Miss Brown~~ A discussion then began on the further winter work of the Society & Miss Brown said that she & Mrs Watson would give a drawing room meeting in the Savoy Hotel during February, & Mrs Turton said that if it were thought desirable she would join as a third hostess. ~~This~~ It was proposed by Mrs Turton & seconded by Miss Bond that this kind offer be accepted & it was carried. It was finally decided that Miss Brown & Mrs Watson should give the drawing room meeting early in February & that a public meeting in the Savoy Hotel should take place in March, Mrs Turton to pay for the speaker.

The March meeting was proposed by Miss Guthrie & seconded by Mrs Rogers.

It was also decided to try & arrange another drawing room meeting in April.

The Committee then discussed the advisability of sending a deputation to the Member for Yarmouth (Mr Fell) to question him on his attitude towards the Government's Reform Bill.[91]

Mrs Turton proposed that a deputation should wait upon the Member seconded by Miss Brown & carried. A discussion ensued on the questions to be put at the deputation, & the Committee finding it difficult to frame questions which would maintain the neutral attitude of the Society as regards the various policies existing in the Suffrage ranks, decided to rescind the ~~motion~~ vote of sending a deputation. This was proposed by Mrs Rogers, seconded by Miss Guthrie & carried.

H E Teasdel

A Public Meeting was held in the Supper-room of the Town Hall on Tuesday March 5th at 3.15, admission free by ticket. The chair was taken by Mrs Combe who moved a resolution "That this Government would pass some

---

91 The Reform Bill, or Government Franchise Bill, finally introduced in March 1912, proposed to give the vote to all adult males. Women were not mentioned: however, many people thought it could be amended, while it passed through Parliament, to include some or all women.

measure of Parliamentary Enfranchisement for Women in 1912" which was carried unanimously & forwarded to the Prime Minister & to Mr Fell. An address was given by Mrs Nevinson[92] from London. At the conclusion of the address Mrs Combe moved a vote of thanks to the speaker, & a vote of thanks was proposed by Miss Brown to Mrs Combe for presiding.

An "At Home held at the Savoy Hotel Monday Feb 12th 1912.

By the kindness of Miss Brown & Mrs Stacy Watson an afternoon meeting was held at the Savoy Hotel at which also vocal & instrumental music was provided for the entertainment of the guests. Miss Brown introduced Mrs Rackham[93] of the N. U who had come from Cambridge to give the address. The audience listened with great attention & showed their appreciation by their applause. A vote of thanks was passed to the speaker.

Committee Meeting held March 15th 1912 at "The Merridans" 4 Wellesley Road

In the chair Miss Teasdel
Present Miss Cooper, Miss Brown, Mrs Rogers, Mrs Turton, Miss Turton, Miss Guthrie, Mrs Waterson representing A Waterson (hon sec)
The minutes of the last meeting were read & confirmed.
The accounts for the last public [meeting] on March 5th were presented & accepted.[94] Mrs Palmer & Miss Aldred very kindly offered to give a Drawing room meeting the date to be April 26th. The selection of a Speaker to be left to the Secretary.
It was also decided to hold the Annual Meeting May 10th or 17th. Miss Brown to ~~arrange the~~ \make enquiries about/ musical programme & the Secretary to provide a Speaker.
It was also agreed to hold another meeting in June.

Ethel Leach

---

92 Margaret Wynne Nevinson (1858–1932). Originally a member of the WSPU she was one of the women who left in 1907 to form the WFL: 'she was a very active member, speaking at meetings on an average of four or five times a week At the beginning of the campaign she felt unable to speak at open-air meetings, but she soon forced herself to overcome the prejudices instilled by her upbringing and endured the gamut of rotten vegetables, eggs, cayenne pepper, rats and indecent heckling'. (Crawford, *Women's Suffrage*, 446). Her husband Henry Nevinson, a journalist was also a passionate advocate of the cause of women's suffrage.

93 Mrs Rackham was Chairman of the Eastern Counties Federation of the NUWSS. The Federation's Annual Report for 1913 gives her address as 18 Hobson St, Cambridge.

94 The word 'meeting' has been inadvertently omitted by the minute-taker.

Committee Meeting held at 4 Wellesley Rd on April 29th 1912

Chair Mrs Leach

Present Mrs Turton, Miss Brown, Mrs Rogers, Miss Bond, Miss Teasdel, Miss K Guthrie,[95] Miss Waterson Sec, Mrs Waterson (by invitation).

The minutes of the last meeting were read & confirmed.

This meeting was called to discuss the arrangement for the Annual Meeting. Mrs Leach proposed & Miss Brown seconded that the meeting be held May 17 Friday, all members to be invited for the business meeting at 7 o'clock, their friends to come to the Social at eight.

Miss Brown to engage a room at the Savoy & arrange for light refreshments.

A Sub committee was formed of Miss Brown, Miss Teasdel, Mrs Turton & the Secretary to arrange the musical programme & select a Speaker.

The Secretary was instructed to write to the ladies on the committee & ask if they wish to be re-elected. Mrs Turton suggested having a G.Y.W.S.S. stall in the Market in the summer from middle of June to the middle of Sept. It was decided to put it before the members at the general meeting, Mrs Turton in the meantime to enquire into the expense of hiring a stall.

Mrs Turton proposed & Mrs Leach seconded that a vote of thanks be passed to Mrs Palmer & Miss Aldred for their kindness in giving a Drawing room meeting.

Miss Brown asked the committee if they would consider the question of Affiliation to the N.U.W.S.S. After a discussion it was decided to obtain more information on the subject & put the matter before the members at the general meeting.

---

95 This was to be Miss Guthrie's last appearance in the group: in May she helped form the Yarmouth branch of the WSPU (of which she became secretary), which just a few days later (3 May 1912) held a public meeting at the Town Hall, with Georgina Brackenbury as the star speaker. There is no mention of Miss Guthrie in the *EDP* report of that meeting, and it is not known whether she joined before, at, or shortly after it, or how many members moved with her to the new Society. This was also the last appearance of Miss Bond, who also probably moved over to the newly-founded WSPU group. No records survive of the new group and it may never have attracted many members: it is only mentioned twice in *Votes for Women* in 1912, in both cases when Kate Guthrie records that she has distributed copies of *Votes for Women* containing the text of important speeches by Mrs Pankhurst. The WSPU conducted summer holiday campaigns in both 1912 and 1913: these take up many pages in *Votes for Women* and *The Suffragette*, but neither Yarmouth nor Miss Guthrie are ever mentioned: Yarmouth is not even shown on the map of 'The Holiday Campaign' in England that made up the front page of *Votes for Women*, 23 August 1912. The suffragette papers contain weekly announcements of meetings throughout the country, but none is recorded in Yarmouth after that of 3 May.

Mrs Castle had offered her garden for a meeting to be held in June. A speaker to be paid for out of the funds proposed by Mrs Turton, Mrs Leach seconded. Carried.

At Home

'At Home' held at the Albion Mission Room April 26th
By the kindness of Mrs Palmer & Miss Aldred the G.Y.W.S.S. held a meeting at the Albion Mission Room, when an address was given by Mrs Tanner of the Women's Freedom League.[96] Mrs Turton was in the chair.

H E Teasdel

Annual General Meeting

On Friday May 17th Members of the Gt Yarmouth W.S.S. met at the Savoy Rooms for business at 7 o'clock. Mrs Leach who was in the "Chair" called for the "Report" for the past year; in the unavoidable absence of the Hony Secretary during the year Miss Waterson, this was read by Miss Brown – it showed that there had been 7 Committee Meetings and some Sub-committee Meetings during the year – also 2 semi-public Meetings, and 4 Drawing room Meetings, at which the following "Speakers" attended, viz Madames Muriel Matters, Nevinson, Hazard, Rackham, Worthington, Tanner and Miss Eva Ward.[97] The membership was declared to be 124 an considerable increase from last year.
The Hony Treas'r next presented her accounts etc. Subscriptions amounted to [blank], donations to [blank]
The following ladies were next elected on the Committee viz Madames Leach, Turton, Teasdel, Stacy Watson, Rogers, Harriss & Brown – with power to co-opt others.
Mrs Turton accepted again the Office of Hony Treas'r, Miss Waterson that of Hon Secy, and Mrs Waterson kindly consented to act as Assistant Secy.

---

96 Mrs Tanner, a member of the mid-London branch of the WFL, and a frequent speaker at meetings; she received several mentions in the WFL annual report for 1912 and in issues of *The Vote*, (none giving her first name), for example, giving a speech in Hyde Park on 21 April 1912, and making 'an excellent speech' at Ipswich a few weeks later. The 'forthcoming events' column in *The Vote* for 27 April 1912 announced that the Yarmouth meeting was to be held at 3 Albert Square, so it was probably moved at short notice.

97 Eva Ward, suffragist speaker for the NUWSS. The 1913 Annual Report for the Eastern Counties Federation (covering events of 1912) mentions her as support speaker on a tour of the region by Lady Frances Balfour (1858–1931), well-known aristocratic suffragist, for example speaking at meetings in Harwich and Felixstowe in October 1912. It is interesting that the Yarmouth society was inviting speakers both from the NUWSS and the WFL – but, of course, none from the WSPU who were now a rival society within the town.

The Application was then discussed.[98] Miss Eva Ward addressed the Members specially on this Subject, at the conclusion of her Address P cards were distributed, returnable to Secy in three days, and to convey the decision of Members in regard to the Application Question. This closed the business meeting.

At 8 o'clock many friends of Members having arrived, the programme for the evening was commenced, when Miss Teasdel took the "Chair" – Vocalists Miss S Wright & Mrs Hare Patterson, \Mrs Collinson/; Reciter Mrs O'Brien; Instrumentalists 1st Violin Miss Bell, Piano Mrs [?]Swinnerton A.R.C.O.[99] Mrs Sayers, "Cello" Organist of St James' Church.[100]

Miss Eva Ward gave a ten minute speech.

Tea & coffee was served about 9 o'clock – the company dispersed at 10 o'clock – having spent a very pleasant evening – four new members were placed on list.

H E Teasdel

On Friday May 24th a Committee Meeting was held at 4 Wellesley Road, time 3.30

When the Minutes of the two last meetings were read, and duly signed. Correspondence from Miss Cooke N.U.S.S.,[101] Mrs Rackham Cambridge on the Affiliation Question, and also announcing the Summer Campaign of the E.C. Federation and pointing out the desirability of joining our forces with theirs for Suffrage Support.

17 Replies in the negative, and 9 in the affirmative were received on the Question of Affiliation not half the membership.[102]

Miss Eva Ward called at 4 Wellesley Road 21st to enquire about matters in regard to a stall for the sale of literature from the middle of July to the middle of September was considered the best time, further enquiries to be

---

98 The application to affiliate to the NUWSS rather than continue as an independent group.

99 Associate of Royal College of Organists.

100 One of several churches built in Victorian Yarmouth to cater for the expanding town. Begun in 1870, not finally completed until 1908.

101 Miss Geraldine Cooke, a paid organiser for the Eastern Counties Federation: according to their annual report, she left in the summer, being replaced very briefly by a Mrs Lucan Davies (not mentioned in these minutes), and then by Eva Ward, a familiar figure to the Yarmouth suffragists.

102 If 26 people represent a little under half the membership, there has been a great fall in the membership from the 124 members of just a week before (in the absence of other records, there is no way of knowing how many have joined Kate Guthrie's new WSPU group and how many may have left the movement). However, it may be that it was a requirement for half the membership to vote on the issue, so it is simply being recorded that less than half had done so, with no comment on what the actual percentage was.

made as to who would assist, and how we should be placed about responsibility for N. Papers etc. The garden meeting organised by Mrs Castle it
was announced could not be held – the Builders would not have finished
alterations to House etc. It was proposed some other lady be asked to hold
such a Meeting. 4 late members were declared off the list viz Miss Hatch,
Miss Daisy Allen, Miss Holmes, Nurse Taylor. 4 Others declared added.
Miss Lawrence, Mrs Bell Market Place, Miss Bell ditto, Miss Last.
A resolution in regard to the Criminal Law Amendment Act was passed
conditionally and, if necessary to be sent to Mr Fell M.P.[103]
Mrs Turton kindly brought 100 cards to send to members announcing the
negative result of appeal for affiliation to the N.U.W.S.S. and E.C. Federation.
– The cards were printed by Master Turton a vote of thanks was passed to
him.[104]
For the Secretary A.L.S.B.[105]
~~Mrs Turton brought 100 cards~~
Present Madames Turton, O.D Turton, Teasdel, Brown & Rogers.

Committee meeting held at 4 Wellesley Rd Oct 23rd 1912 at 3.30 p.m.

Chair Miss Brown
Present Mrs Turton, Miss Teasdel, Mrs Rogers, Miss Harris, Mrs Waterson,
Miss Waterson.
The Committee proposed to hold a general meeting at the Savoy for
the discussion of affiliation to the ~~W~~ N.U.W.S.S. which proposition was
afterwards cancelled.
It was arranged to hold a Drawing room meeting at 3 Albert Square, the
date to be left to the Speaker.
The Speaker to be selected by Mrs Turton.

Drawing room meeting held at 3 Albert Sq Nov 20th 1912 at 3 p.m.

On Wed Nov. 20th Mrs Waterson lent her rooms for a meeting at which Mrs
Combe of St Olaves spoke.[106] Mrs Turton was in the chair & introduced

---

103 The act related to procuring, and to the punishments for brothel-keepers. The
trafficking and enforced prostitution of young – sometimes very young – girls was a scandal
that many suffragists wrote and spoke about in the strongest terms. Many male M.Ps, also
felt strongly on the issue.
104 The Turtons had three sons living with their parents at the Vicarage. The eldest,
Neville Harry was 19 at the time of the 1911 census, so unlikely to be referred to as 'Master':
the card maker would have been either Richard Dacre Turton or Kenneth Arvan Turton
(respectively 13 and 9 in 1911).
105 The initials of Anastacia [L.B.] Brown.
106 Seven miles south of Yarmouth, within the parish of Herringfleet.

the Speaker to an audience of about forty. After a much appreciated address a discussion followed when five new members were enrolled. Miss Brown proposed a vote of thanks to the Speaker.

Committee Meeting held at 32 Wellesley Road (Mrs Skinner's) on Friday afternoon Jan 17th.[107]

When Mrs Turton brought forward the following "Resolution", That we pray Mr A. Fell M.P. for the Borough of Great Yarmouth to support Sir E. Grey's "Amendment" for the deletion of the word "Male" from the "Franchise Bill".[108] Which was duly seconded and carried. The Secretary pro tem be asked to forward the Resolution to Mr. Fell.
The Committee then passed a Vote of Sympathy with V.P. Mrs Ryley who had met with a severe accident through falling down.
Miss Brown to write to Mrs Ryley expressing the regret felt.
On the question of co-opting some more Members for Committee it was decided to ask two or three ladies to take Office.
The Sec then presented Read & Co's a/c of 3/6 which the Treasr paid, and in the matter of Stationery it was thought better to wait awhile to see if an Amalgamation of the two Non-Militant Societies could be carried – the Gt Yarmouth W.S.S. and the Federation Cambridge Branch N.U.W.S.S.
The typed "Notices" sent to Committee having been in some cases charged double Postage – the Sec said she would write to the Postmaster and ascertain the right of the matter.
This concluded the business for the Gt Y.W.S.S.
Miss Teasdel then announced a Meeting of ladies to be addressed by Dr Mary Bell on Thursday afternoon Jan 23rd inst – the time of assembling 3 o'clock and cards were given to those present in order that they might distribute the same.
This Meeting was arranged by Miss Teasdel on or for the Federation Branch.[109]

---

107 1913. That the rival groups could work together is shown by *The Suffragette* (3 January 1913) where contributors to the WSPU campaign fund in December included Kate Guthrie, as might be expected, but also Mrs Leach, Miss Brown, Mrs Harbord and Miss Aldred.
108 Sir Edward Grey (1862–1933), foreign secretary 1905–16. When the amendment came before Parliament, the Conservative leader, Andrew Bonar Law, immediately asked the Speaker of the House of Common if it was constitutionally legal to amend the Bill in such a drastic way. The Speaker begged time to consider his ruling in the matter. See below, note 111.
109 At some time in late 1912, a branch of the NUWSS had been formed in Yarmouth which was affiliated to the Eastern Counties Federation, a subdivision of the NUWSS. It extended from Bedfordshire to North Essex, and was centred in Cambridge where its membership

Present, in the Chair ~~Mrs Turton~~ \Miss Brown/; also Miss Teasdel, Mrs Rogers, Miss Browne

A.C. Turton (Chairman)

At a Committee Meeting held at 4 Wellesley Road on Monday 17th inst \February/ (time 3.30)

Chairman Mrs Turton

The Minutes of the last Meeting were duly read, and signed, also correspondence that had been received in the interim. A discussion was then held as to the advisability of holding some Meeting or the other. Miss Turton proposed a Meeting be held at the Supper Room Town Hall, and a Speaker engaged. This was not seconded so the matter lapsed for the present. On further consideration it was proposed by Miss Teasdel and seconded by Miss Harris that a Business Meeting of the Members be summoned in order to lay before them the state of the two local S. Societies, and to advise the membership now to amalgamate with the N.W.S.S. owing to a different set of conditions prevailing to what was the case last year – this was carried unanimously.[110] Miss Teasdel to write to Head Quarters for Speaker. Place Savoy Rooms, date of enquiry from March 4th to 11th printed tickets or circulars.

Replies from Mrs Ryley, A Fell Esqre, Read & Co.

Present Madams Palmer, Harris, Rogers, Teasdel, Turton, C Turton & Brown.

The following Resolution was proposed to be sent to the Speaker of the House of Commons, That this Committee wishes to record its indignation at the Ruling of the Speaker in regard to the Amendment concerning women re the Franchise Bill, date thereof Jan 23rd.[111] Unanimously adopted – and forwarded by the Secy. Proposer Mrs Rogers, Seconder Miss A Turton

A.C. Turton (Chair)

---

included the suffrage societies of the two women's colleges, Newnham and Girton. In sharp contrast to the establishment of the WSPU earlier in the year, the founders of this new group remained leading members of the GYWSS. Miss Teasdel was both Hon Secretary and Hon Treasurer. The other committee members of the 'new' organisation were Miss Brown, Mrs Rogers, Mrs Turton and Mrs Palmer (Source: *Second Annual Report* of the E.C.F.).

110 The difference could be the much-increased activity of the WSPU over the previous year, or could reflect the changed Parliamentary situation: see following note.

111 On 23 January 1913, the Speaker had ruled that it was not constitutional for the Franchise Bill to be altered by an amendment to include women. The Government immediately withdrew the Bill. Supporters of the women's 'Cause' felt that they had been betrayed: the ruling caused consternation among suffragists, and led to increased militancy among the suffragettes.

A general Committee Meeting was held at the Savoy Rooms on Tuesday evening March 11th inst.

President of the Meeting Mrs Turton. The Members had been summoned by circular to decide the Question of Affiliation to the N.U.S.S. Eastern Counties Federation.
Miss Creak,[112] Organiser of the Federation attended to address the Membership and to explain both financial & other details – the advantages etc to be secured from union with the N.U. At the close of her speech Miss Creak said that she would be glad to answer any questions, after which the H Sec Gt. Yarmouth So said a few words on the moral advantage sought and the expence of carrying on two societies on the same lines & "Rules" etc. Miss Teasdel H Sy Yarmouth Branch E.C.F. then gave a few items of information, this finished, the following "Resolution" was put from the Chair, viz That the time has arrived when the question of affiliation to the N.U.W.S.S. must be settled, therefore those in favour of the Union will please signify their assent in the usual way. The Resolution was carried with only one dissentient. In regard to Offices & Committee it was arranged that the Executive of both Societies should remain in office until July next when the Affiliation takes place.
The Annual Meeting \?/
October was spoken of for commencement of Winter Session

H.E. Teasdel (Chair)

A Committee Meeting was held at 4 Wellesley Road on Monday April 7th

To discuss matters appertaining to the Success of the Gt Yarmouth Society, and to arrange for the future governance of the same. Items Executive to be elected at the forthcoming Annual Meeting, instead of in July, the present Committee to try to obtain fixtures for Garden Meeting in the Summer and drawing room ditto for the Winter. The Committee to visit those members whom they are acquainted with during the Recess – also distribute the recent pamphlets. Urgency Committee left for appointment at the Annual. Title of the Society fixed for printing of stationery.
Subscriptions renewable at the Annual Meeting – Affiliation to be paid in July about 4/-.
The time for Autumn Meeting and Scheme for Winter work may possibly be arranged at the Annual Meeting.
Gentlemen to be invited to join us.

---

112 Miss Ellen Creak, Organising Secretary of the Eastern Counties Federation of the NUWSS. The 1913 annual report of the Federation gives her address as 71 Panton St, Cambridge.

Mrs Turton proposed to ask Mrs Buxton to become President of the Society this was unanimously agreed to, Mrs Turton also consenting to write to Mrs Ed Coombe,[113] & Mrs Ryley to invite them to continue their vice presidentships, under the new arrangement.

The Annual General Meeting, it was decided to hold if possible on Friday evening May 2nd – 1913 and, at the Savoy Rooms. Programme Music, Refreshments, short speech, Report and Election of the Executive for the forthcoming year.

Invitation by card, personally delivered. Mrs Turton kindly offered her son's assistance to print cards of Invitation, which was gratefully accepted.

In the "Chair" Miss Teasdel. Present Mrs Turton, Miss Turton, Miss Brown, Mrs Rogers.

The Annual General Meeting was held on Friday May 9th Inst at the Savoy Rooms.

The Members assembled at 7.30 when Mrs Palmer (of the Committee) took the "Chair". After some introductory remarks that lady called upon the Acting Sec to read the "Report" for the last year, this showed that although the Society had lost some of its members by Marriages or through others leaving the town to take up Appointments elsewhere, yet there had been additional Members to our "Roll" leaving the Membership at 128. The reading of the "Report" finished, the Chairman called upon the H Trear for the financial accounts – which Mrs Turton gave, and announced a small balance in hand 13/10 and that the subscriptions for the year were due to add to this.

The following ladies having consented to serve on Committee, their names were put to the Members who elected them by the usual show of hands, viz Madame Palmer, Harris, W Bunn, Leach, Hurrell, Diboll, Rogers, Brown (8) That the Hon Treasr also H Sec pro tem together with Miss Teasdel H Sec were to be in Office as at present until June Affiliation.

This concluded the business.

The Chairman then introduced Mrs Ponder (Hon Sec of the Lowestoft W Suf Society) to the Meeting, this lady had very kindly come over \at very short notice from Mrs Turton/ to address the Members. She gave a most interesting account of "the Sweated Industries, and the necessity for the P.[114] Enfranchisement of Women to enable us to remove this "blot" on our Social System – the speech lasted about twenty minutes when Mrs Ponder had to leave for return home. A vote of thanks was passed to her for her kindness.

---

113 Incorrectly spelled: should be 'Combe'.
114 Abbreviation for Political.

After this, the Chairman announced that the musical part of the programme would be proceeded with – several items having been rendered, Refreshments were then served, and the remainder of programme performed, the Company then separated after spending a very enjoyable evening.

A.C. Turton (Chair)

A Committee Meeting was held at 4 Wellesley Road on ~~friday~~ Monday June 9th inst.[115]

The Hony Treasr occupied the "Chair", the two Hony Secys conducted the business. The Agenda was as follows. The Minutes of the Annual Meeting were duly read, and signed. When item one was discussed, it was decided that the official title of the Society should be thus, National "Union of Women's Suffrage Societies", "Great Yarmouth Branch" \Non-Militant, Non-Party/.

No. 2, proposed by Miss Teasdel, seconded by Mrs Rogers that Rule 4 be amended to include men, as well as women. Also, to read as follows, "Any Parliamentary Candidate who does not declare himself in favour of the political enfranchisement of women. No. 3 in regard to the subscription to E.C. Federation on our amalgamation this month, proposed by Mrs Hurrell that 10/- be the sum allotted, seconded by Miss Brown & carried unanimously. No. 4 the Urgency Committee was decided on the proposition of Mrs [blank] Seconded by Mrs Hurrell to be three Ms of Committee chosen by the Hy Sec.

No. 5, to settle visiting members with literature during recess, also No. 7, to find a President and Assist Secy were left over for want of time.

No. 6, Fixtures: it was stated by H Sec pro-tem that any Mems who could hold a Meeting for Jun[e] Address etc would assist the "Cause" much in doing so.[116]

No.8 to arrange for a Garden Meeting at Mrs Bunn's Sefton House this "Fixture" to be was altered by the kind courtesy of Mrs Bunn on account of a proposal coming from Mrs Ponder H Sec Lowestoft W.S.S. This lady

---

115 This meeting was held the day after the death of Emily Davison, who four days earlier (on 4 June) had thrown herself in front of the King's horse during the Derby. Her death and funeral created enormous publicity, but a society committed to constitutional means would not have approved. Unfortunately the minutes for Kate Guthrie's 'rival' WSPU group do not survive so we do not know how they reacted: the Norwich WSPU certainly sent a wreath to Emily's funeral, and the Yarmouth WSPU may well have done something similar.

116 The minutes do not mention that Hetty Teasdel had applied, on behalf of the Society, to hold a meeting on Yarmouth Beach. The Town Clerk refused, saying that the Borough Council did not allow political meetings 'or any meetings of a like nature' to be held there. (*Yarmouth Independent*, 12 Jul. 1913).

had sent to Miss Teasdel informing her that Miss Waring, Organiser to the E.C.F.[117] was about to visit Lowestoft and that she would also come over to Gt. Yarmouth to address our Members, if a Meeting could be arranged. Mrs Bunn having informed the Committee she would receive the Members at some future date, Mrs Turton announced that she would hold the Meeting at Mary's Vicarage, Friday June 13th Inst, at 3.30 being fixed for the same.[118]

Proposed from the "Chair" that each M of Committee take a certain number of names of members of the Society to notify to them of the visit of Miss Waring – this to be done by invitation card – Hostess Mrs Turton – who kindly said she would provide Afternoon tea – the member list was then read through by the H.S. pro-tem. In reference to Rule no 10 a quorum of four C Members instead of five was unanimously appointed, Mrs Diboll being the Proposer and Mrs Bunn the Seconder of the same.

Ladies present Madames Bunn, Diboll, Hurrell, Palmer, Rogers, Turton, Teasdel & Brown.

A.C. Turton (Chair)

The first Committee Meeting of the Autumn Session was held at 4 Wellesley Road, on Wednesday afternoon September 10th–13.

The minutes of the former meeting being duly read and signed, It was proposed by Miss Brown & seconded by Mrs Bunn that the H Secretary should be asked to draw up a Resolution, and send the same to the Conference – re the retaining the services of the Organiser Miss Creak (carried unanimously)

Proposed by Miss Teasdel & seconded seconded [sic] by Mrs Diboll that Mrs Turton attend the Colchester Conference on the 23rd of Sep,[119] carried nem con – Mrs Turton acceding to the request of Committee. It was

---

117 Miss L.F. Waring was a full-time NUWSS official: she had been secretary of the Warrington branch on its foundation in 1907, and a founder of the suffrage society at Carmarthen in 1911. As Ellen Creak is described as Organising Secretary of the ECF in the 1913 annual report, and continued to be so described in these minutes, Miss Waring's role as 'Organiser' was presumably a separate and additional position. It was Miss Waring who contributed the description of the Pilgrimage to *The Common Cause* quoted in the Introduction, above, p. 262.

118 According to the local newspaper, about sixty ladies attended the event. Miss Waring spoke about the proposed Grand March to London being organised by the NUWSS to take place in July (*Yarmouth Independent*, 21 Jun. 1913): see Introduction, above, p. 262.

119 Affiliating to the NUWSS meant sending a delegate to the meetings of the Eastern Counties Federation. These were usually held in Cambridge, but there were occasional exceptions. The Colchester group had affiliated to the NUWSS in January 1912, and had the time a membership of eighty (1912 *ECF Annual Report*).

announced by the H Treasurer that there were a few shillings surplus from "Pilgrimage fund",[120] the amount the Committee decided should be placed to the "general fund" local.

Cards from Head Quarters having been sent to Secretary, some Members of Committee took them to find out who was represented on them as favourable to "The S. Movement" in Gorleston.

Some discussion also took place relative to the Winter Scheme of Work, but no decision was arrived at Suffrage Socials once a month were proposed.

Present in the Chair Mrs Turton. Also present Madames Diboll Bunn Waterson Teasdel Brown Rogers.

Mrs W Emma Palmer Chairman signed.

A Committee Meeting was held at 4 Wellesley Rd on Monday aftern Oct 13.

Present Mrs Waterson, Turton, Rogers, Palmer, Hurrell, Misses Waterson, Brown, Teasdel.

The minutes of last meeting were read & signed.

It was proposed by Mrs Turton seconded by Mrs Hurrell that Mrs Palmer should be the permanent Chairman for the session, this was unanimously agreed to.

It was then proposed by Mrs Rogers, seconded by Mrs Hurrell that Committee Meetings should be held monthly, & agreed to.

The formation of a study circle was then proposed by Mrs Turton, seconded by Miss Waterson. This was discussed, the Secretary was instructed to write to head quarters for information as to suitable books to read, & Mrs Turton was to inquire for a convenient room to hire for the meetings. Miss

---

120 The Pilgrimage was one of the greatest events organised by the NUWSS: supporters of suffrage marched from all over England to London, including Yarmouth, culminating in a huge rally in Hyde Park on 26 July 1913: 'The Pilgrimage raised consciousness of the constitutional suffrage movement and £8777', (Crawford, *Women's Suffrage*, 550). The Yarmouth contingent was not large: The *EDP* for 11 July 1913 refers to 'a little band of women' and says that there were about a score of marchers, not all of whom went all the way to London. According to other newspapers, the departure of pilgrims from the town was not without incident: 'one policeman on his beat who met the pilgrims as they were driving away refused to arrest a boy who hit one of them with the result that the boys thought that they could do as they liked and got on to the back of the carriage hitting one of the pilgrims on the head.' (A.W. Ecclestone, *Great Yarmouth 1886–1936* (Yarmouth, 1977), 125). The *Yarmouth Independent* does not mention the incident but notes that the meeting included 'several from Great Yarmouth and district' and adds: 'this demonstration on Saturday certainly made a favourable impression.' (*Yarmouth Independent*, 2 Aug. 1913). The Yarmouth women caried with them a large banner stressing the peaceful nature of the campaign: it read 'Women's Suffrage Pilgrimage. Non-Militants, Great Yarmouth Branch. By faith not force.'

Romero[121] was to be asked to approach Mrs Brownsword[122] on the question of becoming President of the Society.

E. Emma Palmer

Mrs Brownsword eventually consented.

A Committee Meeting was held on Dec 8th at 32 Wellesley Rd after the conclusion of the Reading Circle.

Present: Mrs W Palmer in the Chair, Mrs Turton, Mrs Rogers, Mrs Diboll, [Mrs] Hurrell, [Mrs] W Bunn; Miss Brown, [Miss] Harris & [Miss] Teasdel. The Minutes of last Meeting were read & signed.

It was arranged that the members of Committee should call on those members of the society who had not paid their subscriptions & collect them. It was proposed by Mrs Turton seconded by Mrs Hurrell that as Norwich was going to have an \afternoon/ speaker in the near future a public Meeting should be held at Yarmouth on the same evening with the same speaker. Enquiries were to be made by the Secretary (Later this fell through as Norwich was unable to obtain a good speaker).

E. Emma Palmer

1914

A Committee Meeting was held at 4 Wellesley Rd. on Friday Jan. 23 to discuss the question of sending a delegate to the Council Meeting of the Federation \in Cambridge/ on Monday Jan 26.[123] There were present Mesdames Turton, Hurrell, Diboll, Rogers, Waterson, and Misses Waterson, Brown & Teasdel, Mrs Palmer was in the Chair. The minutes of last meeting were duly read and signed.

Miss Teasdel proposed & Mrs Hurrell seconded that a delegate should be sent, this was carried unanimously. It was then proposed by Mrs Hurrell & seconded by Miss Waterson that Mrs Turton should represent the Yarmouth Society & this was also carried unanimously. There was then some discussion about having a public meeting in March, & it was eventually proposed by

---

121 The 1908 Trade Directory lists 'Madame Romero' as living at Rosemary House, Marine Parade North, Great Yarmouth. Her name was Eva Romero, an American, born in 1853. She married Malcolm Wright Niven in London in 1899 (and appears in the 1901 census as Eva Niven, then in residence in a sanitorium in Somerset), but soon reverted to her former name. In 1911, she was living at Roseacre, Ormesby St Margaret, with her daughters.

122 Mabel Brownsword, born 1863, the wife of Harry Anderson Brownsword a retired lace manufacturer from Nottingham. Still in Nottingham at the time of the 1901 census, they soon afterwards moved to Dilham, Norfolk, and then (in about 1909) to Rollesby Hall, eight miles north of Great Yarmouth.

123 The Eastern Counties Federation of the NUWSS.

Mrs Turton seconded by Mrs Diboll that some kind of Meeting should be held in the middle of March with a good speaker to give an address & that Mrs Turton would make enquiries at Cambridge.

A.C. Turton (Chair)

On Monday eveng March 23rd a Public Meeting was held in the Supper Room Town Hall, when Miss Sheepshanks,[124] of the International Women's Suffrage alliance,[125] gave a very excellent address.

Mrs Richard Worthington of Lowestoft took the chair & introduced the lecturer in an interesting speech. Miss Sheepshanks gave information about suffrage work in many foreign countries, & about the good effects of women's enfranchisement in the countries that already have the vote. There was a good attendance & the sale of tickets & collection at the door was very satisfactory.

A Committee Meeting was held on Monday May 4th at 4 Wellesley Rd. There were present – Mrs Turton in the Chair, Mrs Rogers & Diboll, Misses Brown & Teasdel. The last minutes were read & signed. It was proposed by Mrs Diboll & seconded by Miss Brown that two representatives should attend the Meeting in Norwich on the 9th, to appoint a County Secretary. It was agreed that Mrs Rogers & Miss Teasdel should go.

The Annual Meeting was then discussed. Miss Brown proposed & Mrs Diboll seconded that the Meeting should be held at 32 Wellesley Rd. about May 18th & this was agreed to. Miss Willis was to be asked to speak, & each Member allowed to bring one friend. Mrs Bunn was to be asked to cater for the tea cakes etc. & Miss Teasdel to arrange about room etc. Miss Brown promised to provide music for the social entertainment.

E. Emma Palmer Chairman

A Committee Meeting was held at 32 Wellesley Rd. on Wednesday April 1915.[126] There were present – Mrs Palmer in the chair, Mesdames Waterson, Diboll, Hurrell, Ward, Rogers, Bunn & the Misses Brown, Waterson & Teasdel. A letter was read from Mrs Rackham asking if Miss Creak,

---

124 Mary Sheepshanks (1872–1960), suffragist and pacifist. She became secretary of the International Woman Suffrage Alliance (see following note) in 1913, and edited its magazine *Jus Suffragii*. Her father John was Bishop of Norwich, 1893–1909: by this time Mary was at Cambridge University, so she was not brought up in Norwich, although she did visit her father in the Bishop's Palace on occasion.

125 The IWSA was founded in 1904 to promote women's rights throughout the world: its first President was Carrie Chapman Catt of the USA. Its headquarters were in London and Millicent Fawcett of the NUWSS was a founder member.

126 Actual date not given (Wednesdays in April 1915 were 7, 14, 21 and 28).

the organising secretary, could come & give an address in Yarmouth. It was proposed by Mrs Hurrell & seconded by Mrs Diboll that the Annual Meeting should take place early in May, subject to Miss Creak's arrangements, & that the secretary should write asking her to speak on a date to be fixed by her. It was agreed that the Meeting should be held at Mrs Skinner's 32 Wellesley Rd, & that refreshments should be given. Music to be provided by Mrs Hurrell.

E. Emma Palmer Chairman.

A Committee Meeting was held at 4 Wellesley Rd. on Monday August 1915.[127] Present Mrs & Miss Waterson, Mrs Diboll, Hurrell, Palmer, Rogers, & Miss Brown & Teasdel. It was proposed by Mrs Hurrell & seconded by Mrs Rogers that Mrs Craig should be asked to be a Vice President & the Secretary was desired to write to her & the other vice presidents to ask for the Annual subscriptions.[128] The Secretary was also to write to Miss Creak & thank her for her Address given in June, & to offer her her expenses. 5/- was agreed to be given to the Eastern Federation. 6 members of Committee agreed to take The Common Cause,[129] & to pass it on to members & friends, & to ask at the same time for the subscriptions.
There was some discussion about holding a Working Womens Meeting & of asking Mrs Craig to give an address in Sept. The emergency Committee to consist of Miss Brown, Mrs Hurrell & Mrs Palmer.

E Emma Palmer

A Committee Meeting was held on Friday Oct. 22nd/15 at 4 Wellesley Rd. Present Mrs Palmer in the Chair Mesdames Bunn, Diboll, Ward, Rogers, Waterson & Hurrell, & Miss Brown and Teasdel. A discussion took place as to whether a Meeting with a Speaker could be held before Xmas, but this was negatived, the times being considered too unsettled to ensure an audience.
It was proposed by Mrs Hurrell & seconded by Mrs Ward that a working party should be held monthly to aid the Scottish Hospital in connection with the National Union W.SS.[130] This was unanimously agreed to. The

---

127 Actual date not given (one of August 2, 9, 16, 23 or 30).
128 Mrs Blanche Craig. She had a lot in common with Ethel Leach, being a resident of Gorleston (85 Century Rd in 1911), wealthy (private means, according to the census), and cultured (at the time of the 1901 census, when she was living in London her occupation was 'musical profession'). However, she was 20 years younger (born 1873, her husband (Graham Craig) was living, and they had a young son, born in 1901.
129 The weekly publication of the NUWSS, first published in 1909.
130 When the First World War broke out, the WSPU immediately suspended all militant operations and the Pankhursts devoted themselves to support of the war (although some

party to meet the 1ˢᵗ Friday in each month during the winter at 2.45 p.m. at various members houses. The first one to take place on Nov. 5ᵗʰ at Mrs Hurrell's.

[At back of book]
List of Members.[131]
Commtte
Chairman Mrs Leach Stradbroke Gorleston
Hon Treasurer
Hon Secretary

Mrs Cooper	Salisbury Rd
Mrs Dye	High St Gorleston
Mrs Hull	Granville Hotel Regent Rd
Mrs Harbord	60 St Peters Rd
Mrs Rogers	4 Wellesley Rd
Mrs [*sic*] Brown	4 Wellesley Rd
Mrs Turton	256 Southtown
Mrs Wenn	Milmont North Quay
Miss St John	Fair Haven The Cliffs Gorleston
Miss Turton	256 Southtown

Members

Miss Seymour	Flanborough Marine Parade
Miss Crown	Tregarren Wellesley Rd
Miss Allston	3 Marine Parade
Miss Bond	56 Southtown Rd
Miss Brown	Edgbaston Wellesley Rd
Mrs McLuckie	38 Northgate St
Mrs Quigley	Churchill Rd

---

members took the opposite line, such as Dorothy Jewson in Norwich, a convinced pacifist). The attitude of the NUWSS was more ambiguous, containing both pro- and anti-war elements. Members dedicated their efforts to raising funds for the Scottish Women's Hospitals for War Services, an organisation founded to supply nurses and support staff for hospitals in allied countries. The first hospital opened in France in January 1915, followed by others in Corsica, Malta, Romania, Russia, Salonika and Serbia. The women operating these hospitals faced considerable dangers – disease, bombing and shelling, capture as a result of an unexpected enemy advance – and there were some fatalities. (Robinson, *Hearts and Minds*, 255–69).

131 The list is not dated, but was clearly drawn up between 22 April 1910 (when Mrs Stacy-Watson and Mrs Quigley joined) and 24 August 1910 (when the vacant positions of Treasurer and Secretary were filled).

Mrs Ward	66 South Market Rd
Mrs Stacy Watson	Luxor Southtown
Mrs White	8 Apsley Rd
Mrs Wood	6 Row 21
Miss Holmes	East Anglia Marine Parade
Miss Barrow	Wellesley Rd
Miss Thorpe	24 Salisbury Rd
Miss Seymour	[*blank*]
Miss Narborough	34 Stafford Rd
Miss Westgate	34 Stafford Rd
Mrs Palmer	19 Nelson Rd
Mrs Stanley	Elm Grove Rd Gorleston

Appendix: Great Yarmouth Women Suffragists

This list includes all known members of the Great Yarmouth Women's Suffrage Society: those marked with an asterisk were at some time on the Executive Committee, the others were 'ordinary' members.

Aldred, Sarah Kett (1848–), 23 Princes Rd (1908 Trade Directory). Unmarried daughter of Charles Cory Aldred, a Yarmouth doctor who served five times as mayor between 1856 and 1882. Sarah was co-opted onto Yarmouth Education Committee in March 1904 and stayed on Committee until she retired in 1911: she and Ethel Leach were the only two women on the 21-person Committee.

Allen, Daisy (1888–), 51 Wellesley Road. Unmarried daughter of Frederic Allen, retired wine merchant and his wife Mary Ann. Would have been 21 in 1909, the youngest known full member. Stopped being a member in 1912 – had she moved into WSPU? Married Harold Thurgood in Yarmouth, 1912.

*Alston, Miss, 3 Marine Parade. Two women called Alstone [sic] are listed at this address in 1911: Violet May (1879–) and Dora (1882–): both are described as secondary school teachers. Head of household is Adaline Charlotte Haig, the headmistress of the school, Great Yarmouth High School for Girls: Violet is described as her 'partner', Dora as a 'boarder'. Violet is described in 1912 trade directory as assistant mistress at the school.

*Armitage, Lilian (1858–), Edgbaston, Wellesley Road. 1908 Trade Directory lists Miss L Armitage L.L.A., B.A. as head mistress of Pupil Teacher's Centre, South Quay (this was for girls: boy pupil teachers were trained at the Grammar School). She was appointed in August 1904. Her employment was terminated when the Centre was closed down: the Education Committee gave her formal notice that her employment would terminate on 14 September 1910 (NRO, Y/ED 17). Her first name is never written out in the Education records but a report in the *Eastern Daily Press*

(2 Dec. 1905) gives her name as Lilian. She is the only known Yarmouth suffragist with university qualifications. Her B.A. was from London University (NRO, Y/ED 478). L.L.A. (Lady Literate in Arts) was a degree offered by St Andrew's University, Scotland, either by correspondence or by attendance at non-university classes. It was equivalent to an English M.A.

In 1901 census described as a 'trained certified teacher' living at 17 Handley Rd Hackney; in 1911 census as a 'teacher' living at 10 Ermington Terrace, Mutley, Plymouth.

Barrow, Emma A. (1861–) Miss, Wellesley Road. No Miss Barrow appears in Wellesley Road in the 1911 census. In the 1901 census, she was living at 32 Wellesley Road, as a boarder: her occupation is given as certified head school mistress, and her birthplace as Norwich. Emma is listed as girls' mistress at Northgate School in 1908 trade directory. She is mentioned as head mistress of Northgate Girls School in February 1911 (when she asked if she could invite the children at her school named Mary or May to subscribe to a gift for coronation of Queen Mary) so her absence from the 1911 census could well be a deliberate act. (NRO, Y/ED 17).

Bell, Alice (1885–), Market Place. Single; teacher of music (violin).

Bell, Susan (1859–), Market Place, Widow, mother of Alice; and described in 1911 census as 'purveyor of meat'.

*Bond, Miss, 56 Southtown Road. Frances Sarah Devorah Bond, (1878–), and/or Bertha Alice Steward Bond, (1889–). Sisters, they lived with their mother Alice, a widow: all three are described as of 'private means'. Most references are to 'Miss Bond', one is to 'Miss B Bond' suggesting that this reference is to Bertha and the others to Frances. Do not appear after April 1912, may have moved into WSPU formed in Yarmouth May 1912.

*Brown, Anastacia Sarah Lucy (1853–), Edgbaston, 4, Wellesley Road. Needlewoman. Unmarried sister of Mary Rogers, lived with her. Once incorrectly called Mrs Brown.

Brown, Miss E. B. Not certainly identified. She was brought to the Society by Lilian Armitage along with Emma Barrow, so could well be an error for one of the two Miss Browns, both schoolteachers, with whom the latter was living at 32, Wellesley Road at the time of the 1901 census. These were Emily M. Brown (the head of the house), born 1868, and Elizabeth Harriet Brown, born 1860. Elizabeth was headmistress at St George's Infant School in 1909, (NRO, Y/ED 6): she is described as infants' mistress there in 1912 trade directory.

Browne, Miss. Mentioned once, not identified: many persons of this name in 1901 and 1911 census returns for Yarmouth. Possibilities in 1911 include Miss Zillah Browne of 17, Crown Road, born 1878, assistant teacher, elementary school, and Miss Sarah Ann Browne of 16, Russell Road, born 1853, lodging house keeper.

*Bunn, Frances (1867–), Sefton House, 55 St George's Road. No occupation given in 1911 census, she was married to William Bunn, elementary school teacher. They had three children at home in 1911, the youngest (Gwendolyn) born 1903. Generally called Mrs W Bunn in the record.

*Cooper, Hannah (1837–). Salisbury Road. Widow, private means. She had two adult single daughters living with her in 1911.

Cross, Clara (1855–), 44 Nelson Street South. The wife of Benjamin Cross, born 1853, described in 1911 census simply as 'employer'. Mrs Cross is noted in the minutes as refusing to serve on the Executive Committee, but was presumably a supporter, otherwise she would not have been suggested.

*Crown, Miss, Tregarren, Wellesley Road. No person named Crown in Wellesley Road in 1901 or 1911 censuses. The Tregarren, a boarding house, has an advertisement in the 1908 trade directory, its proprietress being a Miss Louisa M Maynard.

Currington, Agnes, Mrs, 59 Marine Parade, born 1865. A boarding-house keeper [1908 trade directory]; described as widow, apartment house keeper in 1911 census, listed at this address in 1910–11 register of (non-Parliamentary) electors. Mentioned only once, as attending an Executive Committee meeting on 19 Oct. 1909.

*Diboll, Mrs. Probably Emily Diboll, born 1857 widow, boarding-house keeper, 73 Marine Parade; possibly Clara Balfour Diboll, born 1850 wife of Joseph, bank clerk, 86 St George Road.

*Dye, Alice Jane (1857–). 169, High St, Gorleston ('The Bank'). Married. Her husband a cashier, electric tramways. Her husband's name was Charles and she is generally called Mrs C. Dye in the minutes.

Elliott, Beatrice (1872–), in 1911 census single, no occupation, lived with her mother Mary Anne Elliott at 59, Church Road, Gorleston: Mary Anne is described as of 'private means'.

Friend, Miss. Not identified. The only people named Friend (or Frend) in 1901 or 1911 census for Great Yarmouth are Robert and Maria Jane Friend, of Row 117, no. 12. Robert was a metal planer in 1901, a mariner in 1911.

Maria, his wife, was born in 1843. If this identification is correct, she was the only suffragist living in the Rows apart from Mrs Woods (*q.v.*). Another Mrs Friend, Sarah, widow, born 1851 was living at St Olaves (at 2, Bridge Cottage Street) at the time of the 1921 census, and had been born in Yarmouth. However, the designation 'Miss' would be incorrect for either of these ladies. It is possible that Margaret St John brought along Kate Peace, introducing her as her friend, which was misunderstood as Miss Friend.

*Guthrie, Katherine Mary (1855–1924). Born in Yarmouth 23 February 1865, daughter of clerk Robert Guthrie and his wife Jane, nèe Boulter: he had died by 1871 and she and her two sisters were brought up in Crown Rd by their mother whose occupation is given in 1881 as 'income from houses'. Jane had died by 1900, and Katharine continued to occupy 21 Crown Road, sharing the house with sisters Ada Jane Margaret (born 1855) and Hannah Maria (born 1861); all are described in 1901 census as having 'private means', and all three are listed as non-Parliamentary voters (as joint owners) there in the 1910–11 electoral register. Kate had literary interests – author of *Merry Ann, or Yarmouth Yarns,* a book of short stories about Yarmouth, published by Jarrold's Norwich in 1903; supporter of Great Yarmouth University Extension Society.

Last appears in the minutes on 29 April 1912: by May 1912, she had become secretary of newly founded WSPU branch in Yarmouth. Kate Guthrie was a leader of Local Voluntary Patrols in the war (*Yarmouth Independent*, 18 May 1918): her sister Hannah received an award for her work in Yarmouth auxiliary hospital in the war. Kate died at Crown Road 28 June 1924.

*Harbord, Charlotte Nellie (1866–1955), 60 St Peters Road. Maiden name Belward, born in Melbourne, Australia, the wife of Arthur Harbord, described in the 1911 census as 'dairyman (she is thus called Mrs A Harbord in the minutes), restaurant and boarding house keeper'. The Harbords, who were at the same address ten years earlier, had three children living with them, aged between 16 and 20 at the time of the 1911 census. Elected to the Borough Council 1920, one of the first two women to achieve this. There are three photographic portraits of her in the National Portrait Gallery, London. Her husband Arthur Harbord (1865–1941) an important figure in Yarmouth politics, town councillor from 1898, later alderman, three times mayor; Liberal (later National Liberal) MP for Yarmouth 1922–24 and 1929–41.

*Harriss or Harris, Miss. If the spelling of the name is Harriss, as it is the first time she is mentioned, she would be Miss Georgina Harriss, of 4 Beaconsfield Rd, New Town, Great Yarmouth. Born 1869, described as governess in 1901 census; listed under 'Schools-Private' in 1908 Trade Directory. Not in 1911 census. Later entries give the spelling as Harris: too many of these in 1911 census for a certain identification.

Hatch, Ellen, born 1862, no occupation in 1911 census, when she was a lodger in the boarding house of Elizabeth Bond at 87, Albion Road.

Holmes, 'Miss', probably Eliza Holmes, born 1845, widow, no occupation given in 1911 census, when she was resident at boarding house run by Pattie Clayton and her sister Florence Seymour. However, the description Miss would be incorrect so possibly the Yarmouth schoolteacher of that name is intended.

*Hull, Sophia A. (1856–), Granville Hotel, 69 Regent Road. In 1901 census, she is described as the wife of Edwin Hull, hotel proprietor. Two adult sons at home, also two female servants, (apparently not members of the suffrage society). Edwin Hull is listed in 1908 trade directory as tobacconist as also running restaurant at 68 and Granville Hotel at 69 Regent Road. Sophia is not in 1911 census.

*Hurrell, Leah (1858–), 60 Albany Rd Gorleston (in 1911 census). No occupation given in 1911 census, the wife of Harry Edward Hurrell, newspaper manager. Harry was Church Secretary at Middlegate Congregational Church, and their daughter Beatrix (also spelled Beatrice) was nominated for membership of the church in 1910. The family appear to have moved fairly frequently; their address was 7 Regent Rd in 1901 census (in which, Leah is described as a dressmaker), 25 Regent St in 1908 trade directory (this is perhaps his office address). The couple had four daughters aged between 26 and 13 at the time of the 1911 census: Hilda, Ethel, Beatrice and Doris. One of these was presumably the Miss Hurrell whose singing was 'much enjoyed' at an event in 1911, and the Miss Hurrell who played at the welcoming of McLuckie to the church (*Eastern Daily Press*, 5 Jun. 1909).

Jarrett, Mary, born 1869, in 1910 living at 211, Lowestoft Road, described as single and as 'cookery teacher'. Listed in electoral registers, 1905–23. Not in 1911 census – through choice? The 1912 trade directory describes her as teacher at Cookery and Laundry Centre, Church Road, Gorleston. In 1921 census her address is 172, Upper Cliff Road, Gorleston she is described as single and as 'teacher, domestic subjects'.

Last, Miss. Either Lilian Last (1885–), no occupation given in 1911 census, living with parents at 60, Admiralty Road (her father was a boat owner), or Louisa Last (1867–), general shopkeeper, living with widowed mother Ruth Last at 59, Howard Square South.

Lawrence, Eleanor, single, born Great Yarmouth 1871, living with Susan and Alice Bell at time of 1911 census, described as 'visitor', no occupation given.

*Leach, Ethel, (1853–1936), Stradbroke, Gorleston. Widow, no occupation. Address given in 1911 census as Lowestoft Rd Gorleston. See Introduction for more information. Her niece Henrietta 'Hetty' Leach, born 1892 and living with her aunt at the time of the 1911 census, is mentioned in the minutes as a steward: Hetty served as mayoress during Ethel's year as mayor.

McLuckie, Mrs Ethel Mary, 38 Northgate Street. The 1911 census lists George McLuckie at this address: he is described as a Congregational Minister and as married. His wife does not appear in the census return: a deliberate act? In 1901, he was in London as a minister: he married in Lewisham in 1904 (wife's maiden name was Carter). McLuckie was minister at the churches in King St and Middlegate: he is not listed in the 1908 Trade Directory but came to Yarmouth in July 1909 (see *Eastern Daily Press*, 17 May 1909).

May, Anne Elizabeth ('Annie'), born 1871, wife of Joseph White May who at the time of 1911 census was headmaster of the teachers' centre: they lived at 4, Queen Street.

Narburgh (wrongly spelled Narborough in the minutes), Miss, 34 Stafford Rd, Gorleston. Helen Narburgh, born 1873, a teacher at Cobholm Infants School from at least 1902 (NRO, Y/ED 5); salary increased to £60 a year 1906 after she passed Certificate Examination, to £65 1907, to £70 1908. (NRO, Y/ED 13,14). At the time of the 1911 census, she was living at 6, Southtown Road, Gorleston.

*Neave, Emma Bugg 'Mrs John Neave' (1851–), 53 Victoria Road. Wife of John G Neave, poor-rate collector. Daughters at time of 1901 census – Ethel, born 1880, music teacher, Charlotte, born 1885, a dressmaker. Emma's occupation given as 'domestic duties' in 1911 census. Her husband was a son of J. F. Neave, see Introduction.

*Neave, Sarah Lilian 'Mrs Joseph Neave' (1858–), Moat House, Northgate Street. Wife of Joseph Neave, fish merchant. Three daughters at time of 1901 census, two of whom (Maud and Lilian Neave) were school governesses. Sarah given no occupation given in 1911 census. Her husband was a son of J. F. Neave, see Introduction.

*Palmer, (Elizabeth) Emma (1847–), 19 Nelson Road. Described in 1911 census as Elizabeth Emma Palmer, widow 'private means'. Lived with nephew and niece (Ada Kendrick b 1895).

Peace, Kate Elizabeth (1871–), Fairhaven, The Cliffs, Gorleston. Born Denby Dale, Yorkshire, 30 April 1871. In 1891 assistant matron at a 'home for inebriates' in Barnsley (her mother was the matron); in 1901, a visitor at an address in Jersey, and occupation given as 'private means'. Unmarried. Lived with Margaret St John from at least 1906 (see her entry). In 1911, her occupation is given as 'house management'. In the 1939 register, she is described as 'retired teacher'.

Quigley, Marie Josephine (1882–), 6 Churchill Road. Lived with her husband Patrick, an inspector for the Society for Prevention of Cruelty to Animals: both were born in Ireland. At the time of the 1911 census they had one child, a son, Patrick Joseph, aged two.

*Rogers, Mary A (1855–), 4 Wellesley Road. Widow, lodging house keeper. Many of the Society's executive meetings were held at her house. Appears in the 1910–11 register of electors (non-Parliamentary). Two of the Yarmouth suffragists were her boarders, Anastacia Brown and Lilian Armitage: see their entries in this list.

Rose, Miss. Either Helen Rose, born 1882, in 1911 a corsetière and boarder at 50 Regent Road (in boarding-house of Frederick and Amelia Mansfield), or Ethel May Rose, born 1885, housekeeper and companion to sisters Sarah Jane and May Elizabeth Brown of 155 Southtown Road.

Seymour, Florence (1875–), Flanborough, 6 Marine Parade. Unmarried sister-in-law of Charles Clayton, marine engineer, head of the household. Listed in (non-Parliamentary) register of electors 1910–11 as at 57, Marine Parade. Florence and her sister Pattie Clayton are both described in 1911 census as 'boarding house keeper', and the address is given as 57, Marine Parade. Only one boarder is listed in the census, Eliza Holmes, widow. A Miss Seymour listed as at 33 Wellesley Road in 1901 could be a different person, but no other Miss Seymour occurs in the 1901 or 1911 census returns for Great Yarmouth, so this may be her address before she moved in with her sister and brother-in-law.

*Stacy-Watson, Catharine Maria (1854–), Luxor, Southtown. Wife of Christopher Stacy-Watson, head of a firm of herring curers and packers, in Yarmouth in 1894, widowed by time of 1901 census. Appears at 25 Southtown Road in 1902 register of electors. She was formerly a member of Middlegate Congregational Chapel: she was crossed off the membership roll in January 1908 for non-attendance (NRO, FC 31/6): however she maintained links, her daughter Hannah Stacy-Watson being married there 27 April 1910. She was the mother (presumably by a previous marriage) of

Charles Campling, laundry proprietor and printer: he served as Mayor in 1908–09 and, as he was unmarried, she acted as his Lady Mayoress.

*St John, Margaret (1875–), Fairhaven, The Cliffs, Gorleston. Born St Faith's Norfolk, her father a banker's clerk. Unmarried. In 1901, a domestic science teacher in Norwich. Margaret appears in electoral registers from 1906 onward, address given as 13 Upper Cliff Road Gorleston. In 1907 she appears under the same address but she also appears with Kate Peace as joint ratepayers at 26 St Peters Road. From 1908 Margaret and Kate appear as joint ratepayers at 6 Marine Parade. In 1911 census she is described as 'laundry proprietor'.

Stanley, Elizabeth (1858–), Elm Grove, Gorleston. Single, boarding house keeper: just one boarder in 1911 (Hannah Barker, single, private means). Wrongly given as 'Mrs' in the list at the end of the minute book.

Taylor, Violet ('Nurse Taylor'). Born 1890, at time of 1911 census, a live-in nurse at Yarmouth Hospital, Estcourt Road.

*Teasdel, 'Netty', Henrietta Ellen (1860–), 77 Southtown Rd Gorleston. Single, no occupation given in census returns, shared house with brother Robert Henry Teasdel 'accountant etc'.

*Thorpe, Catherine Calvert (1879–), 24 Salisbury Road. Spelled Thorp in 1911 census where she is described as a boot retailer's assistant, her father Henry a retired boot retailer's manager: unmarried, she is living with her parents.

*Turton, Alice C. E. (1859–), St Mary's Vicarage, 256 Southtown. The wife of Zouch Turton, clerk in holy orders, vicar of Southtown. Not in 1911 census.

Turton, Beryl A. (1894–), St Mary's Vicarage, 256 Southtown. Younger daughter of Zouch and Alice. Not in 1911 census. Only mentioned once, in 1911, acting as a meeting steward, at which time she was 17 so perhaps not a full member.

*Turton, Dorothy O. (1888–), St Mary's Vicarage, 256 Southtown. Elder daughter of Zouch and Alice. Not in 1911 census.

Ward, Elizabeth, 'Bessie' (1861–), 66 South Market Road. Wife of Arthur Ward, 'tailor maker'. No occupation given in 1911 census.

*Waterson, Anna (1853–), 3 Albert Square. Widow, boarding house keeper.

*Waterson, Annie (1885–), 3 Albert Square. Single, daughter of above, no occupation given, perhaps helped her mother.

*Wenn, Mrs (?1853–), Milmont (72) North Quay. Probably the wife of Frederick Wenn, timber merchant who appears in 1910–11 register of electors and 1911 census at the address: she does not appear in the latter, perhaps deliberately boycotting it. The family are recorded at 22, Row 54 in 1901. Her name is given there as Maria, and she was born in 1853: she is described as married, but her husband is not listed: the fact that one of their children is named Frederick strengthens the identification.

Westgate, Clara Margaret (1860–), 34 Stafford Rd, Gorleston. 1908 Trade Directory lists Miss C Westgate as infants' mistress at Cobholm Island School. In 1910, she obtained a diploma from the College of Preceptors and asked for an increase in salary but this was declined, 'the diploma obtained by Miss Westgate not being recognised in the Scale of Salaries'. (NRO, Y/ED 17). 1911 census lists her as 'school mistress', 1912 trade directory as 'infants' mistress'.

*White, Mrs Alice (1841–), 8 Apsley Road. Widow, living alone, 'lodging house keeper', according to 1911 census.

Wood or Woodes, Mrs, 6 Row 21. No one of this name at this address 1901 or 1911: many people named Wood or Woods (no Woodes however) elsewhere in the town. The 1909 rate book has this property as owned by a Mrs Herbert and gives the occupier as Ernest Ribbans, so Mrs Wood(e)s perhaps a sub-tenant and/or short-term resident of this house (NRO, Y/TR 290).

Select Bibliography

Trade Directories

Kelly's Directory of Cambridgeshire, Norfolk, and Suffolk, 1892.
Eastern Counties of England Directory, 1901.
Kelly's Directories of Norfolk, 1896, 1900, 1904, 1908, 1912.

Newspapers

Local
Eastern Daily Press
Lynn Advertiser
Lynn News
Yarmouth Independent

Labour and Socialist
The Clarion
Justice
The Labour Leader

Women's Suffrage
The Common Cause
The Suffragette
The Vote

Secondary Works

Socialism and the Labour Movement
Philip S. Bagwell, *The Railwaymen: the History of the National Union of Railwaymen* (London, 1963)
Steven Cherry, *Doing Different: politics and the Labour movement in Norwich 1880–1914* (Norwich, 1989)
Alan Haworth and Dianne Hayter, eds, *Men who made Labour* (Abingdon, 2006)

Alun Howkins, *Poor Labouring Men: rural radicalism in Norfolk 1872–1923* (London, 1985)

Keith Laybourn, *A history of British trade unionism* (1997 edition, Stroud)

Keith Laybourn, *The evolution of British social policy and the welfare state* (Keele, 1995)

Frank Meeres, *George Roberts MP, a life that 'did different'* (Lowestoft, 2019)

Charlotte Paton, *A Portrait of Walter Dexter, an enigmatic man* (Guist, 2014)

Henry Pelling, *A short history of the Labour Party* (London, 1961)

Martin Pugh, *Speak for Britain: a new history of the Labour Party* (2011 edition, London)

John William Raby, *The Allotted Span in King's Lynn* (King's Lynn, 1950)

John Shepherd and Keith Laybourn, *Britain's First Labour Government* (2013 edition, London)

Emanuel Shinwell, *The Labour Story* (London, 1963)

William Stewart, *J Keir Hardie* (London, 1921)

Jacqueline Turner, 'The Soul of the Labour Movement – rediscovering the Labour Church 1891–1914' (unpublished University of Reading PhD thesis, 2010)

Rhiannon Vickers, *The Labour Party and the World: the evolution of Labour's foreign policy 1900–51* (Manchester, 2003)

Michael Wadsworth, 'The Independent Labour Party in Great Yarmouth, 1906–14', *Yarmouth Archaeology*, 2006

Francis Williams, *Fifty Years March, the rise of the Labour Party* (London, c. 1949)

Women's Suffrage

Elizabeth Crawford, *The Women's Suffrage Movement, A Reference Guide 1866–1928* (London, 1999)

Elizabeth Crawford, *The Women's Suffrage Movement in Britain and Ireland, a regional survey* (Abingdon, 2006)

Patricia Hollis, *Ladies Elect: Women in English Local Government, 1865–1914* (Oxford, 1987)

Jill Liddington, *Vanishing for the Vote: Suffrage, citizenship and the battle for the census, with a Gazetteer of Campaigners*, complied by Jill Liddington and Elizabeth Crawford (Manchester, 2014)

Frank Meeres, *Suffragettes – how Britain's women fought & died for the right to vote* (Stroud, 2013)

Frank Meeres, *Dorothy Jewson, suffragette and socialist* (Cromer, 2014)

Emmeline Pankhurst, *My Own Story* (London, 2015 edition)

Sylvia Pankhurst, *The Suffragette Movement* (London, 1977 edition)

Antonia Raeburn, *Militant Suffragettes* (London, 1973)

Harold L. Smith, *The British Women's Suffrage Campaign 1866–1928* (Abingdon, 2007 edition)

Index

Members of socialist and suffragist societies are indexed at point of first mention, together with any references in introductions and appendices. All other names are fully indexed. Places named are in Norfolk except where otherwise indicated.

Previous volumes published by The Norfolk Record Society

Volume	Title
Vol. I	Calendar of Frere MSS.: Hundred of Holt. Muster Roll, Hundred of North Greenhoe, circa 1523. Norwich Subscriptions to the Voluntary Gift of 1662
Vol. II	St. Benet of Holme, 1020–1210. The eleventh and twelfth century sections of Cott. MS. Galba E. ii. The Register of the Abbey of St. Benet of Holme
Vol. III	St. Benet of Holme, 1020–1210. Introductory essay on the eleventh and twelfth century sections of Cott. MS. Galba E. ii. The Register of the Abbey of St. Benet of Holme
Vol. IV	The Visitation of Norfolk, Anno Domini 1664 made by Sir Edward Bysshe, Knt. Clarenceux King of Arts, Volume I, A–L
Vol. V	The Visitation of Norfolk, Anno Domini 1664 made by Sir Edward Bysshe, Knt. Clarenceux King of Arts, Volume II, M–Z
Vol. VI	The Musters Returns for divers Hundreds in the County of Norfolk, 1569, 1572, 1574, and 1577 (Part I)
Vol. VII	The Musters Returns for divers Hundreds in the County of Norfolk, 1569, 1572, 1574, and 1577 (Part II)
Vol. VIII	A Norfolk Sessions Roll, 1394–1397. The Maritime Trade of the Port of Blakeney, Norfolk, 1587–1590. A Norfolk Poll List, 1702
Vol. IX	Records of the Gild of St. George in Norwich, 1389–1547
Vol. X	Norwich Consistory Court Depositions, 1499–1512 and 1518–1530
Vol. XI	The First Register of Norwich Cathedral Priory
Vol. XII	The Norfolk portion of the Chartulary of the Priory of St Pancras of Lewes
Vol. XIII	East Anglian Pedigrees
Vol. XIV	The Correspondence of Lady Katherine Paston, 1603–1627
Vol. XV	Minutes of the Norwich Court of Mayoralty, 1630–1631
Vol. XVI (Part 1)	Index of Wills Proved in the Consistory Court of Norwich, 1370–1550 (A to Hi)
Vol. XVI (Part 2)	Index of Wills Proved in the Consistory Court of Norwich, 1370–1550 (Hi to Ro)
Vol. XVI (Part 3)	Index of Wills Proved in the Consistory Court of Norwich, 1370–1550 (Ro to Z)